O1

D0706574

DISCARD

Rainbow Rights

New Perspectives on Law, Culture, and Society

ROBERT W. GORDON AND
MARGARET JANE RADIN, SERIES EDITORS

*Rainbow Rights:
The Role of Lawyers and Courts in the
Lesbian and Gay Civil Rights Movement,*
Patricia A. Cain

The Congressional Experience, Second Edition,
David E. Price

*Citizens, Strangers, and In-Betweens:
Essays on Immigration and Citizenship,*
Peter H. Schuck

Limits of Law: Essays on Democratic Governance,
Peter H. Schuck

Stewards of Democracy: Law as Public Profession,
Paul Carrington

A Philosophy of International Law, Fernando Teson

Thinking Like a Lawyer, Kenneth J. Vandevelde

*Intellect and Craft:
The Contributions of Justice Han Linde to American Constitutionalism,*
edited by Robert F. Nagel

*Property and Persuasion:
Normativity and Change in Jurisprudence of Property,*
Carol M. Rose

*Words That Wound: Critical Race Theory, Assaultive Speech,
and the First Amendment,*
Mari J. Matsuda, Charles R. Lawrence III,
Richard Delgado, and Kimberlè Williams Crenshaw

Feminist Legal Theory: Readings in Law and Gender,
edited by Katherine T. Bartlett and Rosanne Kennedy

Rainbow Rights

*The Role of Lawyers and Courts
in the Lesbian and Gay
Civil Rights Movement*

PATRICIA A. CAIN

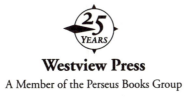

Westview Press
A Member of the Perseus Books Group

New Perspectives on Law, Culture, and Society series

Copyright © 2000 by Westview Press, A Member of the Perseus Books Group

Published in 2000 in the United States of America by Westview Press, 5500 Central Avenue, Boulder, Colorado 80301-2877, and in the United Kingdom by Westview Press, 12 Hid's Copse Road, Cumnor Hill, Oxford OX2 9JJ

Visit us on the World Wide Web at www.westviewpress.com

Library of Congress Cataloging-in-Publication Data
Cain, Patricia A.
    Rainbow rights : the role of lawyers and courts in the lesbian and gay civil rights movement / Patricia A. Cain.
        p.   cm. (New Perspectives on Law, Culture, and Society)
    Includes bibliographical references and index.
    ISBN 0-8133-2618-4
    1. Homosexuality—Law and legislation—United States—History.   I. Title.

KF4754.5 .C35 2000
342.73'087—dc21   00-043264

The paper used in this publication meets the requirements of the American National Standard for Permanence of Paper for Printed Library Materials Z39.48-1984.

10   9   8   7   6   5   4   3   2   1

Contents

Preface

Although this book is finished, gay rights litigation continues. Since *Bowers v. Hardwick* was decided in 1986, the U.S. Supreme Court has agreed to hear only three cases involving legal claims pressed by lesbian or gay litigants. The most recent case, *Dale v. Boy Scouts of America*, was handed down as recently as June 26, 2000, while this book was in production. Lower courts, both federal and state, hear lesbian and gay rights cases much more frequently. I have updated the discussion of all cases, including *Dale*, through July 15, 2000.

The reader should be aware that several cases discussed in this book have not yet reached their final conclusion. In particular, there are at least three cases challenging state sodomy statutes that may yet be appealed, conceivably even to the U.S. Supreme Court, thereby creating an opportunity for the Court to reconsider its opinion in *Bowers v. Hardwick*.

In addition, the Supreme Court has not yet ruled on whether the equal protection clause of the Fourteenth Amendment protects lesbian and gay employees from government-imposed discrimination. The *Romer* case can be cited as evidence that the Court will answer the question affirmatively, but as of the completion of this book, the Court has denied certiorari in every case posing the question directly.

Finally, I predict that there will be a flurry of post-*Dale* litigation in which landlords and employers, as well as allegedly private clubs, will claim that they have a First Amendment right to discriminate on the basis of sexual orientation. A case that is currently before the Ninth Circuit Court of Appeals, *Thomas v. Anchorage Equal Rights Commission*, may well tell us more about the strength of such First Amendment claims than the *Dale* case does. Stay tuned. The struggle for "rainbow rights" is far from over.

Patricia A. Cain

Acknowledgments

This book has been in the making for many years. During that time it has been improved by my ongoing conversations with colleagues in law, history, and gay and women's studies. In addition, a number of my Iowa students have worked on this book. The three who helped bring it to fruition when deadlines were approaching deserve special recognition. They are Lisa Clay, Marci Lowman, and Faith Pincus.

For their wisdom and their energy, I thank the many lawyers at Lambda, the ACLU, and the National Center for Lesbian Rights whom I have come to know over the years. All of us who care about gay justice owe these brave crusaders the highest respect and gratitude for the time they have spent in the trenches. It is not an easy life to swim upstream for so many years.

Three colleagues deserve special thanks for reading the entire manuscript and offering not only wise advice but also thoughtful editorial suggestions. I am particularly grateful to Rhonda Rivera, whose gay legal scholarship I have admired for years; to Linda Kerber, who always asks the right questions and insists on historical context to tell the full story; and, most of all, to my partner, Jean Love, whose penchant for perfection inspires me on a daily basis. Jean, you are my rainbow.

P.A.C.

Introduction

This book is about the legal battles in the courtrooms around the United States that have been part of the struggle for lesbian and gay rights. As other activists did in earlier civil rights movements, lesbian and gay activists have argued their causes in federal and state courts throughout the nation and, on rare occasion, before the Supreme Court of the United States. The role of the lawyers, the legal arguments they construct, and the fine-tuning of these arguments in response to judicial opinions is a central part of any civil rights movement. Recent academic debate among legal and political science scholars, however, questions whether civil rights litigation victories actually do contribute to positive social change. Some scholars argue that courts do not cause social change and that civil rights movements do not make their biggest gains from litigation. One of the strongest contemporary legal advocates for gay rights, Tom Stoddard, agreed with this assessment, and before his untimely death from AIDS, cautioned us to work harder in the legislative bodies of the country in our fight for lesbian and gay equality.

Whether one believes that courts do in fact cause social change, courts are nonetheless crucial in any battle over equal rights. As Gregory Peck said, playing the role of attorney Atticus Finch in the film version of Harper Lee's *To Kill a Mockingbird:* "Our courts are the great levelers in this country."[1] What Finch meant, and what Lee tried to demonstrate in her novel, is that courts understand and apply the notion of equality much more readily than legislatures or than members of society in general. Justice Hugo Black made a similar point in a 1940 Supreme Court case, when he said: "Under our constitutional system, courts stand against any winds that blow as havens of refuge for those who might otherwise suffer because they are helpless, weak, outnumbered, or because they are non-conforming victims of prejudice and public excitement."[2] What civil rights litigators understand is that, even if courts are imperfect as agents of change, they are important arenas for making civil rights claims, for arguing about equality and rights, and for educating legislatures and the broader society about injustices experienced by minorities.

A history of any civil rights movement would be incomplete without the stories of legal battles in the courtrooms across the country. And yet, most histories of the lesbian and gay civil rights movement focus more on political activity and legislative lobbying than they do on the litigated cases. This book is an attempt to correct that imbalance. This book will tell the stories of the lawyers and of the cases that have been central to the lesbian and gay civil rights movement. This book poses the question: How are our courts doing as "the great levelers in this country"?

WHY RAINBOW RIGHTS?

After I began work on this book and started to use "Rainbow Rights" as a working title, several people asked: "Why call it 'Rainbow Rights'? What does 'rainbow' mean, especially as a modifier of rights?"

First, I use the term "rights" because my focus is on the legal arguments that have been made in courtrooms. Those arguments are derived from explicit or implicit guarantees of rights that are constitutionally granted to all "citizens," or, in some cases, to all "persons." Lesbians and gay men are citizens and persons; that characterization has never been seriously questioned. And yet, as the law has developed, gay men and lesbians have not enjoyed the same constitutional rights or protections as they would have enjoyed had they been nongay persons. On the surface, this result sounds like a denial of "equal rights." Yet some argue our very difference from heterosexuals prevents us from enjoying equal rights. Indeed, some argue that to give gays any rights means giving them "special rights." To avoid the equal rights/special rights rhetorical debate, I have settled on "rainbow rights," that is, rights for lesbians and gay men, whether viewed as equal or special.[3]

Why "rainbow"? Many people outside the lesbian and gay community assume that the word "rainbow," when used in a discussion involving politics or rights, refers to Jesse Jackson's Rainbow Coalition. But the gay movement claimed the rainbow first, and it remains the foremost symbol of gay pride, replacing the pink triangle, which was used to identify homosexuals in Nazi Germany and which has always carried negative connotations of the homosexual as victim. In her book *Another Mother Tongue*, Judy Grahn explains the symbolism of the rainbow in the lesbian and gay movement in several ways. Some in the movement embrace the rainbow as a fitting tribute to much-loved gay icon Judy Garland, who gave us the most well-known rainbow song ever, a song whose lyrics capture the hope of a better world. Grahn also provides us with myths from various cultures about the transformative power symbolized by the rainbow. In one such myth, an uncle tells a tomboyish girl that if she walks under the rainbow, she will be transformed into a boy.[4]

Although the rainbow as a symbol of gay pride has its roots in ancient myths and modern fairy tales, it did not become the official symbol of the modern lesbian and gay rights movement until 1978, when Gilbert Baker, a renowned gay seamstress in San Francisco, conceived of the rainbow flag as a worthy symbol for San Francisco's gay pride parade. Baker claims to have been thinking of diversity and not *The Wizard of Oz,* according to lesbian columnist Deb Price. "We (gay people) are so different," he says. "We're men and women. We're black and white and brown, every color . . . and every class. It's a spectrum, and that's why it caught on."[5]

I mean to capture all these meanings in my title *Rainbow Rights.* I am looking for legal arguments that are transformative, that can bring us to that place over the rainbow where even bluebirds fly, and I am not the least bit interested in legal arguments that are not capable, in the end, of bringing us all there—black, white, brown, every color, male, female, able-bodied or not, rich or poor, English-speaking or not, gay, nongay, bisexual, and transgendered.

MAKING "RIGHTS" ARGUMENTS

Civil rights movements succeed when they make arguments that win. The arguments may be ethical (e.g., all persons are deserving of equal respect), legal (e.g., no state can deny a person equal protection of the law), or economic (e.g., discrimination creates economic waste). Perhaps the most successful argument, and one that includes ethical, legal, and economic considerations, is this: Individual merit ought to be evaluated on the basis of one's ability. Blanket proscriptions on the basis of race, gender, or any other irrelevant characteristic have been struck down by the courts when civil rights lawyers have made arguments based on this concept of individual merit. The legally recognized remedy of "affirmative action" is currently under attack, in part, because some view it as a violation of the principle of individual merit.

"Equal opportunity" is another principle that is closely related to the concept of "individual merit." Stated in its individualistic form, the principle of equal opportunity means that all persons ought to be on a "level playing field," so that each individual has an equal shot at benefits such as jobs and education, and so that such benefits will not be allocated on the basis of some characteristic unrelated to the benefit. Stated as a principle of class-based rights, the equal opportunity principle means that one class of people ought to be given the same opportunity as another class of similarly situated people—that women should have equal opportunities with men (and vice versa) and that nonwhites should have equal opportunities with whites (and vice versa).

The lesbian and gay civil rights movement has used these two types of arguments (individual merit and equal opportunity) in its efforts to gain public sphere benefits for gay, lesbian, and bisexual people. The arguments have been successful in court cases that have established employment rights and rights to public accommodations and to housing. In the legislatures, eleven states[6] and the District of Columbia[7] have enacted civil rights protections for lesbian, gay, and bisexual people in the public spheres of employment, public accommodations, housing, and education.

But the principles of individual merit and equal opportunity have been less valuable in the struggle to gain those rights that we typically identify with the private sphere, that is, rights to same-sex intimacy and the right to have our families recognized and protected by the state. To make the legal and moral argument in favor of private-sphere rights, gay rights activists have relied on a different principle, one that is derived from our notion that the government should not unduly interfere in certain private realms. This principle is the basis of the constitutional rights of privacy and liberty.

Privacy and liberty include the right to be left alone and the right to make individual choices about personal morality that differ from the majority. The values attached to privacy and liberty are strong traditional values in our heritage. The Bill of Rights was adopted to protect individual private spheres of life and conscience from unwarranted governmental intrusion. The right to speak in dissent, to keep government troops out of our homes, and to remain silent when questioned by government officials about wrongdoing all evidence the great concern the founders had for protecting the private sphere.

As many feminist writers have shown, however, state or governmental protection of the private sphere can serve to benefit the dominant members of society and to harm the subservient and less powerful members. This situation occurs, in part, because the private sphere deemed worthy of protection has tended to be defined by the dominant class, in particular nongay white men. Thus, the liberty and privacy interests of the dominant and the powerful have been protected, while the liberty and privacy interests of nonwhites, females, and lesbians and gay men have been ignored or debased.

In the history of civil rights movements, the success of liberty and privacy arguments has lagged behind the success of individual merit and equal opportunity arguments. This trend is as true for the antiracism civil rights movement and for the women's liberation movement as it is for the lesbian and gay civil rights movement. For example, *Loving v. Virginia,*[8] the U.S. Supreme Court case that recognized the right to engage in mixed-race marriages, was not decided until 1967. That was almost two decades after the Supreme Court struck down segregated neighborhoods *(Shelley v. Kraemer)*[9] and segregated law schools *(Sweatt v. Painter)*[10] and thirteen years after *Brown v. Board*[11] called for an end to public school segregation in elementary and secondary schools.

Public sphere rights are important to individuals. Jobs, education, and housing are all necessary for individuals to lead productive lives. But private sphere rights are also important. Without the ability to create intimate relationships that support and foster our individual creativity and our capacity for human empathy and love, we, as individuals, are unable to develop our full promise as human beings. A responsible government must protect both sorts of rights. The challenge for government with respect to the protection of private sphere rights is to find the right balance between noninterference with private choice and affirmative support for productive private relationships. Although the government has faced that challenge in the context of other civil rights movements, the lesbian and gay civil rights movement poses the challenge most directly.

COURTS VERSUS LEGISLATURES

Every civil rights movement has two forums in which it can make effective legal arguments: courts and legislatures. This book will focus on the arguments made in courts. Courts hear cases. They do not make broad policy decisions about what is best for society. Their decisions, instead, focus solely on the controversy that is before them. This focus makes their task different from that of legislatures.

Legal scholarship is brimming with discussion about the limitations on courts and whether they should play an active or constrained role in civil rights movements that seek to create change by expanding rights. Without fully summarizing that literature, I do want to make a few key observations about the role of courts, observations that are central to the themes I develop in this book.

Courts are constrained because they can only rule on the case before them. Further, they can only rule if the case is a real one. Thus, the plaintiff in the case must have "standing." To have standing, a person must have suffered a real injury or be imminently threatened by a real injury. Because courts cannot give "advisory opinions," a group of concerned citizens cannot just walk into the courthouse and complain that certain laws are unfair. Rather, those complaints should be taken to the legislature, which has the power to repeal old laws or to enact new ones.

Once an individual or group has asked a court to resolve a real dispute over which the court has jurisdiction, the court must rule. Courts cannot avoid making decisions. Although it is true the Supreme Court can elect not to hear a case, trial courts and most appellate courts have no such option. By contrast, a legislative body, after hearing arguments about how laws ought to be changed, can decide to do nothing. Doing nothing will, of course, maintain the status quo. At the same time, inaction may simply be a means of deferring decision on an issue. Courts cannot defer. Issues before them must be decided.

Because courts must act when an individual has invoked the court's jurisdiction, one can get one's cause more easily considered by a court than by a legislature. When legislatures do not respond to citizen complaints, citizens can complain to the courts. Thus, for example, when legislative bodies refused to enact legislation that would desegregate schools, courts were asked to rule that school segregation was unconstitutional. When certain school boards refused to comply with the Supreme Court's mandate to end segregation, courts were asked to develop judicial remedies to desegregate the schools. Similarly, when some state legislatures refused to repeal their laws criminalizing abortion, courts were asked to rule that the laws were an unconstitutional invasion of a woman's right to choose.

Observers of the Supreme Court have opined that Court decisions recognizing new constitutional rights have very little effect unless society is ready to accept such social change. Gerald Rosenberg's book, *The Hollow Hope*,[12] is perhaps the most important piece of scholarship focusing on the role of the courts in bringing about social change. He demonstrates that, despite the moral victory in *Brown v. Board of Education,* the case did very little to desegregate schools. Similarly, he takes the position that the Court's decision in *Roe v. Wade*[13] appears to have had little impact on the availability of legal abortion. And, despite Supreme Court decisions championing the rights of women in the public sphere,[14] women are still paid less than men and still bump their heads on a "glass ceiling."

Girardeau Spann, in *Race Against the Court,* has argued that the Supreme Court's ability to support minority claims for expansions of civil rights is severely limited by the Court's necessarily conservative nature. He explains:

> Life tenure and judicial independence cause the Court to function as a political force for preservation of the status quo. However, because racial minorities in the United States are disadvantaged by the socioeconomic status quo, the Court's inherent conservatism impairs minority efforts to achieve racial equality. The Court has manifested its inherent conservatism in subtle, yet effective, ways. *Brown v. Board of Education,* the case most often lauded as the icon of judicial sensitivity to minority interests, has had the ironic effect of luring racial minorities into a dependency relationship with the Court that has impeded minority efforts to acquire political power.[15]

I do not wish to challenge Rosenberg's statistics nor debate Spann's observations about the conservative nature of the courts. The work of both of these scholars, and of others who question the efficacy of the courts in bringing about social change, demonstrates that courts alone will never get the job done. And, certainly *Brown v. Board of Education* did not immediately desegregate schools in the South. But without the decision, or if the decision had gone the other way, surely school desegregation would have taken much longer.

Brown, after all, only outlawed de jure segregation. It did nothing to alter individual racist attitudes that continue to produce de facto segregation right up to the present time. Although Robert Carter, one of the NAACP lawyers in the *Brown* case, has said that perhaps the lawyers litigated against the wrong evil, segregation rather than racism, I doubt whether any litigation strategy could have successfully changed racist attitudes. Ending de jure segregation was a reasonable first step in the eyes of most NAACP litigators.

Further, although *Brown* may not have accomplished immediate desegregation or a significant reduction in racism, the decision did make material differences in people's individual lives. I have in mind not only the lives of those who were the direct beneficiaries of the decision—black students admitted to previously all-white schools—but also individuals for whom the decision created new visions of the possibility of equality. Consider, for example, Barbara Jordan's story.[16] In 1954, Jordan was in her junior year of college at Texas Southern, a historically black college in Houston. After a short period of elation over the decision, she realized that nothing was changing in Texas. She then decided she would have to leave the South, so she applied to and was accepted by Boston University Law School. She understood that something more than legal cases were needed to change entrenched patterns of segregation and to improve the condition of black people. She was prepared to add her own personal efforts to that cause. If *Brown* had not been decided in 1954, would Barbara Jordan, inspired by *Brown*'s promise and committed to seeing its promise fulfilled, have become the first black woman to be elected to the Texas Senate? Would she have been elected to Congress in time to play the important public role that she played in the Nixon impeachment process?

Statistics cannot capture these defining moments in individual people's lives—moments that often occur in the wake of a momentous decision like *Brown*. The statistics show that desegregation occurred slowly, but, in the end, due in large part to the continuing efforts of NAACP lawyers, the *Brown* decision was implemented, city by city, school district by school district, university by university.

Rosenberg argues that many of the key participants in the civil rights movement were ignorant of the *Brown* decision. He reports that students who participated in sit-ins and similar demonstrations in the 1960s never cited *Brown* as a motivating factor in their political activities. But times have changed since *Brown*. In an era of televised news, cases such as *Bowers v. Hardwick*[17] and *Roe v. Wade* have quite literally become household words. Today, movement lawyers who take cases to court have a very direct impact on the nature of the nation's dialogue about the rights of minorities.

So, yes, what the courts say on the issue of gay rights matters. Although federal and state lower court opinions are less well publicized than U.S. Supreme Court opinions, those decisions also matter, especially rulings that empower activists in the movement to continue their work. Lower court opinions recognizing the rights of gay organizations and the right of lesbian and gay individuals to congregate in public, for example, have provided crucial support to the organization of the movement. Lower court decisions protecting the public speech rights of lesbian and gay activists have helped to ensure that the movement's claims are heard in the political arena.

This book is about the role of courts generally in the lesbian and gay civil rights movement. I will look at court cases over a fifty-year period, beginning in 1950. I divide these cases into three primary classifications: cases that focus on public sphere rights, cases that focus on private sphere rights, and cases in which the litigants are asking for public recognition of their private relationships.

ORGANIZATION OF THIS BOOK

This book has several themes. One theme is the direct comparison of the lesbian and gay civil rights movement with the earlier struggles for race equality and sex equality. Another theme is the relative success of legal arguments in obtaining public sphere rights as compared with private sphere rights, a phenomenon that also occurred in earlier civil rights movements. Another theme, prevalent in earlier civil rights movements, is the tension between making litigation arguments based on a group's similarity to other groups and making arguments based on the group's difference.

The book is intended as a history of the litigation that has been central to the progress of the lesbian and gay civil rights movement. As I focus on specific cases, I identify legal arguments that touch on the public/private divide as well as arguments that raise tensions over the sameness/difference thesis. Because this book is a history, its organization will be primarily chronological.

By focusing on court decisions, legal theories, and litigation strategies, I highlight the role of the courts in bringing about change. I also hope to demystify litigation and court decisions for nonlawyers who are interested in gay and lesbian rights. Thus, although this book may be more easily read by lawyers and law students, it is written for a broader audience as well.

To address the various themes and to maintain the chronological nature, the book is organized as follows: Chapter 1 provides a brief overview of two earlier civil rights movements, the African American civil rights movement and the women's movement. After that, the primary focus is on the lesbian and gay civil rights movement, but I explore some of the similarities and differences among the movements in each chapter. Chapter 2 introduces the notion of public interest lawyering and describes the key public interest lawyers and their organizations, both for the earlier civil rights movement as well as for the lesbian and gay civil rights movement. In Chapter 3, I begin the story of lesbian and gay rights litigation by focusing on what I call "public sphere rights." These rights include the rights of equal access to employment, public accommodations, housing, education, and credit. Chapter 3 chronicles the litigation efforts that have increased public sphere rights for lesbians and gay men from the early days of the movement, circa 1950, until 1986, when the Supreme Court handed down its decision in *Bowers v.*

Hardwick. Chapter 4 focuses on litigation efforts relating to "private sphere rights" during the same pre-*Hardwick* period. In Chapter 5, I question the public/private divide and focus on those rights that I believe most challenge that divide. Marriage rights are the best example.

Chapter 6 focuses on the *Bowers v. Hardwick* case and puts it in the context of earlier gay rights litigation that had challenged sodomy laws. Then, Chapter 7 focuses on legal arguments post-*Hardwick* in the public sphere. Chapter 8 focuses on legal arguments post-*Hardwick* in the private sphere. Chapter 9 once again questions the public/private divide by focusing on the right to marry and similar couple or family rights. In Chapter 10, I provide a short conclusion that focuses on two of the themes raised in this book: the public/private divide and the sameness/difference thesis. In the conclusion, I identify four obstacles that the lesbian and gay civil rights movement faces, obstacles that will make it more difficult for this movement to obtain the same successes in litigation that earlier civil rights movements for race and gender equality were able to obtain.

NOTES

1. See also Nixon v. Condon, 286 U.S. 73 at 89 (1932), where Justice Cardozo says "The Fourteenth Amendment, adopted as it was with special solicitude for the equal protection of members of the Negro race, lays a duty upon the court to level by its judgment these barriers of color."

2. Chambers v. Florida, 309 U.S. 227 at 241 (1940).

3. The "special rights" versus "equal rights" debate was central in the passage of Colorado's Amendment 2, later held unconstitutional in Romer v. Evans, 517 U.S. 620 (1996). The antigay supporters of Amendment 2 had characterized civil rights laws as laws aimed at giving special protection to certain minorities. They argued that gay rights ordinances in certain Colorado cities gave gay men, lesbians, and bisexuals a form of special protection. Legal experts in civil rights law testified at trial that civil rights laws did not provide special protection to minorities, but rather prohibited discrimination on the basis of certain classifications, such as race and gender. Under such laws, all racial groups are protected, not just minority groups. Similarly, both women and men are protected under laws that forbid sex or gender discrimination. And laws that forbid discrimination on the basis of sexual orientation protect both gay and nongay persons. See Lisa Keen and Suzanne B. Goldberg, *Strangers to the Law*, at 137–141. Justice Kennedy rejected the special rights argument, pointing out that Amendment 2 "withdraws from homosexuals, but no others [i.e., heterosexuals], specific legal protection from the injuries caused by discrimination." *Romer*, 517 U.S. at 627.

4. Judy Grahn, *Another Mother Tongue: Gay Words, Gay Worlds* at 272–273 (1984).

5. Deborah Price, "Rainbow Flag is a Symbol of a United Gay People," *Star Tribune,* April 19, 1995, at 4-E.

6. The eleven states are California, Connecticut, Hawaii, Massachusetts, Minnesota, Nevada, New Hampshire, New Jersey, Rhode Island, Vermont, and Wisconsin. See Cal. Lab. Code § 1102.1 (Deering Supp. 1998); Conn. Gen. Stat. Ann. § 46a–81c (West 1995); Haw. Rev. Stat. Ann. § 378–2 (Michie 1988); Mass. Ann. Laws, ch. 151B, § 4 (Law. Co-op. 1989); Minn. Stat. § 363.03 (West 1991); Nev. Stat. §613.330 (Michie 1999); N.H. Stat. § 354-A:6–17 (1999); N.J. Stat. Ann. S 10:5–12 (West 1993); R.I. Gen. Laws S 28–5–7 (1995); Vt. Stat. Ann. tit. 21, S 495 (1987); Wis. Stat. S 111.36(1)(b)-(d) (West 1997).

7. See D.C. Code Ann. S 1-2512 (1998).

8. 388 U.S. 1 (1967).

9. 334 U.S. 1 (1948).

10. 339 U.S. 629 (1950).

11. 347 U.S. 483 (1954).

12. Gerald N. Rosenberg, *The Hollow Hope: Can Courts Bring About Social Change?* (1991).

13. Roe v. Wade, 410 U.S. 113 (1973).

14. See, for example, Reed v. Reed, 404 U.S. 71 (1971) (striking down a state statute that established a preference for male executors of estates); Meritor Savings Bank v. Vinson, 477 U.S. 57 (1986) (construing Title VII to prohibit sexual harassment in employment).

15. Girardeau A. Spann, *Race Against the Court: The Supreme Court and Minorities in Contemporary America* 3 (1993).

16. See Barbara Jordan and Shelby Hearon, *Barbara Jordan: A Self-Portrait* (1979)

17. 478 U.S. 186 (1986).

1

Earlier Civil Rights Movements: Lessons to Be Learned

The lesbian and gay civil rights movement has focused on two primary themes or arguments: (1) that gay people are similar to all other human beings and should be treated equally, and (2) that gay people are different in ways that the law ought to respect and protect. In this regard, the movement is no different than earlier civil rights movements that also emphasized the themes of sameness and difference. The "sameness" thesis leads to an argument based on the Aristotelian notion of equality, that similarly situated persons ought to be treated similarly. The "difference" thesis leads to the use of arguments based on notions of libertarianism and the freedom of the individual to define self and live according to individual conscience.

The first argument, based on sameness, is easier to articulate, both politically and morally. If A and B are equally talented at designing bridges, then a city who is looking for a competent bridge designer should not care whether the designer is black, female, or gay. The talent of designing bridges is all that is relevant. The second argument, based on difference, is tougher. A person embracing the difference thesis will argue that, because each individual is unique, the law must respect the ways in which individual A is different from B. Disagreements abound over what sort of state action is required to give equal respect to differences. For example, does the state give sufficient respect to individual choices about sexuality simply by not judging what occurs in private (e.g., no regulation of consensual sex in private)? Or must the state do more—for example, accord public recognition for couples who have chosen to experience sexual intimacy and commitment with someone of the same sex? Jean Bethke Elshtain, a renowned professor of ethics, explains the problem as follows:

The argument that gays are oppressed . . . results in two different claims: either that society has no business scrutinizing the private sexual preferences of anybody, including gays; or that government *must* intrude in the area of private identity because gays, like women, require a unique sort of public protection and "validation." . . . The politics of democratic civility and equity holds that all citizens, including gays, have a right, as individuals, to be protected from intrusion or harassment and to be free from discrimination in such areas as employment and housing. They also have a right to create their own forms of "public space" within which to express and to reveal their particular concerns and to argue in behalf of policies they support. This I take as a given when a public-private distinction of a certain sort is cherished and upheld. . . .

But no one has a civil right, as a gay, a disciple of an exotic religion, or a political dissident, to full public sanction of his or her activities, values, beliefs, or habits. To be publicly legitimated, or validated, in one's activities, values, beliefs, or habits may be a political aim . . . but it is hardly a civil right. Paradoxically, in his quest to attain sanction for the *full* range of who he is, the crossdresser [and presumably the homosexual] puts his life on full display. He opens himself up to *publicity* in ways that others are bound to find quite uncivil. . . .[1]

Elshtain either misunderstands the public/private divide in the lives of gay people or she misunderstands the arguments that gay activists make. Gay people can and do argue that government should not intrude in the private sexual sphere. Government should not act in that sphere to limit free moral choices, that is, choices regarding sexual intimacy that are respectful of others. This argument takes the form of a "rights" argument, in particular a right to privacy argument. At the same time, gay people can ask the government to accord equal respect to the private choices of both gay and nongay couples regarding sexual intimacy and commitment. This argument is an "equality" argument. The request for equal respect is not a demand for governmental intrusion in "the area of private identity" as Elshtain suggests, but rather a demand for equal public recognition and facilitation of that private commitment. Recognition of the commitments of opposite-sex couples facilitates the "togetherness" of the partners, a "togetherness" that government generally values. Same-sex couples ask for similar or equal treatment, not "unique" protection or "validation" as Elshtain suggests.

Both arguments, privacy rights and equality, can be made before courts. Elshtain's assertion that "full public sanction of [individual] activities, values, beliefs or habits" is not a civil right is reminiscent of early arguments raised in the battle over racial equality. The Fourteenth Amendment, it was argued, guarantees only equal civil rights, not equal acceptance in society. The lesbian and gay civil rights movement often runs up against similar arguments. The response to such arguments is that the immediate battle, as it was in the civil rights movement for race equality, is over equal treatment by the government. Social acceptance may follow, and indeed is more likely to follow once a group is treated with equal respect by the government. The first Mr. Justice Harlan made a similar point in 1896 regarding racial minorities when he insisted that with respect to "civil rights, all citizens are equal before the law."[2] To the extent gay couples can demonstrate similarity with nongay couples, equal treatment "before the law" should be the rule. Whereas Elshtain appears to view arguments that support public sanction as political, I view such arguments as legal ones based on equality. Equality of treatment by government *is* a civil right.

The lesbian and gay civil rights movement is not the first civil rights movement to wrestle with the sameness/difference question and the public/private divide. Other movements have debated these issues, both internally and externally, and crafted arguments, some political, some legal, to deal with both issues. Other movements have produced their own win/loss records in the courts using both equality arguments and privacy or rights arguments. The purpose of this chapter is to examine two earlier civil rights movements in order to learn lessons from the past—to observe the contexts in which these two movements sounded the themes of sameness and difference, of public and private, of equality and rights, and to observe the responses of the courts to the legal arguments crafted by the litigators in these movements.

The two earlier civil rights movements that are of particular interest for the lesbian and gay civil rights movement are the African American civil rights movement and the women's movement. Advocates in both these movements litigated cases arguing for equal rights in the public sphere and for the right of individual dignity in the private sphere. In an attempt to obtain national and uniform recognition of such rights, both movements pursued litigation to establish rights under the federal constitution. For rights in the public sphere, advocates relied primarily on equality arguments supported by the Equal Protection Clause of the Fourteenth Amendment. For rights in the private sphere, they relied on privacy arguments derived from the liberty rights protected by the Due Process Clause. The lesbian and gay civil rights movement has crafted legal arguments based on the successes of the arguments made in these earlier civil rights movements, thereby arguing for the extension to gay men and lesbians of rights that had been earlier won for racial minorities and for women.

CIVIL RIGHTS MOVEMENT
FOR RACE EQUALITY

At the time of the founding of this country, the Declaration of Independence pronounced: "All men are created equal." But the debates that occurred in the drafting of the Constitution indicated that "all men" did not include black men. In 1857, the U.S. Supreme Court agreed when it announced that Dred Scott, a slave, was not a citizen of the state of Missouri, nor of the United States, and thus could not bring a case in federal court claiming his freedom under the Missouri Compromise.[3]

The *Dred Scott* decision was ultimately reversed by the Fourteenth Amendment, passed in 1868, which states that "all persons born or naturalized in the United States . . . are citizens of the United States and of the State wherein they reside." Slavery was abolished by the Thirteenth Amendment, which had been ratified three years earlier in 1865. The Fourteenth Amendment, in addition to defining citizenship, protects citizens against state abridgments of privileges and immunities and declares that no state should deny a person equal protection or deprive a person of life, liberty, or property without due process of law. The Fifteenth Amendment secures the right to vote in every male citizen regardless of race. These three amendments have all been crucial in crafting legal arguments for racial equality. Constitutional amendments are not self-executing, however. Both litigation and legislation were necessary to effectuate the principles embodied in these Reconstruction amendments.

Relying on the principle of equal access embodied in the Fourteenth Amendment and on section five of that amendment, which authorizes Congress to pass legislation required to enforce the substantive provisions of the amendment, Congress passed the Civil Rights Act of 1875. This legislation guaranteed equal enjoyment of public accommodations regardless of race, thereby prohibiting racial discrimination by privately owned enterprises that opened their doors to the public at large. In response to charges made by some legislators that blacks were asking for something Congress could not provide, the right to socialize with white people, African American congressman John Lynch from Mississippi replied: "No . . . it is not social rights we desire. . . . What we ask is protection in the enjoyment of public rights. Rights which are or should be accorded to every citizen alike."[4]

Note the similarity to current arguments used against gay men and lesbians. When gay people ask to participate in the public arena as gay people, we are viewed as asking for social acceptance. Yet the reality is that when a gay Boy Scout asks not to be stripped of his status as an Eagle Scout, he is asking for protection in the enjoyment of a public right. When partners in a lesbian couple ask that their relationship be acknowledged by hospital workers so that one partner might provide emotional support to the partner in intensive care, they are asking for rights that should be accorded every citizen who is part of a couple. These requests are forms of equality arguments.

Shortly after the passage of the Civil Rights Act of 1875, the Supreme Court thwarted the congressional goal of equal racial access by entertaining a constitutional challenge to the Civil Rights Act of 1875. In 1883, the Court handed down its opinion in the *Civil Rights Cases,*[5] holding that the Fourteenth Amendment addressed only *state* action that denied equal protection and due process.[6] Because the Civil Rights Act attempted to prohibit racial discrimination by privately owned businesses, the legislation exceeded the power granted to Congress under section five of the amendment. Thus, the Court struck down the statute, ruling that Congress had no power to enact it.

With the Court's holding in the *Civil Rights Cases,* the state action doctrine of the Fourteenth Amendment became official. Under this doctrine, race discrimination claims brought in federal court would succeed only if the discrimination could be traced to a state official or state statute. The Thirteenth Amendment, by contrast, contains no "state action" language. Although litigators had argued in the *Civil Rights Cases* that racial discrimination in public accommodations was a "badge of slavery" and thereby prohibited by the Thirteenth Amendment, the Court rejected the argument. Thus challenges to race discrimination, other than challenges to slavery itself, had to be pursued under the Fourteenth Amendment, now burdened with the state action requirement. The state action doctrine had the effect of drawing a sharp line between public and private discrimination and became the first roadblock to realizing the goal of equal access to the public sphere, much of which is controlled or owned by private employers and businesses.

The second "roadblock" to equal access for racial minorities was created by the famous case of *Plessy v. Ferguson,*[7] decided in 1896, in which the Court held that a black man could be barred from a white railroad carriage without offending the Equal Protection Clause of the Fourteenth Amendment. This case created the "separate but equal doctrine," a doctrine that validated segregation in public until *Brown v. Board of Education*[8] was decided in 1954.

Litigating Against the "Separate but Equal" Doctrine and the "State Action" Doctrine

In 1914, the Supreme Court handed down a decision that greased the wheels for the subsequent battle by the NAACP against the "separate but equal" doctrine. In *McCabe v. Atchison, Topeka & Santa Fe Railway,*[9] the Court ruled against a railroad that maintained segregated rail cars, but failed to provide first-class sleeping and dining cars for black travelers. The justification for the unequal facilities was that there was less demand from black travelers for such accommodations. The Court rejected the justification, holding that the right to equal protection was an individual right, that is, the right to be protected regardless of group membership and, in this case, regardless of group demand for first-class service. This emphasis on the individual's right set the stage for later challenges involving individual demands for graduate school education.

Shortly after *McCabe* came another major legal success for the black civil rights movement. In 1917 the Supreme Court decided the case of *Buchanan v. Warley,*[10] which struck down a city zoning ordinance that prevented a white person from selling his home to a black purchaser. The ordinance was not found to violate principles of racial equality since it applied equally to black and white owners by requiring all sellers to restrict their sales to purchasers of the same race. This view of the matter was consistent with the "separate but equal" doctrine, which supported racial segregation. Racial segregation was not the problem in *Buchanan*. Rather, the problem was that the restriction on who could sell to whom violated the white seller's liberty of contract. Since "liberty of contract" was protected by the Due Process Clause of the Fourteenth Amendment, the zoning ordinance was held to be unconstitutional. Although celebrated as a major success at the time, the case was a Sisyphean victory for the African American civil rights movement because it did not advance the meaning of racial equality, nor make any normative statements about segregation. The narrow basis of its holding (that white people could freely choose to sell to black people) did little to further the notion that apartheid, in and of itself, was unequal. The decision was handed down during a short period in constitutional history when liberty of contract was entitled to strong constitutional protection. That period ended in the 1930s. Thus, after that period, even the narrow legal principle established in the case was no longer available to black civil rights lawyers. In addition, the state action doctrine prevented the *Buchanan* ruling from being extended to instances of private zoning, that is, private covenants that restricted property ownership to members of a particular race.

The victory in *Buchanan,* even though it produced no long-term benefit in the form of legal doctrine that might support black civil rights, did produce another sort of long-term benefit. Encouraged by this victory, the NAACP proposed to launch a broader litigation effort to attack racial discrimination. The legal committee of the NAACP developed a proposal to attack segregation in housing, the exclusion of blacks from juries, and to combat segregation in public schools. The Garland Fund provided a $100,000 grant to support the campaign. In 1934, Charles Hamilton Houston, then the dean of Howard Law School, was hired to head the NAACP legal team that would be responsible for conducting this litigation campaign against racism.

Originally organized in 1909 by a small biracial group of New York citizens concerned about racial justice, the NAACP initially fought for legislative changes, in particular the enactment of antilynching laws, and represented black defendants in individual cases. This focus changed significantly under Houston's direction. His plan was to end segregation in education, which he considered "symbolic of all the more drastic discriminations."[11] In 1940, the NAACP Legal Defense and Educational Fund, Inc. was officially incorporated and its charter, authorizing practice of law as a corporation, was approved by the Appellate Division of the Supreme Court of New York County. African American lawyers in the organization at that time, in particular Houston, William Hastie, Thurgood Marshall, and Constance Baker Motley, developed the legal agenda and the legal arguments needed to attack segregated education.

The decision to use the courts was a conscious choice. The details of the NAACP's strategy have been provided by other authors, most notably Richard Kluger[12] and Mark Tushnet.[13] The attack focused primarily on educational opportunities. Two different legal arguments were pursued. Early cases argued that schools for black children were not in fact equal to schools for whites, that black teachers were not paid as much as white teachers, and that graduate school opportunities for blacks were often nonexistent when compared with opportunities for whites. In these cases, equalization was a permissible remedy. By the late 1940s, however, Thurgood Marshall, now at the helm of the NAACP legal team, began a frontal attack on segregated education itself, arguing that separation of the races could never result in equal educational opportunity. This latter strategy ultimately succeeded when the Supreme Court ruled against segregation in *Brown v. Board of Education.*

The litigation efforts of the NAACP were not aimed at ending segregation so much as they were aimed at combatting racial discrimination in its many forms. Although segregated education ended up as a primary focus, the NAACP lawyers pursued other cases that also enlarged and protected the rights of black Americans. Attacks on the state action doctrine began to result in positive decisions as early as the 1940s with victories in the "white primary cases"[14] and the restrictive covenant case, *Shelley v. Kraemer.*[15] In *Shelley,* the Court ruled that private covenants to restrict property ownership on the basis of race violated the Equal Protection Clause even though the discrimination originated with the private landowners who had created the restrictions; the Court found the requisite "state action" in the judicial enforcement of the private covenants. Throughout the 1950s and 1960s, in cases that arose before the passage of the Civil Rights Acts of the 1960s, the NAACP litigated cases that continued to chip away at the state action doctrine, thereby enabling them to reach instances of private discrimination. Thus, a restaurant that leased space from a governmental agency was found to violate the Equal Protection Clause when the owner discriminated on the basis of race, despite the fact that the restaurant itself was privately owned.[16] And department stores that enlisted police aid in ejecting blacks from lunch counters were found to violate the Fourteenth Amendment, despite the fact that the stores were privately owned.[17] "Entanglement" with government officials became a sufficient nexus to turn a private actor into a state actor for equal protection claims.

This broadening of the state action doctrine came to an abrupt end when the political makeup of the Court changed in the late 1960s. The shift from the Warren Court[18] to the Burger Court[19] ended the expansion of the concept of state action.[20] By that time, however, the black civil rights movement had achieved legislative gains that made the state action doctrine less relevant to the attainment of its goals. The Civil Rights Acts of 1964 and the Fair Housing Act of 1968 established the principle of nondiscrimination on the basis of race in the arenas of private employment, education, accommodations, and housing. When civil rights opponents challenged these statutes on constitutional grounds, citing the late-nineteenth-century *Civil Rights Cases,* the courts upheld the legislative action under both the commerce clause and the Thirteenth Amendment, neither of which contains a state action requirement.[21]

More important than chipping away at the state action doctrine was the NAACP's decision to wage a full-scale litigation battle against the separate but equal doctrine in the arena of public education. The first case to reach the Supreme Court was a case challenging the state of Missouri's practice of providing out-of-state scholarships for black graduate students who were unable to obtain graduate degrees in the segregated universities of the state. In 1938, the Supreme Court ruled that the state of Missouri was under an obligation to provide equal graduate education itself, rather than rely on other states to perform that function.[22] Ultimately, the state of Missouri complied, not by admitting the black law student to the white law school, but rather by creating a separate black law school. In subsequent cases, the NAACP legal team challenged the notion that a separate black law school created in a short amount of time could ever be truly equal to a fully established white law school. Finally, in 1950, the Supreme Court agreed and ordered the state of Texas to admit Heman Sweatt to the University of Texas Law School.[23] Furthermore, in its decision, the Court indicated that educating black law students apart from white students resulted in intangible harms to black students that could not be eradicated by spending more money on buildings, faculty, or books. In essence, the Court pointed out that there was only one University of Texas Law School and no comparable school could be built in less time than the time it had taken to establish the reputation of the existing school.

These cases finally led to *Brown v. Board of Education,* a case attacking the separate but equal doctrine directly in the context of elementary and secondary education. The key argument was that the state's separation of the races was inherently unequal because it was based on a system of white supremacy, thereby creating a stigmatic harm to each and every black child who was told that he or she was unworthy to attend the white school. The Supreme Court agreed:

> To separate [children in grade and high schools] from others of similar age and qualifications solely because of their race generates a feeling of inferiority as to their status in the community that may affect their hearts and minds in a way unlikely ever to be undone. . . .
>
> We conclude that in the field of public education, the doctrine of "separate but equal" has no place. Separate educational facilities are inherently unequal.[24]

In the years following *Brown v. Board of Education,* lawyers brought additional cases arguing that apartheid in other public arenas was equally harmful. As a result, municipal golf courses and parks maintained only for the use of whites had to be integrated.[25] Some southern states resisted, but in the end, with the help of federal troops called in to enforce the rulings of the federal courts, de jure segregation of the races was eliminated.

Race as a Suspect Classification

Litigation in the 1960s challenging explicit racial restrictions was aided by another doctrinal development in Fourteenth Amendment jurisprudence: The idea that legislative classifications on the basis of race are inherently suspect and thus rarely constitutional. This doctrine, which requires "strict scrutiny" of racial classifications, did not develop through the litigation efforts or strategy of the NAACP lawyers who battled segregation. Modern constitutional scholars trace the doctrinal development to a 1938 case, *Carolene Products,*[26] which had nothing to do with race discrimination. The *Carolene Products* case, in which a lower court had struck down a state economic regulation on grounds that it interfered with the constitutional right to freedom of contract, reached the Court shortly after the Court had begun to reverse its freedom of contract decisions. Known as the "switch in time that saved nine," the new judicial philosophy of a majority of the Supreme Court justices supported "New Deal" statutes enacted for the public welfare that had previously been vulnerable to constitutional attack because the statutes restricted individual freedom of contract. The new Court philosophy called for judicial deference to legislative decisions to set minimum wages or maximum work hours or provide safe working conditions.

But the Court also realized that it should not readily defer to all legislative choices, for such deference would render judicial review meaningless. How to draw the line between those cases deserving of deference and those not deserving required the development of a new judicial doctrine. Justice Stone, in *Carolene Products,* offered a theory. In footnote four, probably the most famous footnote in the history of constitutional jurisprudence, Stone explained that legislation was suspect when it impinged on specifically guaranteed rights (e.g., freedom of speech or religion)[27] or when the legislative choice resulted from an imperfection in the legislative process.[28] Of crucial importance to supporters of racial justice was Stone's theory that certain discrete and insular minorities, who had suffered from prejudice and discrimination, were likely to be excluded from the normal political process and thus would be unable to express their interests adequately before a legislative body. Blacks, for example, were unable to vote for a long period of our history and remain underrepresented in legislative bodies. Thus, if a legislative body were to enact a statute disfavoring blacks, the Court would view that statute as suspect, as perhaps resulting from racial bias. Stone's theory supported close judicial scrutiny of such statutes and a striking down of such statutes if their justifications did not survive the close judicial scrutiny applied by the Court. By contrast, statutes that merely regulated economic behavior and did not burden a racial minority could be easily upheld under the lower level of scrutiny accorded them.

Carolene Products and its famous footnote were handed down in 1938. The first race case to suggest that racial classifications enacted by legislatures might bear some higher degree of justification was the 1944 Japanese internment case, *Korematsu*.[29] The Court did not mention footnote four in its opinion. However, the Court announced, for the first time, that "legal restrictions which curtail the civil rights of a single racial group are immediately suspect."[30] Then, after giving lip service to the notion that racial classifications were suspect, the Court readily upheld the conviction of Korematsu, a loyal Japanese American citizen by all accounts, for his defiance of the race-based evacuation order.[31]

Some commentators have suggested that the Court could not fully endorse the concept of a different standard of judicial review for racial classifications until *Brown v. Board of Education* had settled the segregation question.[32] For, if racial classifications were inherently suspect, then all statutes requiring racial segregation were subject to serious constitutional challenge. Yet constitutional challenges to secondary school segregation had failed consistently prior to *Brown*. Race as a suspect classification was not a sufficient theory to justify striking down segregation and reversing almost a hundred years of Supreme Court precedent on the specific question of school segregation. *Brown* focused on a different theory, a theory that focused on the fundamental nature of the rights of schoolchildren to education and the negative message that state enforced segregation delivered to those children.

Once segregation had been declared unconstitutional, the Court was free to develop the theory that race was a "suspect" classification for purposes of equal protection analysis. That theory began to take hold in the 1960s. Under this theory, a racial classification will be struck down as a violation of equal protection unless the classification is necessary to accomplish a compelling state interest. Rarely will a racial classification pass this "compelling state interest" test.

Litigating Against Race Discrimination in the Private Sphere of Home and Family

By the time the compelling state interest test was available to help litigants challenge race discrimination on constitutional grounds, Congress had provided a statutory basis for litigating against most instances of race discrimination in the public sphere. But a key barrier to full equality among the races remained in the private sphere, a sphere unaffected by congressional acts or by the court decisions that had dismantled public segregation. This remaining barrier affected the private sphere of marriage and personal intimacy. In 1960, over one-third of the states continued to enforce antimiscegenation laws and related laws that prohibited interracial intimate relationships. These laws had been insulated from a successful equal protection challenge by the doctrine of "equal application" that had first been recognized in *Buchanan*. Antimiscegenation statutes generally prohibited a person of a "colored" race from marrying a white person. As applied, the prohibition equally burdened both racial groups. Furthermore, asking the court to lift the ban on interracial marriage came perilously close to asking the court to *validate* interracial marriages.

The test case that would put an end to miscegenation laws began in the late 1950s when Mildred Jeter and Richard Loving fell in love. Mildred was black and Richard was white. Because they knew interracial marriages were prohibited in their home state of Virginia, they went to Washington, D.C., and got married. Shortly after they returned to Virginia, the local sheriff burst into their bedroom in the middle of the night, arrested them for violating the Virginia law against interracial marriages, and threw them in jail. Citing God's plan of creation as the justification for separation of the races, the trial judge sentenced them to prison, but offered to let them go if they promised not to return to Virginia for twenty-five years. They moved to Washington, D.C., where they began raising a family, but they continued to yearn for their home in Virginia, and they missed their family and friends.

Emboldened by the success of the black civil rights movement in the mid-sixties, the Lovings appealed by letter to Attorney-General Robert Kennedy for help in returning to their native state. The letter was ultimately passed on to civil rights attorneys with the American Civil Liberties Union

(ACLU). ACLU attorney Bernard Cohen took their case to the U.S. Supreme Court, which held the Virginia law unconstitutional on both equal protection and due process (liberty) grounds. The Court rejected the state's argument that because the racial restriction equally burdened blacks and whites, no equal protection violation occurred. Rather, the Court said, "there can be no question but that Virginia's miscegenation statutes rest solely upon distinctions drawn according to race." Because the classification was based on race, the Court applied strict scrutiny and held the statute unconstitutional despite the state's justification that the statute was intended to protect the integrity of both the white and the black races. As an additional rationale for its decision, the Court reiterated its view that

> marriage is one of the 'basic civil rights of man,' fundamental to our very existence and survival. . . . To deny this fundamental freedom on so unsupportable a basis as the racial classifications embodied in these statutes, classifications so directly subversive of the principle of equality at the heart of the Fourteenth Amendment, is surely to deprive all the State's citizens of liberty without due process of law.[33]

One More Constitutional Roadblock: Washington v. Davis

In 1976, the Supreme Court added one more hurdle for litigators seeking redress for discrimination claims under the Fourteenth Amendment. In *Washington v. Davis*,[34] the Court ruled that state action that placed an unintended burden on racial minorities did not violate the Equal Protection Clause. Under this ruling, explicit racial classifications would continue to be subjected to strict judicial scrutiny. But neutral rules, such as those based on education or wealth, would not trigger strict scrutiny even though the enforcement of the rule might more heavily burden one racial group. The fact that years of state-enforced and explicit discrimination against black Americans had reduced their educational and wealth opportunities was not a relevant consideration in judging the constitutionality of classifications based on education or wealth. Only if a litigant could show that the classification was a subterfuge, masking an otherwise clear intent to discriminate on the basis of race, would the neutral rule be subjected to strict judicial scrutiny. Thus, it was no longer sufficient to show that the discrimination resulted from state action. Now litigators had to prove that the state action was based on intentional racial animus.

Making Difference Arguments in
Support of Affirmative Action

Despite legal victories that effectively reversed a century of de jure racial discrimination and that helped to establish both a constitutional and a national legislative norm of racial equality, the material reality of the day-to-day living conditions of black Americans was clearly not equal to that of white Americans. Inferior schools, inferior medical services, segregated housing that had suffered from a lack of government services, economic disparities stemming from years of employment discrimination, and social attitudes about black people that had been formed in an era when blacks were presumed to be unequal all served to perpetuate their material inequality. Ending de jure segregation did not immediately improve the lives of most black Americans.

In an attempt to respond to the reality of continuing material inequality, which could be characterized as "black difference," a new legal argument found its way into the legislatures and the courts: the affirmative action argument. The starting point of the argument is that race should not matter in the allocation of public benefits such as jobs, education, credit, and housing. But so long as material inequalities continued to burden black Americans, the nation should recognize that material inequality and engage in affirmative efforts to overcome it. There are three steps to the traditional affirmative action argument: (1) the persistence of racial difference (i.e., material inequality) contradicts the normative ideal of equality; (2) the material inequality of racial minority groups resulted primarily from past wrongs committed by the dominant race; (3) therefore, government is under an affirmative obligation to right the wrong by acting affirmatively to reduce this manifestation of racial difference.

Court-ordered busing resulted from a form of this argument. Affirmative action in hiring and government set-asides for minority contractors also resulted from this argument. The argument met with some success in the 1960s and 70s. But in the 1980s and 90s, the argument has been attacked by claims that affirmative action of any type is just another form of race discrimination. Specifically, the Court has ruled that race, whether white, black or other minority, is always suspect.[35] Thus statutes that benefit one race (blacks) to the detriment of another race (whites) are subject to the same exacting scrutiny and will only be upheld if they meet the compelling state interest test. This approach to statutes that allegedly disadvantage the majority in favor of a minority is difficult to justify on the basis of Justice

Stone's political process theory set forth in the *Carolene Products* footnote. Replacing the political process theory, the affirmative action decisions instead appear to embrace a normative theory that race preferences are always evil. As a result, in the current legal landscape of the civil rights movement for race equality, the equality principle has trumped the difference argument.

CIVIL RIGHTS MOVEMENT FOR GENDER EQUALITY

The fight for gender equality is often viewed as occurring in two different waves. The first wave of feminism, or the early women's rights movement, known as the "woman movement," occurred in the nineteenth century. In this chapter, I focus primarily on the modern women's movement and the arguments its leaders have made in the courts. The arguments constructed in favor of women's rights in the first wave, however, deserve some comment because they reveal the important role of separate spheres ideology, as well as the sameness/difference thesis, in making legal arguments for gender equality.

The First Wave of Feminism

Nineteenth-century feminists[36] often analogized their plight to that of the African American slave. Acknowledging that woman's bondage was different, they argued that women, like slaves, were human beings entitled to equal respect. The plight of women, unlike that of slaves, stemmed from Victorian notions of women's superiority in the private sphere. Thus a principal cause of women's inequality was private sphere rules that pretended to glamorize women and yet, in reality, stripped them of autonomy. Appropriating male political discourse, early feminists argued in favor of self-ownership, even for women, and even in the private sphere. Arguments for equality in both the private and public spheres were primarily based on sameness. Yet some feminists also relied on the difference thesis—"invoking women's distinctive moral sensibility and mission and their special domestic concerns and competencies"[37] in order to strengthen their claims to additional rights in both the public and private spheres.

During most of the first wave, feminists argued for private law reforms that would enable women to own their own property, their own wages, and their own bodies. Under the common law doctrine of coverture, a woman's legal existence merged into that of her husband at marriage. Only he could own property and contract for the benefit of the family. This arrangement left women at the mercy of their husbands and created a stark imbalance of power within the personal and intimate sphere of home and family. By reforming marital property laws, feminists hoped to strike a more equal balance between husband and wife. Early feminists accomplished their goals regarding marital property reform, but the reform was not sufficient to equalize the balance of power in personal relationships, except perhaps for the most wealthy women. Men still controlled the public sphere and access to wealth. Wives lacked the ability to acquire wealth on their own in the public sphere through employment. Thus they still depended on men to provide them with property.

Early feminists accomplished their legal reforms in legislatures, not in courts. Because property law is within the purview of the state, these reforms took place in state legislatures. Thus, the movement, although national in organization, was local in its politics and its lobbying. Suffrage, another goal for early feminists, started in the states and only later became a national campaign that finally ended in the passage of the Nineteenth Amendment in 1920. Some feminist activity continued after 1920, but there was no readily identifiable unified national effort on behalf of women after passage of the Nineteenth Amendment. Women's groups were often split on strategies and agendas. For example, opinions about the proposed Equal Rights Amendment were quite diverse, with some feminists embracing the concept that women were entitled to the same rights as men and other feminists concerned that equality would not take account of women's differences from men.

The Second Wave of Feminism

The second wave of feminism is often said to have begun in the 1960s. By this time, women who had been encouraged to return to the domestic sphere of home and family after World War II were entering the labor market in increased numbers. In 1960, Esther Peterson, a labor organizer and lobbyist, became active in the Kennedy campaign. When Kennedy was elected president, he appointed Peterson to head the Women's Bureau and created a cabinet post for her as assistant secretary of Labor. In 1961, at Peterson's urging, Kennedy created the President's Commission on the Status of Women. The commission focused on women's equal access to employment, education, financial security, and child care. In struggling with the sameness/difference question, the commission's approach was to recommend equal treatment for women at times and special or different treatment at other times. For example, in recognition of women's special role in childbearing and rearing, the commission recommended that primary financial responsibility for the family should remain with the husband. But whenever women and men were equally situated, such as holding the same jobs, they were to be treated equally, such as receiving equal pay.

In 1963, Betty Friedan's book, *The Feminine Mystique,* hit the stands and quickly became a bestseller. Her arguments resonated with a significant portion of the female populace, especially white, married women, who stayed home while their husbands earned wages to support the family. Friedan argued that a woman's role in the private sphere of the home had been socially constructed in such a way as to prevent her from full participation in the public sphere. Second wave feminists, challenging this private/public divide, made sameness arguments and asked for equal access to the public sphere. Their arguments plugged into the existing feminist network that had become more visible with Esther Peterson's appointment as head of the Women's Bureau and Eleanor Roosevelt's appointment as head of the President's Commission on the Status of Women. These arguments met with early success in the legislative arena with the passage of the Equal Pay Act in 1963,[38] guaranteeing equal pay for equal work regardless of sex, and Title VII of the Civil Rights Act of 1964,[39] prohibiting sex discrimination in private employment.[40]

Because Congress acted so early in the modern women's rights movement to prohibit sex discrimination by private employers, the state action doctrine was never as serious a roadblock to legal actions for gender equality as it was to legal actions for racial equality.[41] The Civil Rights Act of 1964, however, did not ban sex discrimination in public accommodations, although it did ban race discrimination in such arenas. Thus, under federal law, clubs and restaurants could and did impose gender restrictions. Riding on the coattails of the black civil rights movements, feminists were successful in their efforts to expand women's rights at the state level, even where they had failed at the federal level. A number of state legislatures included sex, along with race, as an impermissible grounds of discrimination toward customers or users of public accommodations. Years after these state public accommodations statutes were enacted prohibiting discrimination on the basis of sex, cases arose in a number of states challenging the gender restrictions in private organizations such as the Jaycees and Rotary Club. When state courts ruled in favor of gender equality under the state statute, the clubs appealed to the Supreme

Court claiming their constitutional right to choose their associates had been burdened. In every such case, the Supreme Court has ruled against the associational claims of the clubs, thereby upholding the principle of gender equality in the state law.[42] Yet the Court has left open the possibility that some organizations might be sufficiently private that intrusion into their membership choices would violate their First Amendment rights of association.

Constitutional Arguments for Women's Equality

Successful litigation for women's rights came much later than legislative success. Feminist litigators were hampered by earlier Supreme Court decisions honoring the presumption that a woman's place is in the domestic sphere of home and family. Just as the NAACP legal team had to battle against early Supreme Court precedents, such as the separate but equal doctrine, feminist litigators in the 1960s and 1970s had to battle against early Supreme Court precedents that had denied women equal access to public forums.

The first negative Supreme Court case on women's rights was handed down in 1873. Myra Bradwell appealed to the Supreme Court to reverse the Illinois Supreme Court's decision dismissing her claim that she should be admitted to the practice of law. Relying on the privileges and immunities clause of the recently enacted Fourteenth Amendment, she had argued that the state could not deny her the right to practice her chosen profession. She met all of the qualifications and it was only the state imposition of a gender restriction that barred her from the profession. Because the Court earlier had ruled that the privileges and immunities clause did not grant citizens the right to work or to choose a profession, Myra Bradwell lost her case. But Justice Bradley, joined by Justices Swayne and Field, who thought the privileges and immunities clause should have been read in the manner Bradwell had argued, found himself in need of a different rationale for denying her claim. He wrote separately to say:

> Man is, or should be, woman's protector and defender. The natural and proper timidity and delicacy which belongs to the female sex evidently unfits it for many of the occupations of civil life. The constitution of the family organization, which is founded in the divine ordinance, as well as in the nature of

things, indicates the domestic sphere as that which properly belongs to the domain and functions of womanhood. . . . The paramount destiny and mission of woman are to fulfil the noble and benign offices of wife and mother. This is the law of the Creator.[43]

The *Bradwell* decision, especially Bradley's concurring opinion, exemplified the judicial attitude of the time. As long as judges deemed it to be the "law of the Creator" that women were confined to the roles of wife and mother, it was virtually impossible for women to invoke the "sameness" argument with any success. Feminist arguments that women should be allowed into the male professions or into higher educational institutions reserved for men or that women should be allowed to vote all failed in the courts. The right to vote was not achieved until 1920, and then only by the enactment of a constitutional amendment.

The seed that eventually sprouted into a successful impact litigation strategy for second-wave feminists was planted when Pauli Murray, a young black college graduate and labor and civil rights activist, decided to become a lawyer. Already conscious of society's racism, her law school experience at Howard in the 1940s, where she was one of only two females, raised her consciousness of society's sexism.[44] Murray graduated from Howard Law School in 1944 and did postgraduate legal work on a fellowship at the University of California because Harvard did not accept women at that time. In 1961, she joined the staff of the Committee on Civil and Political Rights of the newly established President's Commission on the Status of Women. She was assigned the task of researching the possibility of making Fourteenth Amendment equal protection claims to assert women's rights.

The most recent rejection of such a claim had come in a 1961 Supreme Court opinion, *Hoyt v. Florida*,[45] a case in which the female defendant challenged the state's laws, which effectively excluded women from jury service. Pauli Murray had seen the connections between racism and sexism from the beginning of her legal career, dubbing sex discrimination a system of "Jane Crow." As a staff member of the Commission on the Status of Women, she had the opportunity to elaborate on those connections. The memo she prepared for the commission grew into a law review article, "Jane Crow and the Law," and was published in the *George Washington Law Review* in 1965.[46] Her thesis was that sexism, like racism, could be attacked in litigation structured under the Equal Protection and Due Process Clauses of the federal constitution. Such litigation could attack state laws and decisions that discriminated against women in employment, jury service, public education, and criminal law. Equal protection arguments might even be used to challenge sexist domestic relations laws.

Murray's thesis, that equal protection litigation could be used for sex cases in the same way it had been used in race cases, was attractive to many legal activists. Murray joined the national board of directors of the ACLU in the mid-1960s and pushed her thesis there, encouraging the ACLU to participate in constitutional litigation to establish equality of rights for women. Prior to this time, most of the ACLU's work on behalf of women had been in the legislative arena or in cases that raised constitutional issues of privacy and reproductive freedom. The ACLU had supported legislation that required equal pay for equal work and it had opposed legislation that restricted the use of contraceptives. In the mid-1960s, the ACLU joined with Planned Parenthood in bringing a constitutional challenge to laws that restricted the use of contraceptives.[47] But it had only once joined litigation that argued for equality for women under the Equal Protection Clause. The ACLU had filed an amicus brief on behalf of Gwendolyn Hoyt in her unsuccessful 1961 constitutional challenge to Florida's discriminatory laws on jury service.

The Women's Rights Project

Finally the ACLU began to focus more directly on equal protection litigation as a strategy to increase women's rights. In 1971, the national organization created a legal program known as the Women's Rights Project of the ACLU. Ruth Bader Ginsburg was appointed its director. She moved from her job teaching courses on sex-based discrimination at Rutgers Law School to join the Columbia Law School faculty and head the new ACLU program. Just as the NAACP had set out to reverse earlier racist Supreme Court decisions, so Ginsburg set out to challenge earlier sexist decisions.

Before the official launching of the ACLU project, Ginsburg became involved in a sex discrimination case that was on the way to the U.S. Supreme Court. The case was *Reed v. Reed.*[48] Ginsburg authored an amicus brief in the case, arguing, along the lines Pauli Murray had suggested, that sex classifications were suspect in the way that race classifications were. She relied on the "discrete and insular minority" language from footnote four of *Carolene Products.* Women, so the argument went, had suffered discrimination over time. Although they made up a majority of the population, they had not been active participants in the political process. First of all, women could not even vote until 1920. In addition, there were very few women holding elective positions in legislative bodies. As a result, women consti-

tuted a discrete and insular group that had not participated equally in legislative processes. Because the political process had failed to represent their
interests, the Court should intervene and scrutinize closely any legislation
that burdened women to determine whether the legislation was justified or
merely resulted from prejudicial thinking.

Although the Court did not adopt Ginsburg's suspect classification argument in *Reed,* it did rule in favor of Sally Reed, the plaintiff. The Court
held that the state of Idaho could not create a legislative preference for
male administrators of decedents' estates. Thus Sally Reed, the mother of
the deceased child, had the right to apply to administer his estate. The opinion was very terse, and the Court appeared to apply low-level scrutiny in
holding that the statute was not rationally related to a legitimate goal.

Recently, when asked about the Court's holding, Ginsburg, now herself a
justice of the Supreme Court, said she was delighted with the holding in
Reed and not at all troubled by the Court's reluctance to apply heightened
scrutiny. She stressed that the Court is an institution that is best suited for
making incremental change.[49] Her strategy as a litigator was to build on
each sex discrimination opinion handed down by the Court in search of
that next bit of change that would bring the Court closer to declaring sex a
suspect classification. In planning such a strategy, the ACLU project had to
keep close tabs on all sex discrimination cases around the country and try
to control the order in which they arrived at the Supreme Court.

Only two years after *Reed,* however, in the first sex discrimination case
argued by Ginsburg before the Court, *Frontiero v. Richardson,*[50] she convinced four justices that sex classifications should be reviewed under the
compelling state interest/strict scrutiny test, only one vote short of a majority. As in *Reed,* the Court ruled in favor of the female plaintiff, striking the
discriminatory law down under a lower level of scrutiny. Ginsburg was
now convinced that four votes in favor of strict scrutiny was the maximum
available at that time. In subsequent cases, she argued for heightened
scrutiny, but not necessarily the same strict scrutiny that the Court had applied to racial classifications.[51]

Ultimately, the Supreme Court hammered out an intermediate level of
scrutiny for sex-based classifications. Intermediate scrutiny allowed the
Court to recognize the sameness argument as a general principle of constitutional interpretation, and yet to honor the difference argument when biological differences made it impossible for the Court to regard men and
women as being similarly situated. Unlike modern race discrimination
cases, which have consistently struck down racial classifications, modern

sex discrimination cases have come out both ways, sometimes upholding the classification and sometimes striking the classification. In 1975, without specifically overruling *Hoyt*, the Court began striking down gender classifications as applied to juries.[52] In other cases, the Court held that the government cannot discriminate on the basis of gender in the sale of beer,[53] in the administration of public benefits programs,[54] or in the provision of public education.[55] The Court ruled that the government can discriminate in the administration of the military draft by requiring only men to register[56] and in the administration of criminal justice by penalizing only men who engage in underage sex.[57]

The Sameness/Difference Thesis

Sameness arguments have worked well for feminist litigators arguing for women's rights in the public sphere so long as women are viewed as being sufficiently similar to men. Although the Supreme Court has never explicitly approved "separate but equal" in the context of gender relations, the notion that the separation of the sexes is proper for some purposes continues to plague the women's rights movement. In the recently litigated case over Virginia Military Institute's (VMI) male-only policy, advocates of the policy argued that separate styles of education, militaristic and aggressive for men, supportive and nurturing for women, complied with constitutional notions of equality. Although the Supreme Court ultimately struck down VMI's male-only policy and ruled that VMI had not successfully created equal opportunity for women at a separate military institution, the Court left open the possibility that it might uphold a truly separate but equal sex-based classification in the future. Furthermore, women and men continue to be separated in the world of public rest rooms, prisons, and college athletic teams. Where separation exists, the risk of unequal treatment arises. Thus, litigators have charged that rest room facilities for women are often inadequate, that prisons for women do not offer the same training and educational opportunities as do prisons for men, and that the financial support provided by colleges and universities to women's sports lags behind the support offered to men's teams.

Thus, in a sense, "separate but equal" is acceptable in the context of gender relations. Biological differences seem to justify the separation of the sexes in certain situations. For example, notions of equality are not offended when women are required to cover their breasts, but men are not. Even when the biological differences are socially constructed, the courts seem more willing to recognize the difference argument if the classification at issue is based on sex rather than on race.

Pregnancy discrimination is another example of the difficult legal issues that arise when men and women are admittedly different. In *Geduldig v. Aiello,*[58] for example, the Court held that discrimination on the basis of pregnancy is not discrimination on the basis of sex and, therefore, is constitutionally permissible, even though the impact of pregnancy discrimination is to deny women equal access to the public sphere. The Court again ruled that pregnancy was not sex discrimination in an employment discrimination case brought under Title VII.[59] Fortunately for pregnant women, Congress took much of the sting out of these cases by enacting the Pregnancy Discrimination Act, as an amendment to Title VII, which has been extended to cover governmental employees as well as private employees.

In short, when women are sufficiently similar to men, they win their legal arguments based on equality in the public sphere. When women are different from men and when they ask for the difference to be honored or "accommodated," the response is that to do so violates the equality principle. The fear seems to be that accommodating women's differences is a form of special treatment, which is a form of affirmative action. Yet rules that conform to women's needs are only special if one views such rules from a perspective that ignored their needs to begin with. "Difference feminists" of the past two decades have been making this latter point as they have attempted to reconceptualize arguments based on equality.

Privacy Arguments and
Women's Reproductive Rights

When equality theory does not work well for women because of their biological differences, they may find success in using privacy theory. Indeed, *Roe v. Wade,*[60] which relied on privacy theory to support a woman's right to abortion, was before the Court at the very same time as *Reed v. Reed,* the first case to use equality theory successfully to support women's rights. Despite the continued assault on its validity, *Roe v. Wade*'s recognition of a woman's right to choose whether to terminate her pregnancy, which made abortion legal throughout the country, still stands as one of the most important gains by women's rights litigators. Litigated as a "right to privacy" case, *Roe* built on earlier Supreme Court cases that had accorded constitutional protection to persons making reproductive choices. The first successful reproductive rights case was *Griswold v. Connecticut,* decided in 1965.[61] The issue in *Griswold* was whether the state of Connecticut could criminalize the use of contraceptive devices. The Connecticut statute dated from 1879 and seemed out of keeping with modern attitudes toward birth control. Nonetheless, the statute remained on the books and continued to be enforced. Challenges to the statute in the 1950s had failed. In 1961, a new challenge was begun by the Planned Parenthood League of Connecticut. The Connecticut Supreme Court upheld the statute, reasoning that the state had the right to regulate private sexual conduct under the general police power, which authorized the state to act in matters of public welfare. The Supreme Court of the United States reversed the Connecticut court in what has come to be the single most important ruling on matters of sexual intimacy.

No specific constitutional provision exists to protect privacy rights, rights to intimacy generally, or sexual intimacy specifically. Writing for the majority of five, Justice Douglas explained that, despite this silence in the Constitution, the right to privacy was lodged in the penumbras of several of the enumerated provisions of the Constitution, notably the general right of association guaranteed in the First Amendment, the right to maintain the privacy of one's home against the quartering of troops in the Third Amendment, the right against unreasonable searches in the Fourth Amendment, and the right against self-incrimination in the Fifth Amendment. Furthermore, the Ninth Amendment specifically says that the rights enumerated in the foregoing amendments are not the only individual rights protected from government interference. Thus in *Griswold* the Court announced a new individual right: the right of privacy. The particular aspect of the right of privacy recognized in *Griswold* was the right of a married couple to make decisions about reproductive sex free from government interference. After *Griswold,* the question was how far could this right of privacy be extended?

Seven years later, in 1972, in *Eisenstadt v. Baird,*[62] the Court extended the right of privacy to unmarried individuals by striking down a Massachusetts anticontraception law. One year later, in *Roe,* the Court relied on *Griswold* and *Eisenstadt* to hold that women had a constitutionally protected right to choose whether or not to have an abortion. The effect of these decisions is to protect women's reproductive choices by according strict judicial scrutiny to state restrictions that burden these choices. If the restriction can't be justified under the compelling state interest analysis, then the restriction will be struck down as a violation of the due process clause.

Although litigated as a privacy case, *Roe v. Wade* can be conceptualized as a case that implicates equality issues. The availability of abortion could be viewed as a necessary prerequisite to attaining sex equality in the public sphere. Giving the pregnant woman the full choice over such an important decision regarding her own body also equalizes the female as full moral agent with males who have the right to make decisions regarding their own bodies. Thus, abortion is not only about privacy, but also about equal access to individual liberty and autonomy. Nonetheless, equality theory, as developed under the Fourteenth Amendment's Equal Protection Clause, fails to work well in the case of abortion and reproductive rights arguments because, as to reproduction, women and men are not similarly situated.

LEGACIES AND LESSONS

The civil rights movements for race and gender equality have both blazed important trails in the courts and established legal precedents that sometimes help and sometimes hinder the litigation efforts of other civil rights groups. Of key import have been those constitutional doctrines that developed in response to litigation that asserted both equality and privacy claims. Litigation efforts on behalf of lesbians and gay men began in the 1960s and 1970s, at a time when some of these doctrines were firmly in place and others were just beginning to develop.

The State Action Doctrine

The state action doctrine, despite its expansion in race cases decided by the Warren Court, remains a roadblock today for claims against private discriminators. Thus, gay people cannot go to federal court and raise constitutional issues about acts of private discrimination. Another interesting question remains as a result of the *Civil Rights Cases,* a case that has never been overturned despite the liberalization of the concept of state action during the Warren Court years. That question concerns the limits of congressional power in reaching acts of private discrimination. The precise holding in the *Civil Rights Cases* was that even though section five of the Fourteenth Amendment gives Congress power to enforce the equal protection guarantee found in section one of the amendment, that enforcement power does not include legislation aimed at private actors.[63] Although commentators have argued that Congress has the power under section five to legislate against private discrimination,[64] the Surpeme Court has never overruled the *Civil Rights Cases* and has never specifically held that Congress has the power to reach private discrimination.[65] The statutes prohibiting private racial discrimination that have been upheld by the Supreme Court have been validated either on the basis of Congress's power under the Thirteenth Amendment (abolition of slavery), which contains no state action requirement,[66] or on the basis of Congress's power to regulate commerce among the states.[67] Should Congress ever pass a statute, such as the Employment Nondiscrimination Act (ENDA),[68] protecting gays from *private* discrimination, that statute's constitutional validity will be subject to attack on the same grounds as the Civil Rights Act of 1875. Because the Thirteenth Amendment covers only racial discrimination, a federal statute such as ENDA could only be validated under either the commerce clause or section five of the Fourteenth Amendment.

In several recent cases, the Supreme Court has struck down statues that exceeded congressional power under the commerce clause.[69] The Court has also reaffirmed the *Civil Rights Cases* and held that Congress does not have the general power under section five of the Fourteenth Amendment to legislate against private discrimination.[70] Furthermore, the Court has held that Congress can only legislate against *state* discrimination if the class discriminated against is a suspect or quasi-suspect one.[71] This latter restriction is based on the Court's Eleventh Amendment jurisprudence[72] and is a recent addition to Supreme Court doctrine. Because both race and sex are suspect or quasi-suspect, the ruling does not affect federal statutes prohibiting the states from engaging in race or sex discrimination. To date the restriction has only been applied to antidiscrimination laws based on age. But the Court recently granted review in a similar challenge to the Americans with Disabilities Act. If ENDA is ever passed and applied to the states, the issue that will arise is whether sexual orientation discrimination is more like race and sex discrimination (both suspect classes) or more like age discrimination (not suspect).

All of these recent decisions affect congressional ability to legislate on behalf of gay men and lesbians and are based on the legacy of the *Civil Rights Cases*. Although Congress probably does have the power under the commerce clause to enact ENDA as applied to private employers, recent cases indicate that Congress probably does not have the power to reach anti-gay discrimination by state employers. Furthermore, Congress probably does not have the power to pass a federal hate crimes law to protect gay men and lesbians from acts of private violence. Thus, unlike the civil rights movements for race and gender equality, the lesbian and gay civil rights movement will have to rely more heavily on states to enact protective legislation.

The Intent Requirement of Washington v. Davis

Under the Court's Fourteenth Amendment jurisprudence, race and sex discrimination require an explicit classification on the basis of race or sex. Other classifications, such as wealth or pregnancy, do not constitute race or sex discrimination even though the effect of the classification may fall more heavily on one race or one gender. A clear parallel in the civil rights movement for gay and lesbian equality occurs in cases in which marital status is the explicit classification. Any benefit or any state law that is limited to married couples necessarily excludes same-sex couples. No state recognizes same-sex marriage. State legislatures are fully aware that laws for the benefit of married couples effectively discriminate against gay couples. When gay rights litigators challenge such rules on grounds that they discriminate on the basis of sexual orientation, courts will respond by saying that the classification is not based on sexual orientation but rather on marriage. Thus, even if sexual orientation discrimination were accorded some form of heightened scrutiny (or specifically prohibited under a civil rights statute), distinctions based on marital status generally would be valid.

Separate but Equal

Although the separate but equal doctrine is no longer available as a defense to race discrimination claims, the doctrine may prove to have some bearing in litigation over lesbian and gay rights. Consider the argument for same-sex marriage. The most recent ruling on the issue was handed down by the Vermont Supreme Court in *Baker v. Vermont*,[73] a case that will be discussed further in Chapter 9. *Baker* suggests that even if there is a state constitutional requirement that same-sex couples be accorded equal treatment with opposite-sex couples, the equality requirement may be met by creating a separate institution, for example, domestic partnership or civil union, for same-sex couples, provided it is sufficiently equal to marriage.

Suspect Classifications

Civil rights litigation on behalf of racial minorities and women has resulted in a bifurcated (or trifurcated) equal protection clause. Only Justice Stevens consistently resists the Court's multi-tiered approach to equal protection, claiming there is only one equal protection clause.[74] As of the 1970s when constitutional attacks on antigay legislation began to enter the federal courts, only race, alienage and national origin had been declared suspect. Later, sex and illegitimacy were declared quasi-suspect. The Court has recognized no new suspect or quasi-suspect classification since the mid-1970s when it hammered out the quasi-suspect status for gender and illegitimacy. Thus, sexual orientation, like wealth, age, and disability, are currently relegated to low level scrutiny, which often means no meaningful judicial review at all. Under this lower level of scrutiny, a test known as rational basis review, discriminatory classifications are held constitutional so long as they can be justified as a rational means to furthering a legitimate governmental objective.

State Antidiscrimination Laws and Private Clubs

When feminist litigators sued private organizations such as the Jaycees and Rotary to include women members, those organizations defended themselves claiming a constitutional right to associate with the members of their choice. In every case that reached the Supreme Court, the Court ruled in favor of the plaintiff and denied the associational claim of the organization. The lesbian and gay civil rights movement finds itself in a similar situation in suits brought under state antidiscrimination laws against private organizations. Such cases have involved the right to be included in a privately-sponsored St. Patrick's Day parade[75] and the right to remain a member of the Boy Scouts of America.[76] Unlike the gender claims, the gays claims have failed. These cases will be discussed later in this book.

Privacy and Sexual Intimacy

Building on the privacy victories of feminist litigators, litigators on behalf of lesbian and gay people have argued that the notion of constitutionally protected privacy rights should be extended to include sexual intimacy of lesbian and gay partners. At its core, this argument assumes that *Griswold*, *Eisenstadt*, and *Roe* were cases that involved more than the question of whether individuals were free to make reproductive choices without undue interference from the government. The argument assumes that privacy entails the right to make individual choices about whether to engage in sexual relations at all and if so, with whom. Yet, as the story unfolds in the following chapters, lesbians and gay men will learn that if sexual privacy is protected under our federal constitution, that protection is apparently limited to heterosexual partners.

The Public/Private Distinction

African Americans and women have won both public sphere and private sphere rights through litigation. In the private sphere, litigation succeeds when the matter being litigated is purely private. But when the private behavior becomes public or when the government is asked to intervene in the private sphere rather than to ignore private sphere activities, the cases become more difficult. Government financial support for abortion is a prime example. Courts are not willing to require that kind of intervention. In part, the difficulty derives from the liberal notion that government ought to remain neutral regarding individual choices about what is good. Neutrality suggests noninterference. Under this view, positive intervention by the government is equated with the coercion of a particular view of the good. Holders of this view, for example, complain that the government's choice to offer positive sex education that includes discussions of homosexuality improperly interjects the government into private family choices about what is good. Similarly, even persons who think the government should not regulate private consensual sexual relations believe that it would be improper for the government to recognize the legality of same-sex marriage. Public recognition would amount to endorsement and thus, as with the case of sex education, interject the government into choices that ought to remain private. What these individuals fail to recognize is that the government has already interjected itself in the debate over the good and has drawn a line that rejects lesbian and gay relationships no matter how similar they may be to relationships that are supported by the government.

I identify cases that fall within this problematic category as cases in which the private becomes public. Courts have supported societal attitudes about sex and family by agreeing that sex and family should, for the most part, be confined to a separate sphere insulated from positive governmental action. Recent exceptions to this rule include cases in which courts have been willing to overrule the marital privilege in favor of a rule that recognizes spousal rape and abuse. The lesbian and gay civil rights movement will likely surpass both the race and gender equality movements in the number of cases that challenge the private/public divide. This arena, this crossover space between private and public, is the arena in which the lesbian and gay civil rights movement will need to break new ground.

NOTES

1. Jean Bethke Elshtain, *Democracy on Trial* at 54 (1995).
2. See Plessy v. Ferguson, 163 U.S. 537 at 559 (1896) (Harlan, J., dissenting).
3. 60 U.S. 393 at 407 (1857).
4. Quoted in Higginbotham, *Shades of Freedom* at 96–97.
5. 109 U.S. 3 (1883).

6. ". . . no *State* shall make or enforce any law which shall abridge the privileges or immunities of citizens of the United States, nor shall any State deprive any person of life, liberty, or property, without due process of law; nor deny to any person within its jurisdiction the equal protection of the laws" U.S. Constitution, Fourteenth Amendment, Section one (emphasis added).

7. 163 U.S. 537 (1896).

8. 347 U.S. 483 (1954).

9. 235 U.S. 151 (1914).

10. 245 U.S. 60 (1917).

11. Mark V. Tushnet, The NAACP's Legal Strategy Against Segregated Education, 1925–1950 at 16 (1987)(quoting Houston).

12. Richard Kluger, *Simple Justice* (1976).

13. Mark Tushnet, *The NAACP's Legal Strategy Against Segregated Education, 1925–1950* (1987).

14. See Smith v. Allwright, 321 U.S. 649 (1944), appealed to the Supreme Court by Thurgood Marshall and William Hastie.

15. 334 U.S. 1 (1948).

16. Burton v. Wilmington Parking Authority, 365 U.S. 715 (1961) (holding that a private actor may be treated as a state actor when the state enables the discrimination through a lease arrangement).

17. See Robinson v. Florida, 378 U.S. 153 (1964) (state rule that restaurant washrooms be segregated on basis of race makes the state a participant in the restaurant's segregation policies); Adickes v. S. H. Kress & Co., 398 U.S. 144 (1970) (state action requirement met when city policeman assists private business in furthering racially discriminatory practices).

18. Earl Warren was chief justice of the Supreme Court from 1953 to 1969.

19. Warren Burger was chief justice of the Supreme Court from 1969 to 1986.

20. By 1970, Warren and Fortas, who had voted in favor of expanding the state action concept in race cases, were replaced by Burger and Blackmun, who voted against expansion. See especially the votes in Evans v. Newton, 382 U.S. 296 (1966) (finding state action) and Evans v. Abney, 396 U.S. 435 (1970) (finding no state action). See also Moose Lodge, 407 U.S. 163 (1972) (finding no state action).

21. See Katzenback v. McClung, 379 U.S. 294 (1964) (relying on commerce clause); Heart of Atlanta Motel, Inc. v. United States, 379 U.S. 241 (1964) (relying on commerce clause); United States v. Mintzes, 304 F.Supp. 1305 (D.Md. 1969)(relying on Thirteenth Amendment).

22. Missouri ex rel. Gaines v. Canada, 305 U.S. 337 (1938).

23. Sweatt v. Painter, 339 U.S. 629 (1950).

24. *Brown* at 347 U.S. at 495.

25. Holmes v. City of Atlanta, 350 U.S. 879 (1955); Hampton v. City of Jacksonville, 304 F.2d 320 (5th Cir. 1962), *cert. denied sub nom* Ghioto v. Hampton, 371 U.S. 911 (1962).

26. United States v. Carolene Products, 304 U.S. 144 (1938).

27. The first paragraph of footnote four, which suggests judicial intervention is more appropriate when specific rights are affected by legislation, is more properly attributed to Justice Hughes than to Stone. For a full discussion of how footnote

four evolved, see Louis Lusky, *Footnote Redux: A Carolene Products Reminiscence,* 82 *Columbia Law Review* 1093 (1982). Lusky was Justice Stone's clerk when the *Carolene Products* case was before the Court.

28. The full text of footnote four, with citations deleted, is "There may be narrower scope for operation of the presumption of constitutionality when legislation appears on its face to be within a specific prohibition of the Constitution, such as those of the first ten Amendments, which are deemed equally specific when held to be embraced within the Fourteenth. . . .

"It is unnecessary to consider now whether legislation which restricts those political processes which can ordinarily be expected to bring about repeal of undesirable legislation, is to be subjected to more exacting judicial scrutiny under the general prohibitions of the Fourteenth Amendment than are most other types of legislation.

"Nor need we enquire whether similar considerations enter into the review of statutes directed at particular religious, or national, or racial minorities; whether prejudice against discrete and insular minorities may be a special condition, which tends seriously to curtail the operation of those political processes ordinarily to be relied upon to protect minorities, and which may call for a correspondingly more searching judicial inquiry."

29. Korematsu v. United States, 323 U.S. 214 (1944).

30. Korematsu, 323 U.S. 214 at 216.

31. See generally Jacobus tenBroek, Edward N. Barnhart, and Floyd W. Matson, *Prejudice, War and the Constitution* at 236 (1968).

32. See, for example, Michael J. Klarman, "An Interpretive History of Modern Equal Protection," 90 *Michigan Law Review* 213 (1991).

33. 388 U.S. 1 at 12.

34. 426 U.S. 229 (1976).

35. The first case to address the issue of level of scrutiny to be accorded affirmative action plans was Regents of the University of California v. Bakke, 438 U.S. 265 (1978). Only five justices reached the issue. Four of them thought intermediate scrutiny rather than strict scrutiny should be applied. One justice (Powell) thought strict scrutiny should be applied. No majority opinon on the question of level of review appeared until 1989. See City of Richmond v. J. A. Croson Co., 488 U.S. 469 (1989) (O'Connor, Rehnquist, White, Kennedy, and Scalia apply strict scrutiny).

36. Activists in that century would not have referred to themselves as feminists, although that is the term we use today to describe them. The word "feminist" was not used by activists until the early twentieth century. See Nancy F. Cott, *The Grounding of Modern Feminism* (1987).

37. Reva Siegel, "Home as Work: The First Woman's Rights Claims Concerning Wives' Household Labor, 1850–1880," 103 *Yale Law Journal* 1073, 1109 (1994).

38. The Equal Pay Act is codified at 29 U.S.C. 206(d).

39. Title VII, which bans discrimination in employment on the basis of race, color, religion, sex, and national origin, is codified at 42 U.S.C. §2000(e).

40. For a good description of the history of passage of both of these statutes, see Cynthia Harrison, *On Account of Sex: The Politics of Women's Issues 1945–1968* (1988).

41. The state action issue was not raised before the Supreme Court in a gender discrimination case until 1994. The case involved the use of preemptory challenges to strike the members of one sex from a jury in a criminal trial. Following its earlier ruling in a racial preemptory challenge case, the Court held that even when a defense attorney who is a private actor uses the challenge system to exclude women, the Equal Protection Clause is violated. J.E.B. v. Alabama, 511 U.S. 127 (1994).

42. See, for example, Roberts v. U.S. Jaycees. 486 U.S. 609 (1984); Board of Directors. of Rotary International v. Rotary Club, 481 U.S. 537 (1987); New York State Club Association v. City of New York, 487 U.S. 1 (1988).

43. 83 U.S.130, 141 (1873).

44. Kerber, *No Constitutional Right to Be Ladies* at 188.

45. 368 U.S. 57 (1961).

46. Pauli Murray and Mary O. Eastwood, "Jane Crow and the Law: Sex Discrimination and Title VII," 34 *George Washington Law Review* 232, 237–238 (1965).

47. The first successful challenge to reach the Supreme Court was *Griswold v. Connecticut.* For the ACLU's record of supporting women's rights generally, see Nadine Strossen, "The American Civil Liberties Union and Women's Rights," 66 *New York University Law Review* 1940 (1991).

48. Reed v. Reed, 404 U.S. 71 (1971).

49. Justice Ginsburg made these remarks in answer to a question that I posed to her at a public question-and-answer session at the annual meeting of the Association of American Law Schools, held in Washington, D.C., on January 8, 2000.

50. 411 U.S. 677 (1973).

51. Martha Craig Daughtrey, "Women and the Constitution: Where Are We at the End of the Century?" 75 *New York University Law Review* 1 at 10 (2000).

52. Taylor v. Louisiana, 419 U.S. 522 (1975); Duren v. Missouri, 439 U.S. 357 (1979). In Taylor, the Court ruled against the state's exclusion of women from juries, holding that such a rule denied the defendant of his Sixth Amendment right to a fair trial. In Hoyt, the claim had been based on equal protection and due process arguments generally and not specifically on any Sixth Amendment right. The Sixth Amendment itself is directed only at the federal government and thus was not relied on in Hoyt. However, a 1968 case held that the Sixth Amendment could be applied against states as well as the federal government. See Duncan v. Louisiana, 391 U.S. 145 (1968). Thus in Taylor the Court could strike the jury exclusion rule without specifically overruling Hoyt since the legal theories in the two cases were different. For all practical purposes, however, Taylor overruled Hoyt because it rejected the notion that a state could constitutionally exclude women from juries on grounds that women were "regarded as the center of home and family life."

53. Craig v. Boren, 429 U.S. 190 (1976).

54. Weinberger v. Wiesenfeld, 420 U.S. 125 (1975).

55. Mississippi University for Women v. Hogan, 458 U.S. 718 (1982).

56. Rostker v. Goldberg, 453 U.S. 57 (1981).

57. Michael M. v. Superior Court, 450 U.S. 464 (1981).

58. Geduldig v. Aiello, 417 U.S. 484 (1974).

59. General Electric Co. v. Gilbert, 429 U.S. 125 (1976).

60. 410 U.S. 113 (1973).

61. Griswold v. Connecticut, 381 U.S. 479 (1965).

62. Eisenstadt v. Baird, 405 U.S. 438 (1972).

63. Section five of the Fourteenth Amendment provides : "... Congress shall have power to enforce, by appropriate legislation, the provisions of this article." Antidiscrimination legislation generally carries out the equal protection provision. However, the equal protection provision is aimed at state, not private, actors.

64. See, e.g., Frantz, "Congressional Power to Enforce the Fourteenth Amendment Against Private Acts," 72 *Yale Law Journal* 1353, 1359–60 (1964); Erwin Chemerinsky, "Rethinking State Action," 80 *Northwestern University Law Review* 503, 504 (1985).

65. The closest the Supreme Court has come to ruling that Congress can reach acts of private discrimination under Section five is United States v. Guest, 383 U.S. 745 (1966)(six justices, concurring in part and dissenting in part, indicated that Section five of the Fourteenth Amendment gives Congress the power to enact laws punishing all conspiracies that interfere with Fourteenth Amendment rights regardless of whether there is state action).

66. See, for example, Jones v. Alfred Mayer Co., 392 U.S. 409 (1968).

67. Heart of Atlanta Motel, Inc. v. United States, 379 U.S. 241 (1964).

68. ENDA would prohibit discrimination on the basis of sexual orientation by certain private employers. A version of this act has been introduced in Congress every year since Bella Abzug first introduced it in 1974. It has never been passed. See William N. Eskridge, Jr., "Challenging the Apartheid of the Closet: Establishing Conditions for Lesbian and Gay Intimacy, Nomos, and Citizenship 1961–1981," 25 *Hofstra Law Review* 817 at 927 (1997).

69. United States v. Lopez, 514 U.S. 549 (1995); *see also* United States v. Morrison, 120 S.Ct. 1740 (2000)(holding that Congress lacked power to enact civil remedy provisions of the Violence Against Women Act under either the Commerce Clause or section five of the fourteenth amendment).

70. United States v. Morrison, 120 S.Ct. 1740 (2000).

71. Kimel v. Florida Board of Regents, 120 S.Ct. 631 (2000).

72. The Eleventh Amendment prohibits the federal judiciary from hearing certain claims against the states and has been interpreted broadly to restrict the federal congress from taking certain actions against the states.

73. 744 A.2d 864 (Vt. 1999).

74. See, for example, Craig v. Boren, 429 U.S. 190 (1976) (Stevens, J., concurring); Cleburne v. Cleburne Living Center, Inc., 473 U.S. 432 (1985) (Stevens, J., concurring).

75. Hurley v. Irish-American Gay, Lesbian and Bisexual Group of Boston, 515 U.S. 557 (1995).

76. Dale v. Boy Scouts of America, 734 A.2d 1196 (N.J. 1999), rev'd 120 S. Ct. 2446 (2000).

2

Lawyers, Legal Theories,
and Litigation Strategy

Civil rights movements have long used litigation successfully to accomplish part of the movement's agenda. Although some people question whether specific court opinions actually contribute to positive social change, the litigation process itself does contribute to the development of a civil rights agenda. High profile cases attract media attention and help to educate the public generally. Movement leaders and spokespeople must be familiar with legal precedent so that they are prepared to give appropriate sound bites to the press when cases are decided. Particular rulings by courts affect later litigation theories and strategies. Negative rulings can contribute to an increase in political activity aimed at legislative changes.

For all of these reasons, one should expect lawyers to play an important role in civil rights movements. Lawyers did play important roles in the NAACP's legal battle over segregation, but they weren't the only activists in the movement for racial equality. Other key participants ranged from public figures like Dr. Martin Luther King Jr. to student protesters in the streets. There were few women lawyers available to play central roles in the first wave of feminism. Indeed, even at the beginning of the second wave, female lawyers were scarce. By the 1970s, however, women lawyers became a more visible part of the movement. The role of lawyers in the lesbian and gay civil rights movement is similar to that of lawyers in the second wave of feminism. The modern gay rights movement was not begun by lawyers, but by grassroots activists, much like the early wave of feminism. Yet it wasn't long before a small group of lawyers in New York agreed to form a legal organization that would litigate on behalf of lesbians and gay men who had suffered discrimination. Unlike Ruth Bader Ginsburg's legal work on behalf of women, however, the lesbian and gay lawyers did not step in at the Supreme Court level to change Supreme Court precedent. Thus, these early lawyers more nearly resembled the early lawyers of the NAACP, who began to fight discrimination by bringing individual cases, with the hope of one day gaining appellate-level rulings that recognized the civil rights of their plaintiffs. Unlike the NAACP, however, early gay and lesbian legal groups were not supported by anything as encouraging as the $100,000 grant from the Garland Fund, which established the NAACP's litigation campaign against school segregation. Gay and lesbian legal organizations turned primarily to the gay and lesbian community itself for their early support. Later, broader financial support occurred as the work of these organizations became more visible and as the AIDS epidemic caught broader public attention. This chapter tells the story of these early lesbian and gay public interest lawyers and the legal groups they helped to form.

PUBLIC INTEREST LAWYERS

A person has to have something special to be a public interest lawyer who fights for rights on behalf of a group that has consistently been denied those rights by the establishment. Individual lawyers in earlier movements have been called crusaders and heroes. Such descriptions are equally applicable to the lawyers who have fought for lesbian and gay civil rights. Civil rights lawyers are visionaries who are passionate about their visions, and they are consumed with the energy and blind faith needed to turn visions into reality.

In addition to being crusaders on behalf of the downtrodden and on behalf of those against whom society discriminates, however, civil rights lawyers are also trained professionals who engage in battle with a certain set of professional skills and within a certain set of professional constraints. Nonlawyer movement leaders may be the great orators or the charismatic politicians who inspire others to join the movement. In some cases, the public interest lawyer may serve this role as well. But in every civil rights movement, the lawyers, who are fighting for clients whose interests converge with that of the larger movement, share some similarities that bear identifying. In his book *Rebellious Lawyering*,[1] Gerald Lopez provides a list of the attributes of public interest lawyers. It includes the following:

1. Lawyers formally represent others, i.e., clients.
2. Lawyers choose between "service work (resolving individual problems) and "impact" work (advancing systemic reforms) and these categories are largely dichotomous.
3. Lawyers litigate more than they do anything else.
4. Lawyers consider themselves the preeminent problem-solvers in most situations they find themselves trying to alter.

There is a danger that public interest lawyers who are committed to the goals of the movement in which they labor will not always listen closely to their individual clients as they are formulating their litigation strategy. Because the public interest lawyer identifies with the goals of the movement, the lawyer may become personally invested in cases that will further those goals. This personal investment in a particular case can cause a lawyer to feel as though the case really belongs to the movement rather than the client. Lopez warns that public interest lawyers often do not understand the nonlegal institutions that are part of the movement for social change. All of these factors suggest that lawyers are not ideal catalysts for social change. They are too isolated, and their vision is often restricted by their own professionalism.

Some public interest lawyers, especially those who represent more radical groups in civil rights movements, are so convinced that law itself will not change society that they are willing to state publicly that they have no respect for the law or legal institutions. In their opinion, litigating cases will never change society sufficiently to bring justice to their clients. These lawyers serve their clients and the movement out of a sense that such service is better than nothing and that occasionally, a legal decision will open up a possibility for minimal progress.[2]

Lawyers, fighting subordination, do convince courts to render decisions, to overturn precedent, and to issue orders that contribute to the ultimate goals of a movement. Furthermore, given the structure of litigation, only lawyers are in a position to play the role of advocate in the courtroom. But given the nature of law, lawyer activists, because they work within the legal system, are often viewed by their constituents as a relatively conservative force in the movement. Ironically, movement lawyers often find themselves criticized publicly by the very people they believe they represent.

Earlier civil rights movements experienced divisions of opinion between those who wanted to act within the confines of the law in order to change the law and those who wanted to act outside the law to bring attention to the problems created by existing law. Thurgood Marshall and the NAACP legal defense team, for example, were critical of the widespread use of civil disobedience by Dr. Martin Luther King Jr. and others in the black civil rights movement. Yet as the lawyers for the movement they were the ones called on to represent activists who broke the law in civil disobedience demonstrations. Lawyering on behalf of arrested activists can cause additional divides between the lawyers and the activists. As Nancy Polikoff, a lesbian feminist activist lawyer who has represented lesbian and gay activists arrested for their demonstration activities, explains: "Clients who see their lawyers behaving as lawyers rather than as activists, as legitimate insiders rather than as daring outsiders, may associate their representatives with the very system they are challenging rather than with the particular civil disobedience action itself."[3]

As in earlier civil rights movements, lawyers for the lesbian and gay civil rights movement have debated their proper role. Can they as lawyers really represent a movement, as the NAACP lawyers were perceived to do? Or is their primary responsibility to the individual client they represent in a given case? Unfortunately, conflicts can arise between the needs of individual clients and what is best for the movement. As a general rule, the rules of professional ethics require lawyers to commit to their individual clients above and beyond anything else. Thus, for example, a lawyer should argue for exclusion of evidence of same-sex sexual conduct on evidentiary grounds if the exclusion will benefit the client. The lawyer must make this argument even though the lawyer would prefer to argue that there is nothing wrong with same-sex relationships.

Another issue facing public interest lawyers is national coordination. There are many lawyers and legal organizations who represent lesbian and gay clients. These lawyers are scattered around the country. Although many of them are dealing with state courts and state law, bad precedent in one case can affect later cases. Ruth Bader Ginsburg experienced a coordination problem within her own organization, the ACLU. Although she tried very hard to see that sex discrimination cases going to the Supreme Court fit a certain model, one case slipped through that she viewed as detrimental to her attempts to get sex classifications elevated to strict scrutiny. The case was *Kahn v. Shevin,*[4] a challenge to a Florida property tax law that favored women over men. The Court ruled that the discrimination was benign and upheld the classification. Although Ginsburg argued that the law disadvantaged women as a whole by stereotyping them as financially dependent, that argument was not a winner and she knew it wouldn't be when she made it.⁵ It is the one case that upheld classifications on the basis of sex during the period that she was arguing for a form of heightened scrutiny that should have struck down most if not all such classifications.

Tensions and divisions have arisen in all civil rights movements. The ones lesbian and gay civil rights lawyers face parallel those of their predecessors. Thus I will begin with some stories of the lawyers in these earlier battles before introducing the lawyers who have fought for lesbian and gay rights.

The NAACP Lawyers

"Crusaders for Change," as Jack Greenberg calls them in his book, seems an apt description of the lawyers who were at the forefront of the black civil rights movement. They include Charles Houston, Thurgood Marshall, Constance Baker Motley, and Greenberg himself. None of these advocates were willing to "accept the things I cannot change," despite its promise of serenity. Rather, they would have agreed with the wry remark of William H. Hastie, the first African American appointed to the federal bench, that "[a]t times it may be better for the Omnipotent One to give men the wit and the will to continue to plan purposefully and to struggle as best they know how to change things that seem immutable."⁶

Charles Houston was dean and professor of law at Howard Law School in the 1930s. Thurgood Marshall, later to become the first black Supreme Court justice, was an early protégé. Greenberg worked with Thurgood Marshall at the NAACP Legal Defense Fund (LDF) in the pre-*Brown* days and later served as director of the organization for twenty-three years after Marshall left to become a federal judge. Motley, whose family did not encourage her to enter the law, decided in 1937 at the age of fifteen to become a lawyer, not just *despite* her family's ambivalence, but *because* of it.

In her autobiography, *Equal Justice Under Law,* Constance Baker Motley, the only female lawyer who worked for many years side by side with Houston, Marshall, Hastie, and their colleagues at LDF, tells stories of turf wars, spotlight grabbing, and all the bickering one might expect from high-profile, high-energy activists who are passionate about their cause. The NAACP had particular problems because it was at the center of the movement as a whole, and not just serving as the litigation team for the movement. Thus, the leaders in the NAACP were simultaneously the spokesmen, the lawyers, and the lobbyists for the movement. The situation changed in 1956 when, in response to threats from the IRS over tax exempt status, the organization had to split into the NAACP and the NAACP Legal Defense

Fund (LDF), also known as the Inc. Fund. The NAACP was the lobbying group with chapters throughout the country. The LDF became the litigation and educational arm. To satisfy the federal tax rules regarding tax-exempt organizations, the two organizations could not be under common control. After the 1956 division, LDF was clearly in charge of the litigation, but which organization would become the chief voice for the movement was less clear.

At this very time, Dr. Martin Luther King Jr., a minister, was becoming prominent in the movement by using boycotts and demonstrations in support of the cause of desegregation. King's rise to prominence can be traced to the 1955 Montgomery bus boycott when Rosa Parks set off the boycott when she refused to give up her seat to a white person on a city bus on a Thursday afternoon in early December. She was arrested and ready to assert a legal challenge to the segregation laws. But with the support of the black community in Montgomery, Rosa Parks used the occasion to make a bigger statement. The following Monday morning, the entire black community boycotted the Montgomery buses, and King seized the spotlight as a dramatic spokesperson for the event. Taylor Branch describes the mood at the NAACP convention that year, where the delegates welcomed King's presence with enthusiasm. "The idea of a mass movement by nearly fifty thousand Negroes in a single city captivated the delegates, whose customary role in the NAACP was limited to support of the lawyers fighting segregation in court."[7] The delegates drafted resolutions in support of nonviolent demonstrations such as the bus boycott. The litigators, in particular Thurgood Marshall, were skeptical of such methods. In their view, the battleground over segregation should be the courtroom and not the streets. They expressed the same reservations years later when college students began participating in sit-ins. The litigators were fighting to change the law. Until the law had been changed, their view was that it ought to be obeyed.

This difference in opinion over appropriate techniques caused a rift in the movement. The NAACP lawyers were not just lawyers for the movement, however, they were lawyers for the individuals in the movement. When Rosa Parks or Martin Luther King Jr. broke the law by peacefully protesting, the NAACP lawyers had to defend them, whether they personally approved of the protester's methods or not.

Furthermore, although the lead NAACP lawyers had settled on a litigation strategy aimed at attacking segregated schools, not everyone in the larger African American community agreed with that goal. Some argued that rather than attack segregation per se, the NAACP should fight for truly equal schools for black children. Even today, some of the people who participated in developing the original strategy to attack segregation question the success of the strategy and suggest that ending segregated schools benefited only middle-class African Americans. Concrete improvement in the material conditions of all African Americans might have been accomplished more quickly by cases demanding increased government funding to improve the schools and the other institutions that served the entire black community.[8]

Lawyers in the Modern Women's Movement

The closest comparison to the LDF in the modern feminist movement was the Women's Rights Project of the American Civil Liberties Union (ACLU), formed in 1971 and headed by Ruth Bader Ginsburg. The women's movement, unlike the African American civil rights movement, which concentrated on its crusade against separate but equal, was never as singly focused on a litigation goal or strategy. Ginsburg, however, did have her eyes set on one overarching objective: to convince the U.S. Supreme Court that women were protected by the Equal Protection Clause. To accomplish this goal, she had to fight for reversals of earlier negative precedents in the same way that the NAACP had had to fight for a reversal of *Plessy v. Ferguson*.

Like the black civil rights movement, the modern feminist movement also had its "bigger than life" political leaders. At first, few of them were attorneys. Betty Friedan, sometimes called the mother of the movement, and Gloria Steinem, journalist, activist, and cofounder of *Ms Magazine*, were not law trained, but they both served as major spokeswomen in the sixties and seventies. Bella Abzug was law trained, but at the time of the rebirth of the women's movement she was voting on legislation in Congress rather than litigating cases in court.

In 1971, Steinem became the first woman invited to speak to the annual banquet of the *Harvard Law Review*. The choice of Steinem indicated that the elite male population of Harvard Law School had a problem identifying "qualified women lawyers." Her lack of legal training, however, did not detract from her ability to deliver a scathing feminist attack on the venerable institution.[9]

In 1966, when Friedan participated in the founding of NOW, the National Organization for Women, she anticipated that NOW would be an organization modeled after the NAACP that would fight for the rights of women, particularly in employment. Furthermore, she imagined that NOW would have a legal arm comparable to the LDF that would be called the NOW Legal Defense Fund. NOW got off to a fast start, but it took four years for NOW's lawyers to work out the details and do the paperwork necessary to gain tax-exempt status for the NOW Legal Defense Fund, which finally began to litigate women's rights cases in 1970. The fund was soon eclipsed by the ACLU Women's Rights Project, which had a more sustained litigation strategy.

Title VII of the Civil Rights Act of 1964 purported to protect women from sex discrimination in the workplace, but sex had been added to Title VII at the last minute, as some commentators report, in an effort to defeat its passage. Even in the Equal Employment Opportunity Commission (EEOC), the agency responsible for carrying out the provisions of Title VII, persons had been heard to quip that Title VII was needed to protect men who wanted to become *Playboy* bunnies. In Washington in 1966, some even talked about taking "sex" out of Title VII.[10] The primary purpose of NOW in its first year was to insist that sex discrimination in employment be taken seriously. To accomplish its goal, NOW focused on the EEOC, which NOW accused of shirking its duty to protect women who were the victims of employment discrimination. In 1967, Friedan made her first report as NOW president, which included a seven-point bill of rights for women. Six of the seven points related to public sphere rights, in particular, the right to equal access to jobs and education, supported by adequate child care and maternity leave. Only one point in the bill of rights, the one referring to reproductive freedom, focused on the private sphere.

By 1970, the leadership of the women's movement, particularly within NOW, was becoming seriously fractured along the fault line of sexuality. Friedan's refusal to wear a lavender armband in support of her lesbian sisters at a march in support of abortion rights occurred in December of that year. Kate Millet had publicly announced her bisexuality and was being criticized by the press. Gloria Steinem and others agreed to pledge their support for Millet and identify themselves as lesbians if need be. Friedan was horrified. The battles between Friedan and Steinem soon became legendary in the movement.

Then, in 1971, feminist activists formed a new national organization to support women's entrance into the political arena. Among the founders of the National Women's Political Caucus (NWPC) were Friedan, Abzug, Steinem, Shirley Chisholm, the first black woman elected to the House of Representatives, and Brenda Feigen, a 1969 Harvard Law School graduate who had worked with NOW and was, in part, responsible for convincing

Steinem to do the *Harvard Law Review* speech. With two national organizations fighting on behalf of women and with the increasing rifts between conservative and radical women, the national leadership for women's rights became more diffuse than the leadership had been for African American rights under Thurgood Marshall and the LDF. Women's goals were also more heterogeneous, encompassing job security, equal educational access, child care and maternity leave, reproductive freedom, sexual freedom, freedom from male violence, and better representation in politics.

In the early 1970s, feminist litigators in various parts of the country began to make significant contributions to the women's movement. For example, in 1973 three visionaries on the West Coast, Mary Dunlap, Wendy Williams, and Nancy Davis, began their own small public interest feminist law firm, Equal Rights Advocates, in San Francisco, aided by Stanford law professor Barbara Babcock and Boalt law professor, and later dean, Herma Hill Kay. Several years later, Nancy Polikoff and Nan Hunter began a feminist law collective in Washington, D.C. And in 1972 a then-unknown young lawyer named Sarah Weddington argued *Roe v. Wade* before the U.S. Supreme Court.

In 1970, New York University Law School hosted the first annual conference on Women and the Law. This national conference continued for twenty-two years. All of the feminist lawyers mentioned in this chapter were active in the conference at some point in their activist careers. In the early years, the conference provided a crucial forum for feminist lawyers, law professors, community activists, and students to share information and brainstorm about strategy. Ruth Bader Ginsburg was a crucial participant in early conferences. Personal and professional relationships formed during the early days of the national conference remain strong today. And many of the feminist lawyers active in the movement at that time have continued their activist lawyering on behalf of lesbians and gay men.

LESBIAN AND GAY
PUBLIC INTEREST LAWYERING

Before Stonewall

Many view the Stonewall Rebellion of 1969 as the beginning of the modern lesbian and gay civil rights movement. However, the battle for gay civil rights began much earlier. Shortly after World War II, a number of homophile organizations began to spring up around the country. Henry Hay, a cofounder of the Mattachine Society in the 1950s, embraced "homophile" as the adjective of choice for the fledgling movement, explaining that the word "homosexual" contained too much negative baggage. Hay and others founded the Mattachine Society in Los Angeles. The name of "Mattachine" was borrowed from secret medieval societies of unmarried men who, while wearing masks, conducted rituals during the Feast of Fools, often as protests against oppression. Hay chose the name in order to signify that gay people in the 1950s were masked and unknown figures, fighting for social change.[11] Hay was not a lawyer, but with his backing, Mattachine made an important legal gain when it supported one of its cofounders, Dale Jennings, in his decision to plead not guilty to a charge of public lewdness. The 1952 trial made headlines when it ended in a hung jury, with eleven jurors believing the police had entrapped Jennings and one juror siding with the police. The charges were dropped and gay men, harassed by police, learned that it was possible to fight back.

In the 1960s, two gay San Francisco lawyers, Herbert Donaldson and Evander Smith, began representing gay men charged with public lewdness and encouraging the defendants to ask for jury trials. In those days, police not only entrapped gay men by propositioning them in gay bars, but, in addition, police often lied about the facts to ensure convictions. Juries did not always believe the police. Most defendants, however, preferred to plead guilty, pay a fine, and put the event behind themselves as quickly as possible. For some, however, police records, especially convictions of sex-related crimes, could ruin their lives. Lawyers, for example, could be disbarred for committing crimes of moral turpitude. Gay sex, or even an invitation to engage in gay sex, was sufficient to constitute moral turpitude. Thus, lawyers, schoolteachers, and other professionals risked losing both their current jobs and any hopes for future employment if they pled guilty to lewd conduct. Even being arrested was, in some cases, sufficient to cause some gay men to lose their jobs since the police saw that names and addresses were included in the newspaper.

Several key gay civil rights organizations were organized in the 1950s and 1960s in San Francisco. The Mattachine Society of Los Angeles had been taken over by Hal Call of San Francisco. Del Martin and Phyllis Lyons formed the first chapter of Daughters of Bilitis (DOB) in 1955, appealing primarily to lesbians. The Society for Individual Rights (SIR) was formed in the early 1960s. All these organizations were aimed at educating the public about homosexuality and fighting for civil liberties for homosexual persons. Of particular interest is the Council on Religion and the Homosexual

(CRH), organized by a number of ministers who thought gay people were being mistreated and who also hoped to bring gay people, who had been alienated by their churches, back into the church. Influenced by the black civil rights movement and in particular by Martin Luther King Jr., this group thought in terms of civil rights as well as in terms of spiritual ministry. To raise money for its activities, CRH, with the support of DOB and SIR, planned to host a gala gay costume ball on January 1, 1965. The mardi gras–style event was to be the first major gay social event in San Francisco and it was to be held at a place called California Hall.

The costume ball became a pivotal moment in gay civil rights history in San Francisco. The police, who had originally agreed to stay away from the event, showed up early. Evander Smith and Herb Donaldson, who were present in their capacity as lawyers to protect the attendees from police harassment, were the first to be arrested. Nancy May, a gay rights activist although she herself was not gay, was the next to be arrested when she tried to keep the police out of the dance by asking if they had a search warrant. Someone called Elliott Leighton, a lawyer they had enlisted as backup. When he arrived at California Hall, the police arrested him as well.[12]

The three lawyers and Nancy May challenged their arrests in a criminal trial. They were represented by the American Civil Liberties Union. The charges were ultimately dismissed, but the arrested lawyers filed their own charges against the city and the county. Although they never pursued the legal claims against the city and the county, the publicity surrounding the events and the claims against the city resulted in important changes in police department operations. Ultimately a liaison to the gay community was appointed to the police–community relations board. SIR continued its civil rights work and became active in a key gay employment discrimination case.[13] On January 1, 1983, Herb Donaldson was sworn in as the first openly gay judge in California.[14]

In 1961, the homophile movement on the East Coast took a turn toward militant activism when Frank Kameny formed the Mattachine Society of Washington, D.C. By that time, the Mattachine Society's national structure had collapsed and Kameny was free to structure his own organization's policy around his concerns. His particular concern was with the federal government, who had fired him from his position as an astronomer with the Army Map Service because he was gay. He sued, and when he lost both his case and his lawyer at the appellate stage, Kameny filed his own petition for certiorari with the U.S. Supreme Court. The Court denied the petition, but the experience for Kameny turned him into an indefatigable gay rights activist. Using the tactics of the black civil rights movement, Kameny planned demonstrations, coined the phrase "gay is good," and coordinated strategic gay rights litigation. Indeed, as the next chapter will demonstrate, Kameny's coordination of litigation efforts on behalf of gay civil service employees was one of the most important early litigation efforts for the movement. In the 1960s Kameny and his local chapter of the Mattachine Society operated much like the public interest law firms of today, giving advice to gays in trouble and referring them to lawyers when possible.

After Stonewall

After Stonewall, with the formation of new organizations committed to political and social change such as the Gay Liberation Front and the Gay and Lesbian Task Force, a need arose for organizations that were committed to litigation. The lesbian and gay civil rights movement would succeed only if it worked on all three fronts simultaneously for social, political, and legal change. This lesson was learned from earlier civil rights movements.

The tax and charitable contribution laws that had plagued the NAACP in the 1950s were much clearer to activists by the 1970s. They understood that lobbying for legislative change could not be supported by tax-deductible contributions, but that litigating for judicial change could be. In 1970, the IRS promulgated "Guidelines Under Which the IRS Will Issue Advance Rulings of Exemption to Public Interest Law Firms,"[15] clarifying its rules for those who wished to obtain tax-exempt status.

When the African American civil rights movement took to the courts in its effort to overturn *Plessy,* it was led by an established organization, the NAACP. When Ruth Bader Ginsburg planned her litigation strategy to overturn prior antifeminist precedents, she did so as part of a long-established civil rights organization, the ACLU. When lesbian and gay lawyers first began to think about litigating for gay rights, they realized that they could either form an alliance with an established civil rights organization, such as the ACLU, or create a new civil rights legal organization of their own to serve the movement.

The ACLU had resisted early pleas from lesbian and gay advocates during the pre-Stonewall days. During the 1950s, the ACLU was periodically asked to provide legal assistance to gay people who had suffered discrimination. Drawing a line between speech and belief, which were constitutionally protected, and sexual conduct, which was not constitutionally protected, the ACLU generally had refused to handle gay rights cases. In 1957, the ACLU issued its first national policy statement on the rights of gay men and lesbians. According to this statement, the ACLU supported the notion that sodomy statutes were constitutional and that homosexuality was a valid concern when granting security clearances.[16] However, the organization did support litigation aimed at protecting some of the due process rights of gay people. Thus, it opposed entrapment and proposals for the compulsory registration of homosexuals.[17]

ACLU affiliates in southern California and Washington, D.C., fought to reverse the national office's position. In 1964, gay rights was on the agenda at the ACLU's national convention. Harriet Pilpel argued that privacy rights should be extended to cover homosexual conduct.[18] The resolution that emerged from the national convention favored the repeal of sodomy statutes, but the national office continued to consider homosexuality a valid concern for security clearances. The national office also repeatedly refused to support Frank Kameny and his Washington chapter of the Mattachine Society in ongoing litigation against the gay exclusionary rule applied by the Civil Service Commission.

By the time of Stonewall, the ACLU's national position on gay rights issues was much improved. Nonetheless, the long battle with the ACLU over whether gay rights was a civil rights issue suggested to many observers that the lesbian and gay civil rights movement needed its own public interest law firm. Although the ACLU would ultimately become a major force in lesbian and gay litigation, it was certainly not the pioneer for gay civil rights that it had been for women's civil rights.

In the early 1970s, two public interest law firms were launched that made important contributions during the early days of the post-Stonewall movement, and continue to litigate on behalf of gays and lesbians today. Lambda Legal Defense and Education Fund, Inc., founded in New York by gay men, is the oldest and largest public interest law firm whose primary focus is to litigate cases on behalf of lesbians and gay men. Simultaneously, Equal Rights Advocates (ERA), a feminist law firm, was being launched on the West Coast. Unlike NOW, ERA embraced lesbian causes from the beginning. One of ERA's founders, Mary Dunlap, was an out lesbian whose feminism had always included a commitment to lesbian and gay causes. In 1977, ERA founded the Lesbian Rights Project, which ultimately became the National Center for Lesbian Rights.

Establishing two new law firms staffed at least in part by gay and lesbian lawyers was not easy in the 1970s. The number of "out" lesbian and gay lawyers was few, and they were true pioneers. To become a member of the state bar, one had to pass certain tests proving moral fitness to practice law. Professor Deborah Rhode, an expert on professional responsibility and the operation of state bar fitness committees, reported in a 1985 article:

> Since disrespect for law remains a rationale for non-certification, and since noncommercial homosexual conduct between consenting adults is unlawful in forty-three states and the District of Columbia, the potential for intrusive and capricious committee action remains substantial. Only California has a formal policy declaring sexual preference irrelevant to practice. Although some state courts have come to similar conclusions with respect to particular applicants, their holdings by no means foreclose extensive and degrading interrogation. For example, in one of these jurisdictions, a 1981 applicant who had been excluded from military service on grounds of homosexuality submitted to an hour and a half of "every tricky question about his sex life [examiners] could dream of."[19]

What was true in 1985 was even more true in 1970. To identify as a gay or lesbian lawyer was to raise questions about one's fitness to practice law because of the presumption that "avowed homosexuals" engaged in criminal misconduct. Although the decision was later reversed, the Virginia Bar, as late as 1979, had refused to admit a woman who was living with a person of the opposite sex.[20] As late as 1981, the Florida Bar refused to admit a male lawyer who had admitted to homosexuality (but not illegal conduct) in his selective service exam with the military. Even though the applicant stated that he intended to obey the laws of Florida, the bar felt that the propensity to engage in illegal conduct was sufficient to deny his application. The Florida Supreme Court ultimately reversed the decision. The court agreed that lawyers should be held to high standards and "should refrain from all illegal and morally reprehensible conduct." Nonetheless, a majority of the judges ruled that "private noncommercial sex acts between consenting adults are not relevant to prove fitness to practice law."[21] Two judges dissented in opinions that would have prevented anyone who identified as homosexual from practicing law as a member of the State Bar of Florida.

Segregation had kept black lawyers out of many of the law schools of the nation, but it did not prevent them from gaining a license to practice as a member of a state bar. Women were initially barred from the practice of law in many states and, in 1873, the U.S. Supreme Court had upheld the

Illinois rule preventing women from becoming licensed attorneys. Nonetheless, by 1917, every state in the country had admitted women to the bar,[22] although some of the top law schools (e.g., Harvard) denied admission to women into the 1950s. Gay men and lesbians were not barred from law schools or from state bars so long as they remained closeted. But "coming out" put a lawyer at risk because of the fear that being gay would be a per se disqualification in the eyes of the state bar examiners.

Fortunately, in some cities, in some states, being "out" or being committed to gay causes was not disqualifying. Thanks to the courage of a critical mass of lesbian and gay lawyers, litigation efforts on behalf of lesbian and gay rights began to increase. By 1982, five organizations across the country were specifically organized as public interest litigation firms for the purpose of supporting the lesbian and gay civil rights movement. Lambda Legal Defense and Education Fund, Inc. is the oldest and largest of these groups. The National Center for Lesbian Rights is almost as old if one counts its predecessor, the Lesbian Rights Project at Equal Rights Advocates. Two regional organizations remain active today: Gay and Lesbian Advocates and Defenders in Boston and the Texas Human Rights Foundation. Only one firm, Gay Rights Advocates, has closed its doors. It was founded by Jerel McCrary and Matt Coles in San Francisco and later moved to Los Angeles, where it disbanded in 1991.

At first, litigation efforts on behalf of gay men and lesbians were primarily reactive, occurring in cases in which individuals were forced to defend the rights that had been taken from them. Some time would pass before the lawyers for the movement would become sufficiently organized to be proactive. In the remainder of this subsection, I focus primarily on the two oldest public interest law firms that sprang up to fight for lesbian and gay rights, Lambda Legal Defense and Educational Fund (LLDEF) and Equal Rights Advocates, which eventually gave birth to the National Center for Lesbian Rights. I will also describe the ACLU's growing commitment to lesbian gay rights.

Lambda Legal Defense and Education Fund. In the early 1970s, William Thom, E. Carrington Boggan, and several other gay lawyers met in New York City to discuss the possibility of forming a public interest law firm whose purpose would be to further the cause of gay rights. New York law at the time forbade the practice of law by a corporation or association unless the organization was "organized for benevolent or charitable purposes, or for the purpose of assisting persons without means in the pursuit of any civil remedy."[23] Basing its charter and petition on that of the recently approved Puerto Rican Defense Fund, Thom applied to the Appellate Division of the New York Supreme Court for approval. The application was rejected unanimously.[24]

Lambda's purposes, as stated in its application to the court, were as follows:

> The attorneys employed by the Corporation will render, provide and carry out the practice of law activities of the corporation as set forth in this paragraph. These activities include providing without charge legal services in those situations which give rise to legal issues having a substantial effect on the legal rights of homosexuals; to promote the availability of legal services to homosexuals by encouraging and attracting homosexuals into the legal profession; to disseminate to homosexuals general information concerning their legal rights and obligations, and to render technical assistance to any legal services corporation or agency in regard to legal issues affecting homosexuals.[25]

The Appellate Division proclaimed: "The stated purposes are on their face neither benevolent nor charitable ... , nor, in any event, is there a demonstrated need for this corporation."[26] The difference between Lambda and the Puerto Rican Legal Defense and Education Fund, said the court, was that the Puerto Rican community was poor and thus could not otherwise afford legal assistance. Admitting that the gay community suffered from discrimination, the court nonetheless reasoned that there had been no proof offered to show that the discrimination prevented gay and lesbian clients from obtaining adequate legal representation. In other words, "charity" does not include attempts to remedy discrimination unless it can be shown that the victims of discrimination are also poor.

The New York Court of Appeals reversed the lower court.[27] Finally, on October 18, 1973, the lower court approved Thom's application and Lambda Legal Defense and Education Fund was officially incorporated and authorized to practice law.[28] Apparently, however, the Appellate Division was not completely happy with the instruction from the highest court to approve Lambda's application. Reasserting its discretionary power to review the specifics of corporate charters, the court mandated the removal of one purpose from Lambda's charter before granting full approval. The purpose to which the court objected was "to promote legal education among homosexuals by recruiting and encouraging potential law students who are homosexuals and by providing assistance to such students after admission to law school." Thus, with this provision deleted from the charter, Lambda was officially incorporated under New York law.

In July 1974, the Internal Revenue Service granted Lambda tax-exempt status under Section 501(c)(3) of the Internal Revenue Code. Lambda is probably the first gay rights organization to earn tax-exempt charitable status from the federal government. In the mid-1970s, a series of general counsel memoranda and private rulings evidenced the discomfort that the IRS was experiencing in admitting that educational efforts related to homosexuality might sometimes be tax-exempt. Not until 1978 did the IRS issue its first public ruling that organizations dedicated to educating the public about homosexuality might be entitled to charitable status under Section 501(c)(3) of the Internal Revenue Code.

In the early days, Lambda was short on staff and did not handle its own cases. Lambda's primary activity in those days was to file appellate briefs as amicus curiae (friend of the court) in cases dealing with lesbian and gay issues, particularly in those cases in which positive arguments on behalf of gay men and lesbians were missing. In addition, because Lambda was short on funds, it could not represent clients directly because it could not afford to carry the litigation costs. The organization was operating on a shoestring budget. Its first newsletter, published in 1976, included a plea for financial support that admits the organization only had enough money to continue operating for the next 60 days. One year later, a similar plea was made, accompanied with an apology that Lambda had insufficient funds to cover litigation costs in key cases. For example, when the ACLU decided not to appeal the *Matlovich*[29] case, an important early case about the military's ban on homosexuals, Lambda's general counsel, E. Carrington Boggan, agreed to handle the case provided Matlovich himself could forward the necessary costs of litigation.

A series of executive directors tried to hold the organization together. During one four-year period, Lambda hired four new executive directors, all of them very young, but with good civil rights experience. Barbara Levy headed the organization until 1979 when she left to become an assistant attorney general for New York state in the civil rights unit. After a nationwide search, the Lambda board appointed Ed Glorius as the new executive director. Glorius had recently graduated from the University of Pittsburgh law school, but he had strong civil rights credentials from his work with the ACLU. In the spring of 1980, Rosalyn Richter, just one year out of law school herself, became the executive director. In 1981, Richter moved to another position in Lambda and Tim Sweeney took over the executive director position. Sweeney was not a lawyer and he was only five years out of college. Richter left Lambda in 1983 to join the Brooklyn district attorney's office and in 1987 became a judge. Sweeney left in 1986 to become deputy director and later executive director of the Gay Men's Health Crisis in New York City.

Sweeney headed Lambda from 1981 to 1986, a key period of early expansion. Sweeney worked to increase Lambda's funding. Rosalyn Richter remained on board to work on legal issues, in particular a project that focused on the potential legal claims against antigay legislation. During this period, Richter developed legal arguments, primarily based on the constitution, to challenge antigay legislation. Of primary interest was legislation that barred federal funds from being used to support anything that carried a gay-positive message. Since 1980, for example, federal legislation had banned legal services lawyers from participating in any litigation that sought to "legalize homosexuality." Initially supported by the N.Y.U. Public Interest Law Foundation, the project drew additional grants from foundations, which in turn helped to increase private donations.

By 1982, with better funding in place, the Lambda Board became concerned about the organization's ability to coordinate lesbian and gay rights litigation through its nationwide network of volunteer cooperating attorneys. At this time, the board decided to hire a managing attorney to oversee Lambda's growing docket. The managing attorney needed to be someone with organizational skills and a vision for Lambda's future. In 1983, the perfect candidate for the position was hired. Abby Rubenfeld has been first at many things. She was one of the first women to attend Princeton after it went co-ed in the late 1960s and she was the first woman class president. Prior to joining the Lambda staff, she had been a cooperating attorney in Nashville, where she was the first openly gay lawyer. Her vision for Lambda was to create better national communication among lawyers and gay rights organizations that were actively representing lesbians and gay men. Rubenfeld helped organize a national legal task force on sodomy laws, an organization that was crucial in the litigation challenging sodomy statutes.

During this critical period in Lambda's history, William Hibsher, who had been an active cooperating attorney for Lambda until he moved into government practice in the late 1970s, returned to private practice in New York. Hibsher was an energetic supporter of using the law to increase gay rights and felt Lambda was in a unique position to make important differences in the way the nation viewed gay people. In 1983, shortly after making partner and with the full support of his law firm, Teitelbaum and Hiller, Hibsher successfully litigated the 1983 Gay Pride case, blocking an attempt by antigay forces to prevent the parade from gaining a permit.[30] Hibsher, with the cooperation of the New York state attorney general, also litigated the first successful AIDS discrimination case, obtaining an injunction that prevented a tenant's association from evicting a doctor who treated AIDS patients.[31] In 1985, as a Lambda board member, Hibsher chaired the search for a new executive director to replace Tim Sweeney. That search culminated in the hiring of Tom Stoddard, who for the next six years led Lambda from being a $350,000-a-year public interest law firm with a staff of six to a firm with a $1.8 million annual budget and a staff of twenty-two. Stoddard also became a leading legal voice of the lesbian and gay civil rights movement and continued in that very public role until his death, of AIDS, in 1997.

Tom Stoddard was both an exceptional lawyer and an exceptional public speaker. He had worked for Lambda even when he was a law student at NYU, drafting an important early memo on the issue of gays in the military for E. Carrington Boggan to use in the *Matlovich* case. After graduation, Stoddard worked for the New York Civil Liberties Union on its legislative efforts to resist the reinstitution of the death penalty. During his time with the Civil Liberties Union, he perfected his legislative lobbying skills, his knowledge of litigation strategy, and his public speaking abilities. In 1981, he began teaching one of the first courses on sexual orientation law in the country as an adjunct professor at NYU Law School.

Stoddard is credited with the successful passage of the 1986 New York City gay rights bill. He drafted the bill and he lobbied it through the city council. Ed Koch, who was mayor at the time, said of Stoddard: "He never retreated, he would find a way to explain, to placate and convince opponents that his approach was reasonable, rational and one they could accept."

But, as one of the larger-than-life public figures in the movement, he was a target for criticism by his constituency. He compared the plight of gay men and lesbians to that of African Americans and, although he acknowledged his own privilege as white and male, the comparisons rankled some people of color in the movement. He defended Lambda's fund-raising event at the theatrical production of *Miss Saigon* and caused a near riot by Asian American gays and lesbians who viewed the selection as particularly insensitive to racial issues, because the show had hired a non-Asian actor for the key role. Stoddard was an early proponent of gay marriage rights, which subjected him to charges from lesbian feminists that marriage would only benefit the already more powerful white gay men in the movement. Radical activists dubbed him too conservative, a lawyer who was out of touch with the community, a charge that is often pressed against public interest lawyers by members of the movement they represent.

Although Stoddard oversaw the full operation of Lambda, Abby Rubenfeld, as legal director, handled Lambda's growing docket of cases. Rubenfeld's tenure with Lambda, from early 1983 until late 1988, coincided with the *Hardwick* litigation challenging Georgia's sodomy statute. To help coordinate litigation challenging sodomy statutes nationwide, in 1983 Rubenfeld organized the Ad Hoc Task Force to Challenge Sodomy Laws. Her plan was to bring together lawyers from other lesbian and gay civil rights groups to develop a coordinated national strategy. Because gay rights litigation covered many other areas as well as sodomy challenges, the original task force quickly grew to become the National Lesbian and Gay Civil Rights Roundtable. The group met three times a year in different locations. Before long it expanded to include some academics and researchers who were also interested in national strategies to obtain equal rights for lesbians and gay men. In the late 1980s, the group had expanded to include over fifty participants at some meetings. In addition to the Roundtable, Rubenfeld organized a monthly conference call among lawyers at lesbian and gay rights organizations around the country. Known as the National Litigators Strategy Project, the conference call enabled each legal organization to stay abreast of each other's docket and to stay informed about possibly good and bad precedent that would affect other cases. Subsequent Lambda legal directors Paula Ettelbrick and Beatrice Dohrn have continued Lambda's role as a key organizer of the national network of lesbian and gay rights litigators.

Under Stoddard and Rubenfeld's leadership, Lambda expanded beyond its New York roots. Rubenfeld committed Lambda resources to cases throughout the country, especially those that reflected Lambda's commitment to fighting all forms of discrimination. The AIDS docket also expanded greatly during this time. AIDS awareness was just developing in the early 1980s and Lambda soon became a key national player in the efforts to protect the rights of persons with AIDS. In a 1987 *New York Times* article, Tom Stoddard credits the AIDS epidemic for much of Lambda's financial success. He said, "Our contributions shot up dramatically as a result of *Bowers v. Hardwick*. . . . But, it has been AIDS that has given the homosexual rights movement widespread legitimation. Without AIDS, Lambda would not be getting grants from mainstream foundations."

The 1987 *New York Times* article was evidence that the lesbian and gay civil rights movement had come of age. The *Times* was covering a major and unprecedented fund-raising event in New York City, cosponsored by three prominent law firms, Skadden, Arps; Wathcell, Lipton; and Nizer, Benjamin. The event raised $50,000 for Lambda and gave it an important dose of media attention that helped cement Lambda's reputation in the New York legal community, a community that Lambda depended on not just for financial support, but also for expert pro bono lawyering in highly visible gay rights cases.

Lambda also expanded its offices beyond its New York City headquarters. Under Stoddard's leadership, Lambda opened its first regional office in Los Angeles in 1990. In 1992, Stoddard left Lambda and Kevin Cathcart became the new executive director. Cathcart joined Lambda after eight successful years as the executive director of Gay and Lesbian Advocates and Defenders in Boston. Under Cathcart's leadership, Lambda has established additional regional offices in Chicago and Atlanta.

Equal Rights Advocates, the Lesbian Rights Project, and the National Center for Lesbian Rights. Equal Rights Advocates was founded in 1973 by Wendy Williams, Nancy Davis, and Mary Dunlap. Its primary purpose was to represent women who were the victims of sex discrimination, particularly in employment. All three founders were recent graduates of Boalt Hall, the law school at the University of California at Berkeley. Within a year of its founding, Wendy Williams found herself arguing before the Supreme Court that discrimination on the basis of pregnancy was sex discrimination and thus a violation of the Equal Protection Clause. The Court rejected the argument, claiming that pregnancy classifications distinguished between pregnant and nonpregnant persons rather than between men and women. Since the nonpregnant person category could contain both men and women, such classifications were not strictly drawn along sex lines. Three years after that, Mary Dunlap took her first case to the Supreme Court, arguing on behalf of pregnant clients that the automatic dismissal of pregnant schoolteachers was a violation of Title VII's sex discrimination provisions. The Court rejected the claim on the basis of its decision in *General Electric Company v. Gilbert*,[32] a case that the Court agreed to hear before Dunlap's schoolteacher case. Therefore, the Court vacated Dunlap's case. In a victory for women's rights, Congress responded to *Gilbert* by amending Title VII to forbid discrimination on the basis of pregnancy.

Mary Dunlap is a fiery advocate for civil rights and an out lesbian. She played an active role from the beginning of the lesbian and gay rights movement by working with her partners, Williams and Davis, to include lesbian women in their representation. Later Equal Rights Advocates would become the home of the Lesbian Rights Project. Ultimately, the Lesbian Rights Project gained sufficient independent funding and became a separately incorporated organization, the National Center for Lesbian Rights.

Before San Francisco had any organization dedicated to the specific purpose of litigating for lesbians and gay men, it had Mary Dunlap. Dunlap was an important force in the shaping of legal arguments on behalf of lesbians and gay men, and, unlike other national players in the movement, she accomplished most of her work on her own, in private practice, often acting as her own secretary. During her association with Williams and Davis, however, she argued her first major gay rights case.

On July 6, 1973, Mary Saal was dismissed from the navy solely on the basis of her own admission that she had engaged in homosexual activity. Under the then existing navy regulations, a person was subject to mandatory discharge proceedings if he or she had committed "a homosexual act," which was defined broadly to include acts that were neither criminal nor explicitly sexual in nature. Dunlap filed suit on behalf of Saal on July 27, 1973, "seeking injunctive relief to prevent the Navy from discharging plaintiff for her homosexual activity as well as damages for back pay and lost promotional opportunities." Saal won at the District Court level. Judge Schwarzer's opinion focused on the fact that the homosexual acts provision in the regulations triggered mandatory discharge proceedings with no opportunity to determine whether the person discharged was actually a threat to navy morale. He said:

> The Navy, along with the other military services, has been in the vanguard in providing equal opportunities to segments of our society that have long suffered discrimination. Without impairment of its efficiency or effectiveness, it has abandoned the stereotypes of the past that have stigmatized women and members of minority races in favor of judging the fitness of individuals on their merits. On the basis of the instant record, its failure to accord the same treatment to plaintiff simply because she has engaged in homosexual acts must be found to be irrational and capricious and thus in violation of the Fifth Amendment.[33]

This case was the first reported progay decision in a case against the military. The victory, however sweet, was short. In 1980, the Ninth Circuit

Court of Appeals reversed the *Saal* decision. But even as it reversed, the Ninth Circuit recognized that intimate sexual association between people of the same sex might, in other situations, trigger heightened judicial scrutiny as a protected right under the Due Process Clause. The court ruled in favor of the navy because of the military deference doctrine.

After Dunlap left Equal Rights Advocates, she continued to litigate civil rights cases. She wrote an important amicus brief in the *Bowers v. Hardwick* case, filed on behalf of the Lesbian Rights Project. In 1987, she argued the Gay Olympics case before the U.S. Supreme Court.[34] As an adjunct professor at several Bay Area law schools, she, along with Tom Stoddard of Lambda, was one of the first in the country to teach courses on sexual orientation and the law.

Shortly before Dunlap left ERA, the Lesbian Rights Project was formed and housed at Equal Rights Advocates. Its first director was Donna Hitchens, who is now a judge of the Superior Court of California in San Francisco. Most of the project's work focused on employment discrimination against lesbians and on lesbian custody cases. During its earliest days, the project served as a clearinghouse for lawyers and plaintiffs involved in lesbian discrimination and custody cases. Because information, especially expert testimony, on lesbian families and their children was scarce, this service proved to be essential to the development of fairer treatment of lesbian mothers. Today, the project's successor, the National Center for Lesbian Rights (NCLR), whose initial director was Roberta Achtenberg, continues this important work. Under the current leadership of Kate Kendell, the NCLR has expanded its program to include advocacy and education on issues of child custody and visitation, adoption, alternative insemination, same-gender marriage, domestic partnership, immigration and asylum, transgender issues, and youth.

The American Civil Liberties Union. The ACLU was founded in 1920 as a national public interest law firm committed to the protection of individual rights secured by the Constitution. The organization did not adopt a positive position on lesbian and gay rights until well into the 1960s. When lesbian and gay military personnel were threatened with dishonorable discharges after World War II, the ACLU responded to pleas for legal help by saying that homosexuality was "relevant to an individual's military service." In its 1957 position statement on homosexuality, the ACLU said that homosexuality "is a valid consideration in evaluating the security risk factor in sensitive positions. . . . It is not within the province of the Union to

evaluate the social validity of the laws aimed at the suppression or elimination of homosexuals." The national board took the position that sodomy
laws were constitutional.

In the early 1960s, during the years that some of the most important litigation challenging the government's exclusionary policies occurred, Frank Kameny, the head of the D.C. chapter of the Mattachine Society, tried repeatedly to get ACLU assistance in cases challenging the government's dismissal
of gay employees. Sometimes a local attorney affiliated with the ACLU was
willing to step in and fight the dismissal at the agency or commission stage,
but was not willing to litigate the case in court.[35] Litigation is expensive and
Kameny's pleas to the ACLU were to provide both counsel and litigation ex-
penses. The national office refused throughout most of the 1960s.

The southern California chapter was the first to issue a public statement
in favor of lesbian and gay rights. In 1964, the board officially adopted the
following statement:

> The American Civil Liberties Union of Southern California believes that the
> right to privacy in sexual relations is a basic constitutional right. In respect to
> private conduct by adults, each individual has the right to decide what kind of
> sexual practices he or she will or will not engage in, what techniques will be
> used, and whether or not a contraceptive should be used. Public regulation of
> sexual conduct should be concerned only with preventing rape and assault and
> protection of minors.[36]

With urging from the southern California and Washington, D.C., affiliates, the national board of the ACLU ultimately adopted the position that
private sexual relations between consenting adults fell within the constitutionally protected right to privacy that the Supreme Court ultimately recognized in *Griswold*. In 1967, with its official policy changed, the ACLU took
part in its first gay rights case at the Supreme Court, *Boutelier v. INS*.[37] The
ACLU argued that homosexuality should not be grounds for deportation
under the then-existing rules applied by the Immigration and Nationaliza-
tion Service (INS) in deporting aliens. The Supreme Court upheld the antigay INS rule.

Although the ACLU was late in establishing lesbian and gay rights as an
official concern of the organization, it is now one of the most active legal
organization on behalf of lesbian and gay rights. Because of its organizational structure, consisting of a national office, with chapters in each state,
and over 300 local chapters in large cities throughout the country, it has

more affiliates than any other national civil rights organization. Moreover, those state chapters are separately incorporated and run by their own state boards of directors.[38] Although the affiliates cannot breach national office policy, the affiliates have a good deal of autonomy in deciding which cases to pursue. Thus, for example, the southern California chapter has been one of the most active ACLU groups on behalf of lesbian and gay rights.

By the 1970s, the national office of the ACLU was actively supporting litigation on behalf of lesbian and gay privacy rights. Harriet Pilpel, who served as general counsel to the Planned Parenthood Federation of America and the ACLU, was the first person to make the connection between reproductive rights and sexual privacy. She encouraged the ACLU to litigate sexual privacy cases. In 1973, the ACLU created the Sexual Privacy Project to work on privacy challenges to government regulation of sexuality. Marilyn Haft, in the national office, headed up the project. In 1974, the ACLU of southern California joined as amicus in a case that challenged California's sodomy statute. The challenge failed, however, when the court dismissed the plaintiff's claim for lack of standing.[39]

Finally, in 1986 the ACLU founded the Lesbian and Gay Rights Project, cementing the organization's commitment to focus on lesbian and gay civil liberties. Nan Hunter, who had been with the Reproductive Freedom Project, became the first executive director of the Lesbian and Gay Rights Project.[40] She also headed up the ACLU AIDS Project. William Rubenstein joined as staff attorney one year later and took over as director of both projects in 1990. Matt Coles, who had founded National Gay Rights Advocates in San Francisco, is the current director. By 1994, the projects had four attorneys in New York, a legislative representative in Washington, D.C., and a budget of nearly $1 million. Today, the ACLU, with its well-organized national system of affiliates, participates in more lesbian and gay rights litigation than any other organization in the country.

LEGAL THEORIES AND LITIGATION STRATEGY

Lesbian and gay civil rights attorneys would rely on the successful legal arguments that had been developed by earlier civil rights lawyers fighting on behalf of racial and gender equality. Under the federal constitution, lesbian and gay rights attorneys would challenge discrimination by government actors using equal protection theories (e.g., all persons should be treated equally regardless of sexual orientation, race, or gender). They would make similar challenges, relying on substantive due process theories, which require that governmental decisions be based on reasonable grounds (e.g., sexual orientation, race, and gender are irrelevant considerations unless they in fact affect the person's qualifications to do a particular job). But, more than in prior civil rights movements, lesbian and gay civil rights attorneys would rely on first amendment, freedom of speech arguments. This fact should not be surprising. Racial minorities and women rarely have to announce their membership in the protected class in order to seek equal protection review of discriminatory actions. By contrast, many lesbian and gay individuals only experience discrimination once they have engaged in expressive activities, either professing their sexual orientation or saying or doing something expressive that signals to others that they may not be heterosexual.

With respect to litigation strategy, the lesbian and gay rights legal community had developed solid networking systems to keep each other apprised of important developments in cases around the country. At the same time, Lambda, one of the key organizers and sustainers of this national network, raised questions within its own organization of whether its primary efforts should be focused on a national litigation strategy. In 1992, shortly before the opening of its Chicago office, the Lambda board appointed a committee to look at these issues in terms of its own long-range planning. At the committee meeting, board members debated, among other items, whether Lambda should be committed to a national litigation strategy to change the status of gay men and lesbians, a strategy that might parallel the national strategy of the NAACP to end racial segregation in education. The report of the board committee on long-range planning, dated September 1992, makes the following observations:

> Lambda is the legal services program for the community. Thus, we must often take on cases that our clients need for us to take on regardless of any "national plan." Furthermore, we *must* provide these services or we will lose the support of our community. In providing such legal services, we distinguish ourselves from the ACLU.
>
> Much of Lambda's impact litigation is not national in scope. There is great geographical disparity in the rights accorded gay men and lesbians. We may do family law cases in Tennessee that qualify as impact litigation for Tennessee, but would not be such in the state of New York.[41]

The following chapters tell the story of the litigation effort on behalf of gay men and lesbians. The story is presented as a national one. But the reader should keep in mind that, although hostility toward lesbians and gay men was fairly uniform throughout the United States at the beginning of the era that is the focus of this book (1950), those attitudes and the laws accompanying them changed rapidly in succeeding years. Litigation at the state level on behalf of lesbian and gay rights begins to vary dramatically in its success rate, state by state, in the 1960s. At the national level, federal constitutional claims were severely hampered once *Bowers v. Hardwick* was handed down in 1986. Thus, lesbian and gay civil rights litigators have been forced back into state courts to pursue their claims in ways that other civil rights litigators have not been forced. In addition, the prolonged unsuccessful attack on antigay military policies has created bad precedent in federal courts, which litigators might avoid in state courts. Finally, many of the core claims for lesbian and gay litigants involve family and relationship issues, topics that are traditionally handled by state, rather than federal, courts.

NOTES

1. Gerald P. Lopez, *Rebellious Lawyering: One Chicano's Vision of Progressive Law Practice* (1992).

2. See generally Marlise James, *The People's Lawyer* (1973), especially statements by Robert Gnaizda, California Rural Legal Assistance Program, at 57, and by Charles Garry, lawyer for the Black Panther Party, at 309–310.

3. Nancy D. Polikoff, "Am I My Client?: The Role Confusion of a Lawyer Activist," 31 *Harvard. Civil Rights-Civil Liberties Law Review* 443 at 448 (1996).

4. 416 U.S. 351 (1974).

5. See Deborah L. Markowitz, "In Pursuit of Equality: One Woman's Work to Change the Law," 14 *Women's Rights Law Reporter* 335, 346–347 (1992).

6. From William H. Hastie, "Toward an Equalitarian Legal Order, 1930–1950," reproduced in A. Leon Higginbotham, Jr., *Shades of Freedom: Racial Politics and Presumptions of the American Legal Process* (Oxford University Press 1996).

7. Taylor Branch, *Parting the Waters* at 189.

8. See generally Robert L. Carter, *A Reassessment of Brown v. Board,* in *Shades of Brown: New Perspectives on School Desegregation* at 21–23 (Derrick Bell ed., 1980).

9. See generally Carolyn G. Heilbrun, *The Education of a Woman: The Life of Gloria Steinem* (1995).

10. Friedan, *It Changed My Life: Writings on the Women's Movement* at 98.

11. See Jonathan Ned Katz, *Gay American History*, at 411–412.

12. See Eric Marcus, *Making History*, at 155.

13. Society for Individual Rights, Inc. v. Hampton, 63 F.R.D. 399 (N.D. Cal. 1973).

14. Ibid. at 165.

15. News Release I. R. 1078, dated November 12, 1970.

16. See generally John D'Emilio, *Sexual Politics, Sexual Communities* at 156; Walker, *In Defense of American Liberties* at 312.

17. Walker at 312.

18. Walker 1990 and D'Emilio 1983.

19. Rhode, Deborah, *Yale Law Journal*, 1985.

20. Cord v. Gibb, 254 S.E.2d 71 (Va. 1979).

21. Florida Board of Bar Examiners v. N.R.S., 403 So.2d 1315 (Florida 1981).

22. Karen Berger Morello, *The Invisible Bar: The Woman Lawyer in America 1638 to the Present* (1986).

23. Section 495 of the Judiciary Law. The exception is in subdivision 5.

24. In re Thom, 337 N.Y.S.2d 588 (App. Div. 1972).

25. Ibid. at 589.

26. Ibid.

27. 301 N.E.2d 542 (N.Y. 1973).

28. 350 N.Y.S.2d 1 (1973).

29. See Matlovich v. Secretary of the Air Force, 1976 WL 649 (D.D.C. 1976).

30. See Catholic War Veterans of the United States v. City of New York, 576 F. Supp. 71 (S.D.N.Y. 1983).

31. People of the State of New York, Joseph Sonnabend, M.D. v. 49 West 12 Street Tenants Corp. (N.Y. Supreme Court 1983)(unreported decision).

32. 429 U.S. 125 (1976).

33. Saal v. Middendorf, 427 F. Supp 192 at 203 (N.D. Cal. 1977), *rev'd* Beller v. Mittendorf.

34. San Francisco Arts & Athletics, Inc. v. U.S. Olympic Committee, 483 U.S. 522 (1987). The case arose because the USOC, vested by Congress with the power to prohibit other organizations from using the word "olympic," enjoined the San Francisco organization from calling its event the "Gay Olympic Games." On appeal, the gay group claimed its First Amendment and equal protection rights were violated by the USOC's discriminatory decision to deny them the right to use the word "olympic." In a 5 to 4 decision, the Supreme Court ruled that the USOC was not a governmental actor and thus not subject to constitutional constraints.

35. See, for example, Richardson v. Hampton, 345 F.Supp. 600 (D.D.C. 1972).

36. Reprinted in Vern L. Bullough, "Lesbianism, Homosexuality, and the American Civil Liberties Union," 13 *Journal of Homosexuality* 23 at 27 (1986).

37. 387 U.S. 118 (1967).

38. September 1, 1992, memo from Ed McAmis to Lambda Long Range Plans Committee (Pat Cain, Chair), describing national/local affiliation of ACLU, NAACP, MALDEF and Lawyers Committee. At the time this research was requested, Lambda was considering opening its regional office in Chicago.

39. People v. Baldwin, 37 Cal.App.3d 385, 112 Cal.Reporter 290 (Cal.App. 1974).

40. Walker, 1990, at 312–313.

41. Report of the Long Range Planning Committee, Lambda Legal Defense and Education Fund, September 1992. I agreed to chair this committee when I was on the Lambda board. Other board members on the committee were Lorri Jean, Andrew Chirls, Nan Bailey, Carol Buell, Harry Harkins, Ed McManis, and Elizabeth McNamara.

3

Public Rights:
1950–1985

Rationing public space and keeping subservient groups separate from dominant groups is one tactic for maintaining power in society. When a dominant group controls space, it can prevent members of subservient groups from banding together and it can insulate members of the dominant group from outside influences and ideas. Battles over the occupation of public space are, therefore, common in civil rights movements. In the early history of this country, as industrialization created more market jobs for men outside the home, women were relegated to the private sphere of home and family. Women who broke with tradition and claimed public space were shunned or, like Anne Hutchinson, condemned as heathen. Women entered the public sphere to protest slavery and later to demonstrate against drinking beer and whiskey. Some women even entered taverns and bars, places that were typically off-limits to women and where their mere presence challenged male customers and changed the political discourse over alcohol use. Other public arenas that were closed to women included wage-paying jobs, seats of government, voting booths, and juries. Feminist legal strategies and legal arguments challenged these exclusionary practices. But before the legal challenges occurred, feminist political action brought women together in spaces where they could meet safely. In the 1800s, those spaces were likely to be churches and schools. In the 1970s, women met in consciousness-raising sessions in private homes. Ultimately, women in both the first and second waves of feminism entered the public streets to demonstrate their solidarity and to announce that they would no longer be confined to the private sphere.

Challenges to racial segregation during the civil rights movement of the 1950s and 1960s were also about access to public space. African Americans and other racial groups had experienced a different sort of segregation, one that forced them into public spaces that were separate from and generally inferior to the public spaces occupied by whites. Black Americans, both male and female, were not separated from each other. They shared the same homes and neighborhoods. They participated in black churches and social organizations. From these organizations, particularly the black church, they founded political groups that took to the streets and sat at previously segregated lunch counters, demanding equal access to public space.

Gay men and lesbians also have suffered from a similar lack of access to public space. Like women, who felt that they were captive in their own homes, gay men and lesbians often have felt that they, too, were captive in their homes. Of course, the source of the feeling of captivity is different in each case. Women felt confined to their homes by the assignment of gender roles and the public/private divide. Gay men and lesbians have felt confined to their homes by society's notions of morality, a morality that forbids any expression of nonheterosexual desire. Thus, although gay people might occupy public space, they have been compelled to disguise their gayness, to remain in the closet. Precious few exceptions have existed to this rule, although George Chauncey has demonstrated that certain parts of pre–World War II New York City, notably Greenwich Village, Harlem, and Times Square, provided some public gay space. Separated from each other in their heterosexual households, gay men and lesbians were similar to the middle-class white women of the 1960s, who were separated from each other in their suburban neighborhoods. As women in the 1800s used the church and schools as safe space to come together, gay men and lesbians in the 1950s used the gay bars. Many gay people had served in World War II and learned for the first time that other people like themselves existed. When they returned to peacetime America, many settled in urban areas and began to lead a secret life in which they were only "out" to other gay men or lesbians.

GAY AND LESBIAN BATTLES
OVER PUBLIC SPACE

Unlike black Americans, gay men and lesbians had no established church or social groups that offered safe spaces to gather and build community. In the 1920s, Henry Gerber had formed an organization called the Society for Human Rights in Chicago for the purpose of protecting those who were ostracized for their different sexual orientation. It lasted for only a short time, however, and disbanded after a police raid of one of their meetings.

As Jonathan Katz details in *Gay American History,* Henry Hay, who founded the Mattachine Society in the early 1950s, had been told about the Society for Human Rights several years after the organization disbanded. He assumed that the group had been formed primarily for social purposes. Hay envisioned an organization that would be educational and political, one that would enable the homosexual minority to engage in productive dialogue with the heterosexual majority. Hay joined with political activists associated with the radical left, the Communist Party, and the labor movement when he founded the Mattachine Society in Los Angeles. Hay and his colleagues formed the organization, with the help of a local attorney, as a nonprofit foundation. Discussion groups explored the nature of homosexuality and talked about the potential contributions to society of homosexual citizens. Word of the organization's existence was spread through the informal networks of the gay subculture, which included gay beaches and bars. Until the federal government threatened to investigate all foundations that might have Communist connections, Hay and his fellow founders ran the Mattachine Society as an organization that was committed to the principle that homosexual persons are different from heterosexual persons and that their difference is something that should be valued by those in power. The threat of a red-baiting investigation caused the more conservative members of the organization to opt for a different sort of leadership that was committed to the principle that gay people are just like everyone else and thus deserving of equal respect.

In 1955, Del Martin and Phyllis Lyon formed the first lesbian organization, Daughters of Bilitis (DOB), in San Francisco. The group defined its purpose as "promoting the integration of the homosexual into society."[1] Three years later, a New York chapter of DOB was formed. Barbara Gittings, reporting on these early meetings, noted that the founders resisted claims that their meetings were social rather than political. Fearful of the charge that their main purpose was to promote sexual relationships or to procure immoral contacts, they insisted that they were not formed for social purposes.[2] In retrospect, however, she admits that the position was silly. Given the isolation of gay people from one another, providing social contact was an essential element of any gay or lesbian organization in the 1950s.

GAY AND LESBIAN BARS

Role in the Community

Lacking safe space to meet and be open with one another, lesbians and gay men turned to the one social meeting space available to them, the gay bar. Although the bar scene was criticized by some of the more political activists in the 1950s,[3] for many gay men and lesbians, the local gay or lesbian bar was the single most important center of lesbian and gay community. In their study of the Buffalo lesbian community of the 1930s, 1940s, 1950s, and 1960s, Elizabeth Kennedy and Madeline Davis recount the central role of the bar scene for most lesbians.

> In the 1930s, 1940s, and 1950s, lesbians socialized in bars for relaxation and fun, just like many other Americans. But at the same time, bars . . . were central to twentieth century lesbian resistance. By finding ways to socialize together, individuals ended the crushing isolation of lesbian oppression and created the possibility for group consciousness and activity. In addition, by forming community in a public setting outside of the protected and restricted boundaries of their own living rooms, lesbians also began the struggle for public recognition and acceptance. . . . [B]ar communities were not only the center of sociability and relaxation in the gay world, they were also a crucible for politics.[4]

Lesbian and gay bars were significant public spaces for the creation of social and political community for a number of reasons. First and foremost, these bars were the one place to which lesbians and gay men could go without being closeted. In their workspaces, they typically had to hide the fact of their sexual orientation. There was no place on the job that lesbians and gay men could appear and have everyone presume that they were gay. Heterosexuality was the presumption. The presumption was so strong that even those who did not hide their gay or lesbian sexual orientation were presumed to be nongay. In the 1940s, 1950s, or 1960s, people did not "come out" at work, to explain that they were, in fact, different. The risk of rejection was too great and the possibility of gaining an understanding ear quite slim. But in the lesbian or gay bar, the expectations were different. Anyone who walked into such a bar was presumed to be gay. Thus, merely walking into such a place was an act of affirmation. One's presence announced, without the necessity of words or explanation: I am lesbian; I am gay.

Secondly, participating in conversation and social dancing with other lesbians or gay men enabled individuals to develop a firmer sense of identity as gay or lesbian. At work, home, church, and so forth, lesbians and gay men had to be careful about the expression of their inner desires and thoughts. But in the bars, they could be themselves and explore those inner desires and thoughts with an honesty and authenticity that is central to developing a healthy concept of self. Also, even though many bars were operated as private clubs, lesbian and gay bars were sufficiently public that they enabled small cliques of friends to meet others and expand their social spheres.

Lesbian and gay bars were important to the development of the lesbian and gay civil rights movement because they created space for building a social community. The early homophile organizations, Mattachine and Daughters of Bilitis, refused to operate as social organizations. Fearful that they would be portrayed as a breeding ground for sexual liaisons, they consistently claimed that their primary purposes were educational and political. And yet, to build a sense of community, public social space was necessary. Not until the Society for Individual Rights was founded in San Francisco in 1964 did a gay organization view its mission as including the creation of safe space for social purposes.

Although gay and lesbian bars provided public space, the space was not particularly safe space. Until the late 1960s, even in the most progressive cities, like San Francisco and New York, police raids were frequent. The crackdowns by mayors and police commissioners against known lesbian and gay hangouts created a certain cohesion among the patrons and eventually led to resistance and political organization. But the fear of raids also scared many individuals away from the bars.

Combating Police Harassment in Gay Bars

The battle over the right to public space in bars and taverns frequented by homosexuals was a legal battle as well as a social and political one. Police harassment was challenged as early as the 1950s, typically by bar owners rather than patrons. Several key court victories in California, New York, and New Jersey made it possible for bar owners to continue operating for the benefit of their gay and lesbian clientele. It is difficult to assess the importance or relevance of these early gay bar cases in the overall battle for lesbian and gay rights, since the victories belonged, for the most part, to the bar owners. In addition, the legal fight in support of gay bars was not a coordinated one and the gay and lesbian community was not itself an active participant in the development of the case law. San Francisco stands as an exception. There, in 1962, owners of gay bars organized and worked with a local gay rights organization, the Society for Individual Rights, to combat police harassment of the bars and their patrons. But even in San Francisco, the crucial gay bar court victories occurred prior to any gay community political organizing. Nonetheless, the early successful gay bar cases stand as the first affirmative legal victories for the lesbian and gay community and, to some extent, indicate the judiciary's readiness to rule sympathetically on gay issues. And, most important, these victories helped to preserve crucial public space needed by lesbians and gay men to form a broad-based political movement.

For example, the gay bars of San Francisco played a crucial role in George McGovern's campaign for the presidency in 1972. To get his nominating petitions turned in to the California secretary of state before other candidates, thereby earning himself a slot at the top of the California ballot, McGovern enlisted the aid of Jim Foster, a local gay activist. Foster organized a band of gay Democrats to register new voters in the bars and then to have the new voters sign the McGovern petitions. In one night, they collected more than a third of the required signatures. Foster's work on the campaign earned him an appointment as a delegate to the 1972 Democratic Convention. Gay bars on a busy weekend have continued to provide political candidates and causes with ready signatures on petitions as well as financial contributions.

The Role of Prohibition on the Establishment of Gay and Lesbian Bars. The cities that gave rise to litigation over improper police harassment of gay bars were all cities in which public bars were legal. The story of gay bars would be incomplete without some acknowledgement that many cities (and counties) prohibited the sale of alcoholic beverages in public barrooms despite the repeal of Prohibition.

When the Twenty-first Amendment repealed Prohibition in 1933, control of liquor sales was returned to the states. Most states opted for strict control of liquor sales and authorized cities and counties to determine whether such sales should occur within their boundaries. In Kansas, home of Carry Nation, over 85 percent of the counties voted to retain Prohibition even after passage of the Twenty-first Amendment. Kansas retained statewide Prohibition until 1948. Liquor by the drink was not authorized in Kansas until 1986 and even today, because local counties have the right to decide whether to legalize saloons or bars within their boundaries (local option), most counties are dry. In many large cities, post–World War II establishments were prohibited from selling drinks to the public in barrooms or saloons. In some cities, sales of beer were permitted, but not sales of liquor by the drink. Private clubs and restaurants were exempted. Strict control of liquor sales in bars and taverns protected against the resurrection of the public saloons that Carry Nation and the WCTU had worked so hard to close. But these rules also made the establishment of public gay bars like the ones in New York City, San Francisco, and Los Angeles impossible in other cities.

The Black Cat and the California Experience. In post–World-War II San Francisco, The Black Cat was probably the most well-known watering hole for gay men on the West Coast. A bohemian bar from pre–World War II days, made more famous by its role in Jack Kerouac's *On the Road* and the patronage of poet Allen Ginsberg, The Black Cat drew the attention of the San Francisco vice squad when it became a central hangout for gay clientele.[5] In 1949, after a yearlong police investigation, the Board of Equalization revoked The Black Cat's license on grounds that it was being used as a "disorderly house." The specific charge was that "persons of known homosexual tendencies patronized said premises and used said premises as a meeting place." The owner of the bar, Sol Stoumen, decided to fight back and hired a lawyer, Morris Lowenthal, to bring suit against the board to reinstate his license. The trial court judge sustained the revocation of the license, explaining:

> It would be a sorry commentary on the law as well as on the morals of the community to find that persons holding liquor licenses could permit their premises to be used month after month as meeting places for persons of known homosexual tendencies with all of the implications that may reasonably be drawn from that last phrase and the people's legal representatives find themselves helpless to take action against the holders of such licenses.
>
> Counsel for Petitioner argue that persons of homosexual tendencies may not lawfully be prohibited from collecting in groups in restaurants for the purpose of securing meals and alcoholic beverages.
>
> An occasional fortuitous meeting of such persons at restaurants for the innocent purpose mentioned is one thing. But for a proprietor of a restaurant knowingly to permit his premises to be regularly used "as a meeting place" by persons of the type mentioned with all of the potentialities for evil and im-

morality drawing out of such meetings is, in my opinion, conduct of an entirely different nature which justifies action on the part of the Board of Equalization.

Counsel for Petitioner spends many pages of his brief in setting forth what appears to be an argument based on the so-called "Kinsey Report" and similar publications to the effect that what he terms the "social taboo" against homosexuals is unjustified.

It will not be necessary to give that phase of Petitioner's argument any extended consideration. The views of the citizens of California on that subject are to be found in Sections 286 and 288a of the Penal Code. Any complaint against those provisions based on the theory that the mores of our times have changed since the enactment of those sections should be directed to the Legislature and not to the courts.[6]

The trial judge's decision was upheld by an intermediate appellate court in 1950.[7] As of that time, the San Francisco police force, the Board of Equalization, and a trial and appellate tribunal were all in agreement that gay and lesbian bars, maintained as a hangout for lesbian and gay patrons, were, as a matter of law, disorderly and illegal.

Stoumen appealed to the California Supreme Court. In 1951, the court ruled in favor of Stoumen and reinstated The Black Cat's liquor license, holding that the state could not revoke a liquor license solely on grounds that a bar caters to a gay clientele. The state officials had argued that because the bar was a hangout for known homosexuals, it was a threat to public morality. The court dismissed that argument, holding that California law allowed every adult of drinking age to patronize any bar of his choosing so long as his conduct was not a threat to public morals.

This case, *Stoumen v. Reilly*,[8] is probably the first successful gay rights case in America. It resulted not only in the continued availability of public space for "known homosexuals" to convene, but it also established a broader principle: that homosexuals had rights of access to business establishments, which included bars, under California's civil rights statutes.

The *Stoumen* decision is particularly noteworthy because the court recognized that the state had erroneously conflated homosexual status and conduct. Demonstrating a common sense that was rare for the time and the topic, the California Supreme Court stated:

The fact that the Black Cat was reputed to be a "hangout" for homosexuals indicates merely that it was a meeting place for such persons. . . . Unlike evidence that an establishment is reputed to be a house of prostitution, which means a place where prostitution is practiced and thus necessarily implies the doing of illegal or immoral acts on the premises, testimony that a restaurant and bar is reputed to be a meeting place of a certain class of persons contains no such implication. Even habitual or regular meetings may be for purely social and harmless purposes, such as the consumption of food and drink, and it is to be presumed that a person is innocent of crime or wrong and that the law has been obeyed.[9]

Despite this early victory supporting the right of gay men and lesbians to hang out with each other in gay bars, state authorities in California and elsewhere continued to harass patrons in gay bars and, at times, to close the bars down. In California, the harassment was carried out pursuant to subdivision (e) of section 24200 of the Business and Professions Code.[10] This statute was enacted by the legislature shortly after the decision in the *Stoumen* case, for the explicit purpose of reversing the result in *Stoumen*. The new statute declared the illegality of gay bars by authorizing revocation of a liquor license if the premises were a "resort for illegal possessors or users of narcotics, prostitutes, pimps, panderers, or sexual perverts."

The new California statute was in direct conflict with the decision in *Stoumen,* which had held that "sexual perverts" had a right to congregate in the bar of their choice. Because the *Stoumen* court had not been clear about the source of this right, however, the new legislation was not necessarily invalid. If *Stoumen* were a ruling based on statutory interpretation, then the legislature could trump the court. But if *Stoumen* were based on either the California or the U.S. Constitution, then the constitutional provision would trump the statute.

The constitutionality of the new statute was finally tested in 1959 in *Vallerga v. Department of Alcoholic Beverage Control.*[11] The California Supreme Court struck the statute down, not based on a finding that gay people have a constitutional right to gather in public, but rather on the more narrow rationale that the provision in the California constitution giving the liquor board the ability to revoke a license for "good cause" did not authorize revocation solely because the establishment catered to homosexuals. Implicit in the decision, however, as in the earlier *Stoumen* decision, was a recognition of the common law right of all people, even "known homosexuals," to consume food, drink, and lodging from proprietors who offer such goods and services to the general public. Indeed, *Stoumen* continues to be cited for the principle that, under California civil rights law, business establishments cannot discriminate arbitrarily against lesbians and gay men.

Vallerga was not a total gay victory. Maintaining the distinction between status and conduct, the court reiterated the *Stoumen* holding that catering to homosexuals was not sufficient "good cause" for the revocation of a license. "Something more" than the *status* of the patrons would be required to demonstrate good cause.[12] The "something more" could, of course, be the conduct of the patrons. Exactly what conduct would be sufficient to constitute "good cause" for revocation of a license was a question left unanswered by the case because the court below had relied solely on the status of the patrons as a justification for the license revocation. Nonetheless, the court indicated how it might rule on the issue in the future:

> Conduct which may fall short of aggressive and uninhibited participation in fulfilling the sexual urges of homosexuals . . . may nevertheless offend good morals and decency by displays in public which do no more than manifest such urges. This is not to say that homosexuals might properly be held to a higher degree of moral conduct than are heterosexuals. But any public display which manifests sexual desires, whether they be heterosexual or homosexual in nature may, and historically have been, suppressed and regulated in a moral society.[13]

John D'Emilio reports that the 1959 mayoral election in San Francisco created a particularly hard time for gay bars. Mayor George Christopher was up for reelection. His opponent charged him with providing too much support for the gay and lesbian community and with turning San Francisco into a gay mecca. Although Christopher denied the allegations and won the election, the charges caused him to institute a crackdown on gay bars, presumably to demonstrate his toughness toward sexual perversion.[14]

These attacks led to the formation of the Tavern Guild in 1962. A group of gay bar owners and employees decided that, if they banded together, they could better fight the assaults. The California Supreme Court's progay ruling in *Vallerga* offered no help for gay bar patrons who were arrested for solicitation or public lewdness. All of the gay bar cases had distinguished between places that were mere hangouts for gay men and lesbians and premises on which "homosexual conduct" occurred. As one California appellate court explained in a licensing case against a bar that allowed its patrons to become too intoxicated: "There is however a basic distinction between the homosexual and the drunkard. Decorum on the part of the former may conceal his unfortunate tendencies."[15] The police in the early 1960s claimed to observe much indecorous behavior. Not only were patrons arrested, licenses were lost. The Tavern Guild provided a lawyer and a bail bondsmen for each and every individual arrested on or near the premises of bars and taverns owned by guild members.

In 1963, Stoumen again found himself before an appellate court, fighting to retain his liquor license for The Black Cat. This time he lost the battle. The court ruled that such conduct as male patrons kissing and caressing each other was sufficient grounds to justify revocation of his liquor license under the court's dictum in *Vallerga*.

The New York City Experience. Similar battles over keeping gay and lesbian bars open occurred in other cities around the country. In New York, the relevant portion of the Alcohol Beverage Control laws prohibited a licensed bar from becoming "disorderly." Robert Amsel reports that, in the 1960s, during Mayor Robert Wagner's administration, the State Liquor Authority interpreted the "disorderly house" statute to include any place where gay people gathered. Such an interpretation found support in an early New York case, *Lynch's Builders Restaurant v. O'Connell*,[16] decided by the highest court of the state in 1952.

In 1950, the New York State Liquor Authority revoked the liquor license for Lynch's Builders Restaurant, finding that the proprietor had run a disorderly house because he "permitted homosexuals to congregate on the licensed premises." In addition the Liquor Authority cited two instances of patrons being arrested for soliciting a policeman in the bar. The intermediate appellate court reinstated the license in an interesting opinion that questioned how the proprietor could be assumed to know that his patrons were homosexual and further questioning whether the private solicitation of an underground vice squad member was a matter that should have been known to the proprietor. Nor, reasoned the court, was it possible to assume that the proprietor had lured individual gay patrons to his premises for the purpose of enabling them to solicit illegal sex acts. Thus, concluded the court, the proprietor could not be held responsible for *permitting* the premises to become disorderly. The case was reversed on appeal in a per curiam opinion by the New York Court of Appeals that failed to address the specific arguments raised by the intermediate court. This decision by New York's highest court was cited by lower courts for the proposition that the mere congregation of gay patrons at a bar was sufficient to cause the proprietor to lose his liquor license under New York law.[17]

Just as San Francisco experienced periodic crackdowns on its gay bars by the police and the mayor, New York City experienced periodic crackdowns, typically resulting from calls in the press to rid the city of an undesirable element. In 1959 the New York State Liquor Authority announced a campaign to revoke the licenses of all bars "patronized by prostitutes and homosexuals." Shortly thereafter, the gay bars of New York City were shut down. Rather than challenge the closings in court, the owners typically reopened either in a new location or sometimes even in the same location under new management.

However, some gay bar cases did reach the courts during this period. From 1952 to 1967, New York court opinions on the propriety of revoking or suspending an establishment's liquor license because of homosexual activity on the premises were mixed. Because the New York statute allowed revocation only if the proprietor permitted the premises to become disorderly, the arguments made on behalf of bar owners were (1) that insufficient conduct existed to constitute disorder, and (2) even if disorderly conduct occurred, such conduct was so isolated that the owner could not possibly have had sufficient knowledge that the conduct was occurring on his premises. In most cases, the State Liquor Authority acted only after a police arrest of a bar patron for solicitation. In those cases in which the court reversed the Liquor Authority's decision, they found either that the solicitations were too few in number to constitute disorder or that they occurred in private without the knowledge or constructive knowledge of the bar owner.

In the meantime, political organizers were challenging the Liquor Authority's position that the mere presence of gay patrons was enough to presume the premises were permitted to become disorderly. In 1966, Dick Leitsch, then president of the Mattachine Society of New York, organized a "sip-in." The plan was for a group of three gay men to appear at various bars in the city, announce that they were gay, and order a drink. If any bar refused to serve them, out of concern about their liquor license, then Leitsch was prepared to sue the bar in order to establish the right of gays to congregate in the bar of their choice. Apparently, the first bars that the three men visited (with the press in attendance) readily served them. Only when they went to a well-known gay bar were they denied service. Under threat of suit, the Liquor Authority voluntarily changed its policy.

In 1967, the New York Court of Appeals issued an important progay ruling in a case against a gay bar whose license had been revoked prior to the

1966 change in policy. The court, which had ducked the issue in *Lynch's Builders Restaurant,* now explicitly ruled that the fact that gay persons were allowed to congregate was not sufficient to convict a bar owner of the knowing operation of a disorderly house. And, more important, the court specifically stated that conduct that fell short of criminal solicitation, such as males dancing with males and kissing each other, was not disorderly conduct under the statute.

Gay bars in New York, including the now famous Stonewall Inn, continued to be subject to some police harassment, especially when illegalities such as serving minors were suspected. Patrons of these bars continued to find themselves potential victims of entrapment. But even if a patron did respond to the entrapment by soliciting the police officer, only the patron risked criminal charges. The bar's license was protected and necessary public space remained available for other gay and lesbian clientele.

The New Jersey Experience. New Jersey has a history similar to New York regarding gay bars. In 1934, the commissioner of the New Jersey Department of Alcoholic Control had adopted Rule 4, which prohibited a licensee from allowing onto the licensed premises "any known criminals, gangsters, racketeers, pick-pockets, swindlers, confidence men, prostitutes, female impersonators, or other persons of ill repute." Pursuant to this rule, the New Jersey authorities closed down gay bars solely on the grounds that the bar at issue was known as a place where homosexuals congregated. Apparently, police at the time viewed effeminate gay men as female impersonators. When that interpretation was called into question, the New Jersey authorities began to regulate gay bars under Rule 5, which prohibited "lewd and immoral activities" on licensed premises.

Finally, in 1967, New Jersey's highest court reversed two license suspensions and one license revocation where the bar owners had been charged with violating Rule 5 solely because they allowed homosexuals to congregate on the premises.[18] After discussing the California cases, the New Jersey court held that Rule 5 as applied was a violation of constitutional due process. The court concluded that the tavern owners had standing to assert the rights of their homosexual patrons because the "asserted rights of the homosexuals to assemble in and patronize licensed establishments are intertwined with the asserted rights of licensed establishments to serve them." The victory was not complete, however, because the majority specifically authorized the filing of new charges under Rule 5 "clearly describing the individual acts" alleged to be lewd and immoral. And the concurring judge wrote to emphasize that the record contained evidence of two men "kissing each other on the lips," which he thought would be sufficient proof of lewd and immoral conduct.

Florida and Other States. Other state Alcohol Control Boards or Liquor Commissions followed rules similar to those in New York and New Jersey, some well into the 1970s and 1980s. The Michigan Commission, for example, had a rule that stated: "No licensee, his agent, or employee shall permit his licensed premises to be frequented by or to become the meeting place, hangout, or rendezvous for known prostitutes, homosexuals, vagrants, . . . " In Las Vegas, Nevada, the Clarke County Liquor Board carried out provisions of a county code that authorized revocation and suspension of licenses of "each licensee, who shall permit his licensed premises to be frequented by or to become the meeting place, hangout, or rendezvous for known prostitutes, homosexuals, vagrants, known hoodlums, . . . " In 1975, the Supreme Court of Nevada, citing the *Stoumen* case, held the provision unconstitutional, saying that it "is established beyond peradventure that the mere presence of prostitutes, homosexuals or other 'undesirable' classes of persons in the licensed premises is not an adequate ground upon which to revoke a liquor license."[19]

The City of Miami had an ordinance, enacted in 1954, which provided:

It shall be unlawful for an owner, manager, operator or employee of a business licensed to sell intoxicating beverages to knowingly employ in such business a homosexual person, lesbian or pervert as the same are commonly accepted and understood. It shall likewise be unlawful for an owner, operator, manager or employee of a business licensed to sell intoxicating beverages to knowingly sell to, serve to or allow consumption of alcoholic beverages by a homosexual person, lesbian or pervert, as the same are commonly accepted and understood, or to knowingly allow two or more persons who are homosexuals, lesbians or perverts to congregate or remain in his place of business.

Officials in Miami called for the closing of gay bars because they were viewed as a "breeding ground for crime." As William Eskridge explains, the crimes cited by these public officials were primarily assaults and murders perpetrated on gay men by straight men who reacted with passionate hatred to homosexuality. In Eskridge's words, the main justification for cracking down on gay bars and beaches was that "homosexuals [needed] to be tracked down and expelled from the area because their existence im-

pelled heterosexuals to kill them."[20] *One Magazine*, a gay publication originally published by the Mattachine Society, reporting on the accompanying
crackdown against gay bars in Miami Beach, offers the following quote
from the Miami Beach Police Chief:

> We had no charges we could book them on, but it's just a question of cleaning
> up a bad situation and letting undesirables know they're not wanted here.
> . . . We intend to continue to harass those men who affect female mannerisms
> in public places and let them know in no uncertain terms that they are unwel-
> come on Miami Beach.

The gay press referred to the 1954 crackdown as the "Miami Hurri-
cane." The Dade County sheriff, Tom Kelly, became known as "Clean-out-
the-perverts" Kelly. On one August evening, eleven gay bars were raided.
All of this harassment was made easy by the passage of the Miami ordinance authorizing the closing of bars that catered to homosexuals. By the
end of the year, most Miami and Miami Beach gay bars had gone out of
business.

But, as is usual with the closing of gay bars, Dade County bars often reopened in new locations or with new proprietors in old locations. The harassment continued into the 1960s. On April 15, 1960, Miami's "E" Club
was raided. With no need to prove the existence of illegal conduct, the police could simply walk in and say "everyone here is under arrest." The
usual crime charged was being a "disorderly person." A Miami ordinance,
enacted in 1945, described a "disorderly person" to include "any person
found loitering in a house of ill fame or prostitution or place where prostitution or lewdness is practiced, encouraged or allowed. . . . " The Miami
police, relying on the 1954 ordinance that criminalized gay bars, interpreted "house of ill fame" to include any bar that was a gathering place for
homosexuals.

The 1954 ordinance became the focus of a gay rights challenge in the
1960s. Unlike the courts in New York, New Jersey, and California, however, the Florida courts upheld the antigay ordinance.[21] The Florida case is
different from the California, New York, and New Jersey cases in several
important respects. In the other states, the tavern owners were the ones
who challenged the liquor laws and the courts recognized the liberty rights
of gay people to congregate in bars only insofar as they were inextricably
intertwined with protecting the property rights of the bar owners. By contrast, the Florida case was pursued by a plaintiff who self-identified as a gay

man. Thus, his liberty right was at the center of the case. Also, most of the cases involving bar owners had challenged the liquor laws "as applied" to the facts of the particular case. By contrast, the Florida case was a "facial challenge" to the constitutionality of the Miami ordinance, which flatly prohibited a bar owner from allowing two or more "homosexuals" to congregate in the owner's place of business. The plaintiff argued that the text of the Miami ordinance constituted a denial of his constitutional right to gather in public with friends of his choice. The court rejected the argument, holding that the ordinance was a reasonable exercise of legislative power because its object was to "prevent the congregation at liquor establishments of persons likely to prey upon the public by attempting to recruit other persons for acts which have been declared illegal by the Legislature of the State of Florida." Thus, the Florida court honored the city's justification for the ordinance, which was based on a line of reasoning that conflated status and conduct—if two or more homosexuals gather together, sodomy will inevitably follow. This line of reasoning was the same one that the state of California had advanced in *Stoumen* and that the California Supreme Court had rejected resoundingly.

Observations About Gay Bars and the Movement

Gay bars were part of the subculture in almost every major city in the United States by the 1950s. They had begun springing up during World War II in places as diverse as San Jose, Denver, Kansas City, Cleveland, New Orleans, and Baltimore. Only a handful of reported cases exist outside of New York, New Jersey, and California in which gay bars were closed down in the 1950s or 1960s. Appellate courts in Pennsylvania,[22] Rhode Island, Louisiana, and Illinois all heard at least one appeal from a gay bar owner who had lost his license or had had it suspended. In all of these cases, the rulings by the state or local liquor authority were upheld.

Even though the reported appellate court cases dealing with gay bars are few, local newspaper accounts show that, during the 1950s, many municipalities exercised police power to arrest scores of gay men and lesbians, often at bars, but sometimes in public parks or elsewhere. The Louisiana opinion affirming the closing of a New Orleans bar notes 250 arrests on the premises over a two-year period.[23] Citywide counts are staggering. In Philadelphia, arrests of gay men and lesbians averaged 100 per month and in Washington, D.C., the arrests averaged 1,000 per year.[24]

Frequent raids on bars were enough to discourage many gay men and lesbians from participating in the bar scene. At the same time, the threat of a raid affected everyone in the bar, whereas gay individuals who cruised public parks or places that were populated by nongay people risked a more individualized jeopardy if their sexual orientation were discovered. The solidarity of the gay bar scene, even though it contained risks, made it the more popular alternative. This solidarity also contributed to the building of a grassroots civil rights movement.

Even in the three states whose highest courts had pronounced that gay persons had the right to frequent the public establishment of their choice, gay men and lesbians could still be monitored for their conduct. Presence at a gay bar subjected one to the possibility of a police investigation for lewd conduct or cross-dressing, both sufficiently amorphous complaints that they tended to be true if the police said they were. Alternatively, undercover policemen could entice gay men in bars to invite them back to their apartments to engage in illegal sex, for example, sodomy. Thus, on the basis of a private conversation that appeared to be welcome, many gay men found themselves under arrest.

Police records in many cities include notations of arrest that often contain nothing other than one word by the person's name—"pervert." The sharp distinction made by judges between status and conduct apparently blurred when it was applied by the people responsible for enforcing the law. Being a patron at a gay bar was often interpreted to mean that one was a sex pervert, which was viewed as sufficient grounds for arrest.

Nor did the gay bar owners in California, New York, and New Jersey feel fully protected by the court rulings in those states. The language of the opinions made clear that allowing immoral conduct to take place on the premises would be sufficient grounds for revocation of a liquor license. Thus, the threat of police raids remained quite real. Concerned proprietors instituted stiff rules that prevented patrons from dancing with each other or showing any affection. As a result, the gay bar cases did not lead to the creation of completely safe public space for gay men and lesbians. One patron in a San Francisco lesbian bar in the 1950s says that a friend of hers was thrown out of the bar for hugging her own sister.

Despite the legal obstacles to their existence, gay and lesbian bars were central to the early development of the lesbian and gay civil rights movement in some of the same ways that the black church was central to the development of the African American civil rights movement. The bars provided a space for coming together and allowed individual members of the community to develop their lesbian and gay identities. Because the bars were subject to attack by local authorities, they also sparked political resistance. In particular, arrests of bar patrons helped to foster both an anger and a sense of commitment to justice that caused those who had been arrested to fight back by creating organizations that would protect other lesbians and gay men from similar fates. At the same time, the centrality of the bars to the creation of a gay political movement proved to be problematic. Because bars were places where alcohol was served and where sexual liaisons were begun, their visible role in the development of the lesbian and gay civil rights movement made it difficult to portray the cause of homosexual rights as a moral one. "Sip-ins" in New York did not result in the same sort of public outrage over discrimination as the "sit-ins" in the South had ignited. Nor was the right to congregate in bars a sufficiently just cause to garner widespread support for a civil rights movement.

Role of the Stonewall Inn

The raid on the Greenwich Village gay bar, the Stonewall Inn, in 1969 is credited as the event that gave rise to the modern gay and lesbian rights movement. Why? There were certainly lesbian and gay political organizations in existence before 1969, as the stories of the founding of Mattachine and DOB make clear. And in New York City, the battle between the local police and the established gay bars had run its course by 1969. The mere presence of homosexuals at a bar was no longer sufficient to warrant the revocation of the owner's liquor license.

The raid on the Stonewall Inn occurred in part because the bar was operating as a private club, with no liquor license. One journalist reports that it was also known to be a dope drop and a firetrap. In addition, it was owned and operated by persons with Mafia connections. Some patrons report that police raids of the Stonewall Inn were common, but none of them had ever been serious before that Friday night in June 1969. The owners were said to have made regular payoffs to corrupt police officials. Some believe the Friday night raid occurred because certain payoffs had not been made. By contrast, the police claimed that the bar had been under surveillance for some time for possible violations of the liquor laws, that they finally had obtained a warrant, and that the Friday night raid was planned. In any event, the police actually entered the premises in the early hours of Saturday morning, June 28, 1969.

Whatever the reason for the raid, the police invasion of the Stonewall Inn sparked an unexpected amount of resistance both from the gay patrons and the bystanders on Christopher Street. Some who were present claim that emotions were running high that night because of gay icon Judy Garland's recent death. Her funeral had taken place in New York that Friday afternoon. Patrons reacted to the police intrusion by camping it up. Queens danced in a chorus line and sashayed around the cops. But before long, the police attitude and their roughness toward several patrons of the bar resulted in more hostile reactions by the primarily gay and lesbian crowd of onlookers. The arresting officers were forced to lock themselves inside the bar to protect themselves from the angry crowd outside. Bottles were hurled at the police, guns were drawn but not fired, someone on the outside tried to torch the bar while the police were barricaded inside, and finally reinforcements arrived from the First Division to quell the riot and rescue the imprisoned members of the police force.

The riots continued in Greenwich Village for several days, with participants calling for "Gay Power." Through word of mouth, news of these riots spread and similar upsurges in support of "gay power" occurred in other cities. The Stonewall Riots marked the beginning of the modern lesbian and gay civil rights movement.

It is ironic that the Stonewall Inn became the landmark for the modern lesbian and gay civil rights movement. The Stonewall Inn had been a popular gay bar for over two years and it catered to people of all classes and races. But gay activists had criticized the bar for its illegal operation and suspected that its unsanitary practices had contributed to a recent hepatitis outbreak in the gay community. Lesbians were not frequent patrons of the Stonewall. Political activists in the pre-1969 gay organizations tended to be leftists and radical, highly educated elitists, mostly white, or they tended to be conservative and upper-class, committed to helping homosexuals assimilate into American society. Gay activists were not the sort of people who would naturally be part of the Stonewall Inn's gay community. Yet it is fitting that the event occurred at a gay bar, a place that symbolized the center of the gay and lesbian social community in cities throughout the country. What the Stonewall riots of June 1969 accomplished was the politicization of the social community—a community that included working-class patrons of the gay bars. Stonewall helped to create a true grassroots activist gay and lesbian political community.

Of course, the founders of the modern movement did not believe that keeping the bars open was the primary goal. Indeed, in the early years of gay liberation, the movement suffered from splintered views over what did constitute the primary goal. Was it, as some argued, to gain the same sort of rights enjoyed by heterosexuals (in which case, arguments needed to be made that gays were just as moral, just as deserving, as were nongays)? Or was the goal, as the more radical forces argued, to gain the right to be our different selves (in which case arguments needed to be made in direct support of the sexual interests that were at the core of our difference)?

STUDENT GROUPS:
ACCESS TO PUBLIC SPACE IN UNIVERSITIES

Universities, which enjoy academic freedom, often find themselves in the center of social and political movements for change. But in the 1950s, the academy as a whole was a collaborator with McCarthyism. Hundreds of liberal professors lost their jobs for no more than asserting their First Amendment rights. The American Association of University Professors was alarmingly slow in responding to individual dismissals and to the general threat to academic freedom posed by McCarthyism. Early student organizations on campus, such as the American Youth for Democracy, were banned on the basis of their Communist affiliations. As historian Ellen Schrecker has shown in her study of McCarthyism and the universities, principles of academic freedom and civil liberty provided no sanctuary for dissidents in the academy. Not until the black civil rights movement and the Vietnam War protests did any significant expression of opposition to the existing orthodoxy occur. "When, by the late fifties, the hearings and dismissals tapered off, it was not because they encountered resistance but because they were no longer necessary. All was quiet on the academic front."[25]

Not until 1957 did the Supreme Court recognize the importance of affording First Amendment protection to academic freedom. In the case of a university professor who had been held in contempt for failing to answer the state attorney general's questions about organizations believed to be subversive, the Court announced that "the essentiality of freedom in the community of American universities is almost self-evident."[26] Throughout the sixties, the Court continued to rule in favor of academic freedom, reversing lower court decisions that had upheld the right of administrators and government to inquire about the political beliefs and associations of teachers and professors. In one case, the Court noted: "The vigilant protection of constitutional freedoms is nowhere more vital than in the community of American schools."[27]

In 1969, this special protection for liberty and difference of opinion was extended to students in the celebrated case of *Tinker v. Des Moines Independent Community School District.*[28] That case arose in the context of protests over the Vietnam War and validated the right of high school students to express their objection to this particular war by wearing black armbands. Just three years later, in *Healy v. James,*[29] the Supreme Court validated another right: the right of a controversial student group, Students for a Democratic Society (SDS) to organize on campus and to use university facilities on an equal basis with all other student groups. This case also arose in the context of the nationwide debate over the war. It forced college administrations to recognize SDS as a valid student organization, and signaled to university administrators that banning radical student groups from campus violated the group's First Amendment freedom of association.

While SDS was asking for official recognition, lesbian and gay students formed clubs and political groups and asked their college or university administrators for official recognition and for use of space for meetings and functions. The first such gay and lesbian student organization was formed in 1967 at Columbia University. It was chartered as the Student Homophile League and received sufficient media attention to encourage the formation of similar groups at Cornell, N.Y.U., and Stanford.

The process took longer at more conservative institutions like MIT. Finally, five gay students with the support of a like number of nongay students formed an official chapter of the Student Homophile League at MIT. The organization requested use of university facilities to host a dance for gay students in the Boston area. The dean of Student Affairs refused, explaining that homosexuality was a disease and that students should be protected from the unhappiness caused by this disease. For a while, the MIT student government supported the request by the Homophile League, but, in the end, they were unwilling to take on the administration.

By 1970 the University of Iowa had formed a student group known as the Gay People's Union and the University of Minnesota had formed a similar group called Fight Repression of Erotic Expression (FREE). In 1971 the *New York Times* reported the increased number of such student organizations around the country and the success that most of them had had in their dealings with university and college administrators.

From conversations with officials and homosexual students on half a dozen college campuses from Boston to Los Angeles, as well as reports from campus correspondents at 15 other schools, it would appear that the gay students have made substantial strides in changing attitudes. To do so, they hold dances and parties, run gay lounges and offices on campus, operate telephone hotlines for emergency problems and counseling services, publish newsletters and provide speakers to address fraternity, dormitory and faculty groups.

The formation of such groups at public universities, however, was a source of consternation for university presidents and regents who had to answer to the state's taxpayers. At the University of Georgia, in 1972, a student group called the Committee on Gay Education requested the use of campus facilities to sponsor a dance. University officials felt uneasy about what the taxpayers of Georgia would have to say about such events. After delaying official recognition of the organization, the university decided that the best policy would be to change its rules regarding the recognition of student organizations generally. Whereas the university had previously required student organizations to seek "recognition" and "approval," the rules were changed to require no more than "registration" of all student organizations.[30] This change prevented university administrators from being part of an approval process that might have caused their conservative constituents to view them as approving an immoral lifestyle. The Committee on Gay Education, which by then was working with a local attorney, Sandy McCormack, immediately complied with the registration process and renewed its request for the use of university facilities. The dance was scheduled for November 11, 1972. Campus officials denied the request for space in a written response dated October 23, which concluded:

> The particular activities for which facilities are requested are not encompassed in the purpose of the University and introduce an element which is believed to be not in the best interest of the University. The activities seem to go beyond and conflict with the educational purpose in apparently promoting and encouraging acts contrary to state law.

The group immediately appealed the decision to the State Board of Regents. Under the board's procedures, the appeal was scheduled for November 24, two weeks after the scheduled date of the dance. In order to protect their rights, the students had to seek a preliminary injunction in federal court. The district court's decision in *Wood v. Davison*[31] is the first reported case recognizing the First Amendment associational rights of a gay and lesbian student group.

Wayne McCormack recalls the events leading up to the case. He and his wife, Sandy, recently had graduated from the University of Texas Law School and moved to Athens, Georgia, where he joined the law faculty and she entered private practice. Sandy McCormack ended up representing the students who sued the university.

I don't have a clear recollection of the student(s) who actually first walked into either Sandy's or my office. I do know that the issue arose because a group of students applied for use of a room on campus to hold a dance (I think in the Student Union). Because the group was not recognized as an official organization, they could not get the use of the space. I believe there was a law student who asked me about it and I sent them to Sandy. I do have a vague recollection of the student named Wood–as you might expect, he was a very nice, quiet kid with a good sense of self–otherwise, he would not likely have had the guts to stand up in public on this issue in Georgia in the early 70's.

The University [argued] the case on two levels–recognition of student organizations and dancing by single-sex couples. Sandy did the preliminary injunction motion with a couple of affidavits and got a hearing scheduled in front of Judge Sidney Smith. . . .

Again my recollection here is fuzzy, but I believe that Ralph Beaird (also on the law faculty at the time) was serving as unofficial university counsel or advisor to President Davison at this point. In "discussions" or "negotiations" prior to the hearing, it became apparent that the university [administrators] understood they had not a leg to stand on. President Davison just wanted an opportunity to get on the stand and justify himself to the conservative constituencies of Georgia. Judge Smith gave him free latitude to do so, and Sandy chose not to question him at any length. It was not necessary for the plaintiffs to put on any testimony, and Judge Smith ruled from the bench. You will notice that the opinion concludes with an apologia for the university so that it appears they acted in good faith but had no choice about allowing this to happen.

The dance proceeded without incident and the students reported they actually enjoyed the whole experience. The final irony in the case was that the local newspaper ran a story the day after the dance with a picture in which they placed a black bar over the eyes of the participants in the picture. After going to the trouble to make a public statement, the students found themselves blanked out.[32]

The "apologia" at the end of the case focused on President Davison's reasons for denying the request of the student organization, concluding that "it is apparent that these defendants acted out of a desire to preserve the integrity of the University as they know it." Judge Smith also noted "University presidents have the unenviable task of trying to maintain a precarious balance between the rights of members of the academic community and the wishes of the taxpayers and alumni who support that community." Nevertheless, Judge Smith made clear that President Davison had to allow the Committee on Gay Education to hold its dance on campus because "it is not the prerogative of college officials to impose their own preconceived notions and ideals on the campus by choosing among proposed organizations, providing access to some and denying a forum to those with which they do not agree."

The judge in this case, Sidney O. Smith Jr., was a graduate of Harvard College and Georgia law school. He served as a federal district judge for the Northern District of Georgia during the 1960s and 1970s, and, for a number of years, served as chief judge of the Northern District. In the 1980s he served on the board of regents of the University System of Georgia, including a term as chair.

A number of other gay student organization cases followed *Wood v. Davison*, all of them arising from the formation of student groups in the early 1970s. In every case the courts ultimately ruled in favor of the gay and lesbian student group.[33] *Gay Students Organization of the University of New Hampshire v. Bonner,*[34]decided by the federal Court of Appeals for the First Circuit in 1974, emphasized that official recognition alone was not sufficient protection of First Amendment associational rights. The court held that the university was required to support the organization's social activities, including dances, explaining as follows: "Considering the important role that social events can play in individuals' efforts to associate to further their common beliefs, the prohibition of all social events must be taken to be a substantial abridgment of associational rights, even if assumed to be an indirect one."[35]

Although some university officials objected to social events sponsored by gay and lesbian student groups on the grounds that the events might lead to criminal activity (i.e., consensual sodomy),[36] this objection was uniformly dismissed by the courts. Georgia had a statute prohibiting sodomy at the time *Wood v. Davison* was decided, but the court refused to assume that a student social affair would lead to criminal activity. New Hampshire also prohibited sodomy at the time of the *Bonner* decision, but the Court of Appeals dismissed the university's concern about inappropriate behavior, stating:

If a university chose to do so, it might well be able to regulate overt sexual behavior, short of criminal activity, which may offend the community's sense of
propriety, so long as it acts in a fair and equitable manner. The point in this
case is that the district court has found no improper conduct, and it does not
appear that the university ever concerned itself with defining or regulating
such behavior. Defendants sought to cut back GSO's social activities simply
because sponsored by that group. The ban was not justified by any evidence of
misconduct attributable to GSO, and it was altogether too sweeping.[37]

Gay Alliance[38] was another case that recognized the constitutional rights
of a gay student group despite the criminalization of sodomy. The case, decided by the federal Court of Appeals for the Fourth Circuit in 1976, involved a student organization in Virginia, a state with a sodomy statute
that had withstood a constitutional challenge in federal court. Just months
before the *Gay Alliance* decision was handed down, the decision upholding
Virginia's sodomy statute, *Doe v. Commonwealth's Attorney,*[39] was summarily affirmed by the Supreme Court of the United States. Citing the Virginia statute, as well as *Doe v. Commonwealth's Attorney,* the *Gay Alliance*
court said:

> There is no evidence that [Gay Alliance] is an organization devoted to carrying
> out illegal, specifically proscribed sexual practices. . . .
>   It follows that even if affording [Gay Alliance] registration does increase the
> opportunity for homosexual contacts, that fact is insufficient to overcome the
> associational rights of members of [Gay Alliance]. Given the right to exclude
> individuals who are convicted of practicing proscribed forms of homosexual-
> ity, or whose homosexual conduct, although not proscribed, materially and
> substantially disrupts the work and discipline at [the university], the suppres-
> sion of associational rights because the opportunity for homosexual contacts is
> increased constitutes prohibited overbreadth.[40]

The only appellate opinion that lent credence to the sodomy argument is
a dissent from the denial of the University of Missouri's petition for a writ
of certiorari to the U.S. Supreme Court in the *Gay Lib* case. The federal
Court of Appeals for the Eighth Circuit had ruled in favor of the student
group, relying heavily on the group's First Amendment right to assemble
for purposes of changing the law, and the U.S. Supreme Court had declined
to hear the case. Rehnquist and Blackmun cast dissenting votes, indicating
they thought the Court should take the case. Rehnquist, putting his views

in writing, identified the issue as whether a group had a First Amendment right to associate for purposes of advocating a change in the law, even though the very association of the group's members might lead to violations of the law. The law at issue was the criminalization of private consensual sodomy. The trial court had found as a matter of fact that the association of gay students for the purpose of overturning sodomy laws was likely to lead to violations of the sodomy law. Rehnquist offered the following analogy to explain why he might refuse to recognize Gay Lib's claim to a First Amendment right to assemble:

> From the point of view of the University, however, the question is more akin to whether those suffering from measles have a constitutional right, in violation of quarantine regulations, to associate together and with others who do not presently have measles, in order to urge repeal of a state law providing that measles sufferers be quarantined. The very act of assemblage under these circumstances undercuts a significant interest of the State which a plea for the repeal of the law would nowise do.[41]

Rehnquist, of course, was not speaking for a majority of the Supreme Court in *Gay Lib*. Nor has a majority of the Court ever spoken to the issues raised by the gay student organization cases. Three petitions for a writ of certiorari have been filed by losing universities in the student organization cases, but none has been granted, perhaps because all of the lower courts have agreed and ruled in favor of the right of association. Thus, the Supreme Court has never been called upon to resolve a difference of opinion amongst the lower courts. With such unanimity in the courts below, it is reasonable to assume that the Supreme Court's silence on the issue indicates that a majority of the Court is content to let those positive rulings stand.

The student organization cases are interesting because they occurred at a time during which university employees could be fired for speaking out on gay rights issues.[42] Even though students had historically enjoyed fewer constitutional rights than other members of society,[43] their right to form gay and lesbian organizations has been upheld consistently under the First Amendment. The gay student group cases succeeded in part because they relied on earlier cases supporting recognition of other unpopular student groups, such as SDS.

The student organization cases provide an interesting contrast to the gay bar cases. In both sets of cases, the issue was access to public space. In all of the student organization cases, even when the litigated claim was over space for social purposes, the federal courts readily recognized the important First Amendment issues at stake. In the gay bar cases, by contrast, those courts that did recognize the rights of the gay patrons to gather in public never elevated that right to a First Amendment one. At best, the right recognized was the right to be served in a place of public accommodation on an equal basis with other members of the public.

THE HIGH SCHOOL PROM:
ACCESS TO PUBLIC SPACE IN SECONDARY SCHOOLS

If gay university students could successfully claim a constitutional right to associate on campus, then why could not high school students do so as well? Aaron Fricke was seven years old when the Stonewall riots occurred, too young to know that a revolution was beginning. By the time he was in high school in Cumberland, Rhode Island, he knew he was gay even though he did not know that other gay people existed. Then he met Paul, who not only talked openly about being gay, but also knew about organizations like the National Gay Task Force. Paul decided to challenge the "heterosexual presumption" and take a male date to the junior prom. Aaron agreed to be the date, but then later backed out. Paul asked a gay male student from Brown as a substitute. The high school principal refused to allow Paul to bring a male date, and Paul, with the support of the National Gay Task Force (NGTF), threatened suit. In the end, however, the suit never materialized. Paul was a minor, and his parents were not supportive. In the end, Paul felt exiled from his school, his home, and his town. He moved to New York City.

The next fall, in 1979, Aaron Fricke entered his senior year at Cumberland High. When it came time for the senior prom the following spring, Fricke, fortified by a sense of what was right and still angered by what had happened to his friend, Paul, decided that he would request permission to bring a male date to the prom. First, he came out to his parents. Next, he talked to friends at the high school. Finally, he saw Paul in New York and asked him to be his date for the prom.

As he had the year before in Paul's case, the principal, Richard B. Lynch, refused permission for Fricke to bring a male escort, primarily on the basis of his concern about potential violence toward Aaron. Fricke had assumed that the principal would refuse his request and immediately got in touch with the NGTF people he knew in Providence. Ultimately, NGTF advised him to file suit and agreed to pay his legal fees and court costs. As Fricke describes his case, the lawyers argued that his "desire to attend the senior prom with [his] male friend was a political and educational statement to [his] classmates and their escorts, to show that [his] dignity and value as a human being [was] unaffected by [his] sexual orientation."[44]

The primary legal arguments were that the school's "state action" violated the first amendment's guarantee to freedom of speech and the right of association, the same legal arguments that had succeeded in the student organization cases. On May 28, 1980, two days before the senior prom, Chief Judge Raymond J. Pettine of the federal district court of Rhode Island handed down his decision in favor of Aaron Fricke. Judge Pettine's opinion is based solely on First Amendment freedom of expression grounds. Finding that Aaron's desire to attend the prom, a public event, with a male escort was a form of protected political speech, the judge ruled that the school could not prevent that speech even though the school officials may have been genuinely concerned about Fricke's welfare. The court explained:

> To rule otherwise would completely subvert free speech in the schools by granting other students a "heckler's veto," allowing them to decide through prohibited and violent methods what speech will be heard. The first amendment does not tolerate mob rule by unruly school children. This conclusion is bolstered by the fact that any disturbance here, however great, would not interfere with the main business of school education. No classes or school work would be affected; at the very worst an optional social event, conducted by the students for their own enjoyment, would be marred. In such a context, the school does have an obligation to take reasonable measures to protect and foster free speech, not to stand helpless before unauthorized student violence.[45]

Aaron Fricke attended the prom with Paul. Although a number of his classmates were clearly uncomfortable around the male couple, the expected violence never occurred. The publicity surrounding the lawsuit and the prom enabled Fricke to carry his gay-positive message well beyond the Cumberland High student body. He received letters of thanks from lesbian and gay young people around the country. And he and Paul danced the night away together at the prom, celebrating the completion of Fricke's high school days.

The *Fricke* case was important because it was the first time that a gay high school student's First Amendment rights had been litigated. Although *Tinker* had established that high school students have free speech rights,

those rights may be constitutionally restricted if the educational and peda-
gogical needs of the institution, the school, outweigh the individual right of
speech. High schools have a strong interest in maintaining order for educational purposes and so it would have been conceivable for the *Fricke* case
to have come out differently, allowing the school's interest to trump Fricke's
speech rights. In a display of candor, Judge Pettine noted the difficulty of
the balancing process:

> As a final note, I would add that the social problems presented by homosexu-
> ality are emotionally charged; community norms are in flux, and the psychi-
> atric profession itself is divided in its attitude towards homosexuality. This
> Court's role, of course, is not to mandate social norms or impose its own view
> of acceptable behavior. It is, instead, to interpret and apply the Constitution as
> best it can. The Constitution is not self-explanatory, and answers to knotty
> problems are inevitably inexact. All that an individual judge can do is to apply
> the legal precedents as accurately and as honestly as he can, uninfluenced by
> personal predilections or the fear of community reaction, hoping each time to
> disprove the legal maxim that "hard cases make bad law."[46]

Unfortunately, the lasting import of the *Fricke* decision as legal precedent
for other cases was diminished when the appellate court, in dismissing the
appeal for mootness, vacated the opinion below. Fricke's lawyers had requested a preliminary injunction, the appropriate legal remedy for enabling
him to attend the prom with a male date. Because the court battle occurred
shortly before the date of the prom, there was no time for a full appeal on
the merits. A preliminary injunction is issued when a judge concludes that
the plaintiff, in this case Fricke, is likely to win on the merits. The district
court opinion was handed down a mere two days before the date of the
prom. Apparently the principal and the school superintendent drove to
Boston immediately after the ruling was issued to appeal the decision, and,
presumably, to ask the First Circuit Court of Appeals to stay the judge's order. No stay was issued. Fricke attended the prom. Thus, by the time the
Court of Appeals for the First Circuit looked at the appeal, the case was
moot because the prom was over. The appellate court vacated the district
court opinion, thereby undercutting the opinion's usefulness as precedent
that can be cited in future cases. This result is not uncommon in cases involving students' rights since litigation can often take longer than the completion of a student's education. The district court opinion in *Fricke* has
only been cited once by another court. Nonetheless, its reasoning stands as

persuasive on the issue of a gay high school student's right to be open about his life and to engage in political speech aimed at educating others about gay and lesbian lives.

A Note on Legal Theories:
Right of Association and Free Speech

We should compare *Fricke* with the gay student organization cases. Both sets of cases involve plaintiffs who are seeking access to public space, but group rights are at the core of the student organization cases, whereas couple rights are at issue in *Fricke*. In both sets of cases, lawyers argued that their clients' rights of association had been violated. The freedom of association at issue is one that is derived from First Amendment speech rights. The contours of the freedom of association were hammered out in several cases litigated by the NAACP in the 1950s and 1960s. When segregationist states wanted to remove NAACP activities from their borders, they enacted laws that made it more difficult for the NAACP to operate, or, in some cases, state officials refused to recognize the organization's right to do business in the state. The NAACP challenged these state restrictions as a violation of the organization's right to associate and carry out its expressive function in challenging segregation. In every instance the courts upheld the rights of the NAACP.[47]

In *Bonner,* the first student organization case to reach the appellate level, the trial court had ruled in favor of the student group on associational grounds, but not on first amendment speech grounds. The appellate court found that both the right of association and the right to free speech had been violated. Since the right of association is derived from speech rights, this appellate court decision seems right. By contrast, Judge Pettine ruled only on the First Amendment speech issue in the *Fricke* case. He did not need to reach the right to association claim to resolve the case. Apparently he was reluctant to address the issue at all, because he did comment on the viability of Fricke's equal protection claim even though he did not have to reach that issue to resolve the case either. One can only surmise that his reluctance stemmed from the perceived difference in recognizing associational rights for organizations compared with couples. Recognizing a right for two people to associate, even if the purpose is political, may suggest recognition of more intimate rights than those implicated in an organization's right to associate for political, cultural, or social purposes.

The lawyers who worked on the student organization cases, many of whom were ACLU lawyers, and the lawyers who worked on Aaron Fricke's case relied heavily on First Amendment rights in constructing their legal theories. They also built on the successes of the NAACP in its civil rights litigation, primarily relying on cases that had recognized the association's right to exist and to press its agenda in unfriendly states. Because these gay student organization cases look so similar to the NAACP cases relying on a First Amendment right of association, they were excellent cases to bring so early in the life of the modern lesbian and gay rights movement. Yet it would be a stretch to claim that gay rights leaders met and decided to start a campaign on college campuses to establish the First Amendment rights of gay organizations. At the same time, it is clear that ACLU lawyers were ready and willing to step in and help in each new case that would solidify the First Amendment precedent in a new jurisdiction.

EMPLOYMENT RIGHTS

The most important cases in the early days of the lesbian and gay civil rights movement were those that enabled the lesbian and gay community to organize. The right to congregate in public, especially in gay bars, was essential. But activists needed further protection. They needed not to lose their jobs simply because they were "out" or "outed" as gay or lesbian.

Federal Civil Service Employees

In 1957, Frank Kameny was fired from the U.S. Army Map Service because someone had reported that he was gay. Kameny challenged the dismissal all the way to the Supreme Court and lost. Kameny not only lost his then-current job, but, as a government scientist, he found himself barred from any meaningful alternative employment. Shortly thereafter, he formed the Washington, D.C., chapter of the Mattachine Society and continued the battle for gay rights by challenging the dismissal of other gay people from federal jobs. His focus of attack was threefold. First on his list of targets was the Civil Service Commission's (CSC) policy of excluding all gay people from civil service employment. His second target was denial of security clearances and the third was exclusion from the military.[48] The problem in all three cases, as he knew from personal experience, was not just losing a job, but being barred from meaningful future employment. His strategy was to challenge dismissals of individual employees in court on grounds that one's sexuality was private and had nothing to do with job competence. He and his organization, Mattachine Society Washington (MSW), handed out leaflets in the gay community outlining Kameny's advice about how to handle investigations into an employee's homosexuality. Emphasizing privacy concerns, he advised employees to say that their sexual activities were of "no proper concern to the Government."[49] Kameny also brought the problem of antigay employment policies to the attention of federal officials and the public. He wrote letters to Attorney General Robert Kennedy and publicized Kennedy's refusal to respond. He also organized the first gay rights picket at the White House in 1965. A handful of men in suits and ties and women in skirts and blouses carried placards protesting the federal government's treatment of gay people. Addressing his concern that the dismissal of gay employees marked them for life, he included the following slogan on one of the placards: "If You Don't Want a Man, Let Him Go, But Don't Throw Him on the Human Trash Heap for the Remainder of His Life."[50] Whether these public demonstrations affected the outcome of individual cases cannot be known. But the litigation spearheaded by Kameny ultimately produced a victory for civil service employees.

To understand the battle for gay and lesbian employment rights, one must understand America's "employment-at-will" doctrine. In most cases, an employer has an absolute common-law right to fire an employee for any reason. The employment is said to be at the "will" of the employer. The employee may gain job security rights in a particular job if the employer has promised those rights in a private contract with the employee or in a labor contract with an employee union or similar employee group. Job security rights can also be obtained through legislation. But in the early 1960s, virtually no legislation existed that secured job rights. Title VII of the Civil Rights Act of 1964[51] created the right not to be fired on the basis of race or sex discrimination, but it did not extend to sexual orientation discrimination. Outside of such specific contractual or statutory rights, no legal theories were available to bring a successful challenge to a wrongful dismissal.

Federal civil service employees, however, were different from the rest of the nation's employees. They were not employees "at-will." Rather, they enjoyed a certain degree of statutory job security in that they could be fired only "for cause." The applicable civil service regulations of the 1960s provided that an employee could be removed whose "conduct or capacity is such that his removal, demotion, or reassignment will promote the efficiency of the service."[52] This restriction on firing federal employees had been the law for fifty years. President Taft first introduced the restriction by executive order in 1911. Shortly thereafter the rule was codified by Congress in the Lloyd-LaFollette Civil Service Act.[53]

The civil service regulations further provided that one ground for disqualification was "criminal, infamous, dishonest, immoral, or notoriously disgraceful conduct."[54] Consensual same-sex sodomy was a crime in most states and in the District of Columbia. Thus, proof of the specific act of sodomy would satisfy the "criminal conduct" portion of the regulations. Employees, however, were rarely dismissed as a result of criminal convictions. Federal agencies customarily dismissed employees for engaging in any sort of homosexual conduct,[55] even being present at a gay bar, because homosexual conduct was viewed as evidence of "immoral conduct." Relying on these regulations, the federal government dismissed civil service employees for unspecified homosexual acts[56] as well as for acts committed prior to government employment.[57]

The CSC continued to apply its exclusionary policy throughout the sixties. In 1963, an internal memo from the personnel director of the CSC confirmed the commission's position that "persons . . . [who] . . . have engaged in or solicited others to engage in homosexual . . . acts with them without evidence of rehabilitation are not suitable for Federal employment."[58] This language mirrored the language of earlier decades. In the fifties, for example, a Senate Subcommittee concluded during the height of the McCarthy era that homosexual persons were morally weak and thus not suitable for positions of responsibility as government employees. Moreover, the subcommittee had concluded that homosexual persons posed security risks, either because they were closeted and subject to blackmail or because they tended to hang out with other sexual perverts who might take advantage of them. The government continued to act on these assumptions in the sixties long after the McCarthy era had passed. Most of the cases challenging the government's policy arose in the District of Columbia.

In a series of cases decided in the 1960s, the Court of Appeals for the District of Columbia developed a rule that restrained the federal government from firing gay employees simply because they were gay. Known as the "nexus test," the rule required the government to establish that the reason for firing was connected to job ability. Three appellate judges played crucial roles in the development of these doctrines. Judge J. Skelly Wright dissented in an early case, setting the stage for later decisions. In the next case, Judge David Bazelon, joined by Judge Carl McGowan, began to turn the Wright dissent into a majority opinion. In the final case, Bazelon and Wright combined to write the opinion that established the "nexus test."

All three of these judges were renowned for their courageous commitment to the rule of law, particularly in civil rights cases. Bazelon had been appointed to the court by President Truman and was best known for his commitment to improving the criminal justice system and protecting the rights of the mentally ill. At one time he wrote: "It is easy to concede the inevitability of social injustice and find the serenity to accept it. The far harder task is to feel its intolerability and seek the strength to change it."[59] Wright and McGowan were appointed by President Kennedy. McGowan, who had been a law professor, quickly became known as a strong center on the court during the turbulent sixties. Wright had been a district judge in New Orleans, appointed by Truman in 1949. He was responsible for most of the opinions that desegregated New Orleans, making him quite unpopular in his hometown. Wright and Bazelon were often labeled activist judges and both embraced the label as descriptive of their commitment to intervene on behalf of justice whenever democratic majorities failed to do so. Many have sung the praises of all three of these judges for their lifetime accomplishments on behalf of minorities, the poor, the incarcerated, and the disabled. Their role in creating justice for lesbians and gay men is less well known.

The facts in the first case are particularly disturbing. William Dew served in the air force from 1951 to 1955. He then obtained a position with the CIA and was asked to undergo a lie detector test to obtain a "secret" security clearance. In response to questions, he admitted that he had engaged in homosexual acts at the age of eighteen. The CIA offered to let him resign his position, and he did so. He was then hired by the Civil Aeronautics Authority, subject to a one-year probationary period and investigation. After twenty months of employment and with a satisfactory performance rating, the agency obtained the old information from the CIA investigation and decided to remove him. The district court and court of appeals ruled for the government. Judge J. Skelly Wright dissented and the Supreme Court granted certiorari. Observers of the litigation read this action by the Supreme Court as a positive sign and assumed that the Court would agree with the dissenting position of Judge Wright. Why else would the Court have bothered to grant certiorari? Wright had pointed out that according to expert testimony offered in the *Dew* case, that is, the Kinsey Report, at least 40 percent of the male population was likely to have engaged in the same adolescent sexual behavior that had caused Dew to lose his job. Thus the ramifications of the Court of Appeals decision were significant. When the Supreme Court agreed to hear the case, the government abandoned the charges against Dew and reinstated him.⁶⁰ Although this was a fortunate result for Dew, the government's action mooted the case and prevented further consideration of the government's policy by the Supreme Court.

Undeterred by the loss in *Dew,* Kameny and his organization continued their strategy. Bruce Scott, secretary of MSW, took the civil service exam and qualified for employment, subject to investigation. The investigation revealed two arrests, one for "loitering" in 1947 and another for "investigation" in 1951. Scott explained the circumstances of the first arrest, which had not led to a conviction and noted that the second arrest had not involved a violation of any law. In response to the commission's questions about his alleged homosexuality Scott responded by saying he did "not believe the Question is pertinent in so far as job performance is concerned."⁶¹ On the basis of the investigation, the commission ruled Scott disqualified for employment on the basis of "immoral conduct." When Scott asked for specifications regarding the "immoral conduct," the commission's Board of Appeals and Review responded that the investigation had revealed convincing evidence of homosexual conduct. Scott challenged the commission's ruling in federal district court and lost. On appeal, he won an interim victory.

The three-judge panel hearing Scott's appeal consisted of Judges Bazelon, McGowan, and Burger. Judge Warren Burger, later to become the Chief Justice of the U.S. Supreme Court, was the lone dissenter. Scott's case raised a new issue for the court. He had not been fired from a job in which he had a vested interest. Rather, he was a mere applicant. Nonetheless, the court ruled that even though he had no right to the job, the government was required to treat him fairly in the application process. Furthermore, the court stressed the very point that Kameny had made countless times before: "The Commission not only disqualified [Scott] from the vast field of all employment dominated by the Government but also jeopardized his ability to find employment elsewhere." In language that suggests elements of both due process and equal protection concerns, the court ultimately held that before the government could so disadvantage Scott, it must provide more specific allegations than that he was "a homosexual or had engaged in homosexual conduct."

The court reversed and remanded to the district court. Because of the narrow grounds for the reversal, the door was left open for the commission to allege more specific allegations regarding Scott's unfitness for federal employment. Indeed, Burger, in dissent, criticized the other two judges on the panel for failing to reach Scott's true claim: that homosexual conduct is not a permissible grounds for disqualification. Burger, in addressing that claim, found that not only did Scott, as a mere applicant for a job, not have constitutional protection, but even if he did, the disqualification on the basis of homosexual conduct was valid. He cited *Dew,* the most recent and controlling authority on the validity of the commission's exclusionary policy.

The commission took advantage of the open door left by Bazelon's opinion and again ruled that Scott was not fit for federal employment. In this round, the commission relied in part on Scott's refusal to answer additional questions about incidents that suggested he had engaged in homosexual conduct. Once again, Scott claimed that such questions invaded his privacy and asked for information irrelevant to his job qualifications. The district court once again upheld the commission. On appeal, Judges Bazelon and McGowan again voted to reverse the district court.[62] But as before their holding was quite narrow and focused on the procedural irregularities, rather than substance. Thus, after four years in litigation and two trips to the appellate court, Scott had the right to seek federal employment, but the lesbian and gay civil rights movement still did not have a definitive opinion ruling against the exclusionary policy.

Finally, in 1969, in the case of *Norton v. Macy,*[63] the Court of Appeals for the District of Columbia ruled that the long-standing exclusionary policy of the Civil Service Commission to dismiss any employee found to have engaged in any sort of homosexual conduct was in violation of the Civil Service Act, enacted by Congress over fifty years earlier. The relevant statute provides that an employee can be dismissed only upon a showing of "such cause as will promote the efficiency of the service."[64] The government had argued that homosexuality alone was sufficient cause because homosexuality is immoral. In an opinion written by Judge Bazelon on behalf of himself and Judge Wright, the court held that neither homosexuality nor homosexual conduct were of themselves the sort of causes that Congress had in mind as being connected to the "efficiency of the service." As in earlier cases, the third judge on the panel, Judge Tamm, dissented.

Clifford Norton, a NASA employee, had been driving around Lafayette Square (a regular hangout for gay men in D.C.) in the late evening. He picked up another man, and they drove around the square once. Then Norton let the other man out of the car. The events were witnessed by police stakeouts, who arrested both men. The man Norton had picked up accused Norton of touching his leg. No further sexual conduct was alleged. Norton was interrogated by the police for two hours, but he steadfastly denied making homosexual advances and was given a traffic summons. The security chief of NASA was called by the police and participated in the interrogation. After the police had finished, the NASA security chief continued separate interrogations until 6:00 A.M. Finally Norton admitted to minimal homosexual conduct during high school and college and claimed to have had blackouts during his adult life, which might have accompanied homosexual acts.

Despite the fact that the conduct at issue occurred away from the job site and in the privacy of the employee's car and despite the fact that the incident led to no sexual conduct because Norton's advances were rebuffed, the government maintained that the conduct was so "immoral, indecent, and disgraceful" as to make the employee unfit. In reversing the district court, Judges Bazelon and Wright demanded proof of some causal connection between the alleged homosexual conduct at issue and unfitness for service. In particular, they required the government to demonstrate an "ascertainable deleterious effect on the efficiency of the service" before terminating an employee for an immoral act. *Norton* established the "rational nexus test" to govern all dismissals of federal government employees who were terminated for off-duty immoral conduct. The language in the opinion was sufficiently broad to cover not only employees with vested job rights, but also applicants for jobs.

A close reading of the opinon suggests that the majority relied on two different grounds in rendering its opinion. The narrower ground was that the agency must follow the congressional directive and only fire employees who threatened the "efficiency of the service." The broader ground was based on due process, a constitutional requirement that applies to all governmental employers, not just those bound by the federal civil service statute. The court held that due process required every governmental employer to make employment decisions based on reason. To deny someone a job on the basis of homosexual conduct in private and unrelated to the job, not only flunked the nexus test under the civil service statute, but also the rationality requirement of due process.

The rule stated by the *Norton* court was clear: homosexuality and homosexual conduct were no longer per se justifications for dismissal or for refusals to hire. But it was not a Supreme Court decision and not all federal employers felt bound by the *Norton* rule. In 1971, Donald Hickerson was hired as a supply clerk by the Consumer and Marketing Service of the U.S. Department of Agriculture. Shortly thereafter, in a routine investigation, the employer discovered that Hickerson had been given an honorable discharge from the army after admitting that he was gay. Upon discovering this fact, the current employer promptly terminated Hickerson's employment. Hickerson, joined by the San Francisco gay rights organization, Society for Individual Rights (SIR), sued in federal district court in California. The case was structured as a class action on behalf of any federal employee or job applicant who had ever or might ever engage in private homosexual conduct. The lawyers asked that the CSC be enjoined from using its exclusionary policy to fire or refuse to hire qualified persons who might have engaged in homosexual conduct. In seeking this remedy, the lawyers were asking a federal court to order the CSC to follow the holding in *Norton.* The district court agreed with the lawyers for SIR and Hickerson and enjoined the CSC to follow the nexus test in *Norton.*[65] Specifically, the district court ruled that Hickerson should be reinstated and that the commission should "cease excluding or discharging from government service any homosexual person whom the commission would deem unfit for government employment solely because the employment of such a person in the government service might bring that service into . . . public contempt," which might affect the efficiency of the service.[66]

Of course, judicial application of *Norton*'s nexus test did not always result in reinstatement of gay employees. The *Norton* court acknowledged in dictum that homosexual conduct might at times be relevant to job performance and, thus, could serve as a rational basis for termination of employment. Such conduct might, for example, invite blackmail, or evidence an unstable personality. Alternatively, if the conduct occurred on the job or was sufficiently notorious, it might affect the employee's relations with other employees or with the public.

One year before the federal district court in Hampton struck down the Civil Service Commission's antigay employment policy, John Singer, a typist for the Equal Employment Opportunity Commission's Seattle office, was fired for being gay. He sued for reinstatement and shortly after the Civil Service Commission had officially changed its policy regarding termination of gay employees, his case reached the Court of Appeals for the Ninth Circuit. The Court upheld the commission's decision to terminate Singer,[67] distinguishing both *Norton* and *Hampton* by pointing out that neither of those cases involved an employee who engaged in public activities. The Court's theory was that by publicly identifying as gay and by taking a position in favor of gay rights, the federal employee, John Singer, would bring discredit to the federal government as his employer. Singer's public activities included speaking to the press, serving on the board of directors of the Seattle Gay Alliance, bringing a legal action claiming he had a right to marry the man of his choice, and openly admitting to being gay on the job.

The Ninth Circuit upheld the CSC's decision to terminate Singer because his "homosexual conduct" was public, rather than private. The public conduct was not sexual. It was expressive. Thus, Singer also pressed a claim based on his First Amendment rights. The Court dismissed the claim saying that government employees, unlike student organizations, have more restricted free speech rights. When an employee speaks out on a topic in a manner that counters the views of his employee a balancing test must be used that weighs the employee's interest in free speech against the governmental employer's interest in running an efficient organization. The Ninth Circuit ruled that the EEOC's interest in efficiency outweighed Singer's right to speak publicly on behalf of gay rights.

The Supreme Court granted certiorari in *Singer*. It may have done so to address the civil service right to exclude persons on the basis of homosexual conduct or it may have done so to address the important First Amendment claims that were raised. We will never know. After the Supreme Court agreed to hear the case, *Norton*'s nexus requirement was codified in the Civil Service Reform Act of 1978.[68] The solicitor general asked the commission to reconsider Singer's dismissal under the new guidelines. The commission held firm, but the Appeals Review Board reversed finding that Singer's activities did not threaten the efficiency of the EEOC.[69] The Supreme Court then vacated and remanded the decision, with Justices Burger, Rehnquist, and White dissenting.[70]

State and Private Employees

State employees could not look to federal civil service regulations for job security since those regulations only applied to federal jobs. Therefore, when they were fired or not hired for being gay, they made constitutional challenges. Several different theories were advanced, including the denial of due process and equal protection.

Faculty Members at State Universities.   One of the more famous state employee cases involved Mike McConnell, who had been offered and who had accepted a librarianship at the University of Minnesota. Shortly thereafter, in May 1970, McConnell and his "fiancée," Jack Baker, a law student, applied for a marriage license in Minneapolis. Although the license was refused, the event was covered by the local press. As a result of the publicity surrounding the event, which the Eighth Circuit Court of Appeals described as an "antic," the board of regents refused to approve the employment contract. McConnell brought suit, claiming a violation of due process rights, and won at the district court level.[71]

Although McConnell was not covered by the federal civil service regulations that specifically restricted the federal government from firing employees at will, his due process claim against the state of Minnesota was based on the same sorts of arguments that had succeeded in the *Norton* case. Due process required that the firing not be arbitrary or capricious, but instead that some reason for it must be demonstrated. Furthermore, the reason ought to bear a reasonable connection to the requirements of the job. The federal district judge accepted this argument and relied on the concept of the nexus test to determine whether McConnell's due process rights had been violated. The court noted that McConell's case was different from Norton's in that McConnell was not yet an employee. He was not being terminated. Rather, the university was refusing to hire him. This fact made his case similar to that of Bruce Scott. The district court in Minnesota, following the lead of the *Scott* court, found that McConnell had sufficient interest in becoming an employee. Thus, he had a constitutional due process right not to be treated arbitrarily or unreasonably by the state employer. The court explained:

> An homosexual is after all a human being, and a citizen of the United States despite the fact that he finds his sex gratification in what most consider to be an unconventional manner. He is as much entitled to the protection and benefits of the laws and due process fair treatment as are others, at least as to public employment in the absence of proof and not mere surmise that he has committed or will commit criminal acts or that his employment efficiency is impaired by his homosexuality. Further, the decided cases draw a distinction between homosexuality, i.e., sexual propensity for persons of one's own sex, and the commission of homosexual criminal acts. Homosexuality is said to be a broad term involving all types of deviant sexual conduct with one of the same sex, but not necessarily criminal acts of sodomy.

The Court of Appeals for the Eighth Circuit disagreed with the district court and reversed.[72] According to the appellate court, McConnell was being treated badly not just because he was gay, but also because he was demanding "the right to pursue an activist role in implementing his unconventional ideas concerning the societal status to be accorded homosexuals and, thereby, to foist tacit approval of this socially repugnant concept upon his employer, who is, in this instance, an institution of higher learning."

Therefore, the university's refusal to hire him was neither arbitrary nor unreasonable.

According to the Court of Appeals, the due process clause protects the self-effacing and closeted gay employee, but not the gay activist. The holding in *McConnell* is not necessarily inconsistent with the dictum in *Norton*. It is in accord with the Ninth Circuit's later holding in *Singer*. Like Singer, McConnell's conduct was more public than Norton's and thus could more readily damage his relationships with coworkers and members of the public, who, according to the Court of Appeals, are likely to view the conduct with repulsion. Moreover, the *McConnell* decision was in keeping with the Supreme Court's view of the right of government employers to control the speech of their employees.[73] The perverse result was that, under *McConnell*'s reasoning, students had greater political rights than university employees, including faculty members. Students could demonstrate on behalf of gay rights. But if faculty members did so, the university could complain that their very position as employees caused their message to be attributable to the university. If the university disagreed with the message, it could move either to silence the employee or to terminate him.

Six years later, a federal district court in Delaware ruled in favor of a gay faculty member who had been fired because of his public statements. Distinguishing both McConnell and Singer, the court in *Aumiller v. University of Delaware*[74] held that a faculty member who was sought out by the press rather than causing the publicity himself, could not be fired for his published statements. Although *Aumiller* is a positive victory compared with *McConnell,* the decision is nonetheless too narrow to protect teachers who participate in rallies and call attention to their public statements in favor of gay rights.

High School and Secondary School Teachers. All states have standards that must be met by public school teachers. In most states those standards include standards of moral fitness. Those standards may be stated in broad terms such as the prohibition of immoral conduct or acts of "moral turpitude." An arrest and conviction for sexual misconduct, whether the conduct is heterosexual or homosexual, would be sufficient grounds for disqualification. But, as was the case with civil service employees, the mere suggestion of a teacher's homosexuality was often sufficient grounds for dismissal. In a series of cases in California, culminating in *Morrison v. State Board of Education*[75] in 1977, the California courts adopted *Norton*'s nexus test in cases involving the dismissal of schoolteachers for homosexuality or homosexual conduct. Thus, if the conduct was not criminal and occurred in private, the teacher was entitled to keep his or her job. The California Supreme Court adopted this narrow interpretation for "immoral conduct" on the basis of due process and privacy concerns. Any broader interpretation would have violated due process in that the employee would have no clear understanding of what sort of conduct might put his job at risk.

But not all states were so enlightened as California. James Gaylord had taught at Wilson High School in Tacoma, Washington, for over twelve years. He had always received excellent teaching evaluations. One day, after hearing a student suggest that Gaylord might be gay, the vice principal of Wilson High confronted Gaylord at his home with the allegation. Gaylord freely admitted that he was gay. Before this time, no one at the school knew of Gaylord's sexual orientation. He was terminated on grounds of immorality. He sued the school board, but lost. The Washington Supreme Court upheld his dismissal, finding that being homosexual meant that a person engaged in homosexual sex acts and that such conduct was understood to be immoral.[76] Thus, Gaylord had fair warning that he might be dismissed. In response to his claim that his sexual orientation had never affected his teaching ability, the court responded that things had changed now that his sexual orientation had become public because of the publicity surrounding his firing. No constitutional claims were addressed by the Washington court. The sole issue was whether or not the school had the power to fire a known gay person for being immoral. The court held that the school's action was in keeping with state statutes setting forth standards for qualified teachers. The U.S. Supreme Court denied certiorari.[77]

Marjorie Rowland, a high school guidance counselor in Mad River, Ohio, lost her job when she confided privately to a coworker that she was bisexual. Rowland pressed two constitutional claims in her suit. First, she argued that her First Amendment speech rights were infringed because she was, in effect, being punished for speaking about her sexual orientation. Second, she argued that the school board's decision violated equal protection because she was being treated differently from heterosexual employees. The Court of Appeals for the Sixth Circuit rejected both claims.[78] As to the First Amendment, the court said that private speech was not protected. As to the equal protection claim, the court said she had not offered sufficient proof of differential treatment. Specifically, she had failed to put on any evidence showing how heterosexual employees were treated. Although it is true that she did not produce direct evidence, one would think that judges could take judicial notice of the fact that school boards do not normally fire their heterosexual employees when the employee communicates her or his sexual orientation by announcing an engagement, a marriage, or by talking about one's spouse at work. Rarely do heterosexual employees "confide" in their coworkers that they are heterosexual.

Other Employees. State employees who were not teachers pursued court cases when their employers discriminated against them on the basis of sexual orientation. Relying on *Norton,* plaintiffs often framed their complaints in due process terms, claiming that the employer's actions were arbitrary or capricious. But by the mid-seventies, more plaintiffs were also pressing equal protection claims, arguing that discrimination on the basis of sexual orientation was irrational. Plaintiffs often filed complaints alleging violations of both the federal and the state equal protection clauses.

The federal equality claims were generally unsuccessful.[79] For example, in a 1981 case, litigated by ACLU lawyers, a Texas district court upheld a negative employment decision by the Dallas Police Department. As had been true in *Singer* and *McConnell,* the prospective gay employee, Steven Childers, was a gay activist. The court upheld the Dallas Police Department's decision not to hire Childers, finding that the decision was based on his public conduct and not just the fact that he was gay. Specifically addressing his equal protection claim, the court said:

> Plaintiff's equal protection claims rest on two bases. First, Childers argues . . . that homosexuals are a suspect class, and that any infringement thereof may not be upheld except upon the showing of a compelling state interest. Alternatively, Childers argues that even if the government's actions are reviewed under traditional equal protection analysis, their actions have been so irrational as to be arbitrary.
>
> . . . Childers is not a member of a protected class. Traditionally, only those classifications based on race, religion, national origin or alienage have been considered suspect. In *Frontiero v. Richardson,* four members of the Supreme Court found sex to be a suspect class. Since the Supreme Court has not definitely ruled that gender is a suspect class, this Court is not prepared to go even further to declare that sexual preference is a suspect class.

The court went on to hold that the police department's action met the lower level rational basis test that was typically applied to the equal protection claims of nonsuspect classes.

Other than *Childers,* the employment discrimination cases claiming violations of equal protection tended to involve teachers or military personnel. Plaintiffs in those cases were hampered not only by the judiciary's refusal to view sexual orientation as a protected class for equal protection analysis, but also by the judiciary's deference to boards of education concerned about maintaining high moral standards for their teachers and deference to military employers concerned about national security.

The first successful equal protection challenge to antigay employment practices was a California case, brought by the Gay Law Students Association of Hastings Law School and SIR, the gay rights organization that had successfully enjoined the CSC from continuing to apply its gay exclusionary policy.[80] The two gay rights organizations were joined by several individual plaintiffs who claimed to have suffered from the antigay hiring practices of the Pacific Telephone and Telegraph Company. The plaintiffs filed suit in state court as a class action on behalf of all gay and lesbian persons who might be discriminated against by the defendant, and they asked the court to enjoin the discriminatory practice. The California Supreme Court ruled in favor of the plaintiffs on their equal protection claim under the California constitution. Because the California equal protection clause contains no express state action requirement, California courts have been willing to extend the principles of equal protection to cases against quasi-public entities such as utilities, which are regulated heavily by the state. In finding a violation of equal protection, the court said, "Protection against the arbitrary foreclosing of employment opportunities lies close to the heart of the protection against "second-class citizenship" which the equal protection clause was intended to guarantee. An individual's freedom of opportunity to work and earn a living has long been recognized as one of the fundamental and most cherished liberties enjoyed by members of our society . . ." Thus, the California court indicated that the right to work was sufficiently fundamental to require closer judicial review in cases in which employment rights are denied. By contrast, the U.S. Supreme Court has consistently held that the right to work is not a fundamental right and thus rational basis review is all that is required in employment discrimination cases brought under the Equal Protection Clause of the Fourteenth Amendment.[81]

By the mid-1970s, some private and state employers (particularly universities), in response to lobbying efforts by their gay and lesbian employees, had adopted antidiscrimination employment policies that prohibited discrimination on the basis of sexual orientation. If such an employer breached its own policy, an employee could sue for a contractual violation, provided the policy was part of the employment contract. But most employers did not have such policies in the 1970s or early eighties. Gay and lesbian activists also lobbied their state legislatures to adopt such policies. In 1984, Wisconsin became the first state to enact statewide civil rights protections for lesbians and gay men. The law prohibits employers, both state and private, from discriminating on the basis of sexual orientation. The term "sexual orientation" includes persons who are heterosexual, homosexual, or bisexual.[82] Thus, all Wisconsin employees, whether gay or non-gay, were given a new statutory cause of action to pursue in the event they suffered job discrimination based on their actual (or perceived) sexual orientation.

Military Employees

In most employment discrimination cases, the employer does not have a per se rule barring the employment of homosexuals. But when the employer is the military, such a rule has been on the books in one form or another for decades. Yet no one had ever challenged the military's rule in court prior to Stonewall.

The early cases challenging the military's policy on equality grounds did not arise because lesbian and gay activists decided that they should begin attacking military policy. Indeed, most gay activists of the early 1970s had also been active in the antiwar movement. None of the early manifestos or lists of goals included ending discrimination in the military so that more gay men and lesbians could enlist. Moreover, gay and lesbian lawyers knew that the Supreme Court has never ruled against the military in a civil rights claim, including cases alleging discrimination on the basis of sex[83] or on the basis of religion. Under *Parker v. Levy*,[84] decided in 1974, the Supreme Court embraced the concept that military decisions should be accorded extreme deference.

Time and again, the Supreme Court has pronounced that the civil rights of military employees may be more restricted than the rights of civilians generally. Even freedom of speech, probably the most protected right under current interpretations of the U.S. Constitution, is curtailed in the case of military employees. As the Court has explained:

> The military is, by necessity, a specialized society separate from civilian society. Military personnel must be ready to perform their duty whenever the occasion arises. To ensure that they always are capable of performing their mission

promptly and reliably, the military services must insist upon a respect for duty
and a discipline without counterpart in civilian life.

Speech that is protected in the civil population may . . . undermine the effectiveness of response to command. Thus, while members of the military services
are entitled to the protections of the First Amendment, the different character
of the military community and of the military mission requires a different application of those protections. The rights of military men must yield somewhat
to meet certain overriding demands of discipline and duty. . . . Speech likely to
interfere with these vital prerequisites for military effectiveness therefore can
be excluded from a military base.[85]

Furthermore, the Court has announced that it will accord more deference
to the military's employment decisions than it does to the decisions of other
employers. Such deference is justified in part because military decisions implicate national security. Judicial deference to military decisions is further
justified because

[i]t is difficult to conceive of an area of governmental activity in which the
courts have less competence. The complex, subtle, and professional decisions
as to the composition, training, equipping, and control of a military force are
essentially professional military judgments, subject always to civilian control
of the Legislative and Executive Branches. The ultimate responsibility for these
decisions is appropriately vested in branches of the government which are periodically subject to electoral accountability. It is this power of oversight and
control of military force by elected representatives and officials which under-
lies our entire constitutional system.[86]

Leonard Matlovich and Copy Berg.   Given these recognized restrictions on
civil rights and judicial deference to the military, challenges to the military
antigay policy were not likely to prevail. Nonetheless, such challenges began
to occur post-Stonewall. Most of the early cases arose, not as test cases, but
rather because of the very real harm caused to individuals by the harshness
of the military's policy. Challenges were brought by individuals who had
been investigated for homosexuality and risked not only losing a job, but
also being marked for life by the discharge. Emboldened by the lesbian and
gay rights movement, some of those investigated were ready to fight back.

One such person was Ensign Vernon E. (Copy) Berg III, who had recently
graduated from the Naval Academy in the top 10 percent of his class. Berg
was the son of a career naval officer. Despite his top performance at An-

napolis and the fact that he was an officer, Berg decided that the navy was not the career for him. He intended to serve out his five-year commitment and then leave. One year into his tour of duty, however, in the summer of 1975, the Naval Investigative Service began an inquiry into his "homosexuality." The investigating officers claimed to have talked with his partner, Lawrence Gibson, also in the navy, who had been pressured to reveal that he and Berg were having a sexual relationship. Berg admitted the fact of the relationship and assumed his navy days were ended. Yet shortly after the initial investigation, he was given a new assignment, one that required he maintain his security clearance. Apparently his immediate supervisors continued to have faith in his ability and loyalty despite the allegations regarding his homosexuality.

By the end of the summer, Berg was back in Virginia facing a discharge from the navy. A few months later, while visiting in New York City, he attended a gay rights conference. By this time, Lambda Legal Defense and Education Fund, the first gay rights law firm in the country, had been formed. He talked to a Lambda lawyer and began to think about fighting his discharge rather than waiting quietly for the inevitable result.

Technical Sergeant Leonard Matlovich, by contrast, had never been investigated for homosexuality. He had been in the air force for twelve years when he made his decision to fight its gay exclusion policy. He wanted to continue serving and he wanted to stop living a lie. At the time that he made this decision, he had accumulated an impressive record. He had won the Bronze Star when he was a mere Airman First Class. He had volunteered for more than one tour of duty in Vietnam. In addition to the Bronze Star, he had been awarded the Purple Heart, two Air Force Commendation Medals, and a Meritorious Service Medal. His superiors consistently rated him at the highest possible ratings in all aspects of his performance.

On March 6, 1975, after consulting with D.C. activist Frank Kameny and ACLU lawyer David Addlestone, who had been an air force lawyer in the 1960s, Matlovich wrote a letter to the secretary of the air force, which began:

> After some years of uncertainty, I have arrived at the conclusion that my sexual preferences are homosexual as opposed to heterosexual. I have also concluded that my sexual preferences will in no way interfere with my Air Force duties, as my preferences are now open. It is therefore requested that those provisions in AFM 39-12 relating to the discharge of homosexuals be waived in my case.

Both Berg and Matlovich were discharged by the military. Both men filed suit, Berg against the navy and Matlovich against the air force, claiming that the military's gay exclusion policy denied them equal protection and due process. The cases were filed in the federal district court for the District of Columbia. While the cases were under consideration, the U.S. Supreme Court issued its summary affirmance in *Doe v. Commonwealth's Attorney*.[87] In *Doe,* gay rights activists from Virginia had challenged the constitutionality of the Virginia sodomy statute on due process/privacy grounds and lost. By summarily affirming the lower court decision, the Supreme Court was on record as ruling against constitutional protection for same-sex sexual intimacy, even when two parties have fully consented to the conduct and it occurs in private. Judge Gerherd Gesell, the trial court judge in the *Matlovich* and *Berg* cases, cited to this summary affirmance and noted that it weakened the plaintiffs' constitutional challenges. Absent constitutional protection for homosexual conduct, he determined that the military policy had to stand unless the plaintiffs could prove that the policy was irrational. Given the doctrine of deference to the military, the judge was unwilling to say that the policy was totally arbitrary. He ruled against both plaintiffs.[88]

The appeal to the Court of Appeals for the District of Columbia took two years. The *Berg* and *Matlovich* cases were consolidated for purposes of argument.[89] At this time both men were represented by E. Carrington Boggan, a lawyer who had helped found Lambda Legal Defense and Education Fund. The Court of Appeals ruled in favor of both Berg and Matlovich, but not on constitutional grounds. Instead, its ruling was based on a much narrower administrative law ground.

DOD directives purported to dismiss all gay persons from military service. However, the Court of Appeals found evidence that the navy and the air force had sometimes made exceptions to the directive that all gays be dismissed. Under administrative law, if exceptions to a rule can be made, they must be made consistently and not arbitrarily. Neither the air force nor the navy had offered any explanation as to why Matlovich and Berg did not qualify for exceptional treatment. The Court of Appeals reversed and remanded both cases, ordering the air force and navy to explain why Matlovich and Berg, respectively, did not deserve to be reinstated under the exception.

For two years, Judge Gesell waited for a sufficient explanation from the military. None ever was presented. In 1980, the judge ordered both men reinstated.

Although the cases represented important personal victories for Matlovich and Berg, they did not increase equal access to the military for gay
men and lesbians. Not only did the appeals court deliver a narrow ruling
on administrative law grounds, but also the decision ordering reinstatement
was only a district court opinion. The navy and the air force still had the
power to appeal the decision all the way to the Supreme Court. To end the
battle, however, the military offered to drop its appeal and pay a cash set-
tlement to both Matlovich and Berg, provided they would resign from the
military. With the advice of their attorneys and knowing that chances for
any lasting court victory were slim, both men accepted the offer and ended
their military careers.

Miriam Ben-Shalom.   The Pentagon reacted to the *Matlovich/Berg* litigation by tightening the rules regarding exclusion of homosexual personnel.
In 1981 new regulations were crafted, and they were published by the
DOD as a directive in 1982. The new regulations stated clearly that homosexuality and military service were incompatible and that no exceptions
would be recognized. Homosexuality was now grounds for automatic exclusion in all branches of the service.

Miriam Ben-Shalom had the opportunity to challenge the military under
both the old and the new regulations. Ben-Shalom, a member of the Army
Reserves in Milwaukee, Wisconsin, had read the press coverage of the *Matlovich* case and asked her commander: Why does the army keep me, since I
am a lesbian? His answer, at the time, was that she was a good NCO, and
besides, the dismissal policy was discretionary.

When she graduated from drill sergeant's school, she decided it was time
to be more open about the fact that she was lesbian. She thought people
should know that a competent lesbian could continue to serve in the military. When she gave an interview to the press, her commander became livid.
A competent closeted lesbian was one thing, but he could not live with
someone who talked to the press about her sexual orientation. He initiated
discharge proceedings against her.[90]

Unlike Matlovich and Berg, Ben-Shalom's primary legal theory was a
First Amendment argument. She claimed that the army was discharging her
because she had exercised her speech rights in proclaiming her lesbianism
and talking to the press. The speech claim seemed a stronger one after the
Supreme Court's summary affirmance in *Doe v. Commonwealth's Attorney,*
a decision that the district court in *Matlovich/Berg* had thought weakened
both their equal protection and due process privacy claims.

Ben-Shalom had admitted that she was a lesbian but had not admitted to same-sex sexual conduct of any sort or even to a propensity to engage in such conduct. By refusing to admit to sexual conduct, she insulated her claim from *Doe v. Commonwealth's Attorney*, which had been interpreted to mean that no constitutional protection existed for homosexual sex. In 1980, a federal district court in Wisconsin ruled in her favor and held the army's regulations unconstitutional as infringements of her rights to free speech, association, and privacy.[91] The applicable regulations, at that time, required the discharge of any soldier who "evidenced homosexual tendencies, desire or interest, but is without overt homosexual acts." Ben-Shalom's only transgression had been making a statement in which she had identified herself as a lesbian. The army failed to appeal the decision but also refused to reinstate her. After several court battles, the Court of Appeals for the Seventh Circuit ordered her reinstated pursuant to the initial decision.[92] Only eleven months of her enlistment period were left. She then sought to reenlist, but the army, relying on the stricter 1982 regulations, refused. The new regulations provided for the discharge of any soldier who had made a statement acknowledging homosexual status. In addition, the new regulations provided for no discretionary exceptions to the discharge policy. She challenged the army's rejection of her request to reenlist. She argued that to the extent the regulations prohibited her from saying she was a lesbian, they violated her First Amendment free speech rights. The Court of Appeals for the Seventh Circuit, in a 1989 opinion, rejected her First Amendment challenge, finding that the regulations did not regulate speech, but only conduct.[93] In the court's view, the speech prohibited (e.g., identifying as a lesbian) was not pure speech, but rather an announcement that the speaker intended to or was likely to engage in same-sex sexual conduct. Since the conduct itself was grounds for dismissal, announcing an intent or propensity to engage in the conduct was also sufficient. Thus, the one gay service member who had successfully mounted a First Amendment challenge to the old regulations was not able to repeat her success when challenging the new regulations.

A Note on Legal Theories:
Equal Protection, Due Process, and Free Speech

Gay and lesbian plaintiffs have relied on three primary legal theories in employment discrimination claims against public employers. All three theories are based on constitutional provisions that apply to governmental employers, whether federal, state, or local. By contrast, African American civil rights litigators relied primarily on one theory: equal protection. In cases that occurred before the Court began to apply strict scrutiny to all racial classifications, litigators argued that classifications based on race were never rational. Similarly, gay and lesbian plaintiffs who have been excluded from employment opportunities might argue that denying someone a job solely because of that person's sexual orientation is never rational. The best employee should always be hired regardless of sexual orientation. But once the Court adopted its two-tiered approach to equal protection claims, under which it accorded race heightened scrutiny as a suspect classification, equal protection claims pursued by nonsuspect groups were doomed to fail. The Court routinely upheld governmental action that discriminated against nonsuspect groups. Thus, equal protection was not a good legal theory for gay and lesbian plaintiffs unless they could convince the courts that sexual orientation, like race, was a suspect classification. In the late sixties and early seventies, when even feminist litigators could not convince the Supreme Court that gender was a suspect classification, arguing that sexual orientation was suspect seemed unlikely to produce litigation victories.

Another means of ratcheting up judicial review to strict scrutiny was to argue that the discrimination impinged upon a fundamental right. During the sixties the Warren Court had expanded equal protection jurisprudence so that certain fundamental rights were entitled to the same judicial scrutiny as suspect classifications. This development became known as the fundamental rights branch of equal protection jurisprudence. Fundamental rights included rights related to free speech, the right to marry, the right to vote, and the right to travel. But the right to work was never recognized as fundamental. Thus, the fundamental rights branch of equal protection law was not available for lesbian and gay employment discrimination cases.

The clearest success in employment discrimination cases occurred in the prolonged and organized challenge to the CSC gay exclusionary policy. Yet, despite the clear victories in *Norton* and *SIR v. Hampton,* judicial rationales for striking down the exclusionary policy were in fact quite murky. Then Circuit Judge Warren Burger was correct in his charge that his colleagues were unwilling to deal directly with the issue on the merits. In his view, Congress had enacted a statute that said civil service employees could be terminated only for reasons that were detrimental to the efficiency of the service. The Civil Service Commission had interpreted that statute in regulations to provide for termination in the event of immoral conduct. There is a certain rationality in the notion that immoral persons are not likely to be trustworthy and thus should not work for the government. The real problem was that the commission considered private, consensual homosexual conduct to be sufficiently immoral. The real question on the merits was whether or not that belief was rational. Burger thought it was, although there is no evidence that he was presented with direct arguments to the contrary. The legal arguments in the cases he reviewed, *Scott* and *Scott II,* focused on a number of different theories. One theory was that Scott need not answer questions about whether or not he had engaged in homosexual conduct because that information was private. But Scott, at one point in the litigation, directed the court to assume that he had engaged in private consensual conduct, presumably wanting to set the stage for a ruling that such conduct was irrelevant to the job. But the *Scott II* court, unwilling to say that refusing to hire homosexual persons is irrational prejudice, instead took a smaller step and said that the decision not to hire Scott was procedurally defective because the commission did not sufficiently communicate to Scott its reasons. And in *Norton,* the court, again unwilling to say that refusing to hire homosexual persons is irrational prejudice, also took a smaller step and said that the policy applied by the commission was beyond the scope of the Civil Service statute. Although that theory appears to have no constitutional basis, the *Norton* court nonetheless claimed that the policy violated substantive due process in that it was arbitrary and capricious.

Thus, by the mid-seventies, it had become clear that claims of irrationality or arbitrary employment decisions were more successful when presented as due process claims rather than as equal protection claims. I can think of no satisfactory explanation of why the outcome ought to be different under substantive due process and equal protection. They both rely on the concept of rationality. Yet because particular judges had chosen to rely on due process notions in particular cases, litigators began to view due process claims as stronger than equal protection in pursuing claims of antigay bias.

Because of this projected difference in outcome under equal protection rationality review and due process rationality review, gay and lesbian plaintiffs, where possible, relied more heavily on due process arguments than on equal protection. But equal protection was not entirely without force. The district court in *Fricke* had noted that equal protection claims have greater force when the right that is being unequally protected is free speech, or some similar right that is fundamental in our constitutional history. Deprivation of a fundamental right on the basis of sexual orientation would probably violate equal protection. But mere denial of jobs did not impinge on a fundamenetal right and thus did not deny equal protection.

Free speech rights are fundamental. The ACLU has fought for the free speech rights of unpopular speakers over most of its history. Because of the ACLU's successful public interest litigation on behalf of Communists and government critics and the NAACP, the nascent lesbian and gay movement benefited from a legal landscape in which lesbian and gay activists had a legally recognized right to call for law reform. The student organization cases benefited from earlier civil rights litigation. Building on this success, lesbian and gay employees crafted their discrimination claims as a combination of free speech and due process violations. Yet employment discrimination cases such as *McConnell, Singer,* and *Childers* suggested that gay political activity, which under normal definitions constituted free speech, might nonetheless be sufficient grounds for job termination. Military cases also challenged the gay exclusionary policy on First Amendment grounds because service personnel could be terminated merely for speaking the words "I am gay." As in *McConnell, Singer,* and *Childers,* the military cases appeared to view personal statements about sexual orientation as unacceptable behavior rather than protected political speech.

DIRECT RESTRICTIONS ON PUBLIC SPEECH

The litigation against the CSC and the successful litigation on behalf of California schoolteachers Marc Morrison[94] and Jack M[95] established some minimal job protection for gay and lesbian employees. During the decade of the seventies, additional protection was provided in the form of municipal ordinances, passed in a number of cities and counties, which prohibited discrimination against gay people in employment, housing, and other public arenas. The backlash against these modest gains garnered national attention when Anita Bryant's "Save Our Children" campaign in Dade County, Florida, resulted in a repeal of that county's gay rights ordinance. Similar antigay grassroots campaigns have sprung up around the country.

In California, responding to the gay-positive court rulings in the schoolteachers' cases, state senator John Briggs forced a referendum on the issue. The Briggs Initiative supported the firing of any schoolteacher or other school employee who advocated, solicited, imposed, encouraged, or promoted "private or public homosexual activity directed at, or likely to come to the attention of, schoolchildren." Although advertised as a referendum on whether gay schoolteachers should be employed at all in California, the question on the ballot more directly prohibited gay-positive speech. Dubbed as the beginning of the "No Promo Homo" backlash by activist lawyer Nan Hunter,[96] the Briggs Initiative raised serious first amendment issues because it was directed at banning a particular viewpoint: that lesbians and gay men were acceptable human beings.

Early reports predicted easy passage of the initiative.[97] The lesbian and gay community responded in force. Thousands of volunteers joined the campaign against the Briggs Initiative. In the end, even conservative Republican Ronald Reagan spoke out against the initiative. The initiative was soundly defeated at the polls with 58 percent of the voters voting against it.

The debate over the Briggs Initiative changed the national conversation about the nature of gay political speech. With a clearer understanding of the feminist slogan, "the personal is political," gay activists argued that "coming out" was in and of it itself political speech. The California Supreme Court adopted this argument when it ruled against Pacific Telephone and Telegraph Company in the 1979 employment discrimination brought by the Gay Law Students Association. In addition to the equal protection claim, the plaintiffs had argued that the antigay policy violated the state's labor code. With respect to this claim, the court said, "[O]ne important aspect of the struggle for equal rights is to induce homosexual individuals to 'come out of the closet,' acknowledge their sexual preferences, and to associate with others in working for equal rights." The court ruled that this "coming out" speech was political speech protected by the state labor code.

In Oklahoma, the language of the Briggs Initiative was adopted by the Oklahoma legislature. Anita Bryant, a former Miss Oklahoma, had supported the legislation. The National Gay Task Force challenged the statute on several grounds. In 1984 the Court of Appeals for the Tenth Circuit struck down the statutory language borrowed from Briggs, language that was broad enough to cover political statements made to legislative bodies, an activity clearly protected by the First Amendment.[98] The majority opinion applied the overbreadth doctrine, a First Amendment doctrine under which a statute restricting speech can be struck down when it infringes upon both protected and unprotected speech. The Supreme Court granted certiorari. Having won at the appellate level and with no other appellate opinions taking a contrary view to the Tenth Circuit, review by the Supreme Court was not something to celebrate. On one hand, litigators hoped for a gay-positive Supreme Court precedent and thought that a First Amendment case was probably the type of case most likely to produce a positive result. On the other hand, a Supreme Court reversal would cause serious problems for future gay rights litigation. As it turned out, Justice Powell did not particpate and the remaining eight justices split the vote four to four.[99] The four justices voting against the positive decision were: (1) Chief Justice Warren Burger, whose views on gay civil service employees were set in the two *Scott* decisions; (2) Justice William Rehnquist, who had compared gay student groups to a group of people with measles advocating against quarantine; (3) Justice Byron White, who along with Burger and Rehnquist had dissented in the Court's decision to vacate the *Singer* case, indicating some uneasiness with the gay employee's reinstatement under the new CSC procedures; and (4) Justice Sandra Day O'Connor, casting her first public vote on the Court on a gay issue.

The split vote preserved the gay positive ruling below. No opinion was issued. Such a decision resolves the dispute between the parties, but has no precedential effect. Furthermore, because there was no written opinion in the case, even the rationale of the four Justices on the gay-positive side of the issue will never be known.

CONCLUSION

The 1960s and 1970s witnessed major legal victories that benefited the lesbian and gay movement and expanded the range of civil rights and civil liberties. The gay bar cases helped to secure public space for creating a social and political community. The student organization cases secured additional public space for building an even wider community. Court battles over employment rights were more mixed. The most solid victories were won by federal civil service employees who were protected by the civil service rules. By extension, the due process rationale of these decisions was available to other governmental employees. But rarely did courts invoke equal protection as a basis for protecting gay employees. In almost all of the public access cases that can be described as victories, there was a nagging hint that gay men and lesbians were just barely worthy of legal protection. The bar cases protected the owners so long as gay patrons did no more than drink on the premises. If they danced or held hands or engaged in any of the normal behavior that opposite-sex couples typically engaged in, the police raids were still a threat. The student organization cases recognized the right of gay students to organize for political purposes, but plaintiffs' lawyers had to contend with the argument that organized students would be more apt to commit sodomy. The civil service employment cases stood for the proposition that one could be gay so long as being gay did not interfere with doing the job. But being too "out" or too political might well affect one's ability to do the job.

The early 1980s saw no major changes in the judicial response to gay rights claims. Equal access to employment claims were litigated primarily against the military and other public employers. The military's special status protected, on national security grounds, its antigay policies from meaningful judicial review. Furthermore, the Pentagon responded to attacks on its exclusionary policies by tightening up the rules barring gay and lesbian service members and increasing its resolve to rid itself of gay and lesbian personnel. The 1980s continued to produce gay rights victories in student organization cases, however, as well as in other cases that relied primarily on First Amendment free speech arguments. Perhaps most significant in light of the litigation yet to come, by 1984 the Supreme Court had indicated that four justices were likely to rule positively in a gay rights case and four justices were likely to rule negatively.

NOTES

1. Jonathan Ned Katz, *Gay American History: Lesbians and Gay Men in the U.S.A.* at 426.

2. Katz at 428.

3. D'Emilio, *Sexual Politics, Sexual Communities* at 106.

4. Kennedy and Davis, *Boots of Leather* at 29.

5. D'Emilio, *Sexual Politics, Sexual Communities* at 186–187.

6. Stoumen v. Reilly, 222 P.2d 678, 683 (Cal. App. 1950) (quoting the opinion of Superior Court Judge McWilliams and upholding his decision to revoke).

7. 222 P.2d 678 (Cal. App. 1950).

8. 234 P.2d 969 (Cal. 1951).

9. 234 P.2d 969 at 971 (Cal. 1951).

10. 1953 Cal. Stat. 986 (codified at California Business and Professional Code § 24200 and repealed 1963).

11. 347 P.2d 909 (Cal. 1959). The *Vallegra* decision cut short Mayor Christopher's crackdown against San Francisco's gay bars.

12. 347 P.2d 909 at 912 (Cal. 1959).

13. Ibid.

14. D'Emilio, *Sexual Politics* at 182.

15. Harris v. Alcoholic Beverage Control Appeals Board, 28 Cal. Rptr. 74 at 84 (Cal. App. 1963).

16. 103 N.E.2d 531 (N.Y. 1952).

17. Gilmer v. Hostetter, 245 N.Y.S.2d 252 (N.Y. App Div. 1963).

18. One Eleven Wines and Liquors, Inc. v. Division of Alcoholic Beverage Control, 235 A.2d 12 (N.J. 1967).

19. Cline v. Clark County Liquor & Gaming Licensing Board, 535 P.2d 783 at 784–785 (Nev. 1975).

20. William N. Eskridge, Jr., "Privacy Jurisprudence and the Apartheid of the Closet, 1946–1961," 24 *Florida State University Law Review* 703 at 728 (1997).

21. Inman v. City of Miami, 197 So.2d 50 (Fla. App. 1967), *cert. denied,* 201 So.2d 895 (Fla. 1967), and *cert. denied,* 389 U.S. 1048 (1968).

22. *See* In re Freedman, 235 A.2d 624 (Pa. Super. 1967).

23. Kotteman v. Grevemberg, 96 So.2d 601 (La. 1957).

24. D'Emilio, *Sexual Politics, Sexual Communities* at 49–50. These arrest figures improved somewhat in the 1960s and 1970s. See generally William N. Eskridge, Jr., "Challenging the Apartheid of the Closet: Establishing Conditions for Lesbian and Gay Intimacy, Nomos, and Citizenship, 1961–1981," 25 *Hofstra Law Review* 817 (1997).

25. Ellen W. Schrecker, *No Ivory Tower: McCarthyism & the Universities* at 341 (1986).

26. Sweezy v. State of New Hampshire, 354 U.S. 234 at 250 (1957).

27. Shelton v. Tucker, 364 U.S. 479 at 487 (1960).

28. 393 U.S. 503 (1969).

29. 408 U.S. 169 (1972).

30. See Wood v. Davison, 351 F.Supp. 543 at 545 (N.D. Ga. 1972).

31. Ibid. Wood cites an unreported California trial court opinion in favor of a similar gay and lesbian student group, Associated Students of Sacramento State College v. Butz (Super. Ct. Sacramento 1971).

32. E-mail correspondence with Wayne McCormack, professor of law, University of Utah, May 25, 1999.

33. Gay Students Organization of the University of New Hampshire v. Bonner, 509 F.2d 652 (1st Cir. 1974); Gay Alliance of Students v. Matthews, 544 F.2d 162 (4th Cir. 1976); Gay Lib v. University of Missouri, 558 F.2d 848 (8th Cir. 1977), *cert. denied* 434 U.S. 1080 (1978); Gay Activists Alliance v. Board of Regents of University of Oklahoma, 638 P.2d 1116 (Okla. 1981) (student group has First Amendment right to organize and be recognized by university); Gay Student Services v. Texas A&M University, 737 F.2d 1317 (5th Cir. 1984) (First Amendment right of association recognized), *cert. denied* 471 U.S. 1001 (1985); Student Services for Lesbians/Gays and Friends v. Texas Tech University, 635 F.Supp. 776 (N.D. Tex. 1986) (university officials not liable for damages for initial failure to recognize gay student group because law not sufficiently clear until Supreme Court's denial of certiorari in Texas A&M case; officials did recognize student group prior to court decision). *See also* Gay Lesbian Bisexual Alliance v. Pryor, 110 F.3d 1543 (11th Cir. 1997) (holding a state statute that prohibited funding for any gay-positive student group unconstitutional because it infringed on the speech rights of a gay student organization).

34. 509 F.2d 652 (1st Cir. 1974).

35. Ibid. at 659–660.

36. See, for example, 351 F.Supp. at 548 and 509 F.2d at 663.

37. GSO v. Bonner, 509 F.2d 652 at 663 (1st Cir. 1974).

38. Gay Alliance of Students v. Matthews, 544 F.2d 162 (4th Cir. 1976).

39. 403 F. Supp. 1199 (E.D. Va. 1975), *aff'd,* 425 U.S. 901 (1976).

40. Gay Alliance of Students v. Matthews, 544 F.2d at 166.

41. *See* Ratchford v. Gay Lib, 434 U.S. 1080 (1978), *denying cert.* in Gay Lib. v. University of Missouri, 558 F.2d 848 (8th Cir. 1977).

42. *See*, for example, McConnell v. Anderson, 451 F.2d 193 (8th Cir. 1971) (university librarian). *See also* Aumiller v. University of Delaware, 434 F. Supp. 1273 (D. Del. 1977) (lecturer was fired based on progay statements he made to the press; district court ruled in favor of reinstatement based on First Amendment principles, but in so doing, the court emphasized that "Aumiller never set out to generate publicity, but was sought out by reporters desiring information about the Gay Community").

43. Students' First Amendment rights were recognized in *Tinker* and in *Healy v. James*. *See generally* Charles Allen Wright, "The Constitution on Campus," 22 *Vanderbilt Law Review* 1027 (1969).

44. Aaron Fricke, *Reflections of a Rock Lobster: A Story About Growing Up Gay* at 81 (1981).

45. Fricke v. Lynch, 491 F.Supp. 381 at 387 (D.R.I. 1980).

46. 491 F.Supp. 381 at 389.

47. NAACP v. State of Alabama, ex. rel. Patterson, 357 U.S. 449 (1958); Bates v. City of Little Rock, 361 U.S. 516 (1960); NAACP v. Button, 371 U.S. 415 (1963).

48. Eric Marcus, *Making History: The Struggle for Gay and Lesbian Rights 1945–1990* at 99.

49. William N. Eskridge Jr., *Gaylaw: Challenging the Apartheid of the Closet* at 126.

50. Eric Marcus, *Making History* at 99.

51. 42. U.S.C. 2000(e).

52. 5 C.F.R. § 9.101 (Rev. 1961) (no longer in effect).

53. 37 Stat. 555, 5 U.S.C. § 652. For a history of the Civil Service Acts, see Van Riper, *History of United States Civil Service* (1958).

54. 5 C.F.R. § 2.106(a)(3).

55. See Norton v. Macy, 417 F.2d. 1161, 1167 (D.C. Cir. 1969).

56. See Scott v. Macy, 349 F.2d 182 (D.C. Cir. 1965) (reversing the decision of the Civil Service Commission, which had excluded an applicant from the civil service solely on the basis that he was a "homosexual" and had engaged in "homosexual conduct." No specific conduct was alleged).

57. See Dew v. Halaby, 317 F.2d 582 (D.C. Cir 1963), *cert. dismissed per stipulation*, 379 U.S. 951 (1964).

58. Eskridge, *Gaylaw* at 402, n55.

59. Abbe Smith and William Montross, "The Calling of Criminal Defense," 50 *Mercer Law Review* 443, 498, n. 375 (1999).

60. See Dew v. Halaby, 317 F.2d 582 (D.C. Cir. 1963), *cert. dismissed per stipulation*, 379 U.S. 951 (1964).

61. Scott v. Macy, 349 F.2d 182 at 183 (D.C. Cir 1965).

62. Scott v. Macy, 402 F.2d 644 (D.C. Cir 1968).

63. 417 F.2d 1161 (D.C. Cir. 1969).

64. 417 F.2d 1161 at 1162 (D.C. Cir. 1969).

65. S.T.R. v. Hampton, 63 F.R.D. 399 (N.D. Calif. 1973).

66. Ibid., 402.

67. Singer v. Civil Service Commission, 530 F.2d 247 (9th Cir. 1976).

68. Pub. L. No. 95–454, § 907, 92 Stat. 1111, 1227.

69. Singer v. Civil Service Commission, United States Civil Service Commission, Federal Employee Appeals Authority, Decision No. SEO 71380002 (July 21, 1978), cited in Judith M. Hedgperth, "Employment Discrimination Law and the Rights of Gay Persons," in Donald Knutson, ed., *Homosexuality and the Law* at 77 (1980).

70. Singer v. Civil Service Commission, 429 U.S. 1034 (1977).

71. McConnell v. Anderson, 316 F. Supp. 809 (D. Minn. 1970).

72. McConnell v. Anderson, 451 F.2d 193 (8th Cir. 1971).

73. Compare Pickering v. Board of Education of Township High School District 205, Will County, Illinois, 391 U.S. 563 at 571–574 (1968) (protecting an employee's speech if the speech is about matters of public concern) with Connick v. Myers, 461 U.S. 138 at 153–154 (1983) (upholding employer's sanction of employee where the employee's speech was about matters of only personal interest). *See generally* Cynthia L. Estlund, "Speech on Matters of Public Concern: The Perils of an Emerging First Amendment Category," 59 *George Washington Law Review* 1 (1990) (discussing the development and implications for First Amendment law of these two cases).

74. 434 F.Supp. 1273 (D. Del. 1977).

75. 461 P.2d 375 (Cal. 1969).

76. Gaylord v. Tacoma School District No. 10, 559 P.2d 1340 (Wash. 1977).

77. 434 U.S.879 (1977).

78. Rowland v. Mad River Local School Dist., 730 F.2d 444 (6th Cir. 1984), *cert. denied*, 470 U.S. 1009 (1985).

79. *See*, for example, Childers v. Dallas Police Department, 513 F.Supp. 134 (N.D. Tex. 1981), *aff'd*, 669 F.2d 732 (1982).

80. Gay Law Students Association. v. Pacific Telephone & Telegraph Company, 595 P.2d 592 (Cal. 1979).

81. Massachusetts Board of Retirement v. Murgia, 427 U.S. 307 (1976).

82. The statute's exact language is: "Sexual orientation" means having a preference for heterosexuality, homosexuality or bisexuality, having a history of such a preference or being identified with such a preference." Wisc. Stat. §111.32.

83. See Rostker v. Goldberg, 453 U.S. 57 (1981).

84. 417 U.S. 733 (1974).

85. Brown v. Glines, 444 U.S. 348 at 354 (1980).

86. Gilligan v. Morgan, 413 U.S. 1 (1973).

87. 403 F.Supp. 1199 (E.D. Va. 1975), *aff'd.*, 425 U.S. 901 (1976).

88. Berg v. Clayton, 436 F.Supp. 76 (D.D.C. 1977), 591 F.2d 849.

89. Matlovich v. Secretary of the Air Force, 1976 WL 649 (D.D.C. 1976), 591 F.2d 849.

90. See Randy Shilts, *Conduct Unbecoming* at 264.

91. Ben-Shalom v. Secretary of the Army, 489 F.Supp. 964 (E.D. Wis. 1980).

92. Ben-Shalom v. Secretary of the Army, 826 F.2d 722 (7th Cir. 1987).

93. Ben-Shalom v. Marsh, 881 F.2d 454 (7th Cir. 1989) *cert. denied* 494 U.S. 1004.

94. See Morrison v. State Board of Education, 461 P. 2d 375 (Cal. 1969).

95. Board of Education of Long Beach v. Jack M., 566 P.2d 602 (Calif. 1977).

96. See Nan D. Hunter, "Identity, Speech, and Equality," 79 *Virginia Law Review* 1695 at 1702 (1993). Much of the discussion in this part of the chapter is derived from Nan Hunter's work. I am indebted to her for providing me with her insights about the connections between the Briggs Initiative, the Gay Law Students Association case, and the suit by the NGTF against an Oklahoma statute fashioned after the Briggs Initiative.

97. Randy Shilts, *The Mayor of Castro Street: The Life and Times of Harvey Milk* 242 (1982).

98. National Gay Task Force v. Board of Education of Oklahoma City, 729 F.2d 1270 (10th Cir. 1984).

99. 470 U.S. 903 (per curiam), *aff'g* 729 F.2d 1270 (10th Cir. 1984).

4

Private Rights: 1950–1985

Individual liberty is a necessary prerequisite to the possibility of moral choice and full personhood. If a person is not free to make certain critical choices in life, such as whether to love, whether or when to reveal her thoughts to others, and what God she will or will not embrace, then she is not capable of becoming an autonomous moral agent. For Jean-Paul Sartre, the key to being an ethical person was the freedom to choose. According to Sartre, if one exercises choice in accordance with a previously embraced ethical code, one is not really acting authentically. Instead, one is merely playing a role, acting in bad faith, and ceding responsibility for the choice to a predetermined code of ethics or a particular rule. Thus, if one acts in accord with a code of ethics, one is not authentically moral in doing so unless one chooses the applicable ethical rule anew in the moment of the ethical decision. The ability to choose freely is a prerequisite to morality, which is a core aspect of personhood. This principle was even true for Kant, who did embrace and develop an ethical code derived from the categorical imperative. The freedom to embrace one moral code over another was essential to Kant's vision of the ethical. Individual liberty is a prerequisite to becoming a moral being.

At the same time, individual liberty is not a value that always trumps other values in establishing authentic personhood. We live in a society that is composed of competing autonomous individuals with varying conceptions of the good. For a Robinson Crusoe, the consequences of free choice have a different meaning than they do for those of us who live in a more populous society. Crusoe's choices affect only himself. But when those of us in the organized society of today make a choice, that choice may affect family, neighbors, and the broader community. My freedom necessarily bumps against your freedom. My choice must be grounded in my freedom, but my freedom cannot be the ethical end of all my decisions.

Liberal political theory recognizes that government must balance the good of the society against the individual needs of the persons who make up that society. For a government to ensure the possibility of full personhood for all its citizens, it must protect a sphere of free choice for all individuals.

In the United States, legal protections for individual liberty can be found in private law and in public constitutional law. All human beings spend some amount of time in a private sphere that may consist of complete solitude or may include others. Private law, such as tort law, regulates individual relationships within this sphere, and when necessary, it recognizes individual privacy rights. But sometimes public law, such as criminal law, also regulates activities within this sphere. When that regulation interferes with individual liberty, claims against government intrusion are mounted as constitutional claims to privacy rights. Gay rights advocates have relied on *Griswold, Eisenstadt, Roe,* and *Loving,* all privacy cases pursued in earlier civil rights movements, to argue for an expansion of constitutional privacy rights. The primary goal has been to protect gay and lesbian intimacy from governmental intrusion. Sodomy laws have been the main target of this project.

CRIMINALIZATION OF SODOMY

The gay bar cases recognized the right of gay patrons to gather at the bar of their choice and the right of bar owners to cater to gay and lesbian persons. But the cases are problematic as pure gay rights cases because they also condemn same-sex expressions of love and sexual attraction. In the 1950s, sex was viewed by society as a totally private matter. People did not talk about sex, no sex education classes existed, and the criminal laws regulating sexual behavior reached a number of private expressions of intimacy that many Americans engage in today. For example, fornication, or sex outside of marriage, was against the law in most states. And sodomy was a crime in all states.

Sodomy was not just a crime for lesbians and gay men. State statutes were quite broad in their prohibitions and usually prohibited all acts of anal or oral sex. In such states, a married couple who engaged in fellatio would be committing a crime. The Georgia sodomy statute was typical of most sodomy statutes of the 1960s: "A person commits the offense of sodomy when he performs or submits to any sexual act involving the sex organs of one person and the mouth or anus of another."[1] The original Georgia sodomy statute applied only to unnatural acts of man with mankind or of man with a woman.[2] In 1939, the Georgia Supreme Court held that the language of the original statute did not cover oral sex between two women. In 1963, another Georgia court expressed incredulity that the legislature could have criminalized cunnilingus between a man and a woman and not between two women and, thus, held that cunnilingus was not covered by the statute, regardless of who committed the act.[3] The legislature responded in 1968 by enacting an amended version of the statute, which criminalized all oral and anal sex acts.[4]

Georgia's experience, characterized by a pattern of narrow interpretations of the sodomy statute by the courts followed by a broadening of the statutory language by the legislature, was not unique. A similar struggle between the judicial and legislative branches occurred in New York in the 1950s. Beginning with *People v. Doyle,*[5] in 1952, the New York Court of Appeals began handing down decisions that narrowed the practical application of New York's sodomy statute. *Doyle* involved an adult teacher who had taught in schools for boys for twenty-five years. Doyle was convicted of private consensual sodomy with a twelve-year-old student. In a surprising procedural move, the court held that since the boy had consented to the "crime," he was an accomplice. Under New York law, a conviction could not stand if the only evidence against the defendant was the uncorroborated evidence of an accomplice. With this decision, the court did not change the definition of sodomy, but it did make successful prosecution of consensual private sodomy much more difficult.

Shortly thereafter, the New York Court of Appeals made another move toward decriminalization. In 1961, in the case of *People v. Randall,*[6] the court read the sodomy statute narrowly in a case of anal intercourse. The defendant had been the passive party. The court, construing the statutory language that prohibited a person from carnally "knowing" any male or female person by the anus, held that only the active participant could be guilty of the crime of sodomy. The passive participant might be an accomplice but could not be guilty of sodomy, since only the person using his penis is capable of committing the act of carnal knowledge. The same narrow interpretation of the statute was also applied to acts of fellatio until the Court of Appeals, by a narrow margin, ruled otherwise in *People v. Maggio* in 1962.[7] The New York legislature amended the sodomy statute that same year to make passive participants equally guilty with active participants.[8]

As long as statutory construction was the issue, progressive judicial interpretations of state sodomy statutes could always be reversed by the legislature. That is certainly what occurred in both Georgia and New York. Only
two ways existed for opponents of sodomy statutes to combat this problem
in the 1960s: (1) convince the courts that a constitutional basis could be
found for protecting same-sex sexual intimacy, in which case the legislature
could not reverse the court's action, or (2) convince the legislature to repeal
sodomy statutes.

Before the Supreme Court's decision in *Griswold,* no strong argument
could be made for claiming that same-sex intimacy was constitutionally
protected. Even after *Griswold,* the argument was not a clear winner, since
the holding in *Griswold* was based heavily on the right to marital privacy.
Not until the early 1970s was the holding in *Griswold* extended to single
persons. In the decades before these breakthrough decisions established a
constitutional right to privacy, the better route for repeal of sodomy legislation appeared to be the legislative route. Moreover, a number of events occurred in the 1950s and 1960s that made legislative repeal seem plausible,
despite the actions taken by the Georgia and New York legislatures.

THE WOLFENDEN REPORT

In 1954 in Great Britain, the secretary of state for the Home Department
and the secretary of state for Scotland appointed a committee to consider
the criminalization of homosexual sodomy and prostitution. Based on in-
tense examination of witnesses and private deliberation, the committee ultimately issued the Wolfenden Report in 1957, recommending that "homosexual behavior between consenting adults in private be no longer a
criminal offense."

The committee was not unanimous in its recommendation. Shortly after
the report was issued, Sir Patrick Devlin delivered a public lecture challenging the recommendation. This lecture sparked the now famous Hart/Devlin
debate over the role of morality in law. Devlin took the position that law
properly expresses and enforces the moral standards of the community.
Hart, relying on John Stuart Mill's harm principle, took the position that
the law ought to prohibit only those acts that cause harm to others.

The committee's recommendation that private homosexual acts be decriminalized finally was adopted in 1967 with the passage of the Sexual Offenses
Act. The change was effective for England and Wales only. Decriminalization
in Scotland and Northern Ireland occurred later, in the 1980s. The

Wolfenden Report and the debates that it triggered affected law reform efforts in other countries as well, most notably the United States and Canada.

THE ALI PROJECT

Relying on the Millian argument that law should only criminalize conduct that violates the harm principle, the American Law Institute, a national elective body of lawyers, judges, and academics who work to improve the law, drafted a Model Penal Code that decriminalized adult, consensual, private sexual conduct. Tentative drafts of this proposal predate the Wolfenden Report by two years. The final proposal was not adopted until 1962. The proposal had no force of law, but merely recommended to the states that they follow the model in the enactment of their own criminal laws. In 1961, Illinois became the first state to adopt the ALI provision, but no state followed in its wake. In most states, consensual sodomy was a felony and carried the same penalty as aggravated or forceful sodomy. In Georgia, for example, the penalty for consensual, private acts of sodomy was twenty years imprisonment. New York, reacting to the ALI proposal, decided to reduce consensual sodomy to a misdemeanor in 1965, even if the act was committed in a semi-private place such as a public washroom. For first-time offenders, a suspended thirty-day sentence was typical.[9] In 1969, Connecticut became the second state to adopt the ALI provision.

EARLY CONSTITUTIONAL
CHALLENGES TO SODOMY STATUTES

Since state legislatures were slow to repeal sodomy statutes, gay rights advocates turned to constitutional challenges, arguing that *Griswold* could be applied to protect gay and lesbian privacy rights. In the late sixties and early seventies, two methods were used to challenge sodomy statutes in court: (1) a defendant arrested and prosecuted for the crime could defend the prosecution on grounds that the statute was unconstitutional, or (2) a person who claimed to be harmed by the threat of prosecution could bring a case in either state or federal court claiming that the statute was unconstitutional and asking the court to so declare and to enjoin the statute's enforcement.

A number of procedural and strategic problems existed with both options, however. The first problem was caused by the doctrine of "standing." As a general rule, a person challenging a law on constitutional grounds must be someone whose rights are affected by the law, or, as we saw in the gay bar cases, someone sufficiently connected to the person whose rights are affected. Arrests for consensual sodomy did not generally occur in the privacy of a defendant's bedroom. Rather, they tended to occur in such places as public washrooms. Thus, the available criminal defendants for lodging constitutional challenges against the statute were not individuals who had "standing" to make the argument that their rights of privacy had been violated. Early challenges to the New York statute failed for this reason.

Standing was also a problem for a gay or lesbian plaintiff who wanted to challenge the sodomy statute by asking a court to declare the statute unconstitutional and enjoin its enforcement. In the sixties and seventies, federal courts were the preferred sites for such suits. Federal courts were believed to be stronger protectors of federal constitutional rights and were believed to be more willing to strike down a state statute that infringed those rights. In those days, any suit brought in federal court to enjoin the enforcement of a state statute had to be heard by a three-judge panel. This requirement of three judges, which was repealed in 1976, helped shield individual judges from local political fallout when sensitive issues were at stake. To bring a case before a three-judge panel, however, the plaintiff would have to satisfy federal standing requirements. As a general rule, to have standing a plaintiff had to be imminently threatened with arrest or be able to show that the state was prosecuting in bad faith. Alternately, if the plaintiff could show that his free speech rights were "chilled" by the statute, he could bring a case challenging the statute even though threat of prosecution was not imminent.

In 1970, a challenge to the Texas sodomy statute was filed in the federal district court for the Northern District of Texas.[10] The three-judge court included Judge Irving L. Goldberg from the Fifth Circuit Court of Appeals and District Judges Sarah Hughes and W. M. Taylor Jr. In the same year, these same three judges comprised the panel that struck down the Texas abortion statute in *Roe v. Wade*. The sodomy challenge had been commenced by a gay man who had been arrested for violating the state sodomy statute in a public washroom. When the American Civil Liberties Union became involved, lawyers immediately realized that this plaintiff presented two procedural problems. First, they doubted that he had standing to challenge the Texas statute on grounds of privacy since he had been arrested for committing the crime in public. Second, although federal courts at that time could enjoin future enforcement of state criminal statutes, they could not, absent evidence of bad faith on the part of the state, enjoin a prosecution already in progress. To solve these problems, three additional plaintiffs were located and added to the case. One plaintiff was a gay man who admitted to committing sodomy in private, and claimed a fear of arrest and prosecution for such private acts. The other plaintiffs were a married couple who admitted to committing sodomy in the privacy of their marital bedroom. They claimed that they feared arrest and that their First Amendment rights were chilled by the statute.

The three-judge panel allowed all plaintiffs to proceed on standing grounds. On the merits, however, only the married couple's privacy rights were honored. At that time, no case had yet extended *Griswold* to protect unmarried couples. The panel was willing to extend *Griswold*'s privacy doctrine to protect marital sodomy, however, which was banned by the Texas statute equally with same-sex sodomy. Because the married couple had challenged the statute on its face under the First Amendment, and not just as it applied to them, the court struck down the entire statute.

The state appealed to the Supreme Court. In those days, determinations by a three-judge district court panel could be appealed directly to the Supreme Court. Furthermore, the court procedures in place in those days required the Court to make a disposition of the case, by either affirming or reversing. Instead, however, the Court held the case until it had rendered its opinion in another case dealing with the right of federal courts to enjoin state statutes. That case, *Younger v. Harris*,[11] was decided in 1971, and it held that federal courts could not entertain jurisdiction in cases challenging state statutes on the grounds that had been alleged by the married couple in the Texas case, namely that their First Amendment rights were chilled. Instead, the plaintiffs would have to meet the traditional standing tests relating to imminent threat of prosecution. Because of its holding in *Younger*, the Supreme Court vacated and remanded the Texas sodomy challenge to the federal district court panel.[12]

Thus ends the story of the first successful gay rights challenge to a state sodomy statute. Shortly after the case was closed, the Texas legislature revised its penal code and amended the sodomy statute to include only same-sex sodomy. Challenges to this amended statute will be discussed in later chapters of this book.

Another constitutional objection to some state sodomy statutes, in addition to invasion of privacy, was vagueness. When a criminal statute threatens a violator with loss of liberty, due process requires that the statute be worded sufficiently clearly to give the defendant fair warning as to what constitutes the criminal act. A number of state legislatures had merely incorporated the old English common law phrase "crime against nature" into their statutes. Florida's statute, for example, prohibited the "abominable and detestable crime against nature." In a nongay challenge to the statute, a defendant who had been convicted for violating the statute brought a habeas corpus proceeding in federal court claiming that the language of the statute was not sufficiently clear to satisfy due process requirements. The case reached the Supreme Court in 1973, and the Court handed down a decision that effectively ended "void for vagueness" challenges to such statutes by reasoning that the statute was not unconstitutionally vague because the Florida courts had specified the content of the crime by construing the statute to prohibit oral and anal sex.[13]

Two years later, another gay rights challenge to a state sodomy statute began in the state of Virginia. As in the Texas challenge, the plaintiffs, a group of gay males, proceeded in federal district court before a three-judge panel. In *Doe v. Commonwealth's Attorney*,[14] the plaintiffs asserted that they regularly engaged in consensual homosexual sodomy in private and feared arrest under the sodomy statute. Their primary argument was that the statute violated their privacy rights.

The potential challenge to the Virginia statute was first discussed by a group of gay rights activists in an open forum with Supreme Court justice William O. Douglas. One of the members of the group was Bruce Voellner, who at that time was president of the Gay Activists Alliance and would later become one of the cofounders of the National Gay Task Force. Voellner became one of the plaintiffs and was the main force behind the suit. The plaintiffs chose to proceed in federal district court, knowing they would have a better chance of success before three federal judges than before a trial judge in a Virginia state court. Randy Shilts, reporting on the case, says: "The case seemed ill-fated from the start. Scheduling problems precluded appointment of a normal federal . . . court panel in Richmond. Instead two elderly judges were brought out of retirement to sit on the three-member panel hearing the case. Both voted in favor of the statute in the two-to-one ruling."[15]

The majority opinion never considered whether the plaintiffs satisfied federal standing requirements. It cited neither *Younger v. Harris* nor the Texas sodomy case, which had been vacated on standing grounds under the holding in *Younger*. Possibly, the state did not sufficiently contest the plaintiffs' standing. For whatever reason, the majority seemed intent on having its say regarding the validity of the statute and expressing its views about the immorality of the plaintiffs.

Relying primarily on *Griswold,* the gay plaintiffs had argued that the Virginia sodomy statute, as applied to such private consensual homosexual conduct, violated their right to privacy under the First and Ninth Amendments, their due process rights under the Fifth and Fourteenth Amendments, their First Amendment right to freedom of expression, and the Eighth Amendment's prohibition of cruel and unusual punishment. The court rejected all of these claims, citing the Bible for proof of the statute's Christian and Jewish heritage and concluding that its ancestry was relevant to the reasonableness of the law. The court also based its decision on a passage from Justice Goldberg's concurrence in *Griswold* that had differentiated homosexuality and adultery on the one hand from marital intimacy on the other. Justice Goldberg had opined: "Adultery, homosexuality and the like are sexual intimacies which the State forbids . . . but the intimacy of husband and wife is necessarily an essential and accepted feature of the institution of marriage, an institution which the State not only must allow, but which always and in every age it has fostered and protected."[16] As the sole dissenting judge of the Virginia panel pointed out, however, Goldberg's emphasis on marriage had not carried the day in later litigation, which had extended the *Griswold* privacy right to unmarried couples.[17]

Doe was appealed to the Supreme Court. The case provided a good opportunity for the Court to expand on its interpretation of the privacy rights of unmarried couples, which had been recognized for the first time in its 1972 decision, *Eisenstadt v. Baird.* However, the Court refused to hear oral arguments in the case. Four votes in favor of oral argument were required for the Court to hear the case in full and only Justices Marshall, Brennan, and Stevens had voted to hear oral arguments. Thus, the case was summarily affirmed, without benefit of argument.[18] Summary affirmances were typical in cases that were appealed to the Supreme Court directly from the district court.[19] They were decisions made on the merits, and, thus, they bound lower courts. Nonetheless their precedential value was unclear because no rationale was ever stated for the affirmance.[20]

The summary affirmance in *Doe* created some confusion in the courts below. For the next ten years, until the Court revisited the issue in *Bowers v. Hardwick,*[21] gay rights litigation was affected by conflicting opinions regarding the precedential value of *Doe.* The Court of Appeals of New York and the Supreme Court of Pennsylvania, for example, both ruled that their state sodomy statutes violated the federal constitution despite the summary affirmance in *Doe*.[22] The Iowa Supreme Court declared the Iowa sodomy statute unconstitutional in a case involving heterosexual sodomy, finding that *Doe* presented no barrier to its decision.[23] By contrast, other state courts relied on the authority of *Doe* to uphold their own sodomy statutes against similar federal constitutional challenges.[24]

People v. Onofre,[25] the New York case holding that state's sodomy statute unconstitutional, had been argued on both state and federal constitutional grounds. Nonetheless, for reasons that were apparent to no one, the Court of Appeals limited its decision to the federal constitutional claim. This limitation gave the state the opportunity to ask the U.S. Supreme Court to grant a petition for a writ of certiorari and review the decision. Most people thought that if *Doe* stood for the proposition that sodomy statutes are constitutional, then the Court should have granted certiorari in *Onofre* and should have reversed the holding of the New York Court of Appeals. Instead, the Court denied certiorari in *Onofre*, much to the simultaneous relief and consternation of the gay rights litigators who were handling the case. Using *Onofre* for all it was worth, lawyers in later gay rights litigation cited the certiorari denial to support their position that the *Doe* affirmance should not be read as a refusal to extend *Griswold* to same-sex sodomy. Although denials of certiorari petitions generally have no precedential value, the denial of certiorari in *Onofre* appeared in a context that appeared to give the decision greater weight. Perhaps *Onofre* was a sign that the *Doe* affirmance had said nothing about the application of *Griswold* to same-sex sodomy. Perhaps, some argued, the Court had affirmed summarily because the plaintiffs in *Doe* had lacked standing since none of them had ever been arrested under the challenged statute.

Prior to the controversial denial of certiorari in *Onofre*, the Supreme Court had denied a string of certiorari petitions in gay rights cases coming to it from other jurisdictions. For example, in 1977, the Court had denied cert in a case that had upheld the dismissal of a gay teacher.[26] In 1978, it had denied cert to a North Carolina sodomy challenge in which the state court had upheld the sodomy statute.[27] In 1978, it had denied cert in a case which had required recognition of a gay student group.[28] This aversion to rule on gay rights issues led Bruce Ennis of the ACLU to comment "that the Supreme Court was not about to expand gay rights, that they didn't even want to have to deal with anything as controversial if they didn't have to, and that it was probably a waste of time to take gay rights cases to the court."[29]

SOLICITATION TO
COMMIT SODOMY AND
LEWD AND LASCIVIOUS CONDUCT

Although gay rights litigators could argue that sodomy statutes were a denial of the constitutional right to privacy as applied to private consensual sexual conduct, other criminal statutes also impinged upon the private sphere that were not so readily subject to a privacy attack. These problematic crimes included solicitation to commit sodomy and lewd and lascivious conduct.

The ALI's Model Penal Code recommended decriminalization of private consensual acts, but the code left certain public conduct subject to criminal prosecution. Solicitation to commit sodomy was the primary offense with which gay persons had been charged in the past. Under the Model Penal Code, solicitation remained a criminal offense. The crime of solicitation involves nothing more than an invitation to commit sodomy. It is not the equivalent of prostitution, where sex is solicited in exchange for the payment of money. A statement by one gay man to another man indicating an interest in having sex is all that is necessary.[30]

Most solicitation cases arose because police decoys entered gay bars or other gay gathering places and seduced individuals into suggesting a sexual liaison. Although the solicitation might occur in a public place, such as a bar, the invitation was normally made in a private conversation, and the sexual liaison was usually to occur in a private place. Nonetheless, because the criminal act of solicitation took place in a public place, the statute was deemed applicable.

The police also relied on laws prohibiting lewd and lascivious behavior to harass and arrest homosexuals. Most state statutes prohibiting lewd and lascivious behavior applied to acts that occurred in public. The statutes were codifications of the old common law crime of public lewdness.

Occasionally, the manner in which these two types of statutes were written allowed for a successful privacy challenge. For example, in Washington, D.C., Arizona, and Florida, the lewd and lascivious conduct statutes applied to private as well as public conduct. And in Washington, D.C., even the solicitation statute applied to solicitations that occurred in private. A 1960 District of Columbia case, however, successfully challenged the solicitation statute as applied to purely private behavior.[31] From that time on, at least in the District of Columbia, solicitation and lewdness had to occur in public before the statutes could be enforced.

Lewdness and solicitation statutes were rarely challenged by the persons arrested for violating them. Most defendants were even unwilling to challenge the arrests, despite the fact that the arresting officer may have been guilty of entrapment or, perhaps, guilty of misrepresenting the actual facts. Arrests for offenses connected to same-sex sexual conduct were often too embarrassing to reveal for people who might have had the wherewithal to mount a challenge, but who preferred to stay in the closet and avoid the public attention that was likely to accompany such a challenge. Most of these arrests occurred at gay bars and other public gathering places in the gay community. The risk of arrest and the reluctance of defendants to claim entrapment or otherwise defend themselves meant that gathering places were not safe. Gay activists needed political action, not legal defenses, to stop the entrapment.

In New York City, the Mattachine Society did mount a successful political campaign to stop entrapment. Three years prior to the Stonewall Raid, police entrapment of gay men for solicitation of lewd conduct ended. After a March 1966 crackdown by police aimed at gay men in Greenwich Village, the New York Civil Liberties Union stepped in at the request of the New York Mattachine Society. A meeting was arranged between Mayor John Lindsay, Dick Leitsch, who was the president of Mattachine, the New York Civil Liberties Union director, and other interested parties. Shortly thereafter, the mayor ordered the police to cease arresting gay men unless, in addition to the arresting officer, a civilian was also present who witnessed the incident.[32]

FAMILY RIGHTS

By contrast with choices about private, consensual sexual relations, other choices about private sphere family matters have been protected by the U.S. Constitution since the early 1920s when the Supreme Court decided two cases, *Pierce v. Society of Sisters*[33] and *Meyer v. Nebraska*.[34] Both cases recognized the liberty interest of parents in making decisions regarding the rearing of their children. In 1965, these two cases were brought back to life when the Court recognized the modern constitutional right to privacy in *Griswold v. Connecticut*. Thus, although the Court generally avoids taking family law cases, by the end of the sixties, the Court had announced in *Griswold* that marital privacy was protected by the Due Process Clause of the Fourteenth Amendment and, in *Loving*, that the right to marry was a

fundamental right protected under the fundamental rights branch of equal
protection jurisprudence.

After its early 1970s sex discrimination cases in which the Court recognized sex classifications as quasi-suspect under equal protection analysis,
the Court found itself faced with a number of family law issues. Thus, for
example, in *Orr v. Orr*,[35] the Court rewrote the domestic relations law of a
number of states by ruling that the obligation of spousal support must fall
equally on husbands and wives.

In addition, the Court began to apply its evolving privacy jurisprudence
to matters of intimate concern in heterosexual families. For example, when
the state of Illinois attempted to remove three children from the custody of
their father after their mother (his companion) had died, the Supreme Court
recognized a substantial interest in the father's desire to maintain custody of
his children, despite the fact that he had never chosen to legitimate the family through marriage.[36] And in 1977 the Court held that a grandmother's
right to live with her grandchildren was a fundamental right that the City of
East Cleveland could not abridge without a compelling reason.[37]

During the 1970s and 1980s, the Court time and again recognized the
fundamental liberty interest of a natural parent to maintain the parent-
child relationship.[38] At the same time, it also recognized that mere biological connection alone was not sufficient to establish a fundamental right
protected by the Due Process Clause.[39] The development of an actual relationship with the child was an important factor in recognizing the liberty
interest.

Lesbian and gay rights lawyers who litigated family law cases on behalf
of their clients paid attention to this "constitutionalization of family law."

Two different types of family law issues that affected lesbian and gay
families began to gain attention in the courts during the early decades of
the movement. With respect to children, a primary issue was the question
of whether a natural parent's homosexuality was sufficient either to terminate the parent/child relationship or to remove the child from the primary
care and custody of the gay or lesbian parent. The second issue, which did
not arise until the 1980s, involved the legal status of the nonbiological parent in a same-sex parent household. This "second parent" problem developed because the legal system only recognized family relationships based
on birth and marriage. Family relationships created by choice or by affinity
were, insofar as the law was concerned, nothing more than relationships
between strangers.

Parental Termination and Custody Decisions

When a father and mother divorce and cannot agree what to do with their children, the family law court will decide which parent is more fit to maintain custody of the child. Custody battles also can occur when the mother and father are unmarried. Losing custody does not terminate the parent-child relationship. The noncustodial parent retains the right to continue developing the relationship through visitation. The family court can place restrictions on visitation, however, and has done so quite often in the case of lesbian and gay parents. A gay parent's legal relationship can be terminated only if the parent is found to be unfit. Some gay and lesbian custody battles become cases about the gay parent's fitness, but such cases are rare. Typically, such cases involve a request for custody by a relative of the child who is not a parent. Since parental custody is presumed to be in the best interest of a child, a court will rarely grant custody to a nonparent unless the court determines that no natural parent exists who is capable of caring for the child. In the more common lesbian and gay custody cases, however, the battle is between two fit parents, one heterosexual and one homosexual, and the litigation is centered on the question of who is more fit.

Custody decisions are usually made by judges, although at least one state, Texas, provides for jury trial if one party requests it. Judges are given great latitude in deciding custody issues. The guiding principle is the best interest of the child. Family courts retain jurisdiction over custody questions after the divorce is final and until the child is of legal age. In the 1950s and 1960s, judges often applied the "maternal preference" rule and awarded custody of children of all ages to their mothers when other factors were equal. Alternatively, judges might apply the "tender years" rule and award the custody of very young children to their mothers when other factors were equal. Thus, fathers were rarely awarded custody in those days and fathers, including gay fathers, rarely even attempted to gain custody of their children. Questions of visitation, however, did arise for gay fathers. And later, in the 1970s and 1980s, as judges began to abandon the custody doctrines that preferred mothers over fathers, gay fathers did sometimes seek custody.

Before Stonewall, mothers regularly lost custody of their children at the time of divorce if the father were able to prove the mother's lesbianism. If her lesbianism were discovered after the divorce, then the father could ask the court to modify the custody order to give him custody, even though the mother had been awarded custody at divorce and even though the change meant uprooting the child from a stable and familiar home.

Because judges usually were the ones responsible for making custody decisions, their own mistaken assumptions about lesbian mothers were a key
factor in the decision-making process. To counter negative judicial attitudes
toward lesbians, expert evidence was necessary. But in the 1950s and
1960s, virtually no reliable studies had been conducted that one could use.
In the 1950s, most studies of homosexuality focused on homosexuality as a
pathological condition, and most of the subjects studied were mental patients or prisoners. In 1953, a breakthrough occurred when Dr. Evelyn
Hooker received a grant from the National Institute of Mental Health to
study the mental health of gay males in the general population. She presented her paper in 1956 to the American Psychological Association and reported that gay men could be just as well adjusted as nongay men.[40] At the
time, her study was the only one of its kind and no comparable studies
were done of lesbians.

Indeed, until 1973, homosexuality was officially listed as a mental disorder in the *Diagnostic and Statistical Manual of Mental Disorders (DSM-
III)*. One of the earliest victories of the modern gay rights movement was to
work with members of the American Psychiatric Association to get homosexuality off this list. Success came on December 15, 1973, when the
trustees of the American Psychiatric Association ruled that "homosexuality
per se implies no impairment in judgment, stability, reliability or general social or vocational abilities" and that "in the reasoned judgment of most
American psychiatrists today, homosexuality per se does not constitute any
form of mental disease."[41]

But this public statement was not sufficient to sway the opinions of biased judges. Nor did all psychiatrists agree with it. Thus, nongay fathers
could hire experts who would opine that a lesbian mother's sexual orientation might be a negative factor in raising her children. In the absence of reliable studies showing otherwise, such opinions were difficult to challenge.
Del Martin and Phyllis Lyon, in their 1972 book, *Lesbian/Woman,* tell a
story that portrays just how huge was this void of information.[42] The lesbian mother in their story was being divorced by a husband who was not
vindictive toward her and valued her ability to be a good mother to their
children. But he had never known any lesbian mothers, and he worried
about what might happen to the children of a lesbian mother. The husband's psychiatrist called Lyon, who was a founder of the lesbian organization Daughers of Bilitis in San Francisco, to ask if she knew of any studies,
any information at all, that he could rely on to allay the husband's concerns
about his children's future. Lyon reported that no such information was

available. Studies on lesbians were hard enough to carry out, but studies on lesbian mothers were even more difficult. Homophobic attitudes kept most lesbians closeted in the 1950s and 1960s. Fear of losing their children kept lesbian mothers even more closeted.

Only after Stonewall and the beginning of the modern lesbian and gay rights movement did things begin to change for the better. In 1971, for example, San Francisco's Family Service Agency added two gay people to its board.[43] New research on gay and lesbian relationships began to occur, and it countered stereotypical views of lesbian mothers.[44] By the 1970s, some lesbian mothers, typically in California, were able to retain custody of their children, although in some instances, only if they agreed to terminate their existing lesbian relationships or keep the children apart from lesbian partners and friends.[45]

The *Koop* case from Oregon, reported by Nan Hunter and Nancy Polikoff, is a good example of the fierceness of one judge's determination to keep two children away from a lesbian mother. Worried about the sexual development of the two girls, ages ten and twelve, the judge ordered them to live with their father despite their stated preference to live with their mother. When the children ran away from the father several times, the mother asked the judge again to award her custody on the basis of a change in circumstances. The judge ruled against her and, since the children refused to live with their father, the judge put the children in a juvenile detention center. In a subsequent hearing in juvenile court, the children were placed with their married half-sister. The juvenile court judge explained: "The living arrangement of their mother is an abnormal and not a stable one. It would be highly detrimental to these girls." He made this determination despite the fact that a psychiatrist, a psychologist, and a juvenile court caseworker all testified in favor of the mother. The judge explained that he "did not believe that statement of opinion."[46] Perhaps the most interesting aspect of this case is that the abnormal living arrangement to which the juvenile court judge referred had been reviewed in a separate custody case by another family law judge in the same county and found to be a positive and stable environment for raising children. Koop was living in a committed relationship with another lesbian mother, who had won her custody battle before a judge who had been willing to believe the opinion of the experts. By contrast, the judge in *Koop* relied on the opinion of the children's father, who testified that he was repulsed by the mother's lesbianism and was afraid his daughters would grow up to be just like her. The *Koop* judge was influenced by at least two myths that often have haunted lesbian mothers seeking custody: their relationships are unstable, and they will influence the sexual preferences of their children. In the growing body of scholarly research on lesbian mothers, both of these myths have been soundly debunked.

Family law varies quite a bit from state to state, and the cases tend to be very dependent on the specific facts. These considerations make family law cases a difficult focus for mounting a national gay rights campaign. Fighting different legal rules in the various states was something that the NAACP, for example, had specifically rejected when it decided to mount a national campaign to end segregation. In addition, the early post-Stonewall days of gay liberation were full of activists calling for sexual liberation. The key spokespeople were not addressing the problems of creating traditional families with parents and children. Some lesbian activists charged that the early movement was too male dominated and that the leaders were not well attuned to the concerns of women, especially those who were mothers.

In 1977, responding to the need for an organization to address the specific concerns of lesbians, Equal Rights Advocates, the feminist public interest law firm in San Francisco, founded the Lesbian Rights Project (LRP). Under the leadership of Donna Hitchens, LRP soon became the central force in supporting lesbian mother litigation. Direct legal representation was one means of providing support for lesbian mothers fighting for custody. But in the early 1970s, the greater need was for litigation tools, such as expert witness testimony and statistical studies that could be used to support the notion that lesbians could be good mothers. LRP was active in developing these tools and sharing them with lawyers across the country.

In 1984, the Supreme Court handed down an opinion in a family law case involving race discrimination that gave new hope to lesbian and gay parents. In *Palmore v. Sidoti*,[47] the Supreme Court reversed the decision of a state court judge who had ordered a change of custody from the white mother to the white father of the child when the mother became intimate with a black man whom she subsequently married. The case arose in Florida, a state not known for its tolerance of interracial marriages. The judge, applying the best interest of the child standard, had determined that it was better for the child to live with the father to avoid the stigma of being part of a mixed-race household. The U.S. Supreme Court reversed. Without finding that the judge had relied on improper personal bias, the Court ruled that a family law judge could not make decisions regarding child custody by taking into account societal discrimination and the risk of stigma that societal prejudice creates. Chief Justice Burger, for a unanimous Court, wrote:

The question . . . is whether the reality of private biases and the possible injury they might inflict are permissible considerations for removal of an infant child from the custody of its natural mother. We have little difficulty concluding that they are not. The Constitution cannot control such prejudices but neither can it tolerate them. Private biases may be outside the reach of the law, but the law cannot, directly or indirectly, give them effect.

Palmore v. Sidoti was immediately invoked by lesbian mothers and gay fathers, who by this time had begun to seek custody, to challenge the two types of rules that family law judges applied to deny them custody of their children. The first rule was a per se rule under which custody was automatically denied to a gay or lesbian parent. Virginia applies this rule. In a 1985 case, involving a gay father, the Virginia Supreme Court said: "The father's continuous exposure of the child to his immoral and illicit relationship renders him an unfit and improper custodian as a matter of law."[48]

The second rule, known as the "nexus rule," required proof that the parent's homosexuality would in fact harm the child in some way. On its face, the "nexus rule" was clearly more positive for gay parents than the "per se rule," but when applied by a biased judge, it could have draconian results. Judges often assumed that societal bias against gay men and lesbians was sufficient to cause harm to a child who was being raised by a gay parent. Thus, under the "nexus rule," a judge could effectively rule against gay and lesbian parents solely on the basis of society's prejudice. The relevance of *Palmore v. Sidoti* to such cases was obvious.

In 1985, the Supreme Court of Alaska became the first state court to apply the *Palmore v. Sidoti* rationale in a lesbian custody case.[49] In 1986, a New York court followed suit and awarded custody to a gay father.[50] These two cases gave new hope to lesbian and gay parents involved in custody battles throughout the country. If the Fourteenth Amendment prohibited consideration of societal prejudice when courts awarded custody in cases involving lesbian and gay parents, then perhaps constitutional challenges could produce progay uniformity in family law decisions. But the U.S. Supreme Court created an obstacle to such constitutional challenges when it handed down the infamous *Bowers v. Hardwick* decision, discussed in full in Chapter 6. In 1985, some states still applied the per se rule to deny lesbian and gay parents custody.[51] Some had adopted the more liberal nexus rule, but often applied it in such a way that it accomplished the same results as the per se rule. In practice, lesbian mothers in most states were advised to remain closeted if they wanted to keep their children, to give up their rights to property, alimony, and child support in order to avoid a custody battle, and to live apart from their female partners. Gay fathers were usually advised not to seek custody and warned that they might have to settle for supervised visitation.

Rights of the Second Parent

Most lesbian households with children included the children who came from prior marriages. As lesbians began to win more and more custody battles and as restrictions on custody loosened, the incidence of children being raised in two-parent households where both parents were of the same sex increased. By the early 1980s, a new phenomenon was occurring, however, a phenomenon that would become known as the "lesbian baby boom."

New reproductive technologies created primarily for the benefit of married couples who had trouble reproducing could also be used by single women in many places. Sperm banks, in particular, could be used by lesbians to impregnate themselves. If sperm banks were not open to lesbians, as they were not in some locations, then known male donors were a possible source of sperm. In 1984, a documentary, *Choosing Children*, told the story of many lesbian couples who had planned to have and raise children together.

The legal issues presented by these arrangements were myriad. If a known donor was used for the artificial insemination of sperm, would that donor be recognized as a parent? Could the parties by contract agree that he would not be recognized as a parent? Could they by contract relieve him of all child support obligations? Could a lesbian couple by contract provide that the nonbiological mother would be a parent, both in the sense of being responsible for the child's support and in terms of having rights to be with the child?

Many lesbians in the 1970s and early 1980s drafted contracts that were intended to resolve these questions, often knowing quite well that no court would enforce them. Family law was controlled by the principle of the "best interests of the child" and clearly did not allow legal parents to waive child support obligations. In addition, family law rigidly recognized only two parents, a father and a mother. Thus, a lesbian couple could not create parental status by contract. Furthermore, adoption of the child by the second parent in the lesbian couple was not realistically possible since most state adoption laws required the biological mother to give up all rights to her child if anyone other than a spouse were to adopt the child. Nonetheless, using the "best interests of the child" principle, some advocates were able to convince lower court judges that having two female parents was better than having only one. The first successful coparent adoptions occurred in unreported cases in 1985 and 1986 in California, Oregon, and Alaska.[52]

The absence of a recognized legal relationship between the child and the second parent created serious problems when relationships ended. Relationships could end in two different ways: by the couple splitting up or by one partner's death. By 1985, no court had recognized the right of any lesbian second parent to seek custody or visitation with a child whom she had helped to raise. Thus, for example, in a Florida case, the biological mother had signed a letter of intent stating her desire that her lesbian partner of eleven years be allowed to raise their child should anything happen to the mother. The mother died when the child was six years old. The surviving partner had been in the role of parent, even before the child's birth, when the two women agreed that they would have a child and raise the child together. Nonetheless, despite the fact that this woman was the only other parent the child had known, the Florida court awarded custody to the deceased mother's parents, a couple in their seventies. This decision was typical of the era.

CONCLUSION

Despite the Supreme Court's promising ruling in *Griswold v. Connecticut,* courts were generally unwilling to extend the right of privacy to protect gay men and lesbians who engaged in private consensual sexual conduct. Some sodomy statutes were struck down on privacy grounds by state courts, relying on the privacy rationale of *Griswold,* but those cases dwindled significantly after the Supreme Court's 1976 summary affirmance in the Virginia sodomy case, *Doe v. Commonwealth's Attorney.* Furthermore, the state-by-state legislative repeal of sodomy statutes stalled. Sodomy challenges remained on the agenda of the lesbian and gay civil rights movement, but court challenges had become significantly more difficult to pursue.

The constitutional right of privacy was also relevant to family law issues involving parents and children. For the most part, however, lesbian custody and other gay parenting issues continued to be decided by state family law judges who, because of their wide discretion on such matters, were able to rule in accord with their own beliefs of what was best for the child. Fortunately, the availability of reliable studies of lesbian parenting had the effect of changing some judicial attitudes on the subject. And *Palmore v. Sidoti* engendered hope that one day the federal constitution would remove anti-gay bias from family law decisions in the same way that it had removed racial bias.

NOTES

1. Georgia Code § 16- 6–2(a). This statute was recently held unconstitutional under the Georgia constitution.

2. Thompson v. Aldredge, 187 Ga. 467, 200 S.E. 799 (Ga. 1939), applying former Georgia law, then Code § 26–5901.

3. Riley v. Garrett, 219 Ga. 345, 133 S.E.2d 367 (Ga. 1963), interpreting former Georgia law, then Code § 26–5901.

4. See Georgia Code, 1968 § 26–2002.

5. 304 N.Y. 120, 106 N.E.2d 42 (1952).

6. 214 N.Y.S.2d 417, 174 N.E.2d 507 (1961).

7. 228 N.Y.S.2d 791 (N.Y. App. Div. 1962).

8. *See* People v. Katt, 234 N.Y.S.2d 988 (N.Y. App. Div. 1962), discussing legislative amendment to statute.

9. *See* People v. Sanabria, 42 Misc.2d 464, 249 N.Y.S.2d 66 (N.Y.Sup.App.Term 1964).

10. Buchanan v. Batchelor, 308 F.Supp. 729 (N.D. Tex 1970).

11. 401 U.S. 37 (1971).

12. Buckanan v. Wade, 401 U.S. 989 (1971).

13. Wainwright v. Stone, 414 U.S. 21 (1973).

14. 403 F. Supp. 1199 (E.D. Va. 1975).

15. Shilts, *Conduct Unbecoming* at 284.

16. Justice Goldberg quoted from Justice Harlan's dissent in Poe v. Ullman, 367 U.S. 497 at 553 (1961).

17. Eisenstadt v. Baird, 405 U.S. 438 (1972).

18. Doe, 425 U.S. 901 (1976).

19. See Charles Alan Wright, *Federal Courts* at 755 (4th ed. 1983).

20. See Hicks v. Miranda, 422 U.S. 332 (1975) stating that lower courts are bound "until such time as the Court informs [them] that [they] are not." *See also* Note, "The Precedential Effect of Summary Affirmances and Dismissals," 64 *Virginia Law Review* 117 (1978).

21. 478 U.S. 186 (1986).

22. People v. Onofre, 415 N.E.2d 936 (N.Y. 1980), *cert. denied* 415 U.S. 987 (1981); Commonwealth v. Bonadio, 415 A.2d 47 (Penn. 1980).

23. State v. Pilcher, 242 N.W.2d 348 (Iowa 1976).

24. See People v. Masten, 292 N.W.2d 171 (Mich. App. 1980), rev'd by 322 N.W.2d 547 (Mich. 1982). *See also* Kelly v. State, 412 A.2d 1274 (Md. App. 1980), judgment aff'd by Neville v. State, 430 A.2d Md. 1981) (heterosexual sodomy).

25. 415 N.E.2d 936 (N.Y. 1980).

26. *See* Gaylord v. Tacoma School District No. 10, 559 P.2d 1340 (Wash. 1977), *cert. denied,* 434 U.S. 879 (1977).

27. *See* Enslin v. Wallford, 565 F.2d 156 (4th Cir. 1977, *cert. denied* by Enslin v. Bean, 436 U.S. 912 (1978).

28. Gay Lib. v. University of Missouri, 558 F2d 848 (8th Cir. 1977), *cert. denied,* 434 U.S. 1080 (1978).

29. *Washington Post,* December 11, 1979.

30. *See* Christensen v. State, 266 Ga. 474, 468 S.E.2d 188 (Ga. 1996) (statement that "all I'm looking for is a blow job" to an undercover police officer constitutes solicitation to commit sodomy).

31. Rittenour v. District of Columbia, 163 A.2d 558 (D.C. Mun. App. 1960).

32. *Sexual Politics* at 207

33. 268 U.S. 510 (1925).

34. 262 U.S. 390 (1923).

35. 440 U.S. 268 (1979).

36. Stanley v. Illinois, 405 U.S. 645 (1972).

37. Moore v. City of East Cleveland, 431 U.S. 494 (1977).

38. *See,* for example, Lassiter v. Department of Social Services of Durham County, N.C., 452 U.S. 18 (1981); Santosky v. Kramer, 455 U.S. 745 (1982).

39. *See* Lehr v. Robertson, 463 U.S. 248 (1983).

40. Marcus, *Making History* at 21–24.

41. Reported in 32 *UCLA Law Review* 852. *See also Making History* at 253–254.

42. Del Martin and Phyllis Lyon, *Lesbian/Woman* at 144.

43. *Lesbian/Woman* at 145.

44. Letitia Anne Peplau, "Research on Lesbian and Gay Relationships: A Decade Review" (paper presented at the 4th International Conference on Personal Relationships held at the University of British Columbia, July 1988).

45. See Hunter and Polikoff, "Custody Rights of Lesbian Mothers: Legal Theory and Litigation Strategy," *Buffalo Law Review* 691 (1976) and Hitchens and Price, "Trial Strategy in Lesbian Mother Cases: The Use of Expert Testimony," *Golden Gate Law Review* 451(1978–1979).

46. Hunter and Polikoff, 25 *Buffalo Law Review* at 699.

47. 466 U.S. 429 (1984).

48. Roe v. Roe, 324 S.E.2d 691, 694 (Va. 1985).

49. S.N.E. v. R.L.B., 699 P.2d 875 (Alaska 1985).

50. M.A.B. v. R.B., 510 N.Y.S.2d 960 (N.Y. Sup. Ct. 1986).

51. For example, Virginia and Missouri. See discussion of custody cases post-*Hardwick* at Chapter 8.

52. Roberta Achtenberg, *Preserving and Protecting the Families of Lesbians and Gay Men* (publication of the Lesbian Rights Project 1986). *See also* the National Center for Lesbian Rights web page (www.nclrights.org).

5

When Private Becomes Public: Coupling in the Public Sphere, 1950–1985

Liberal political philosophy, which informs much of American political history, is based on the concept of a society made up of individuals. As citizens, individuals participate equally in the polity. As people with private lives, they also inhabit a sphere of personal space removed from the polity. In each sphere, each individual possesses certain rights and obligations. "Equal rights" and "equal access" are the arguments used to obtain public sphere rights such as employment and education. The "right to be left alone" is the argument used to obtain private sphere rights such as the right to chose whether or not to procreate. Public sphere obligations include military service and jury duty. Private sphere obligations include obligations of spousal and child support. However, the public/private divide is not as clearly delineated as liberal theorists often assume.

Feminists have understood the problem with liberalism's public/private divide since the early days of the first wave of feminism. Modern feminists, as well, grapple with issues that are not easily confined to one sphere or the other. For example, although choices about reproduction may be private, they implicate public resources when abortion is the choice. The decision by the woman may be private, but her access to abortion is dependent on the public sphere of professional doctors, hospitals, and clinics. Furthermore, reasonable access to abortion by poor women is dependent on public funding. Feminist advocates for women's rights question the current structure of the public/private divide every time they argue for public support of abortion.

The lesbian and gay civil rights movement has also felt the need to question the public/private divide. Lesbians and gay men, exercising their private right to choose, have selected domestic partners, and often they have voiced lifetime commitments to each other. But once such intimate relationships have been formed, some of these lesbian and gay couples have requested government support for their private choices in the form of marriage or some comparable form of public recognition. The standard response has been that the government has no obligation to support their private choices.

MARRIAGE

Marriage is a legal relationship that creates obligations that are typically characterized as belonging in the private sphere. In truth, however, marriage is a very public affair. Not only do states decide who can marry, states also regulate many aspects of marriage, including the private behavior of the spouses. But it is not only the state's involvement that adds a public dimension to marriage. Spouses themselves "come out" in public as a couple each time they present themselves as husband and wife. Sometimes this "coming out" is voluntary, but often spouses are forced to "come out" by routine questions asked about marital status on everything from tax forms to health club memberships.

Marital status can have both positive and negative effects, as feminists have long understood. For early feminists, the most negative effect was the harsh application of the English doctrine of coverture. Under coverture, once a woman married, her separate legal identity ended. She was no longer capable of owning property or entering into contracts. Instead, her identity was said to merge into that of her husband, who was accorded full legal power over her property and could contract on her behalf.

Even after individual states began to enact married women's property acts that allowed a wife to own property, vestiges of coverture remained. At the federal level, for example, the Expatriation Act of 1907 provided that when an American woman married a foreign national, she ceased to be an American citizen. At the state level, even as late as the 1960s, married women experienced discrimination in access to credit. Banks and financial institutions presumed that within a married couple, the husband was the breadwinner. Thus, a wife's credit application would not be honored unless her husband was a coapplicant. In community property states, where the common law rules of coverture had never applied, the husband continued as the manager of any property brought into the marital community by the wife. In such states, wives could not even manage their own earnings. Some community property states began changing these sexist property management rules in the 1960s. However, in Louisiana, the husband was the sole manager of the married couple's property until 1981, when the U.S. Supreme Court finally struck down the sex-biased rule in *Kirchberg v. Feenstra*.[1]

Because marriage historically has denied the existence of the wife as an independent person, both de jure and de facto, feminists in both the first and second wave fought to erase the role of marriage in the subjugation of woman. The main thrust of feminist arguments regarding marital status was that a woman's marital status should be irrelevant with respect to public sphere rights such as employment, housing, credit, and education. These arguments eventually resulted in the passage of federal and state statutes prohibiting discrimination on the basis of marital status in such public sphere arenas as credit and housing.

Marriage also provides numerous benefits, a fact that has been problematic for feminists. The government provides many spousal benefits on the presumption that, within marriage, one spouse is likely to be dependent on the other spouse. For some feminists, gender equality will be accomplished so long as the presumption of dependency is a nongendered one. Other feminists believe that, given our history of coverture and the fact of actual dependency of wives on husbands under that system, the adoption of a new nongendered system of spousal benefits would not result in actual equality between husbands and wives. Thus, for some feminists (i.e., those who embrace the notion of formal equality), there should never be gendered rules. For others (i.e,. those who embrace the notion of substantive equality), gendered rules that favor women may be necessary until substantial equality between the sexes has been achieved.

But marriage produces benefits apart from those based on assumptions about spousal economic dependence. Marriage also produces benefits that protect the intimacy of the spouses. Governmental recognition of the marital relationship as superior to other relationships creates an intangible benefit in that it values and honors the commitment that the two individuals have made to each other. And sometimes, governmental recognition of the relationship offers tangible support for the couple's decision to be together. For example, ever since passage of the War Brides Act of 1948, the government has given special preference to foreign spouses of Americans, male or female, allowing them to immigrate in order to continue their spousal relationship unhindered by the national borders that often divide other couples.

The women's movement and the lesbian and gay civil rights movement have approached the issue of marriage from very different perspectives. For women, the battle has been to diminish the importance of marriage so that a woman will be viewed as an individual and not as part of a couple. Thus, a woman's marital status should not affect her ability to borrow money. Nor should it affect her ability to continue her education. Nor should marital status prevent a wife from claiming abuse or rape by her husband. All of these arguments center on respecting a married woman as an individual. Such arguments tend to push marriage back into the private sphere by making marital status irrelevant in the public sphere.

For the lesbian and gay civil rights movement, by contrast, the government's refusal to honor and support same-sex committed relationships reflects the government's negative view of lesbians and gay men as individuals by presuming their private commitments are less worthy than those of non-gay persons. Thus, denial of public benefits to same-sex couples is viewed as a denial of equal respect. More radical gay activists, who care nothing of gaining the government's respect, reject same-sex marriage as a legitimate goal for the movement. But even radicals believe that an individual's choice to share a life with another person should not be thwarted by governmental action. Thus, at the very least, government should honor and support such individual choices when they are challenged by immigration laws, hospital visiting rules, and even prison regulations that allow spouses, but no others, to maintain their close personal connection.

The radical activists who were most vocal after Stonewall talked of sexual liberation and the right to be different. Many of them trashed the concept of marriage because they viewed it as an oppressive institution, in much the same way that radical feminists viewed marriage. But many gay and lesbian Americans, who lived their lives alongside their neighbors, always wanted what their neighbors had: public recognition of the most important personal and private relationship in their lives. At the grassroots level, marriage was a right that lesbians and gay men generally thought their movement should strive to win.

In the early 1970s, a wave of lesbian and gay activity commenced around the marriage issue. Gay activist Tim Mayhew of the Seattle Gay Alliance prepared a detailed "Position Statement on Marriage" for the ACLU of Washington.[2] His primary focus was to explain the discriminatory effect of marriage on lesbians and gay men and to call for the total abolition of marriage, a position consistently supported by the more radical gay activists in the post-Stonewall era. For example, "A Gay Manifesto," a document from the early days of the movement in San Francisco, denounced traditional marriage, describing it as "a rotten, oppressive institution" that is "fraught with role playing," and called for gay couples to resist mimicking heterosexual marriage.[3] Similarly, a statement by the Third World Gay Revolution of New York City called for "abolition of the bourgeois nuclear family."[4]

At the same time, individual lesbians and gay men across the country, who were not part of any national lesbian and gay political movement, were appearing in their local clerks' offices demanding marriage licenses. Most of their demands were denied, but a clerk in Boulder County, Colorado, actually issued licenses after receiving an attorney general's opinion that said Colorado law was not clear on the issue of whether marriage licenses were only available to opposite-sex couples. Although state legislatures no doubt viewed marriage as a union between one man and one woman, most state marriage statutes at the time did not specifically provide that marriage was an institution only for opposite-sex couples. In some cases, state legislatures had recently redrafted marriage statutes to degender them in response to feminist arguments for statutes to require gender-neutral responsibilities in marriage. Thus, some statutes that used to define marriage in terms of "husband and wife" or "male and female" now referred only to "persons." This sort of statutory language enabled gay marriage plaintiffs to argue that they had a statutory right to marry on the theory that the statute did not say the right was restricted to opposite-sex couples.

If the statute explicitly limited marriage to one man and one woman, or if the state so construed its marriage statute, then litigants challenged the statute on constitutional grounds. Some conceptual difficulties arose, however, in constructing a constitutional theory to challenge these statutes. Equality arguments were the most attractive, especially if the equal protection claim could be crafted as discrimination on the basis of sex, a classification that was just beginning to receive closer judicial scrutiny under the Supreme Court's developing equal protection jurisprudence. But an analytic problem existed in articulating this sort of equality argument. Although these statutes contained an explicit sex-based classification, it was a classification that burdened men and women equally. That is, both men and women were prohibited from marrying someone of the same sex. Although

Loving v. Virginia had ended the vitality of this "equal application" argument in the context of racial classifications in the context of marriage, it was not certain the argument could be avoided when the classification was sex. Because of this weakness in the equality argument, gay rights advocates also advanced right to privacy arguments, claiming that marriage was a fundamental right.

The first reported gay marriage case was handed down by the Supreme Court of Minnesota in 1971, shortly after the first gender discrimination victory in the Supreme Court, *Reed v. Reed,* but before the adoption of heightened scrutiny for sex classifications. The Minnesota case, *Baker v. Nelson,*[5] was the result of litigation by Mike McConnell and Jack Baker, the Minnesota couple that also sued the University of Minnesota when Mike lost his university librarian position on account of the publicity surrounding their attempted marriage. Their story is a simple one. Mike McConnell and Jack Baker fell in love and wanted to be together. Jack was beginning law school at the University of Minnesota. Mike followed him to Minneapolis and interviewed for a job in the university's library located on the St. Paul campus. The couple wanted public recognition of their love and commitment. They talked to their priest and ultimately married each other in a religious ceremony on September 3, 1971. They were both active members of the Newman Center, the Catholic chapel at the University of Minnesota.

McConnell and Baker were also activists. Baker was the leader of the gay student group, FREE, at the University of Minnesota. Without the backing of FREE and without any real warning to other activists in the community about their intentions, Baker and McConnell decided to make a public statement about gay commitment by applying for a marriage license prior to their wedding. Baker, a law student, knew that the Minnesota statute did not state explicitly that marriage was only between a man and a woman.[6] Nonetheless, the local clerk refused to grant the license. On the basis of this refusal, Baker and McConnell sued in the Minnesota courts. The court first ruled that the absence of specific statutory language defining marriage as a relationship between a man and a woman did not mean that the statute applied to same-sex couples. The very definition of marriage, reasoned the court, embodied the notion that it was an institution designed for opposite-sex couples only. As for the constitutional arguments, the court rejected both of them. The court concluded that the equality argument failed owing to the equal application doctrine. It distinguished the race-based classification in *Loving v. Virginia* by explaining that the Supreme Court struck down Virginia's antimiscegenation statute because it supported white supremacy and thereby stigmatized African Americans. Minnesota's marriage statute, by contrast, contained a sex-based classification that stigmatized neither men nor women. Rather, the court found the sex-based classification perfectly justifiable. After all, marriage always had been defined as a union between one man and one woman. Therefore, limiting marriage to opposite-sex couples was entirely within the state's power. As for the privacy argument, the court ruled that the right to privacy recognized in *Griswold* was a constitutional right enjoyed only by married couples and not by unmarried, same-sex couples.

In addition to losing their battle to have their marriage legally recognized, Baker and McConnell suffered secondary harms from their decision to go public about their relationship. As reported in Chapter 3, the publicity surrounding their request for a marriage license caused McConnell to lose his job as a librarian with the university. McConnell sued to retain his job, but lost his case before the federal Court of Appeals for the Eighth Circuit, where the judges viewed his attempt to marry a man as an "antic."

While their marriage case was on appeal to the Minnesota Supreme Court, McConnell and Baker were apparently able to obtain a marriage license from the Blue Earth County court clerk. With the marriage license in hand and with the formalization of their commitment in a religious ceremony, Baker applied for increased benefits from the Veterans' Administration on the grounds that McConnell was now his dependent spouse. This application resulted in a third round of litigation, this time against the Veterans' Administration. The Court of Appeals for the Eighth Circuit, citing the Minnesota Supreme Court decision as determinative, held that McConnell was not Baker's spouse.

Another familiar gay civil rights plaintiff pursued equal marriage rights in the state of Washington. John Singer, whose employment discrimination case is discussed in Chapter 3, was fired for being openly gay. One of his employer's complaints was that Singer had attempted to obtain a marriage license to marry another man and when refused, had filed suit. In 1974, the Washington Court of Appeals ruled that Singer and his partner, Paul Barwick, had no legal right to wed in the state of Washington. Although the Washington statute did not explicitly require spouses to be of opposite sex, the court construed the statute to apply only to opposite-sex couples. Citing *Baker v. Nelson,* the court also rejected Singer's equal protection and due process arguments. But Singer had one additional legal argument. Washington had recently added an equal rights amendment to the state constitution. Singer argued that the language of the equal rights amendment absolutely forbade any distinctions based on sex. He also argued that the people of Washington approved same-sex marriages when they adopted the amendment because opponents of the amendment had clearly stated that passage of the amendment would require recognition of such marriages. The court responded to this argument by citing its own understanding of what the people of Washington were voting for when they adopted the equal rights amendment. The opinion cites press reports that claimed the same-sex marriage result would not occur and that opponents of the amendment were using the threat of same-sex marriage to coax people into voting against the amendment.

Singer's brief contained an additional argument rejected by the court. He claimed that the trial court's order "was based on the erroneous and fallacious conclusion that same-sex marriages are destructive to society." To counter this conclusion of fact, Singer's lawyers prepared a brief full of sociological, theological, scientific, and medical expert information that described homosexual relationships in positive terms. The court rejected the argument, claiming that there was no evidence that the trial court had made its determination on the basis of the alleged conclusion. Thus, the information, although informative, was not relevant to any legal point raised in the case.

The saga of these plaintiffs demonstrates how the private sometimes becomes public. In order to obtain government recognition of their relationship, these two couples had to apply to a public governmental agency. Most marriages are celebrated as public events in order to announce to the public the couple's commitment and to receive the support of the community in which the members of the couple participate, whether that community is religious or social. Instead, when Baker and McConnell made their public statements about their commitment to each other, McConnell lost his job. Singer also lost his job in part over his attempt to marry. When McConnell became dependent on Baker for support, Baker, as a veteran, applied for increased benefits in order to be able to stay in law school and still support his newly dependent partner. Yet neither the Minnesota Supreme Court nor the Eighth Circuit Court of Appeals completely understood the need for public recognition of their private relationship. Indeed, the Court of Appeals dismissed the entire affair as no more than an "antic."

IMMIGRATION

An even stronger case involving the need for public recognition of our private relationships is the case of Richard Frank Adams and his partner, Anthony Corbett Sullivan. Adams was an American citizen. Sullivan was not. The two men shared an intimate and committed relationship that had begun in 1971. Sullivan, an Australian, entered the United States on a visa. When the visa was about to expire, Sullivan went through a marriage ceremony with a female and sought permanent residence status based on that marriage. The marriage, however, was a sham because Sullivan was personally committed to Adams. The INS discovered the nature of the marriage and revoked its permission for Sullivan to remain in the United States. After annulling the sham marriage, Sullivan "married" Adams, having first obtained a marriage license from the helpful and sympathetic clerk in Boulder County, Colorado. Sullivan applied again for permanent residence status based on his marriage to Adams.

To no one's surprise, the INS denied the application and refused to recognize the marriage. After all, the INS had operated for years on a policy under which homosexuality alone was grounds for refusing entry to aliens or for ordering their deportation. Furthermore, the policy had been upheld by the Supreme Court as recently as 1967.[7] But what really irked the gay couple was the written notice from the INS that said the two men had "failed to establish that a bona fide marital relationship can exist between two faggots."

The couple decided to fight that decision by the INS in federal court and to fight deportation proceedings at the INS administrative level on the additional grounds of extreme hardship. Challenging the INS ruling that they did not qualify as spouses, they filed suit in federal district court in California. In addition to claiming that their marriage should be recognized, they argued that failure to recognize it would violate their right to equal protection. Suing the INS was about as foolhardy as suing the military in those days because the INS was at least as impervious to constitutional claims, maybe even more so. As the federal district court explained: "Congress has virtually plenary power in immigration matters and is not bound by otherwise applicable equal protection requirements."[8] Even if the INS were subject to equal protection constraints, their refusal to recognize same-sex couples was viewed as completely rational by the appellate court. The court said:

In effect, Congress has determined that preferential status is not warranted for the spouses of homosexual marriages. Perhaps this is because homosexual marriages never produce offspring, because they are not recognized in most, if in any, of the states, or because they violate traditional and often prevailing societal mores. In any event, having found that Congress rationally intended to deny preferential status to the spouses of such marriages, we need not further "probe and test the justifications for the legislative decision."[9]

This decision was the end of round one of Sullivan's fight for the right to remain in the United States. At the same time, round two was gearing up at the INS. With no valid visa, Sullivan was subject to deportation. He requested a continuance from the INS in order to make a case for a suspension of deportation on grounds of extreme hardship. He made two arguments: (1) severing the personal relationship by deporting him would cause personal anguish to both him and his partner of twelve years, and (2) deportation to Australia would cause him "undue hardship because homosexuals are not accepted in that society and because the members of his own family who live in Australia [had] turned against him."

The Board of Immigration Appeals (BIA) rejected both claims. Responding to his plea regarding the personal anguish of being separated from a life partner, the BIA said that his separation from Adams did not amount to extreme hardship because "[s]eparation from those upon whom one has become dependent is common to most aliens who have spent a considerable amount of time in the United States."

The Court of Appeals for the Ninth Circuit upheld the BIA, agreeing with its reasons for not honoring Sullivan's claim.[10] With respect to the importance of the personal relationship, the Court merely observed, "Deportation rarely occurs without personal distress and emotional hurt. Various courts have previously upheld orders of the BIA that resulted in the separation of aliens from members of their families."[11] By contrast, Judge Pregerson, in dissent, noted that the majority opinion was out of line with earlier Ninth Circuit cases stressing that family ties and relationships were crucial considerations in determining whether to deny deportation. As to the requirement that the BIA give attention to the specific facts in each case, Pregerson pointed out that it had failed to consider the fact that Sullivan's partner was unlikely to be able to immigrate to Australia because, in addition to his homosexuality, he was of Filipino ancestry, and likely to be subjected to racial discrimination there. Furthermore, he concluded: "The BIA gave no recognition to the strain Sullivan would experience if he were forced to separate from the person with whom he has lived and shared a close relationship for the past twelve years. This failure to recognize Sullivan's emotional hardship is particularly troublesome because he and Adams have lived together as a family."[12]

Sullivan appealed to President Reagan for intervention, but never got a response. Rejected by both of their countries, the two men left their friends and family in Los Angeles and flew to London to avoid separation. The couple reappeared briefly in Washington, D.C., in May 2000 for the Millennium March on Washington.

Gay marriage may not be the only solution for couples like Richard Adams and Tony Sullivan, but such couples need some sort of public recognition of their relationships in order to be able to stay together. Any couple that spends nine years in a protracted legal battle just to remain together certainly has demonstrated the sort of commitment that warrants public recognition.

ADULT ADOPTION

Some lawyers, responding to the concerns of their clients over the lack of public recognition for their relationships, began to advise gay men and lesbians to use the adoption process to create a legal relationship. Using the adoption process, one partner in the couple would become the parent, and the other would become the child. Parent/child relationships are not given the same preferential treatment as spousal relationships, but for many gay men and lesbians, a legal connection of any sort seemed preferable to none.

According to news reports, after the Minnesota courts refused to honor the marriage between Mike McConnell and Jack Baker, McConnell, the older of the two, adopted Baker, thereby creating a family relationship of father and son. The story, as reported in the press, explained:

> A judge in Minneapolis allowed McConnell to adopt Baker. The Gay Activists Alliance believes the ruling to be the first of its kind—at least between publicly admitted homosexuals. McConnell and Baker were basically trying to legitimize their association as best they could, but they say that they also had inheritance rights in mind. And Baker now should be able to get a $300 quarterly resident's discount on his tuition since his nonstudent "father" can establish a state domicile. McConnell (who is suing to regain the university job he lost because of his homosexuality) may also be able to gain a head-of-household deduction [for income tax purposes].[13]

Adult adoption would not have helped Richard Adams and his partner, Tony Sullivan, with the immigration officials. Nor would it have provided the increased veterans' benefits that Jack Baker claimed for his "spouse," although apparently he gained that benefit indirectly by being able to establish Minnesota state residency for tuition purposes. The ability to claim head of household reporting status for tax purposes will also produce a short-term benefit in the form of lower taxes so long as son Jack is under the age of twenty-four and a full-time student. But once Jack finishes law school and starts earning income, that benefit will end because Jack will no longer qualify as a dependent.[14]

There are only a handful of additional benefits that can be obtained using adult adoption. For probate law purposes, the child in the couple will be recognized as the legal heir of the parent and the parent will become a legal heir of the child. Absent a will, this status will entitle one partner to claim an intestate share in the other partner's estate at death. However, a better way to ensure inheritance is to draft a will naming the intended beneficiary and describing his or her share of the estate. Some gay couples, worried about an estranged family member's ability, as an heir, to contest the will, will opt for adult adoption to protect against such will contests.

Also related to probate are concerns about inheritance taxes. Although most states have repealed such taxes, where they remain, the existence of a legal family relationship between the decedent and the heir or beneficiary can create a significant reduction in taxes. Inheritance taxes are levied at the lowest rate when property passes to a child, and at the highest rate when property passes to an unrelated individual. In some states, no inheritance tax is levied against transfers of property from parent to child. A legal adoption would avoid the tax completely in such states.

Concerns over rent control and rent subsidization can also encourage same-sex couples to consider adoption. In New York City, for example, rent control laws protect the current tenant as well as any family member who was living with the tenant at the tenant's death. Establishing a legally recognized family relationship could prevent a surviving gay or lesbian partner from being evicted from his or her home when the deceased partner was the only tenant on the lease.

One additional benefit may arise from adult adoptions. Many doctors and other medical personnel are hesitant to recognize the unrelated partner of a patient as a person who has any valid interest in the patient's medical condition. Unless the doctor is the family physician for both partners, there is no way for the doctor to know the true nature of the relationship. And if the partner who is being hospitalized is comatose or unable to communicate clearly, then the doctor has only the word of the unrelated partner. Although a better way to address this problem is for each partner to execute a durable power of attorney for health care naming the other partner as the agent entrusted with making medical decisions, establishing kinship through adult adoption can also be useful.

For many gay and lesbian couples, however, the acquisition of financial benefits was not what drove them to adult adoption in the 1970s and 1980s. Rather, the desire for some public recognition of their relationship motivated them. Most such adoptions occurred in California, and most were routinely granted. In the early 1980s, courts in New York began to question the public policy implications of allowing a gay man to adopt his adult same-sex partner. After positive rulings had been issued by lower New York courts on the question,[15] the New York Court of Appeals put a stop to the practice in 1984 by ruling that such adoptions were not contemplated by the New York statute.[16] Although the statute included no explicit requirements for one adult to adopt another other than a willingness to enter into the relationship, the court read into the statute a requirement that the two adults not have a sexual relationship. Thus, the very nature of their private relationship prevented them the public recognition they sought.

CONCLUSION

During the first decades of the modern lesbian and gay civil rights movement, activists sought legal recognition for same-sex relationships. All attempts to secure marriage rights were soundly rejected by the courts. A number of same-sex couples, mostly gay men in California, sought an alternative route to official recognition: adult adoption. But when the issue of using adult adoption as a means of gaining legal recognition of gay and lesbian relationships reached the highest court of New York, that court ruled against such attempts for public recognition.

A comparison of all the legal gains from this era shows that the greatest gains were in the public sphere, particularly with respect to the public speech rights of student organizations. Some gains occurred in the private sphere. These gains, however, primarily in the form of decriminalization of sodomy, occurred only in some states. No national case occurred to protect lesbian and gay privacy. In fact, the one case to reach the U.S. Supreme Court on this issue, *Doe v. Commonwealth's Attorney,* resulted in a summary affirmance upholding Virginia's consensual sodomy statute. Finally, the least amount of positive change occurred in the area of family law. No court ruled in favor of recognizing the legal right of lesbian and gay partners to share their lives, to be together, to claim that they were family. Modest gains occurred for some gay and lesbian parents who sought custody or visitation of their children upon divorce. But in most states, homosexual parents were presumptively unfit.

NOTES

1. 450 U.S. 455 (1981).

2. Tim Mayhew, position statement on marriage, prepared for the ACLU of Washington, December 5, 1971 (Mayhew Collection, Box 12, University of Washington Libraries, Manuscripts & University Archives Division).

3. Karla Jay and Allen Young, *Out of the Closets: Voice of Gay Liberation* at 331 (twentieth anniversary edition 1992).

4. Ibid. at 365.

5. 191 N.W.2d 185 (Minn. 1971).

6. The Minnesota marriage statute has been amended twice since the couple pursued their marriage claim in the courts. It was amended in 1977 to insert the words "a contract between a man and a woman" and then again in 1997 to say that lawful marriages can only exist between people of the opposite sex. Both amendments seem superfluous given the Minnesota Supreme Court's clear holding in the case brought by Baker and McConnell.

7. Boutelier v. INS, 387 U.S. 118 (1967).

8. Adams v. Howerton, 486 F. Supp. 1119 at 1124 (C.D. Cal. 1980).

9. 673 F.2d 1036, 1042–1043 (9th Cir. 1982), *cert. denied* 458 U.S. 1111 (1982).

10. Sullivan v. INS, 772 F.2d 609 (9th Cir. 1985).

11. Ibid. at 611.

12. Ibid. at 612.

13. See "The Law," *Time*, September 6, 1971, at 50, reported in Lynne Marie Kohm, "A Reply to 'Principles and Prejudice': Marriage and the Realization that Principles Win Over Political Will," 22 *Journal of Contemporary Law* 293 at n36 (1996).

14. *See* Sections 2, 151, and 152 of the Internal Revenue Code. A person can claim head of household status so long as he is supporting a dependent. An adopted child qualifies as a dependent so long as: (1) the parent provides over half the support for the child, and (2) either (a) the child is under nineteen, or (b) the child is under twenty-four and a full-time student, or (c) the child has insignificant amounts of gross income, for example, under $2,000.

15. *See*, for example, In re Adult Anonymous II, 452 N.Y.S.2d 198 (App. Div. 1982).

16. In re Robert Paul P., 471 N.E.2d 424 (N.Y. 1984).

6

Bowers v. Hardwick

THE EARLY SODOMY CHALLENGES: THE ROAD TO *BOWERS V. HARDWICK*

In the 1970s and 1980s, gay legal activists increasingly concluded that sodomy statutes had to be challenged by gay rights lawyers. In 1977, Lambda and the ACLU joined together to challenge the New York State sodomy statute, the constitutionality of which was before the New York Court of Appeals in *People v. Mehr*.[1] *Mehr* presented a constitutional challenge to New York's consensual sodomy statute that forbade unmarried couples from engaging in "deviate sexual intercourse."[2] The case was before the court on defendants' motion to dismiss the criminal information that had been issued against them. The trial court held the statute in violation of the Equal Protection Clause, finding no rational basis for distinguishing between married and unmarried couples.[3] That decision was reversed on appeal.[4] The appellate division held that marital privacy interests recognized under *Griswold* supported the marital/nonmarital distinction. The New York Court of Appeals ultimately avoided the constitutional questions, refusing to rule on so difficult an issue "without a trial record and solely on the informations filed." Thus, the Court denied the defendants' motion to dismiss, without prejudice, and reserved review of the constitutional issues in the event the defendants were actually convicted.[5]

Focusing on the right to privacy, the two organizations continued to mount challenges to sodomy statutes.[6] The New York sodomy statute was ultimately ruled unconstitutional in *People v. Onofre*,[7] a Lambda case. And on November 20, 1983, Lambda and the ACLU hosted a national meeting of gay and lesbian legal organizations to develop a national strategy for eradicating sodomy laws across the country.[8] This was the first meeting of

the Ad Hoc Task Force to Challenge Sodomy Laws. Participating organizations in addition to Lambda and the ACLU included the Lesbian Rights Project (San Francisco), Gay and Lesbian Advocates and Defenders (Boston), Texas Human Rights Foundation, National Committee for Sexual Civil Liberties, National Gay Rights Advocates (Los Angeles), and various ACLU affiliates.

Mainstream lawyers and activists have not always understood why gay and lesbian legal organizations chose to focus their attention on sodomy laws. After all, sodomy laws are rarely enforced against consenting adults in private. Surely fear of prosecution is not the main concern of most gay men and lesbians. Was the focus on sodomy challenges determined by the fact that, in light of *Griswold* and *Roe,* such challenges seemed the most promising for setting constitutional precedent? In answer to these questions, which came both from without and within the gay and lesbian community, Lambda's legal director, Abby Rubenfeld, maintained that "sodomy laws are the bedrock of legal discrimination against gay men and lesbians."[9]

Associating homosexuals with sodomy and, thus, with criminal activity had been at the core of earlier governmental action against gay men and lesbians. Raids on gay bars were often justified on grounds that criminal activity might result where gay persons congregated. The 1950 Senate Subcommittee report recommending that all homosexual persons be dismissed from government service relied in large part on the assumption that same-sex sexual conduct was both criminal and immoral. Persons who engaged in such conduct were presumed to be morally weak and, thus, unfit for employment in responsible positions. So long as consensual same-sex sodomy remained a crime, these justifications for discrimination against gay people were more difficult to attack.

The role played by sodomy laws in antigay discrimination in the 1980s was much the same as in earlier decades. The risk of prosecution for sodomy was not the main concern of gay men and lesbians. Rather, their concern was the risk of being branded as a criminal once one's sexual orientation became known. So long as gay men and lesbians were presumed to engage in criminal acts of sodomy, employers could argue that they should not be forced to hire criminals, and landlords could argue that they should not be forced to rent to criminals.

Many lesbians identified sodomy statutes as a concern primarily of gay men since the statutes were often applied to gay men who were arrested for engaging in gay sex in semipublic places such as rest stops. Thus, within the gay and lesbian community, sodomy challenges were often perceived as a male issue. Lesbians were more concerned with family issues such as custody and domestic partner benefits. Lambda's Rubenfeld spoke to lesbian activists about the importance of sodomy challenges to lesbian lives.[10] As an example, she described a custody case in which her lesbian client was branded as a criminal in open court by counsel for the husband. Although sodomy statutes are rarely enforced when the sexual conduct occurs in private, one of the more outrageous convictions for consensual sodomy involved two women who were arrested for engaging in sexual conduct in the privacy of their own tent on public camping grounds.[11]

The campaign to erase sodomy statutes from the books was consistent with the original impulses of the gay liberation movement. As the lesbian and gay civil rights movement developed beyond its original grassroots beginnings, exemplified by the 1969 Stonewall riots, more radical factions of the movement accused mainstream groups such as Lambda of ignoring the original purpose of gay liberation. Gay liberation was always about sexual freedom and about the breaking down of stereotypes. Thus, supporters of sexual freedom, who might have opposed legal arguments for equal lesbian and gay participation in such conservative organizations as the military, fully agreed with the legal challenges to sodomy laws. So long as state laws criminalizing lesbians and gay men for engaging in intimate sexual behavior remained on the books, the state's repressive power was legitimated. This state power to define good and bad sex was a barrier for gay and lesbian individuals who sought to redefine themselves publicly as good, moral, and noncriminal. And it was a legitimate target for the more radical segments of the grassroots movement, who may not have cared about dominant definitions of morality, but certainly cared about individual freedom to transgress. For all these reasons, the attack on sodomy laws was the one focus that could best unite what had become a very diverse movement.

From the time of Stonewall through the mid-1980s, the Supreme Court had ruled in only two gay rights cases, *Doe v. Commonwealth's Attorney* and *National Gay Task Force v. Board of Education of Oklahoma City*.[12] Neither ruling had produced a written opinion; both were summary affirmances. The affirmance in *Doe* could be explained on procedural rather than substantive grounds, but, in the absence of an opinion, no one could be sure of the Court's motives. The *NGTF* case provided a better gauge of current Court opinion, because it was a more recent decision. In that case, at least four justices had ruled on the side of gay rights. If litigators could get the Court to take the right case and if they could get one more justice to

join the four that had evidenced some support for the movement in *NGTF,*
they might experience their first Supreme Court victory. The right case, or
so the movement lawyers thought, was put on the Supreme Court docket in
1985.

BOWERS V. HARDWICK

On August 3, 1982, Michael Hardwick was arrested by an Atlanta policeman for committing the crime of sodomy with a consenting adult male in
the privacy of his own bedroom. Such arrests are rare for, despite the existence of state sodomy statutes, policemen rarely have sufficient cause to enter a private bedroom to see if the offense is being committed. The policeman who arrested Hardwick happened upon the event because he was
there to issue an unrelated warrant. A slightly groggy houseguest had answered the door and admitted the policeman into Hardwick's home. The
policeman witnessed the commission of the crime (oral sex) through a bedroom door that was slightly ajar. Charges were brought as a result of the
arrest and, after a hearing in the Municipal Court of Atlanta, Hardwick
was bound over to the Superior Court. Hardwick consulted a local ACLU
attorney. At that point the district attorney's office decided not to prosecute
the case further. Hardwick, with the help of the ACLU, decided to bring
suit in federal court asking for a declaratory judgment that the Georgia
statute criminalizing sodomy was unconstitutional.[13]

The time seemed ripe for a constitutional challenge, despite the Supreme
Court's 1976 summary affirmance of the early gay rights challenge to the
Virginia sodomy statute. A number of courts had been willing to avoid that
summary ruling by explaining that the plaintiffs in that challenge, not having been arrested for violating the statute, probably did not have sufficient
"standing" to bring the case. The Supreme Court had, in the 1970s, begun
to narrow its view of appropriate plaintiffs in cases that challenged the constitutionality of statutes. In order to challenge the constitutionality of a
statute, a plaintiff must suffer more than an abstract threat of harm from
the statute. The threat must be more concrete, thereby ensuring that this
plaintiff has a real grievance and is in a sufficiently adversarial position to
make the best factual and legal arguments against the statute. The Supreme
Court may well have summarily affirmed in *Doe* because it did not view the
plaintiffs as sufficiently threatened by the statute. Since the lower court in
that case had upheld the Virginia statute, the summary affirmance by the

Supreme Court was really no more than a decision that maintained the status quo.

Michael Hardwick clearly had standing to challenge the statute under the recently tightened Supreme Court interpretations of standing doctrine. He had been arrested in his own home and, although the charges were dropped, he certainly had reason to fear additional arrests in the future. The facts of the case made it an attractive one for challenging the Georgia statute.

In addition, the Supreme Court had not made any clear statements about where it stood on the question of constitutional protections for same-sex private intimacy. In a 1977 opinion dealing with reproductive freedom issues, *Carey v. Population Services*, the Court had said *in dicta:*

> The Court has not definitively answered the difficult question whether and to what extent the Constitution prohibits state statutes regulating [private consensual sexual] behavior among adults, . . . and we do not purport to answer that question now.[14]

Given this statement, one could view the 1973 affirmance in *Doe,* since it predated *Carey,* as saying nothing about this "difficult question."

To strengthen their constitutional claim, the ACLU lawyers representing Hardwick, primarily Kathy Wilde, decided to include a married couple as additional plaintiffs in the case. The Georgia statute, by its language, applied equally to same-sex and opposite-sex couples, and it included no exemption for married couples. Thus, John and Mary Doe joined the challenge and asserted in their portion of the petition that they wished to engage in sexual activity that was criminalized by the Georgia statute but were "deterred" from doing so by the statute.

Citing *Doe v. Commonwealth's Attorney,* the district court dismissed Hardwick's claim on a preliminary motion. There was no trial. The Court of Appeals for the Eleventh Circuit reversed as to Hardwick, explaining that the Supreme Court had stated that it had not yet answered the "difficult question" posed by Hardwick's claim. The Court of Appeals upheld the dismissal of the claim of the married couple, explaining that the threat of arrest to them was not particularly imminent, and, thus, they did not have sufficient standing to join the challenge. As for Hardwick, the court ruled that the "Georgia sodomy statute infringes upon the fundamental constitutional rights of Michael Hardwick. On remand, the State must demonstrate a compelling interest in restricting this right and must show that the sodomy statute is a properly restrained method of safeguarding its interests."[15]

On July 25, 1985, Georgia attorney general Michael Bowers petitioned the Supreme Court for discretionary review of the decision and the writ of certiorari was granted on November 4, 1985.[16]

Note that *Bowers v. Hardwick* did not present an opportunity for lesbian and gay activist lawyers to debate whether the time was ripe to go to the Supreme Court or not. That decision was made by the attorney general for the state of Georgia who was appealing his loss in the case. The Court's decision to grant certiorari and thus hear the appeal was met with mixed reactions by the lesbian and gay legal community. The Eleventh Circuit, after all, had ruled in favor of gay rights. Why should the Supreme Court grant certiorari in this case? Was the Court considering a possible reversal of the progay holding? Or did a majority of the Court feel that the time to speak out positively in a gay rights case had arrived?

Lesbian and gay lawyers across the country began counting the votes on the Court as soon as the decision to take the case was announced. Justices Brennan and Marshall were the only certain votes. Blackmun was a good possibility and so was Stevens. All four of these justices had voted in favor of gay rights in the *National Gay Task Force* case in 1985. Four justices had voted against gay rights in that case. They were Chief Justice Burger and Justices Rehnquist, White, and O'Connor. Justice Powell had not participated in the *NGTF* case. He was the unknown and his was the needed vote to turn the probable plurality of four into a majority of five. The outcome was not clear, and so gay and lesbian civil rights lawyers had cause to be worried.

Justice Marshall's papers, released in 1993, reveal the uncertainty of the situation. For the Court to grant certiorari, four justices had to vote in favor of hearing the case. On the first round of voting only Justices White and Burger cast votes in favor of granting review. Marshall and Brennan, who both supported gay rights, were tempted to add their names, but they could not be certain that the ultimate vote on the merits would produce the five votes needed to affirm the court below. Some indication existed that Justice Powell might side with Brennan and Marshall, but Brennan, overcautious, decided not to vote in favor of reviewing the case. Then, Rehnquist signed on in favor of granting review, and Marshall decided to add his name as the required fourth vote, fully realizing that his vote created a risk that the case would be reversed.

Michael Hardwick had been represented by Kathy Wilde, an ACLU affiliate attorney in Atlanta in the litigation below. Litigation strategy and the development of arguments in the case quickly became an agenda item for the Ad Hoc Task Force to Challenge Sodomy Laws and Wilde readily agreed to consult with the task force regarding the case. National meetings of gay rights litigators included Wilde and attorneys from other ACLU affiliates in states possessing sodomy statutes.[17] The task force debated the question of who should represent Hardwick before the Supreme Court. Kathy Wilde had represented him successfully before the Eleventh Circuit panel and some task force members supported her continuation in the role as lead counsel. Others questioned whether it would be appropriate to have anyone other than a gay man represent Hardwick before the Supreme Court. After all, Thurgood Marshall had argued *Brown*. Sarah Weddington had argued *Roe*. Ruth Bader Ginsburg had argued a string of sex equality cases. Michael Hardwick was a gay man who had been arrested in his bedroom and the attorney general of Georgia was arguing that so long as the sodomy law was on the books he would continue to enter the bedrooms of gay and lesbian Georgians. Some lawyers in the movement were convinced that the justices of the Supreme Court would understand the threat to privacy better if the person standing in front of them were someone who was actively threatened by the sodomy statute.

Ultimately the task force focused on Harvard law professor Laurence Tribe as a possible advocate on behalf of Hardwick. Although he might not have been able to provide the desired gay perspective, his experience in arguing before the Supreme Court was impressive. Indeed, in past cases the justices had sided with his arguments enough to earn him the nickname of "Tenth Justice." When contacted, Tribe readily agreed to represent Hardwick. Tribe and a young Harvard colleague, Kathleen Sullivan, later to become the dean at Stanford Law School, coauthored the brief in support of Hardwick. Tribe agreed to make the oral argument. Kathy Wilde, the ACLU lawyer who had represented Hardwick from the beginning, graciously agreed to turn the case over to the Harvard team, who now became active members in the task force.

Hardwick was not the only sodomy challenge in the court system at that time, nor the only case on the agenda of the Ad Hoc Task Force. Another active participant in the think tank was Jim Barber, a Dallas attorney representing Donald Baker in a suit that challenged the Texas sodomy statute. Although certiorari was granted in *Hardwick* first, the Dallas case had been in the court system longer.

Two weeks after Michael Hardwick was arrested in August of 1982 and well before he filed suit in Georgia,[18] a federal district judge in Dallas,

Texas, had ruled that the Texas sodomy statute was unconstitutional both under a right to privacy analysis and under equal protection. The Texas case, *Baker v. Wade*,[19] unlike *Hardwick*, was decided after a full trial.

Baker v. Wade followed a tortuous route to the Supreme Court; thus, *Hardwick* landed there first. Donald Baker, the individual plaintiff in the case, had filed suit against the district attorney of Dallas County, Henry Wade (the same Wade of *Roe v. Wade* fame) and Lee Holt, Dallas city attorney. To assure that any affirmative ruling would be binding against all law enforcement officers in the state of Texas, the class of defendants included all city, county, and district attorneys in the state of Texas. The state of Texas intervened via its attorney general—all city, county, and district attorneys were notified of their right to intervene and not one of them elected to do so. Thus, Wade and Holt were certified as the class representatives for the defendant class. When the court ruled in favor of the plaintiff on his constitutional claims, all then-existing members of the class of defendants were given notice of the court's ruling. Danny Hill, a newly elected district attorney of Potter County, then filed a motion to intervene. Initially the attorney general filed notice of appeal, but then withdrew the notice. District Attorney Hill then asked the Texas Supreme Court to require the attorney general to file an appeal. The Texas Supreme Court refused. Hill then pursued a direct appeal on his own, asking the Fifth Circuit to reverse the pro-gay decision of the district court. The three-judge panel of the Fifth Circuit held that Hill was not a proper representative of the class and, thus, had no legal standing to challenge the lower court opinion. Upon reconsideration en banc, the full bench of Fifth Circuit judges, in an 9 to 7 vote, ruled that Hill was a proper party and, that, on the authority of *Doe v. Commonwealth's Attorney*, the district court must be reversed. Baker requested a rehearing. After the rehearing was denied, Baker filed a cert peitition with the Supreme Court, a petition that reached the court while *Bowers v. Hardwick* was under consideration.[20]

In discussing litigation strategy, the Ad Hoc Task Force considered whether the two cases, *Hardwick* and *Baker*, should be consolidated at the Supreme Court level. The lawyers focused on the legal theories in the two cases. The Virginia sodomy statute, which had been at issue in the 1976 Supreme Court affirmance of *Doe v. Commonwealth's Attorney*, prohibited both homosexual and heterosexual sexual conduct. The Georgia statute in *Hardwick* similarly covered heterosexual and homosexual sodomy. By contrast, the Texas statute applied only to "deviate sexual intercourse" between persons of the same sex. Thus, only the Texas case squarely presented an equal protection argument that gay people were treated differently from nongay people. Because the cases raised different constitutional issues, only privacy in *Hardwick* and both privacy and equal protection in *Baker,* the litigators thought that keeping the arguments separate was preferable.

The Tribe and Sullivan brief in the *Hardwick* case focused narrowly on the right of privacy. The crucial fact underlying Hardwick's claim was that he had been arrested in the privacy of his own bedroom. The brief argued that this case was not about sodomy or even about homosexuality. Instead, the case was about the right of every American, including gay and lesbian Americans, to feel safe and secure in the privacy of their own bedrooms.

Those who were concerned that the justices might not understand that gay men and lesbians are Americans just like everyone else felt that there needed to be a progay brief filed in the case, a brief that would put a personal face on the lives of the many gay men and women whose lives are destroyed by the continued existence of sodomy statutes. Mary Dunlap authored such a brief on behalf of amicus, the Lesbian Rights Project.

AIDS was of recent origin. The threat of AIDS had not been part of the state of Georgia's justification for the sodomy statute, nor had it been addressed in the arguments below. But everyone knew that the AIDS issue was lurking behind any claim of constitutional protection for gay male sex. The American Public Health Association was solicited to write an amicus brief to address the AIDS issue. The brief argued that the continued criminalization of sodomy was the worst policy decision for purposes of containing the AIDS epidemic. Specifically, the association argued that individuals threatened by criminal laws are less likely to be honest about their sex practices and less likely to learn what they need to learn to protect themselves and others.

Oral arguments in the case occurred on March 31, 1986. In a packed Supreme Court chamber, Assistant Attorney General Michael E. Hobbs began his argument on behalf of the state of Georgia. In his opening statement, he identified the issue before the court as whether or not the Constitution protected a fundamental right to engage in "consensual private homosexual sodomy." Twenty-two minutes later Professor Tribe opened his argument on behalf of Michael Hardwick. Tribe identified the main issue in the case as one about the limits of governmental power. Both attorneys aimed many of their remarks toward Justice Powell. In *Moore v. City of East Cleveland,* an earlier fundamental liberty/privacy case, Powell had expressed concern about the need to limit the concept of fundamental liberty. Without limits, he feared the Court would be enticed to recognize new fundamental rights in each privacy case brought before the Court. Hobbs, for the State of Georgia, argued that history and tradition were the limiting principles, just as Powell had suggested should be the case in *Moore*. Absent a tradition of homosexual sodomy, the Court had no basis for finding that homosexual sodomy was protected under the Liberty Clause of the Fourteenth Amendment. Tribe offered more specific limits. First, he argued that Michael Hardwick's conduct occurred in the home. Thus the place of the conduct was one limiting factor. Second, the conduct at issue was an expression of personal intimacy, freely chosen, and harmful to no one. Then, to solidify the connection to history and tradition, Tribe explained that tradition included a strong expectation of privacy in the home and that this country had historically honored the principle of "autonomous personal control over intimacy."

Tribe also argued that the Georgia statute flunked both strict scrutiny and rational basis review. The state of Georgia, he claimed, had offered no better explanation for its criminal statute than that the people of Georgia thought the conduct was wrong. Several justices suggested that a law prohibiting homosexual sodomy, like other laws prohibiting nonmarital sex, might be justified as part of a state policy to encourage marriage. Even so, Tribe responded, the state must show that the means it has chosen to encourage marriage is at least rational. Banning this particular form of sexual conduct (i.e., oral and anal sex) no matter who engages in the conduct seems far removed from the goal of encouraging marriage.

Only Justice O'Connor raised the possible justification of protecting public health. Tribe, citing the American Public Health Association brief, responded that even though public health is a compelling state interest, the means chosen by the state of Georgia (i.e., banning all oral and anal sex) is not tailored to accomplish that purpose. At the very least, the state ought to consider the effect that its sodomy statute has on public health. Since there had been no trial, there was no record, and no evidence that Georgia had ever considered the effect on public health.

In rebuttal, Hobbs identified none of the purposes suggested by the justices as Georgia's purpose. Instead, he said, the purpose of the state of Georgia in criminalizing homosexual sodomy was to maintain a decent and moral society.

On June 30, 1986, at the very end of the term, the Court handed down its decision. By a vote of 5 to 4, the Court announced that the constitutional right to privacy did not extend to private consensual homosexual sodomy. The risk that Justice Marshall had taken in voting in favor of review had been realized. Justice Powell, the necessary fifth vote for gay rights, had sided with those who voted against Hardwick. Years later, after he had retired, Justice Powell would publicly recant and admit that his vote in that case was a mistake.

Bowers v. Hardwick produced three specific legal holdings. To understand the opinion, one must consider all three holdings. They are: (1) homosexual sodomy is not a fundamental right, (2) a state legislature need only show a rational basis for criminalizing homosexual sodomy, and (3) the promotion of public morality is a sufficiently rational basis to justify the criminalization of homosexual sodomy. Justice White, writing for the Court, explained the decision by saying: "Proscriptions against that conduct have ancient roots."[21] Old law is good law. The gay community was stunned.

THE AFTERMATH

Tom Stoddard called the decision the gay community's *Dred Scott* decision. Abby Rubenfeld pronounced it the equivalent of *Plessy v. Ferguson*. To make ourselves feel better, some of us in the lesbian and gay legal community ignored the White opinion that placed same-sex intimate expression in the same category as drug use and incest and focused instead on the Blackmun dissent that recognized our humanity. But in the end, nothing could erase the feeling of betrayal. The Supreme Court of the United States had pronounced that gay people had no constitutionally protected right of privacy even in their own bedrooms.

Was the decision disastrous? Several years afterward, at a conference at the University of Southern California Law School, Judge Richard Posner of the Seventh Circuit suggested what the Supreme Court decided did not really matter. The Supreme Court, after all, did not cause social change. Public discourse did that. Win or lose, *Bowers v. Hardwick* had made gay rights a visible cause in the United States. Americans who had never discussed sodomy or thought about the regulation of private sexual conduct were suddenly faced with an event that caused them to enter the public discourse.

Shortly after the opinion was handed down, Michael Hardwick, his ACLU lawyer, Kathy Wilde, and Lambda executive director Tom Stoddard appeared on the Phil Donahue show. Donahue posed the question that should have been addressed by the Supreme Court: does the state of Georgia have the right to enter your bedroom, even if you are married, to determine whether your sexual practices are in violation of state law? The Georgia statute made no distinction between single persons, married persons, gay persons, and nongay persons. Assistant Attorney General Hobbs, in response to questions from the bench, had admitted that the state of Georgia could not constitutionally apply the statute to married couples who engaged in sodomy in the privacy of their own bedrooms. He was immediately asked to explain why a married couple might have a fundamental right to engage in sodomy, even though under his "tradition as a limiting factor" principle, marital sodomy did not qualify as a tradition. His reply was that "marital privacy rights" trumped. Since the *Hardwick* decision did not mention marital sodomy, the ultimate effect of the ruling was to uphold the entire Georgia statute, which on its face prohibited all acts of sodomy, even when the participants were married.

On the Donahue show, Michael Hardwick, who had never appeared on national television and who had only appeared before the Supreme Court through his lawyers, told the American public his version of the story. He presented himself as a man who cared enough about his privacy that he was reluctant to litigate the case. He was personable and easy to identify with. He told us about his mother and his mother's concerns for his safety because of the risks of gaybashing. Most of the audience expressed outrage at what had happened to him and at the Georgia sodomy statute. In some ways, Judge Posner was right. The movement got an amazing dose of positive, supportive publicity after the loss in *Hardwick*.

Lambda legal director Abby Rubenfeld also questioned whether the decision was truly disastrous. Yes, she had dubbed it our *Plessy v. Ferguson*. We would now have to begin our fight for an ultimate reversal of *Bowers v. Hardwick*, just as the NAACP had fought to overturn the doctrine of "separate but equal." At the same time, as she accurately pointed out, we had not asked for something that we already enjoyed. We were trying to move forward, to obtain a right that had not yet been extended to us. And we lost. In one view, then, we simply did not get what we asked for. Nothing was any worse. And if Posner's view of the matter was correct, the movement was actually better off because of the publicity surrounding the decision.

Time would tell. The decision certainly had some immediate negative effects. Before *Hardwick*, some lower courts had been willing to rule that the criminalization of sodomy violated the federal constitution. Now, no court could rule that way again because the U.S. Supreme Court had spoken.

Hardwick also had repercussions with respect to arguments that did not directly involve challenges to sodomy statutes. The very reason the movement had focused on sodomy challenges had been with the hope of making it easier to win arguments in other arenas such as employment discrimination and family law. But with the constitutional validity of sodomy statutes firmly established, arguments for equal rights in the areas of employment, housing, and child custody became more difficult to win.

Notes

1. Lambda and the New York Civil Liberties Union filed a joint brief when the case was before the New York Court of Appeals. See *Lambda News* (April 1977).

2. Penal Law §§ 130.00, subd. 2, 130.38.

3. People v. Rice, 363 N.Y.S.2d 484 (N.Y. Dist. Ct. 1975).

4. 383 N.Y.S.2d 798 (N.Y. App. Term 1976).

5. People v. Rice, 363 N.E.2d 1371 (N.Y. 1977).

6. *See* People v. Onofre, supra, (a Lambda case,) and New York v. Uplinger, which was argued before the Supreme Court by Lambda board member Bill Gardner. ACLU amicus brief was filed in Uplinger. New York v. Uplinger, 467 U.S. 246 (1984).

7. 415 N.E.2d 936 (N.Y. 1980).

8. Lambda Update at 3 (February 1984).

9. Ibid.

10. In 1985–1986, before the Supreme Court handed down its decision in Bowers v. Hardwick, Rubenfeld addressed various lesbian groups across the country on the importance of the *Hardwick* case to lesbians. I was present at a speech she gave in Austin, Texas, in the spring of 1986.

11. State v. Livermore, 155 N.W.2d 711 (Mich. App. 1967) (Livermore was sentenced to a term of one and a half to five years for this crime).

12. 729 F.2d 1270 (10th Cir. 1984).

13. The Georgia statute provided, in part:

(a) A person commits the offense of sodomy when he performs or submits to any sexual act involving the sex organs of one person and the mouth or anus of another. . . .

(b) A person convicted of the offense of sodomy shall be punished by imprisonment for not less than one nor more than 20 years. . . .

Section 16-6-2, Georgia Code.

14. Carey v. Population Services, 431 U.S. 678 at 688, n.5 (1977).

15. Hardwick v. Bowers, 760 F.2d 1202 at 1211 (11th Cir. 1985).

16. Brief of Petitioner, Michael J. Bowers, Bowers v. Hardwick, 478 U.S. 186 (1986).

17. In particular, Louisiana, Arkansas, and Missouri. *See* Lambda Update at 5 (Winter 1985).

18. Hardwick was arrested on August 3, 1982. *See* "Statement of the Case" in Brief for Respondent, Bowers v. Hardwick. Baker v. Wade was decided by the district court on August 17, 1982.

19. 553 F.Supp. 1121 (N.D. Tex. 1982).

20. See Baker v. Wade, 563 F.Supp. 1121 (N.D. Tex. 1982), *rev'd769* F.2d 289 (5th Cir. 1985) *(en banc); cert. denied* 478 U.S. 1022 (1986).

21. 478 U.S. 186 at 192.

7

Public Sphere Rights Post–
Bowers v. Hardwick

Justice White's opinion in *Bowers v. Hardwick* held that no constitutionally protected right to engage in homosexual sodomy existed. The entire argument in the case had centered on the question of whether Michael Hardwick's privacy rights were violated by a statute that authorized the Atlanta police to enter his home and arrest him, provided of course reasonable cause existed for believing he might be committing the crime of sodomy. The state of Georgia had argued in its brief that the state intended to continue enforcing the law even if it meant entering private bedrooms. At oral argument, Assistant Attorney General Hobbs stressed over and over again that the antisodomy law was important to the people of Georgia and that it would continue to be enforced. The clear message of the *Hardwick* decision was that gay men and lesbians had no reason to feel secure in the privacy of their homes. The police determine reasonable cause; thus, would one's identity as a gay person, coupled with the fact that one lived with a partner, be sufficient to warrant intrusion by law enforcement personnel? After all, the cohabitation of a white man and a black woman had been sufficient in Virginia to warrant the local sheriff's intrusion into the bedroom of Richard and Mildred Loving. Or perhaps the police could keep an eye on gay bars and follow same-sex couples to their homes and, after a sufficient amount of time, presume the crime was being committed.

Absolutely no evidence has been found that sodomy arrests escalated after the *Hardwick* decision, and no reason exists to believe that police officers have increased their surveillance of gay bars looking for potential sodomites. As this lack of interest by law enforcement suggests, the real battle in *Hardwick* was not over privacy and protection from arrest; the real battle was over the public consequences of being labeled a sodomite or a homosexual.

Discrimination was at the core of the *Hardwick* decision. Although the case was not litigated as an equal protection case and, on its face, said nothing about discrimination on the basis of sexual orientation, lesbian and gay rights litigators immediately understood the case's reach. A column by Ruth Marcus in the *Washington Post* just two days after the decision was announced captured the core of the problem. Her headline announced: "Sodomy Ruling's Implications Extend Far Beyond Bedroom."

Bert Neuborne, professor of law at New York University and longtime ACLU leader, explained that the decision was unlikely to cause "midnight raids into the bedroom." Rather, the decision would be "read as a signal by people who believe that homosexuality is sinful" and they will "use the decision as a justification for making life as hard as possible for homosexuals." Lambda's Tom Stoddard said:

> [Sodomy] statutes are the centerpiece of discrimination. They have been used to justify denial of parental rights, of employment, of apartments. That is why this case has a special sting for gay people.

Nan Hunter, director of the ACLU's Lesbian and Gay Rights Project, presciently predicted what lay ahead when she said that the court's decision "will not doom every gay-rights case in every context in the future. . . [but will provide] an excuse for the courts to invoke" when they side with antigay employers or when they wish to deny gay parents custody of their children.

The Ad Hoc Task Force to Challenge Sodomy Laws understood that the challenge to sodomy laws must continue to protect gay people from discrimination. After *Hardwick,* the task force met and adopted new strategies for the continuing battle against sodomy laws, a battle that would focus on legislative repeal and state constitutional challenges.

Although the *Hardwick* decision clearly necessitated a change in strategy toward sodomy law challenges, the decision also created havoc in equal protection challenges to antigay discrimination. Gay and lesbian civil rights lawyers, surprised by the loss in *Hardwick,* spent some time regrouping after the decision. The publicity that surrounded the decision kept many of the spokespeople for the lesbian and gay civil rights community focused on the details of the *Hardwick* decision. What the community needed, however, was an impetus for focusing on the equal protection cases to come.

Within a year of *Hardwick,* the Ad Hoc Task Force to Challenge Sodomy Laws had been transformed into the National Lesbian and Gay Civil Rights Roundtable. Three times a year lawyers from the major lesbian and gay civil rights organizations met to discuss litigation in process. They were joined at times by attorneys from private practice who were also lititigating gay rights cases. Lambda Legal Defense and Education Fund hosted the meetings, but provided no travel support. The Roundtable would grow in future years to serve as an important brainstorming session for a wide range of gay rights lawyers and to offer national leadership and coordination. But in 1987 the Roundtable's ability to reach private attorneys involved in gay rights litigation around the country was hampered by the underfunding and understaffing of the public interest groups who sponsored the Roundtable.

At the time *Hardwick* was handed down, Lambda's docket included about twenty-five cases. The Lambda legal department consisted of the legal director, Abby Rubenfeld, and one staff attorney, Paula Ettelbrick. Cooperating attorneys from private practice provided much of the needed legal work on these cases and some of the cases were joint efforts with other gay rights organizations. However, in 1986 not a single Lambda case involved a pure equal protection claim. The docket included AIDS cases, family law cases, gay student organization cases, cases that raised First Amendment speech and religion issues, and discrimination cases that relied on state or local gay rights laws banning discrimination on the basis of sexual orientation.

Although movement lawyers certainly thought about the connection between *Hardwick* and equal protection claims, their own dockets did not immediately force them to tease out the legal arguments that would be needed to prevent the privacy/due process holding in *Hardwick* from affecting discrimination claims. By the time these organization lawyers became fully engaged with equal protection claims against discriminatory government employers, they would have to grapple with negative precedent produced in litigation over which they had had very little control.

HARDWICK'S EFFECT ON
EQUAL PROTECTION CLAIMS:
ONE COURT MAKES THE CONNECTION
BETWEEN SODOMY LAWS AND DISCRIMINATION

Equal protection claims are tested either under heightened scrutiny, as in the case of suspect classifications such as race, or under low-level scrutiny.

Just as feminist litigators in the 1970s had argued that sex, like race, was entitled to heightened scrutiny, lesbian and gay civil rights litigators in the 1980s pressed the argument that gay people were also entitled to heightened scrutiny. Relying on *Carolene Product*'s footnote four, litigators argued that gay people constituted a discrete and insular minority that had suffered discrimination for centuries. A growing body of scholarship in the law journals pressed this argument,[1] and litigators incorporated these arguments into their briefs.

Absent a finding that classifications based on sexual orientation were suspect, lawyers had to convince the courts that discrimination on the basis of sexual orientation was irrational. Nonsuspect classifications were accorded low-level scrutiny, but even low-level scrutiny required some justification for the government's decision to discriminate. All government decisions must, at a minimum, satisfy the principle of rationality.

When courts applied low-level scrutiny to equal protection claims, they rarely ruled in favor of the plaintiff. In 1985, however, the Supreme Court added teeth to its low-level scrutiny approach when it reversed a city's denial of a "permit for the operation of a group home for the mentally retarded." In *City of Cleburne*,[2] the Court rejected the argument that the mentally retarded should be classified as a suspect group and, thus, be entitled to strict scrutiny. Nonetheless, applying only low-level scrutiny, the Court found that the City of Cleburne had acted unconstitutionally. Based on the facts of the case, the Court concluded that the city had made its decision on the basis of irrational prejudice.

Four years before *Hardwick* reached the Supreme Court and shortly after she had graduated from law school, Margaret Padula applied for a position with the FBI. She took the tests required to qualify for the position and ranked in the top 25 percent. After a routine investigation revealed that she was a lesbian, a fact that she confirmed when asked, her application was denied. Believing that the FBI had improperly considered her sexual orientation in making its decision, she decided to sue. Judge Gerhard Gesell, the district court judge who heard the case, granted summary judgment to the FBI on November 15, 1985. Padula appealed. She was represented by two Washington, D.C., lawyers from private practice, who served as cooperating attorneys with the ACLU.

The lawyers crafted the legal theories in the case before the *Hardwick* decision was announced by the Supreme Court. The original theories included privacy and due process claims, both of which were abandoned on appeal, presumably in response to *Hardwick.* The remaining legal theory was equal protection, which required the lawyers to identify the class of persons targeted by the FBI's discriminatory policy. The FBI claimed that it did not discriminate against anyone on the basis of sexual orientation alone, but rather was concerned with an applicant's conduct. The FBI had been drawing this line between status and conduct for more than five years in response to queries from law school placement offices. Understanding that law schools prohibited prospective employers from interviewing their students if the employer discriminated on the basis of race, sex, color, national origin, or sexual orientation, the FBI issued statements that it did not discriminate on the basis of orientation, but only on the basis of conduct.

Padula's lawyers could have argued that since the FBI had no evidence of sexual conduct of any sort in this case, the agency's decision, at least as to Padula, was based solely on her status as a lesbian. Instead they argued that "homosexual status is accorded to people who engage in homosexual conduct, and people who engage in homosexual conduct are accorded homosexual status." This conflation of status and conduct is accurate in most cases, although no one bothered to point out that "homosexual conduct" does not necessarily mean "homosexual sodomy," which had been the focus in the *Hardwick* case.

Intent on making the argument that classifications based on sexual orientation should be strictly scrutinized, the Padula lawyers neglected to make the rational basis argument, based on *Cleburne,* that bias against a group was never a legitimate reason for discriminating against members of the group. In addressing the suspect class argument, the Court of Appeals for the District of Columbia ruled definitively that *Bowers v. Hardwick* prevented gay men and lesbians from claiming heightened scrutiny as a suspect class.[3] As the court explained: "It would be quite anomalous, on its face, to declare status defined by conduct that states may constitutionally criminalize as deserving of strict scrutiny under the equal protection clause."[4] Or, more precisely, "there can hardly be more palpable discrimination against a class than making the conduct that defines the class criminal."[5] Under rational basis due process review in *Hardwick,* public morality had been sufficient to justify a criminal statute that carried with it the possibility of twenty years in prison. The *Padula* court thus concluded that the same rational basis justification ought to be sufficient to support the lesser penalty of job loss.

RESPONDING TO *PADULA:* THE BIRTH OF THE STATUS VERSUS CONDUCT DISTINCTION

The *Padula* decision confirmed every fear that gay rights litigators had had when *Hardwick* was handed down. From now on, *Hardwick* and its public morality rationale could be used to justify any discrimination against gay people. If carried to its logical conclusion, the *Padula* argument would treat all gay people as criminals whether they were or not.

Yet, to be gay or lesbian had never been illegal. Furthermore, earlier Supreme Court decisions had clearly established the principle that to criminalize one's status was unconstitutional. Thus, one cannot be arrested because one is a drug addict or an alcoholic, although one can be arrested for using illegal drugs or for violating public drunkenness statutes. Similarly, no one can be arrested for merely *being* gay. Because the Supreme Court had so clearly distinguished between status and conduct in past decisions, lesbian and gay legal theorists and activists began to consider this bifurcation an attractive means to limit the effect of the *Hardwick* decision.

Another possible way to limit the effect of *Hardwick* in the run-of-the-mill discrimination case would have been to distinguish the sexual conduct (i.e., sodomy) at issue in *Hardwick* from whatever sexual acts the plaintiff in a discrimination case might admit to having committed. For example, a plaintiff might admit to sexual conduct that did not constitute sodomy. Holding hands, kissing, even genital stimulation by hand all fall short of the definition of sodomy in most states.[6] If the lesbian plaintiff has not actually engaged in criminal sodomy, then *Hardwick* should provide no justification for the discrimination levied against her. This form of argument had its attractions. Lesbian and gay plaintiffs could fight the "sodomite" label, distance themselves from *Hardwick,* and educate the judiciary about gay sexual intimacy. If all went well, sexually active lesbian and gay plaintiffs could admit the sexual nature of their relationships and find constitutional protection under the Equal Protection Clause. Eventually, courts would realize that all expressions of sexual intimacy other than sodomy had been effectively protected under the resulting equal protection rulings. These equal protection rulings, when viewed as a whole, would produce differential treatment between gay "nonsodomites" and gay "sodomites." Such differential treatment should be sufficient to set up an equal protection challenge on behalf of the "sodomites," whom equal protection had failed to protect. Presumably at that point, a now wiser Court would overrule its decision in *Bowers v. Hardwick.*

Of course, the risk in such a strategy was that courts would not be sufficiently enlightened to rule in favor of gay people who openly admitted to sexual intimacy with members of their own sex, even when that intimacy fell short of criminal sodomy. If that were the case, then individual clients would lose their cases and eventually the courts would have developed an equal protection jurisprudence that endorsed discrimination against all people who engaged in any sort of same-sex sexual intimacy. Many public interest lawyers, feeling that they should be cautious after the loss in *Hardwick*, were unwilling to have their clients admit to any sexual conduct if such admissions could be avoided. Thus, distinguishing between conduct and status became the preferred argument in equal protection cases. The federal government, as employer, aided gay rights litigators in this bifurcation project. The FBI stated quite clearly that it was only concerned about conduct, not status. Later the military would follow this example and similarly claim that gay people themselves should not be denied jobs in the military solely on the basis of their status. But if gay service members engaged in homosexual conduct, broadly defined, they would be terminated.

Shortly after *Padula*, other cases rejected the argument that sexual orientation should be considered a suspect or quasi-suspect classification. The Court of Appeals for the Tenth Circuit had held in a pre-*Hardwick* opinion that heightened scrutiny was inappropriate for cases involving sexual orientation discrimination.[7] It reaffirmed that position, citing *Hardwick*, in 1992.[8] And, in 1989, the Court of Appeals for the Seventh Circuit rejected Miriam Ben Shalom's claim that lesbians were a suspect class, reversing the district court opinion in which the judge had ruled in favor of Ben Shalom. In these cases, the courts rejected the argument for heightened scrutiny because they were unwilling to distinguish between status (i.e., sexual orientation) and conduct (i.e., sodomy).

Despite these losses, lesbian and gay rights litigators held out hope that more progressive judges elsewhere in the country would accept their equal protection argument that sexual orientation, like race and gender, was a suspect or quasi-suspect classification. In California, their hopes were met in a number of positive decisions, none of which survived appellate review. Federal appellate decisions are issued by panels consisting of three judges. The makeup of the panel in any given case is random. More than in any other civil rights movement, lesbian and gay activists have been apprehensive about the judges assigned to hear their cases. The successful litigation in the 1960s before the D.C. Circuit Court of Appeals forcing the CSC to abandon its antigay employment policies can be explained in part by the fact that some of the early cases went before panels that included Judges Skelly Wright, David Bazelon, and Carl McGowan. In addition, the early challenges against the military brought by Matlovich and Berg were aided by the fact that they began before district court Judge Gerhard Gesell, a fearless trial judge who gave the military no more slack than he would have given any other litigant in his courtroom.

In the 1980s post-*Hardwick* period, gay litigators bringing cases in California felt positive about their cases if they were litigating before Judge Thelton Henderson, an African American judge on the federal district court for the Northern District. In 1987, in a case brought by a group called High Tech Gays against the Department of Defense over the department's antigay policy with regard to security clearances, Judge Henderson accepted the analogy between sexual orientation and other suspect classes. He ruled that sexual orientation, like gender, was a "quasi-suspect" class.

Litigators remained concerned, however, about which judges they might draw on appeal before the Ninth Circuit. One year later, while *High Tech Gays* was on appeal, gay rights litigators in a gay military case convinced an appellate panel of the Ninth Circuit that sexual orientation was a suspect classification entitled to strict scrutiny. Ruling in favor of Perry Watkins, a black gay soldier who had enlisted in 1967, fully disclosing his homosexuality, and had reinlisted three times since then and earned an exemplary service record, two judges, William A. Norris and William C. Canby Jr., held that sexual orientation, like race, was a suspect classification. Both judges had been appointed by President Carter in 1980 and both had served in the military, Norris with the navy and Canby with the air force. Canby had also served with the Peace Corps in Ethiopia and Uganda.

The third judge on the panel in the *Watkins* case was Judge Stephen R. Reinhardt, often described as one of the last crusading liberals on the bench. Reinhardt, whose ancestors escaped Nazi Germany, is the son of Gottfried Reinhardt, who directed and produced a number of World War II films including *Town Without Pity* and *Betrayed*. In response to questions about his zealous efforts to protect individual rights, Judge Reinhardt recently explained that "the horrors of the Nazi era helped shape his unshakable conviction about the need for vigilance in upholding basic human rights."[9] Reinhardt, who wins high praise from his more conservative colleagues on the Ninth Circuit despite his reputation as the judge most reversed by the Rehnquist Court, was also appointed by Carter in 1980. He is married to Ramona Ripston, who has been the Executive Director of the Southern California ACLU since 1972. Judge Reinhardt also served in the air force. To the surprise of many, Reinhardt dissented in *Watkins,* explaining that he felt constrained by the Supreme Court's opinion in *Bowers v. Hardwick,* which he construed to be an opinion authorizing discrimination against gay people on the basis of public morality. Nonetheless, he added his personal views about the *Hardwick* opinion:

> . . . as I understand our Constitution, a state simply has no business treating any group of persons as the State of Georgia and other states with sodomy statutes treat homosexuals. In my opinion, invidious discrimination against a group of persons with immutable characteristics can never be justified on the grounds of society's moral disapproval. No lesson regarding the meaning of our Constitution could be more important for us as a nation to learn. I believe that the Supreme Court egregiously misinterpreted the Constitution in *Hardwick.* In my view, *Hardwick* improperly condones official bias and prejudice against homosexuals, and authorizes the criminalization of conduct that is an essential part of the intimate sexual life of our many homosexual citizens, a group that has historically been the victim of unfair and irrational treatment. I believe that history will view *Hardwick* much as it views *Plessy v. Ferguson.* And I am confident that, in the long run, *Hardwick,* like *Plessy,* will be overruled by a wiser and more enlightened Court.

This panel opinion was a high point for lesbian and gay rights litigators. Unfortunately, the opinion did not stand. The Ninth Circuit agreed to rehear the case en banc. A majority of the eleven-judge en banc panel refused to reach the equal protection issue, ruling instead that since the army had known that Watkins was gay when he enlisted, the army was now prevented (or in legal terms, estopped) from claiming that Watkins was ineligible to serve. The effect of this decision was to nullify, rather than reverse, the earlier panel decision holding that gay men and lesbians deserved heightened scrutiny under equal protection doctrine.

Now that the Canby and Norris opinion in *Watkins* had no legal effect, hopes became pinned on the *High Tech Gays* appeal. The litigants in that case, however, drew a more conservative panel of judges, which included two Reagan appointees, Edmund Leavy and Melvin Brunetti. They were joined by Senior District Judge Jesse W. Curtis, sitting by special designation. Curtis was a Kennedy appointment. Four days after the panel handed down the opinion in *High Tech Gays,* he retired from the bench at age eighty-four. The panel unanimously reversed Judge Henderson and held that sexual orientation was neither suspect nor quasi-suspect.[10] Citing the en banc decision in *Watkins* for the proposition that the court had failed to find that sexual orientation was a suspect classification, a finding totally irrelevant to the estoppel holding, the three-judge panel in *High Tech Gays* cited *Hardwick* and said: "because homosexual conduct can . . . be criminalized, homosexuals cannot constitute a suspect or quasi-suspect class entitled to greater than rational basis review for equal protection purposes."[11]

The plaintiffs' lawyers requested a rehearing of the case before an en banc panel. The Ninth Circuit denied the request, with Judges Canby and Norris dissenting from that denial.

To avoid *Hardwick,* lawyers continued to make the conduct/status distinction. Although they won no cases, the argument seemed the best alternative available in equal protection cases. Lesbian and gay civil rights lawyers knew that the distinction was a difficult one to make. Lesbian and gay identity has always been connected to choices about sexual intimacy. To protect the person and not the choice often seemed pointless. But lawyers are ultimately committed to the client in the individual case. Lawyers make legal arguments on behalf of those clients, and they must ethically employ any available legal argument that might produce a victory for the client. The conduct/status distinction was a legal argument capable of producing victory. The argument was especially effective in cases in which the employer admitted to discriminating solely on the basis of status. In the 1980s the military was such an employer.

THE MILITARY CASES

Ironically, discharged gay and lesbian military personnel in the 1980s presented the most ideal "test" cases. Their cases were ideal because, at least until adoption of "don't ask, don't tell" in the 1990s, the military explicitly discriminated solely on the basis of homosexual status. The irony stems from the fact that although these cases present perfect facts for arguing the status/conduct distinction, these facts occur against the most nonideal defendant. The military, because of the doctrine of deference to the military, is never a good target for impact civil rights litigation.

The 1980s Regulations

The years following the *Hardwick* decision witnessed an increase in the litigation challenging the military's gay exclusion policy. Each branch of the service had its own regulations, but they all mirrored the general policy that "homosexuality is incompatible with military service." That policy called for automatic exclusion from the military of any person who met one of three tests: (1) stating that one is homosexual, (2) engaging in a homosexual act, or (3) marrying someone of the same sex.

In 1982, the Department of Defense (DOD) issued a directive to create uniformity among the various branches of the service and to strengthen the military's position in cases that challenged the gay exclusion.[12]

Each branch of the service conformed its regulations on homosexuality to meet the requirements of the DOD directive. The new regulations purported to require discharge only for persons who engaged in homosexual conduct, in particular "homosexual acts." The term "homosexual act" was defined broadly to include any bodily contact "for the purpose of satisfying sexual desires."[13] Such acts might include kissing or holding hands, acts that fall far short of sodomy. Furthermore, the new regulations contained an affirmative defense. Even if one had engaged in homosexual conduct, one could avoid discharge by proving that one was not in fact homosexual. Specifically, a service member would have to meet the following five-prong test: (1) that the conduct was a departure from normal behavior, (2) that the conduct is unlikely to recur, (3) that the conduct did not involve force, coercion, or intimidation, (4) that continued service is in the best interest of the armed forces, and (5) that the service member has no intent or desire to engage in homosexual acts.

Under this five-prong test, commission of the criminal act of homosexual sodomy was not sufficient grounds for discharge unless the act was committed by a gay person. A heterosexual who committed sodomy with a person of the same sex could defend himself by relying on the five-factor test to prove that he was not, in fact, gay.

Thus, despite the claim that the new regulations targeted conduct, they in fact only targeted gay people who engaged in the conduct. The operative distinction in that event is status, not conduct. Here was an employer, the military, with an explicit antigay hiring policy based solely on status. That made the policy a perfect target for attack by lawyers who were trying to litigate around the *Hardwick* decision by bifurcating conduct from status.

A major problem existed, however, in planning a litigation campaign against the military: the doctrine of deference to the military. Despite the rather formidable hurdle created by this doctrine, gay rights lawyers decided to challenge the military policy. One reason for this decision was that the military's intolerance produced a spectacular array of highly qualified men and women who were impressive plaintiffs. The educational benefit of getting their individual stories before the American public was viewed by many as worth the entire litigation effort, whether or not a single case was won. At the same time, enforcement of the policy was literally ruining the lives of real people who had more at stake than just educating the public. These individuals deserved the best legal representation available to help them protect their jobs and their reputations. Cooperating attorneys for Lambda Legal Defense and ACLU affiliates around the country offered to provide the needed legal expertise, and, later, they were joined by the Servicemembers Legal Defense Network.

The military's status-based policy was challenged by a number of service members, including some who announced their sexual orientation publicly and by others who only admitted their sexual orientation in response to questions from the military. Despite pleas from immediate supervisors on behalf of some of the most outstanding officers and enlisted personnel whose continued service was threatened by the antigay rule, the top brass continued to apply the mandatory exclusion rule. One of the most celebrated cases from these days was that of Colonel Margarethe Cammermeyer. Colonel Cammermeyer had entered the Army Student Nurse Corps in 1961. She married in 1966 and became pregnant with the first of her four sons in 1968. At that time, she experienced her first discriminatory rejection from the army based on its then-existing rules requiring pregnant women to resign. She was able to reenlist in 1972 and served until 1986. She then transferred to the Washington State National Guard. She was at that time a well-respected nurse who had obtained a Ph.D. degree and published articles in national journals. She was also a distinguished member of the armed services who had volunteered for duty in Vietnam and who had been awarded the Bronze Star. She became chief nurse of the Washington State National Guard. While she was under consideration for an even more important post, Chief Nurse of the National Guard Bureau, she was forced to submit to a security review in order to obtain a top-secret clearance. In response to a question about her sexual orientation, she admitted that she was a lesbian. She admitted no conduct, and no conduct was ever reported in her case. Solely on the basis of her honest admission that she was a lesbian, the army moved to dismiss her. Dismissal from the army would make her ineligible to serve in the Washington National Guard. She continued to serve as chief nurse in the Washington National Guard, however, while her appeal was under administrative review. Booth Gardner, then the governor of Washington, made a plea in writing to Secretary of Defense Cheney that Cammermeyer be allowed to continue serving the state of Washington. His letter stated: "If Colonel Cammermeyer's discharge becomes final, this would be both a significant loss to the State of Washington and a senseless end to the career of a distinguished, long-time member of the armed services."[14]

Claiming that it no longer had the authority to recognize an exception to its policy, the army dismissed Colonel Cammermeyer in 1992. Cammermeyer filed suit in federal district court in the state of Washington, charging that the army regulations, to the extent they required her discharge for merely stating she was a lesbian, denied her equal protection of the laws. The district court agreed with Cammermeyer and ruled in her favor, applying low-level rational basis review. The opinion by the district court is a paradigm of clarity.

Because the court felt compelled by *Hardwick* to apply low-level scrutiny, the issue before the court was whether there was a rational basis for the military's sexual orientation-based classification. As the court explained: "A discriminatory classification that is based on prejudice or bias is not rational as a matter of law." Cammermeyer had the burden of proving that the military's policy was not rational. The burden of proof was a heavy one, given the principle of deference to the military. If she could prove that the regulations were based on prejudice, then the court would rule in her favor.

The army offered eight justifications for its antigay policy, including the protection of unit cohesion, of the chain of command, and of future recruitment. Lambda lawyer Mary Newcombe, aided by attorneys from several cooperating public interest legal groups, attacked each justification one by one, ultimately proving that the justifications were all based on prejudice. A high point occurred when lawyers asked General Otjen to assume, hypothetically, that no one in the military had any fear or prejudice against gay people, and to assume further that no one morally disapproved of the homosexual lifestyle. If that were the case, asked the lawyers, "would there be any problem with unit cohesion in the military as a result of permitting open homosexuals to serve?" Otjen admitted, that if these assumptions were true, if no one felt prejudice against gay people, then "there would be no problem with unit cohesion."[15] The charge that the DOD's exclusionary policy was based on prejudice was further supported by the comments of another defense witness, former assistant secretary of defense Dorn. Dorn testified that "[a]s with the racial desegregation of the military, much of the resistance to gays is grounded in fear and in prejudice."[16]

The trial court ruled that Cammermeyer had met her burden of proof. The antigay regulations were based on prejudice and thus they were unconstitutional as applied to her. He ordered the army to reinstate Cammermeyer.

The army did reinstate Colonel Cammermeyer, but it also appealed the District Court decision. The Court of Appeals for the Ninth Circuit avoided ruling on the merits by holding that the case had become moot. It had become moot because Colonel Cammermeyer had been reinstated, and the regulations that the army had used to discharge her had been replaced by a new set of regulations, the so-called "Don't Ask, Don't Tell" policy. Presumably, if the army had wished to discharge Cammermeyer at this point in time, it would have had to do so under the new policy. Thus, the constitutionality of the old 1980s regulations was irrelevant to her current situation. If the court of appeals were to reverse the ruling below regarding the constitutionality of the regulations, the army would gain nothing because it could no longer use the old regulations to dismiss Cammermeyer. And if the Court of Appeals were to uphold the ruling below, Cammermeyer would gain nothing, because she was now subject to discharge under the new policy. Because the case had become moot, the appeal was dismissed. The Court of Appeals, however, refused to vacate the decision below. Thus, that decision continues to stand as citeable precedent.

The 1990s Regulations

When President Clinton was elected in 1992, he thought that he could carry out his election promise to lift the military's ban on gays and lesbians by issuing an executive order as commander-in-chief. After all, President Truman had ended racial segregation in the armed forces by executive order. But, the Clinton plan ran into difficulty immediately. The Pentagon and Congress both objected. In the end, an alleged compromise was hammered out in 1993. That compromise policy, known as "Don't Ask, Don't Tell" is not only reflected in current military regulations, it was also enacted into statutory law by Congress.[17]

Throughout the negotiations over the compromise, the White House described the new proposals as being based on conduct, not status. Adopting a status/conduct distinction seemed to be consistent with the argument movement lawyers were making in cases like Colonel Cammermeyer's. The only problem is that President Clinton's characterization of the new proposal as one that punishes conduct rather than status turns out not to be true. Janet Halley has demonstrated this point brilliantly in her recent book, *Don't: A Reader's Guide to the Military's Anti-Gay Policy.*

The 1990s policy, like the 1980s policy, authorizes discharge from the military on the basis of a homosexual statement, a homosexual act, or a same-sex marriage. Under the 1990s policy, as under the 1980s policy, a person who has committed a homosexual act can defend against the discharge by relying on the five-prong test to prove heterosexual status. Both policies discharge a person who has stated that he or she is gay. Under both policies a service member can avoid discharge provided she proves that the statement is false, that she is not gay.[18] Under the new policy, to prove that she is not gay, the service member must prove that she does not intend to engage in homosexual acts, and, further, that she has no propensity to engage in homosexual acts. How one proves this "negative" (i.e., no propensity), other than by proving that one is heterosexual is unclear. As Janet Halley points out, this rebuttal option creates a defense based on status.[19] And a defense based on status certainly suggests that the reason the service member is being booted out in the first place is because of status, that is, because the service member is *not* heterosexual.

The only real difference between the old and new policies is that the military may no longer ask about a person's sexual orientation. But if that person's sexual orientation is discovered through some other route, the grounds for discharge remain the same. The claim that the 1990s policy is based on conduct seem disingenuous at best. Clearly, the grounds for discharge under the 1990s policy are not confined to the type of conduct that President Clinton talked about when he struck the alleged compromise, namely the commission of sodomy and other illegal acts.

Because the 1990s policy appears to be based on status as much as the old policy was, one would have expected a case like Cammermeyer's, which had been brought under the 1980s policy, to have been just as successful under the 1990s policy. In fact, however, not one intermediate appellate court has struck down "Don't Ask, Don't Tell" and the U.S. Supreme Court has not yet been willing to review the constitutionality of the 1990s policy.

Many gay rights activists viewed the Ninth Circuit as the best forum for challenging the 1990 regulations. The Ninth Circuit is the largest of the thirteen circuit courts of appeal and hears appeals in cases brought in nine states, California, Washington, Oregon, Arizona, Montana, Idaho, Nevada, Alaska, and Hawaii. When all judicial positions are filled, there are twenty-eight active judges on the court and almost as many senior judges. Senior judges are judges who have retired and volunteer their services to the court. Although they participate fully in any panel to which they are assigned, senior judges do not vote on whether or not a case should be referred to an en banc panel. By the mid-1990s, all thirteen circuits were dominated by Reagan/Bush appointees. The Ninth Circuit, however, was fairly evenly split and, when senior judges are added to the calculation, had a higher percentage than any other circuit of judges appointed by President Jimmy Carter. In addition, a number of Ninth Circuit judges had written decisions that were viewed as progay. In addition to the original panel in *Watkins,* consisting of Norris, Canby, and Reinhardt, Judge Betty Fletcher, also appointed by Carter, had written a progay opinion in a 1991 military case.[20] She was joined by Canby and a Reagan appointee, Judge Diarmuid F. O'Scannlain. In 1994, another three-judge panel, consisting of judges who had been appointed by Presidents Carter, Reagan, and Bush, ruled in favor of a gay service member, albeit on fairly narrow grounds.[21] No other circuit had issued so many gay-positive opinions.

The next best forum was thought to be the Second Circuit because it was perceived as relatively more liberal than other circuits and because it had not yet ruled negatively in a gay military case. By 1996, cases were in litigation in seven different circuits, but gay rights litigators had their hopes pinned on *Holmes,*[22] the case before the Ninth Circuit, and *Able,*[23] the case before the Second Circuit.

The *Holmes* panel included Judges Charles Wiggins and Stephen Reinhardt from the Ninth Circuit and Tom Reavley, a senior judge from the Fifth Circuit sitting by designation. Reinhardt's presence on the panel was encouraging. Wiggins was a 1984 Reagan appointee who had not yet participated in a gay rights case. Reavley was a Texan, appointed by President Carter. Nonetheless, gay rights activists were pessimistic about his participation. Reavley had written the 1985 en banc opinion in *Baker v. Wade,* the pre-*Hardwick* challenge to the Texas sodomy statute. Because the Texas statute applied only to same-sex sodomy, Baker had made a strong equal protection claim. Judge Reavley had replied: "In view of the strong objection to homosexual conduct, which has prevailed in Western culture for the past seven centuries, we cannot say that [the sodomy statute] is totally unrelated [to the implementation of] morality, a permissible state goal."[24]

Lieutenant Andrew Holmes had been discharged solely for making a homosexual statement. This fact made his case similar to that of Colonel Cammermeyer, who had admitted she was gay in response to an investigation. Holmes, by contrast, had volunteered the information regarding his sexual orientation. Holmes, with the advice of counsel, sent a memo to his commanding officer in which he said, "[A]s a matter of conscience, honesty and pride, I am compelled to inform you that I am gay." His commanding officer then initiated proceedings that culminated in Holmes's discharge. The "Don't Ask, Don't Tell" policy explicitly provides for the discharge of any service member who "has stated that he or she is a homosexual . . . unless there is a further finding . . . that the member . . . is not a person who engages in, attempts to engage in, has a propensity to engage in, or intends to engage in homosexual acts." Holmes had offered no affirmative defense to show that he had no propensity to engage in homosexual acts. He challenged the policy directly, claiming that discharge on the basis of a statement alone was a constitutionally impermissible infringement of both his equal protection and free speech rights. Judge Wiggins, writing for the majority, denied both of Holmes's claims. He distinguished earlier cases in which the court had found in favor of the gay or lesbian service member by pointing out that they had all been decided under the old military policy. Judge Reinhardt dissented, finding that the presumption and resulting discharge constituted an impermissible restriction on free speech.

Judge Reinhardt then called for rehearing en banc. The matter was then referred to the full court to determine whether an en banc rehearing should occur. On April 6, 1998, the motion for a rehearing en banc was denied. Five judges voted in favor of the rehearing and issued a written opinion dissenting from the decision not to hear the case en banc. The Supreme Court denied certiorari in the case in early 1999.[25]

At the same time that *Holmes* was under consideration by the Ninth Circuit, the other crucial military case, *Able v. Perry,* was moving forward in the Second Circuit. *Able,* like *Holmes,* was a true "test case." However, unlike *Holmes,* not one of the plaintiffs had been terminated based on conduct, status, or statements. Rather, the plaintiffs in *Able* were seeking a declaratory judgment that the 1990s policy was unconstitutional. Their first hurdle was to prove that the plaintiffs had sufficient "standing" or threat of harm to bring the lawsuit. The lawyers quickly figured out that merely by bringing a lawsuit, the plaintiffs would be "coming out," and thereby subjecting themselves to possible discharge. Highlighting the First Amendment arguments against the new policy, the lawyers entered a motion asking the judge to restrain the armed forces from discharging any plaintiff solely on the grounds of bringing the lawsuit. After all, if one could not even ask a court to consider the constitutionality of the policy without risk of losing one's job, something was surely wrong. In addition, the lawyers decided that the lead plaintiff should be identified only by a pseudonym, and further, that the pseudonym should not be Doe or Roe, but rather should be something that better captured the real nature of the plaintiff. Able was the name chosen.

The *Able* case has a long and tortured litigation history, with several appeals to the Second Circuit.[26] At first, the plaintiffs in *Able* focused on their free speech claim, arguing that they could not be discharged solely on the basis of speech. In an early appeal, the Second Circuit ruled that speech was not at the core of the case. The speech at issue was the plaintiffs' statements admitting that they were gay. The Second Circuit concluded that, on the basis of such self-identification, the military was justified in presuming the likelihood of homosexual conduct. Then, the Second Circuit remanded the case to the trial court and instructed the plaintiffs to focus on the "real issue," which was whether a denial of equal protection occurred under a rule that appeared to discharge gay service members for their homosexual acts when nongay service members were not discharged for comparable heterosexual acts.

At last, in *Able,* a federal court judge was being asked to focus closely on the specifics of the homosexual conduct rules that the armed forces claimed would disrupt the military. Judge Nickerson, of the federal district court for the Eastern District of New York, reviewed the rules on conduct and determined that the 1990s policy was, indeed, a denial of equal protection.[27] He issued an opinion that gets it just right. In his view, the military rules call for the discharge of personnel if they engage in (or have a propensity to engage in) homosexual acts, including romantically holding hands in private with a person of the same sex. The rules do not call for the discharge of personnel if they romantically hold hands in private with a person of the opposite sex. The difference in treatment raises equal protection issues because it creates a classification on the basis of sexual orientation that disfavors gay men and lesbians.

Applying low-level scrutiny, the next question addressed by Judge Nickerson was whether the sexual orientation classification was rational. To answer this question, Nickerson had to focus on why the category of *homosexual* acts for which one can be discharged (e.g., holding hands) is so much broader than the category of *heterosexual* acts for which one can be discharged (e.g., sodomy and adultery). Why, muses Judge Nickerson, does the definition of "homosexual act" include holding hands in private? Can such conduct destroy the military mission? Or, as he concludes, is the answer more likely that the act is not inherently dangerous on its own, but rather says something dangerous about the actor, namely, that the actor is gay.

Having concluded that "Don't Ask, Don't Tell" has nothing to do with conduct, but is really a policy that prevents persons who are discovered to be gay from serving in the military, Nickerson then asked the crucial question: Why does the military allow closeted gays and lesbians, but not open ones, to serve in the military? Why did the military decide to stop asking about homosexual orientation in the 1990s while continuing to enforce a rule, no different from that contained in earlier policies, that booted gay people out for making a statement or engaging in an act that identified them as gay?

As the district court in *Cammermeyer* had done, Judge Nickerson went through each justification offered by the military and rejected it. Many of the justifications were rejected for the same reasons they were rejected in *Cammermeyer*; that is, that they were based on prejudice. As Judge Nickerson noted: "The fact that the prejudice arises in the military context does not legitimate the discrimination. The Constitution does not grant the military special license to act on prejudices or cater to them."

Also, because the 1990s policy allows closeted gays to serve, Nickerson was able to identify additional irrationalities in the 1990s policy that were not ever present in the 1980s policy. For example, the military advanced its usual justification of "unit cohesion." But given the military's concern about how heterosexual service members will react to the presence of gays and lesbians in their midst, Nickerson astutely asked whether unit cohesion is facilitated or destroyed by allowing only closeted gay persons to serve in the military. If unit members must wonder about each other's sexuality because they cannot ask, will they feel closer to each other or more distanced?

Nickerson determined that the policy made no sense and that it thus flunked the rational basis test. With such a strong opinion dealing with all the right issues, gay rights activists were heartened and awaited a positive affirmance of his position when the case went up on appeal to the Second Circuit. Hopes were dashed when the three-judge panel reversed Nickerson's opinion, primarily on grounds of deference to the military.

Enough was enough. The Supreme Court had denied certiorari in every single military case, whether litigated under the old 1980s policy or the new 1990s policy. Not a single court of appeals had ruled against the 1990s policy. In consultation with each other, the public interest gay rights lawyers that had been fighting the military for over a decade finally decided it was time to quit. No writ of certiorari would be requested in *Able*.

Military litigation is not over. Challenges must continue to be made because people's lives and reputations are still at stake. That fact has not changed. Loss of pension and retirement benefits are at issue for some personnel who are discharged under the new policy. The Servicemembers Legal Defense Network has documented violations of the "Don't Ask" part of the policy by each branch of the armed forces. This "outing" of gay service members is often accompanied by harassment and violence. Gay rights lawyers will continue to represent individuals who suffer under the military's policy. But given the current judicial attitude of deferring to the military, there will no longer be an orchestrated attack against the 1990s policy in an effort to further the constitutional rights of lesbians and gay men.

SUPREME COURT VICTORY:
ROMER V. EVANS

As fate would have it, not a military employment discrimination case, but rather a ballot initiative case created the opportunity for the U.S. Supreme Court to rule on the question of whether gays and lesbians could claim equality under the Constitution of the United States. And much to the surprise of some, the case, *Romer v. Evans,* was a clear victory for the gay rights movement.

Romer began in a Colorado courtroom on November 12, 1992, shortly after the voters of the state of Colorado had approved an amendment to their state constitution. The antigay initiative, known as Amendment 2, singled out a class of persons defined as homosexual, lesbian, or bisexual and prohibited any municipality or other governmental unit from enacting antidiscrimination measures to protect the group. Specifically, the amendment provided:

> No Protected Status Based on Homosexual, Lesbian, or Bisexual Orientation. Neither the State of Colorado, through any of its branches or departments, nor any of its agencies, political subdivisions, municipalities or school districts, shall enact, adopt or enforce any statute, regulations, ordinance or policy whereby homosexual, lesbian or bisexual orientation, conduct, practices or relationships shall constitute or otherwise be the basis of or entitle any person or class of persons to have or claim any minority status, quota preferences, protected status or claim of discrimination. This Section of the Constitution shall be in all respects self-executing.

Fifty-three percent of the voters had approved the amendment in the November general election. The vote had followed a bitter political battle between gay rights activists and the conservative right. This ballot was not the first time an antigay initiative had been put before the people. The first backlash ballot measure occurred in 1974. In 1977, such measures gained national attention when Anita Bryant campaigned against the Dade County gay rights ordinance in the state of Florida. Although the lesbian and gay community successfully fought against the antigay Briggs Initiative in California in 1978, conservative and fundamentalist groups in various states around the country continually tried to repeal hard-won votes in favor of gay rights or block future votes by passing initiatives like Colorado's Amendment 2.

Until the Colorado measure, these battles occurred at the local municipal or county level, not at the state level. This "battle at the local level" aspect of the lesbian and gay civil rights movement is often characterized as something unique to the gay movement, in that women and blacks are thought to have gained their rights at the national level first. Several gay rights activists over the years have described their movement as one that is building from the "bottom up," as compared with other movements that are perceived to have first won their rights at the top. Although this comparative description is certainly true regarding the modern women's movement and its battle for equal employment opportunities,[28] it ignores the earlier feminist battle for suffrage. Unable to pass a constitutional amendment and often unable to win the vote at the state level, feminists fought and were sometimes successful at the municipal level in obtaining the vote. Similarly, the modern African American civil rights movement can be viewed as a "top-down" movement with respect to integration. President Truman issued an executive order in 1948 ending segregation in the armed forces and, in 1954, the Supreme Court of the United States set in motion more local efforts to desegregate schools. But the battle over race discrimination in employment was won at the bottom first. In 1945, the city of Chicago enacted the first modern fair employment legislation banning discrimination on the basis of race, color, or creed. Milwaukee and Minneapolis followed. By the time Congress finally passed Title VII, twenty states had passed similar fair employment legislation.[29]

Two different sorts of battles occur at the local level in civil rights movements: First, a battle to obtain a civil right, whether it is equal access to employment, housing, or some other right, and second, a battle to keep that right. At the local level, lesbian and gay activists have met with relative success over the years in the first battle, obtaining the civil right. One of the reasons for the lesbian and gay movement's political success at the local level was that certain municipalities had larger and more active gay communities. San Francisco and New York City, for example, were more amenable to gay rights than were the states of California and New York. But neither of these cities was the site of the first gay rights law. Instead, the honor goes to East Lansing, Michigan, a college town of 50,000. In March 1972, after much lobbying by the officially recognized gay student group at Michigan State University, the city council voted 3 to 2 to ban discrimination on the basis of sexual orientation in city personnel decisions.[30] University campuses around the country were crucial in this early battle and the movement's progress owes much to the political organizing that occurred at the student level, organizing that was protected by federal court decisions recognizing the constitutional right of such groups to associate for political purposes. The University of Iowa gay student organization was a central force in the adoption of a gay rights ordinance by the Iowa City City Council in 1977. New York City did not pass a gay rights bill until 1986.

Most of these successes were won by lobbying elected officials, such as city councilpersons. Success at the local level occurred only where gay rights groups were well organized. Measures were often debated for years before they were finally enacted. In some cases, the issue was so hotly debated that city councils decided to pass the buck and ask the local voters to decide the issue. In Boulder, Colorado, the first such popular vote soundly defeated gay rights. But years later, the same voting public endorsed the antidiscrimination principle. By 1993, 126 gay rights ordinances were still in effect and more were on the way. Political discourse at the local level was a successful route for gay men and lesbians. They were making their arguments to their neighbors, teachers, fellow employees, and friends. No one at the local level could cast an antigay vote and claim, as Justice Powell did after he had voted against gay rights in *Bowers v. Hardwick,* that he or she had never met a gay person.

Lesbian and gay rights groups have had a more difficult time in the second type of local battle: keeping the civil right once it has been won. In most cities around the country, two ways exist to repeal a local civil rights ordinance. The city council can vote to repeal it, or the people, by popular vote, can vote to repeal it using the initiative process. By initiative, the general public can either repeal a specific legislative enactment or amend the city charter to prevent any future enactment. In the latter case, legislative power on the topic is removed from elected representatives and lodged in the public as a whole. Although this form of popular democracy sounds good in the abstract, researchers have shown that initiative measures passed by popular vote tend to be based on ideology and tend to discriminate against minority groups. History shows that gay men and lesbians are not unique in experiencing the brunt of popularly enacted prejudice. "During the last 30 years, ballot measures addressing issues affecting racial and ethnic minorities have resulted in significant rejection of the rights of minority groups in housing and public accommodation (80 percent [success rate]), school desegregation (71 percent [success rate]), and English language laws (100 percent [success rate])."[31] During the twenty-two-year period from 1974 to 1996, antigay initiatives won sixty out of eighty battles at the ballot box.[32] Ballot measures restricting the rights of racial and ethnic minorities ceased for all practical purposes in the late 1960s. In 1967, the Supreme Court ruled such measures unconstitutional if they were enacted as amendments to state constitutions.[33] In 1969, the Court made a similar ruling regarding racially discriminatory amendments to city charters.[34]

Approximately half the states have constitutional or statutory provisions authorizing popular or direct democracy through the use of ballot initiatives.[35] In these states, any group can put a matter before the general public provided the group can obtain sufficient signatures on a petition. In Colorado, a right-wing religious group, Colorado for Family Values, gathered approximately 55,000 signatures and thereby put Amendment 2 on the November ballot to be voted on by the entire state.[36] The amendment passed by a vote of 53 percent to 46 percent.

At that time, three Colorado cities, Aspen, Boulder, and Denver, had ordinances that prohibited discrimination in employment on the basis of sexual orientation. Amendment 2 effectively repealed these ordinances, at least to the extent the ordinances protected gay men, lesbians, or bisexuals, and prevented those cities from ever passing any new protections so long as Amendment 2 was in effect. If the amendment stayed in place, lesbian and gay rights activists could no longer lobby at the local level, or even before their state legislature, but instead would have to take their case to the full voting public of the state of Colorado.

But cutting short the best political tactic that the movement had known, that is, local lobbying, was not the only problem with Amendment 2. Because of the breadth of its language, it appeared to block any claim of discrimination brought by a gay man, lesbian, or bisexual person before any political subdivision of the state of Colorado. At the same time, the amendment did not affect the right of nongay persons to bring discrimination claims on the basis of their heterosexual orientation. The language of the amendment singled out persons with a homosexual, lesbian, or bisexual orientation, thereby burdening only some sexual orientations and not all.

A lawsuit challenging the constitutionality of the amendment was filed by a coalition of local and national gay rights lawyers. Suzanne Goldberg from Lambda's New York office participated from the beginning of the suit. Mary Newcombe, from Lambda's Los Angeles office, had participated earlier in legal challenges to keep the measure off the ballot before it went to the voting public. Bill Rubenstein and Matt Coles represented the ACLU. Local groups had asked Jean Dubofsky, a Colorado attorney and prior Colorado Supreme Court justice, to represent their interests. Although Dubofksy had represented some gay and lesbian clients and supported gay rights, she was not a gay rights lawyer as such, and, moreover, she was not gay. But the case was a local one, to be fought in the courts of Colorado, and her stature in Colorado made her the perfect choice for lead attorney.

The original petition claimed numerous violations of the federal and state constitutions. The primary legal argument against the amendment was that it prevented a class of persons, gay men, lesbians, and bisexuals, from equal participation in the political process. The thrust of the argument was to describe the interest at issue, participation in the political process, in such a way that it could fit within the fundamental rights category recognized by the U.S. Supreme Court under the fundamental rights branch of equal protection. If the amendment burdened a fundamental right, then it could only be justified under the compelling state interest test. Alternately, if the amendment did not burden a fundamental right and only discriminated against a nonsuspect class of persons, then it would receive only low-level scrutiny. Since no case had ever finally held gay men and lesbians to be anything other than a nonsuspect, low-level scrutiny group for equal protection purposes, the fundamental rights argument seemed the best route.

The argument worked. The Supreme Court of Colorado held that Amendment 2 burdened a fundamental right, participation in the political process. Upon remand to the trial court, the state, representing the voters of Colorado, was unable to justify by compelling reasons its decision to place that burden on lesbians, gay men, and bisexuals. The justifications offered were six in number:

1. deterring factionalism;
2. preserving the integrity of the state's political functions;
3. preserving the ability of the state to remedy discrimination against suspect classes;
4. preventing the government from interfering with personal, familial, and religious privacy;
5. preventing government from subsidizing the political objectives of a special interest group; and
6. promoting the physical and psychological well-being of Colorado children.[37]

The trial court ruled the amendment violated the federal constitution and enjoined its enforcement. The Supreme Court of Colorado affirmed.

Then the state of Colorado asked the Supreme Court to review the case, and the Supreme Court agreed. Jean Dubofsky continued to serve as lead counsel and argued the case before the Supreme Court. Suzanne Goldberg and Matt Coles organized amicus briefs, including briefs from the American Bar Association, the NAACP, and the National Organization of Women. In all, over two dozen amicus briefs were filed, representing "almost 100 organizations, cities, and individuals."[38]

Two primary legal arguments were made in the case. The first was that Amendment 2 burdened the fundamental right of lesbians, gay men, and bisexuals to participate in the political process. Under this amendment, only this group, and no other, was prevented from asking its city council, county commissioners, or even state legislators to pass antidiscrimination laws for its benefit. As Matt Coles, director of the ACLU's Lesbian and Gay Rights Projects, explained it, the basic theory was: "You have seriously weakened or diluted somebody's right to participate in democratic self-government if you take away the legislature's power to pass protective legislation as to them."[39] The second argument was that the amendment discriminated against lesbians, gay men, and bisexuals, thereby violating their equal protection rights. Briefs were organized to develop fully both arguments. The key question, no matter which argument prevailed, was whether the amendment would be subject to strict or low-level scrutiny by the Court.

Although the Colorado Supreme Court had endorsed the fundamental rights theory, thereby triggering strict scrutiny and requiring a compelling justification for the amendment, gay rights scholars and litigators were nervous about the theory. One problem was that the Supreme Court had never recognized this particular fundamental right except in cases affecting suspect groups such as racial minorities. And in fact, in a 1971 case, *James v. Valtierra,*[40] dealing with a California constitutional amendment that required a vote of the people rather than the appropriate legislative body to approve low-income housing measures, the Supreme Court had said it was okay to restrict the political access of nonsuspect groups, such as the poor. Arguments were constructed to avoid the *James* holding, but the concern remained that the Supreme Court would not find a fundamental right and would confine itself to standard equal protection analysis where level of review depended on the classification.

A series of amicus briefs were coordinated around the equal protection issue. One brief argued that the classification on the basis of sexual orientation, even subjected to rational basis review, was unconstitutional. Another argued that, despite *Bowers v. Hardwick,* gay men and lesbians were entitled to a higher level of scrutiny based on their history of discrimination. In addition, Professor Laurence Tribe, the Harvard law professor who had argued the *Bowers v. Hardwick* case on behalf of Michael Hardwick, submitted an equal protection brief arguing an entirely new theory: that Amendment 2 was a per se violation of the Equal Protection Clause.

The Tribe brief was unique in another respect as well. Although originally planned as a brief to be submitted on behalf of himself and a national organization of law professors that often filed amicus briefs in discrimination cases,[41] the brief was ultimately submitted by a group of five individual law professors. The five were some of the most well-known and respected constitutional scholars in the United States, and they taught at three of the top law schools in the country: Laurence Tribe of Harvard, Kathleen Sullivan, Gerald Gunther, and John Hart Ely of Stanford, and Philip B. Kurland, now deceased, of the University of Chicago. Both the argument and the select group of professors who signed onto the brief indicated to the Court that this brief was a special one.

The following is a summary of Tribe's argument, as outlined at the beginning of the brief:

> This brief argues that Colorado's Amendment 2 constitutes a per se violation
> of the Equal Protection Clause of the Fourteenth Amendment, which provides
> that "[n]o state shall . . . deny to any person within its jurisdiction the equal
> protection of the laws." That command is violated when a state's constitution
> renders some persons ineligible for "the . . . protection of the laws" from an
> entire category of mistreatment—here, the mistreatment of discrimination,

however invidious and unwarranted. If Colorado had declared some people within its jurisdiction completely ineligible for the protection of its laws, existing or future, from some other form of mistreatment—unjustified physical assault, for example—no one would doubt that such state action would constitute a per se denial of the equal protection of the laws. Selectively decreeing some "person or class of persons," to use Amendment 2's language, ineligible for legal protection from mistreatment in which the wrong charged takes the form of discrimination as such is every bit as offensive on its face to the principle of equality before the law.

States have no affirmative duty to enact or retain special laws for each individual or group who might be victimized by discriminatory treatment . . . just as they may well have no affirmative duty to enact or retain laws directed at other forms of wrongful treatment. But it is quite another matter for a state's constitution absolutely to preclude, for a selected set of persons, even the possibility of protection under any state or local law from a whole category of harmful conduct, including some that is undeniably wrongful.

On May 20, 1996, the Supreme Court handed down its opinion and struck down Amendment 2 by a vote of 6 to 3, concluding that "Amendment 2 classifies homosexuals not to further a proper legislative end but to make them unequal to everyone else. This Colorado cannot do. A State cannot so deem a class of persons a stranger to its laws."[42] Reacting to the decision, Matt Coles of the ACLU quipped that the lawyers in the offices of Lambda Legal Defense were popping champagne while he and his lawyer cohorts at the ACLU Lesbian and Gay Rights Project were reading the footnotes. The 6 to 3 vote was a decisive victory and worthy of good champagne. But figuring out exactly what the Court had ruled required a close reading and parsing of the opinion—and the footnotes.

Clearly the Court had ruled on equal protection grounds and not on the basis of a fundamental right to participate in the political process. At one point, the Court says: "A law declaring that in general it shall be more difficult for one group of citizens than for all others to seek aid from the government is itself a denial of equal protection of the laws in the most literal sense."[43] This statement sounds like it came from the Tribe brief. But the Court also offers an alternative rationale: that Amendment 2 by "its sheer breadth is so discontinuous with the reasons offered for it that the amendment seems inexplicable by anything but animus toward the class that it affects; it lacks a rational relationship to legitimate state interests." This statement sounds like the Court is applying standard equal protection analysis, and further, it sounds as though the Court believes the real motive for enactment is prejudice, which is never a legitimate interest.

Unfortunately, the Court never clearly states the animus/prejudice theory for striking down Amendment 2. Later in the opinion, the Court cites two justifications offered by the state in support of the measure: (1) protecting the rights of nongay Colorado citizens who for personal and religious purposes wish to discriminate against gays and lesbians, and (2) the state's interest in preserving resources by not having to entertain discrimination claims on the basis of sexual orientation. In response to these two justifications, the Court merely says:

> The breadth of the Amendment is so far removed from these particular justifications that we find it impossible to credit them. We cannot say that Amendment 2 is directed to any identifiable legitimate purpose or discrete objective. It is a status-based enactment divorced from any factual context from which we could discern a relationship to legitimate state interests; it is a classification of persons undertaken for its own sake, something the Equal Protection Clause does not permit.[44]

This part of the opinion sounds as though it is based on an argument made in the brief for Respondents, Evans, and the other gay, lesbian, and bisexual Coloradans who were the plaintiffs in the lawsuit. That brief argued that the amendment merely singled out gay, lesbian, and bisexual Coloradans for the sake of discriminating against them. "Such a law declares a characteristic to be sufficient justification for discrimination regardless of any specific purpose. Such discrimination for the sake of discrimination is illegitimate."[45]

Matt Coles, who participated in the brief writing, has described the argument more fully and called it the principle of "it's the classification, stupid!" The Colorado measure drew a line, a classification. It put gays, lesbians, and bisexuals on one side of the line and everyone else on the other side, including those with sexual orientations other than gay, lesbian, or bisexual. The Colorado amendment was not an amendment about discrimination on the basis of sexual orientation in general and whether protections against such discrimination were needed or whether it was wise to have those protections enacted at the local or state level. Everyone has a sexual orientation. Statutes and ordinances that protect individuals from sexual orientation discrimination protect everyone. Gay men and lesbians certainly need the protection more than heterosexuals and so the absence or repeal of a law banning discrimination on the basis of sexual orientation will *affect* gays disproportionately. But the Colorado amendment was more explicit. It took away protection from only some sexual orientations. Indeed, as a logical matter, after passage of the amendment, the cities of Aspen, Boulder, and Denver presumably had their sexual orientation laws transformed into laws that protected its heterosexual residents, but not its homosexual citizens. What is the sense in drawing such a line other than to disadvantage one particular group? To draw a line for the purpose of disadvantaging a group is animus-based and thus illegitimate under the Equal Protection Clause.

Justice Scalia was disdainful of the majority decision's mere suggestion that the good people of Colorado were acting from improper motives in exercising their popular will. In his dissent, he wrote: "The Court's opinion contains grim, disapproving hints that Coloradans have been guilty of 'animus' or 'animosity' toward homosexuality, as though that has been established as Unamerican." The only animus suggested by the Coloradans who voted in favor of Amendment 2 was, in Scalia's opinion, their moral disapproval of homosexuality and, under *Bowers v. Hardwick,* moral disapproval of a group of people that engage in homosexual conduct is quite all right.

The full import of *Romer* cannot be known until its boundaries are tested in future litigation. But one message rings loud and clear: despite *Bowers v. Hardwick,* gay men and lesbians are now entitled to meaningful judicial review of their equal protection claims. The majority opinion in *Romer* never mentioned *Bowers v. Hardwick.* At oral argument, Justice Scalia had asked Jean Dubofsky, counsel for the plaintiff/respondents, whether she was asking the Court to overrule *Hardwick.* She answered "no." The litigation strategy, agreed upon by the coalition of national and state lawyers working on the case, had been that it was too soon to ask the Court to overrule *Hardwick.*

In dissent, Scalia indicated that he did not believe the two decisions, *Hardwick* and *Romer,* could be reconciled. Repeating the argument that gay rights litigators had faced in earlier gay discrimination cases, Scalia reasoned: "If it is constitutionally permissible for a State to make homosexual conduct criminal, surely it is constitutionally permissible for a State to enact other laws merely disfavoring homosexual conduct." And further, "If it is rational to criminalize the conduct, surely it is rational to deny special favor and protection to those with a self-avowed tendency or desire to engage in the conduct." In Scalia's view, the majority opinion in *Romer* was totally incompatible with the decision in *Hardwick*. If one agrees with Scalia, then *Hardwick* has been effectively overruled by *Romer.*

Such a conclusion is far-fetched. Although courts can overrule by implication, that usually happens when the court does not have the earlier case in mind while it is deciding the later case. *Bowers v. Hardwick* was certainly in the minds of everyone during the briefing, the oral arguments, and the crafting of the final opinion in *Romer.* The real question post-*Romer* is whether *Hardwick's* continued vitality has been weakened only in equal protection status cases or also in equal protection and due process cases involving conduct. Or, as some constitutional scholars have argued, *Romer* may be a very narrow decision that has nothing to do with *Hardwick.* As Professor Laurence Tribe has explained:

> Even convicted felons are sometimes the victims of what can only be regarded as utterly purposeless and purely prejudiced treatment—and would ordinarily be free to seek, through any branch of the state or local government, protection—including protection specific to the relevant felony category—against such discrimination.[46]

Under this view, *Romer* is not cause for champagne after all because the decision indicates no willingness to offer greater constitutional protection to gay men and lesbians than was offered in *Hardwick.* Rather, *Romer* merely states that some laws are so prejudicial that, even when applied to criminals, they are unconstitutional.

The immediate import of *Romer,* however, lay not in its contribution to constitutional theory. Rather, the decision made it possible for the gay and lesbian civil rights movement to continue its work. Backed by the Supreme Court's affirmative ruling in *Romer,* gay and lesbian activists across the country were empowered to continue their fight for antidiscrimination laws. Movement lawyers could more quickly respond to the increasing number of antigay initiatives in states across the nation by citing *Romer* as precedent for their constitutional infirmity. As Suzanne Goldberg, the Lambda lawyer on the case reports, shortly after the decision in *Romer,* "the Oregon Citizens Alliance, the group that had promoted antigay initiatives in Oregon for nearly a decade, announced it would be withdrawing a series of antigay amendments."[47] A similar decision by antigay forces in Idaho followed several weeks later. The decision by the Supreme Court thereby freed up movement lawyers to spend more time on core substantive issues, such as employment and family rights. In the short run at least, the decision enabled gay lawyers and activists to debate the meaning of equality for gay men and women in political arenas that remained open to accept or reject their arguments on the merits rather than simply ruling them out of order.

ROMER'S LONG-TERM EFFECT ON ANTIGAY BALLOT INITIATIVES

Although *Romer*'s short-term effect was positive with regard to other antigay ballot measures, the decision did not go far enough to create any lasting impediment to antigay forces around the country. The decision did cause some retreats by antigay forces, but these retreats were more likely explained by a need for the forces to rethink the drafting of new initiatives to work around the *Romer* holding. Unlike the Supreme Court opinions in the late 1960s that struck down racially discriminatory ballot measures and put a stop to that practice, *Romer,* by its vagueness and its refusal to apply anything other than rational basis review, left huge holes for antigay forces to use to their advantage.

Recent events show that antigay forces have not given up on the use of ballot initiatives. When Maine's legislature enacted legislation protecting employees from discrimination on the basis of sexual orientation, antigay forces used the initiative process to repeal the legislation. In Fort Collins, Colorado, when the city council voted to include sexual orientation to the list of protected classes in its civil rights ordinance, antigay forces quickly responded with a petition to put the matter before the public for a vote. In November 1998, the antigay forces won. In the cities of Seattle and Spokane, where gay rights legislation is in effect, antigay forces are pushing to put the matter to a popular vote. And Colorado for Family Values is also collecting signatures to reverse a city council resolution that extends antidiscrimination protections to include "sexual orientation."

To the extent that these efforts merely operate to repeal existing legislation, they are unfortunate but not in violation of the ruling in *Romer.* To the extent these efforts make it more difficult for lesbians and gay men to lobby for legal protections in the future by amending city charters or state constitutions to prohibit protection from discrimination, they arguably violate the ruling in *Romer.*

Some scholars have argued, however, that *Romer* is a "minimalist" decision that should probably be limited to its very specific facts.[48] If that is the correct reading of *Romer,* then antigay forces will be free to pursue antigay amendments to city charters without violating *Romer* because *Romer* dealt with amendments to a state constitution. In addition, antigay forces will be free to pursue antigay amendments to state constitutions so long as they are carefully worded to apply to all sexual orientations and not just gay, lesbian, and bisexual ones.

Already evidence exists that *Romer* may indeed be of little help in fighting future antigay initiative measures. At the same time that the Supreme Court was considering *Romer,* the Court of Appeals for the Sixth Circuit ruled that an amendment to Cincinnati's city charter barring future antidiscrimination measures that would benefit lesbians, gay men, and bisexuals did not violate the equal protection clause of the federal constitution.[49] The Supreme Court granted certiorari in the Cincinnati case and, on the basis of its decision in *Romer,* vacated the case and remanded it to the Sixth Circuit to reconsider in light of the Court's decision in *Romer.*[50] The Court of Appeals for the Sixth Circuit again ruled that the amendment to the city charter was constitutional, distinguishing *Romer* as a case involving a statewide rather than citywide measure.[51] The language in the Cincinnati amendment was very similar to that of Colorado's Amendment 2. It specifically singled out lesbians, gay men, and bisexuals. However, whereas Amendment 2 prevented gay or bisexual people from making any claim of discrimination, the Cincinnati amendment prevented them from claiming protected status. The Sixth Circuit construed the language to prevent gays and lesbians from claiming "special rights." Although this construction would make the Cincinnati language different from the Colorado language, this construction ignores the context in which the term "protected status" is being used. In an amendment intended to speak about employment discrimination matters, "protected status" merely means "a claim to be protected from discrimination." In this case, the language has the same meaning as the Colorado language. But even if the Sixth Circuit is correct in its "special rights" construction, the Court ignored the *Romer* opinion by never asking why heterosexual persons, and not homosexual persons, might be entitled to "special rights."

The U.S. Supreme Court denied certiorari in the *City of Cincinnati* case.[52] This surprise result has left gay rights litigators puzzling over whether the *Romer* opinion can be applied to stop antigay initiatives aimed at city charters.

ROMER'S EFFECT ON EQUAL PROTECTION CLAIMS

In the three years following the *Romer* decision, the case has been cited in support of a positive result in only four gay rights cases. In other losing cases, it has either had no noticeable impact or has been cited to support low-level scrutiny in lesbian and gay discrimination claims. In every case challenging the military's antigay policy on the basis of equal protection, for example, the post-*Romer* decisions by the courts of appeal cited to *Romer* for the principle that only rational basis review was required. Since *Romer* had struck down an antigay measure using only rational basis review, however, some courts felt it necessary to distinguish the military cases from *Romer* in order to uphold the military policy. In *Holmes,* the Ninth Circuit distinguished *Romer* by saying it was a very limited opinion; it was not an employment discrimination case; and, most important, it did not involve the military. In *Able,* the Second Circuit relied primarily on the fact that *Romer* did not arise in the military context and also argued that whereas the measure in *Romer* was status-based, the military policy was based on conduct. Specifically addressing the argument that *Romer* said antigay animus was never a permissible purpose under rational basis review, the *Able* court replied:

> In this case, plaintiffs' reliance on *Romer* . . . is misplaced. [That case] did not arise in the military setting. In the civilian context, the Court was willing to examine the benign reasons advanced by the government to consider whether they masked an impermissible underlying purpose. In the military setting, however, constitutionally-mandated deference to military assessments and judgments gives the judiciary far less scope to scrutinize the reasons, legitimate on their face, that the military has advanced to justify its actions.[53]

At best, this response means that because the goals seem legitimate on their face, the court will not even ask whether the means chosen to accomplish that goal is legitimate. For example, unit cohesion was one of the justifications offered for the military policy. Unit cohesion is certainly a legitimate concern on its face. Whether barring known gays from the military is a rational or a prejudicial means of accomplishing unit cohesion will simply not be questioned by the court. Presumably, if the military had been direct enough to say, "we are barring gays from the military because we dislike them," the Second Circuit would have been willing to apply the antigay animus rule of *Romer.* The result under the *Able* decision is that the military will only be subjected to meaningful equal protection scrutiny if it actually says that its motive is based on prejudice, an event unlikely to occur, given the high-quality legal advice that the Pentagon receives. In effect, the equal protection test applied to the military will only look at goals and not at the means chosen to accomplish those goals. This result makes the equal protection test for the military different from that applied to other state actors and certainly a different test from the one applied in *Romer*. There, the Supreme Court looked at the means chosen (barring gays from making discrimination claims) and found that the means were too loosely connected to any of the governmental purposes put forward by the state. By not even looking at the connection between means and ends in *Able*, the court never addressed the ultimate question: under rational basis review, can an employer take into account the prejudices of its other employees or customers to avoid hiring gay people?

Taking into account the prejudices of others has certainly not been an adequate defense for employers who wish to discriminate on the basis of sex or race.[54] And the Supreme Court has ruled that society's racial prejudices are not a sufficient justification for placing a child with his white father and stepmother rather than his white mother and black stepfather.[55] Even in a low-level, rational basis case, the Court ruled that the state actor could not take into account the irrational prejudices of neighbors when determining where to locate a group home for the mentally retarded.[56] The military's justifications for excluding gays and lesbians are clearly based on concerns about the prejudice of nongay military personnel. Such concerns on behalf of the military are not themselves irrational concerns. A nonprejudiced person can legitimately be concerned about another person's prejudice and the effect that prejudice will have on others. But when the military deals with its own concerns by contributing to the prejudice, that is an impermissible choice. The government cannot decide to combat homophobia by ridding its ranks of gay people. Instead, it should offer homophobia training to reduce the prejudice. After *Romer*, one would have hoped that the *Able* court would either have found the antigay bias impermissible or honestly ruled that, in the military at least, antigay bias is permissible because, after all, we must defer to military choices.

While *Romer* was making its way through the courts, another equal protection/gay discrimination case was also making its way through the courts. *Shahar v. Bowers*[57] would not be finally decided until after the Supreme Court decision in *Romer*.

Robin Shahar graduated at the top of her law school class at Emory Law School where she was the Note and Comment editor of the law review.[58] During the summer before her final year in law school, she clerked for the attorney general of Georgia, Michael Bowers. Michael Bowers is the same attorney general who successfully defended Georgia's sodomy statute in

Bowers v. Hardwick. At the time of her clerkship, Robin went by the name of Robin Brown. Based on her outstanding record plus her job performance, she was offered a permanent job as a staff attorney with the Criminal Division of the Attorney General's Office.

That same summer, she and her partner of four years met with their rabbi to discuss their desire to have an official ceremony signifying their commitment to each other. With his support, they began planning the ceremony for the following summer. Shahar wanted to bring her partner to the summer picnic that was hosted for members of the department in which she was working. Concerned about how others would view her relationship with another woman, she confided in one of the female attorneys, who advised her not to bring the partner to the picnic.

Several months later, in November, Shahar filled out the required forms for a staff attorney position. Under marital status, she wrote "engaged." She marked through "spouse's name" and wrote in "future spouse's name," and named her partner, "Francine M. Greenfield." The form also asked: "Do any of your relatives work for the State of Georgia?" Shahar identified her partner, who worked for a state university.

That June, after graduating from law school, Shahar called Bob Coleman, the deputy attorney general for administration. She and her partner had decided to adopt the same last name, "Shahar," which means the "act of seeking God."[59] She wanted to inform Coleman of the marriage, the name change, and that she would prefer to start work after the honeymoon in Greece. She did not tell Coleman she was marrying another woman. Coleman shared the information about the marriage with another attorney in the AG's office, who in turn mentioned it to another attorney, Susan Rutherford. Rutherford knew, from a chance meeting with Shahar outside the office, that the person Shahar was marrying was another woman. Apparently, Rutherford mentioned this fact and, before long, the entire AG's office was in a stir. Shortly thereafter, Shahar received a letter from Attorney General Bowers withdrawing the offer of permanent employment because of information received concerning "a purported marriage between you and another woman." Shahar brought suit, claiming that the withdrawal of the job offer violated her free exercise and free association rights and her rights to equal protection and substantive due process.

Bowers, who had never met Shahar personally, justified his action by asserting that Shahar's employment in the criminal division would interfere with that division's ability to enforce the laws of Georgia. In the pleadings, he elaborated as follows:

Regardless of whether [p]laintiff has actually committed sodomy, [p]laintiff's Amended Complaint admits that she has purportedly "married" her female companion, and that she made such "marriage" public knowledge. On these facts alone, the Attorney General is justified in withdrawing the offer of employment in order to ensure public perception (and the reality) that his [d]epartment is enforcing and will continue to enforce the laws of the State.[60]

The district court ruled in favor of Bowers on the pleadings and dismissed all claims. On appeal, a panel of the Court of Appeals for the Eleventh Circuit ruled in favor of Shahar on her intimate association claim and dismissed all other claims. The court of appeals ruling was quite limited. The court did not rule that lesbians in general, no matter how committed, have a right of intimate association. Rather, the court stressed that Shahar and her partner, who had both grown up in the Jewish faith and were quite committed to Judaism, had shared a religious ceremony of that faith with intimate friends and family. Their marriage was not a legal one, recognized by any state. However, it was a union that was recognized by the Reconstructionist Movement in Judaism. As their rabbi testified, "The union in which they joined is a public affirmation of their commitment to each other and to the Jewish people, having no legal significance but only personal and religious significance, and it can be terminated only by the church."[61]

Because the withdrawal of the job offer burdened Shahar's right of intimate association, the court of appeals required that Bowers justify his action by showing a compelling reason. The panel split 2 to 1 on this holding. Judge Phyllis A. Kravitch wrote separately to concur that Shahar's right of intimate association had been burdened. Indeed, in Judge Kravitch's opinion, the intimacy and commitment of the relationship was central and not the religious nature of the ceremony. But rather than require Bowers to satisfy the compelling state interest test to justify his action, Kravitch would require a lesser test that balanced both parties' interests. Known as the *Pickering* balancing test, this test is usually applied in cases in which government has restricted a free speech right of its employees. It has been applied in other cases in which "out" gay employees bring discrimination charges against their governmental employers. Because government has a legitimate interest in maintaining the trust and confidence of its citizens, government has a legitimate interest in seeing that its employees, by their behavior and speech, maintain the same trust and confidence. Bowers had a legitimate interest, as an elected public official, in the efficient operation of his office. When the state is acting as employer, rather than sovereign, it is entitled to more discretion in carrying out its duties. Nonetheless, after fully considering the interests of Bowers, Judge Kravitch ruled in favor of Shahar. Thus, although she applied a different legal test, something greater than rational basis review, but less than compelling state interest, she came to the same conclusion as the other two judges who had applied the higher compelling state interest test.

Attorney General Bowers asked for a rehearing, a standard procedure before asking for review at the Supreme Court level. A majority of the judges voted in favor of rehearing the case en banc. This decision to grant en banc review was not a good sign for Shahar because it meant that, in all likelihood, a majority of the court disagreed with the panel decision. Her lawyers remained hopeful, however, because the en banc hearing might mean something else: that a majority of the judges agreed with Judge Kravitch that a balancing test, rather than the compelling state interest test, was the appropriate legal test to apply in the case. Thus, the court could still rule in favor of Shahar but choose to clarify that the *Pickering* balancing test was the correct test to apply in determining the outcome.

One year after the Supreme Court victory in *Romer,* the en banc panel of the Eleventh Circuit handed down its opinion in *Shahar,* reversing the panel decision and ruling in favor of Attorney General Michael Bowers. Three judges dissented.[62]

Solely for purposes of argument, the majority opinion assumed, but did not find, that Shahar had a First Amendment right of expression or of intimate association and that it had been burdened by the attorney general's action. However, because of the nature of her employment, the court agreed that the appropriate test to apply was the *Pickering* balancing test. Unlike Judge Kravitch, however, these judges felt that Bowers had satisfied that test. The equal protection claim was dismissed because Shahar had not proved that Bowers dismissed her on the basis of status alone. Rather, he had dismissed her on the basis of her choice to marry another woman and her choice to make that information known. Bowers was justified in making this decision based on her conduct because, in marrying another woman, Shahar created the impression that she engaged in sodomy. Sodomy was a crime in Georgia at that time. Shahar was to work in the criminal division. The people of Georgia would lose faith in the attorney general once they knew he had a presumed sodomite working to enforce the criminal laws of the state.

The *Romer* decision had no effect in *Shahar* because *Romer* was a pure status equal protection claim. Besides, applying *Romer* would only have provided Shahar with rational basis review. Instead, the court applied a higher level of review under the *Pickering* balancing test. At least the court claimed to be applying a higher level of review. But a close review of the decision suggests otherwise. The opinion is replete with references to the amount of deference that ought to be accorded the attorney general. The court required no evidence from him to support his conclusions. The judges in the majority concluded that he had the power to hire and fire employees based on his personal sense of whether he trusted the person. The court mandated no requirement that the trust be based on reason rather than prejudice. The court also found reasonable the attorney general's assertion that employing Shahar would compromise his office since his office dealt with issues of homosexuality, sodomy, and domestic partner benefits. Presumably, the fact that she was a lesbian, that she might engage in sodomy, and that she had a domestic partner would create a conflict of interest in such cases.

The court stressed the importance of the sodomy law in its decision. Because Michael Bowers had defended Georgia's sodomy statute before the Supreme Court and had received so much public attention, the possibility that his staff would include a sodomite seemed a legitimate and important concern. Regarding the presumption of sodomy, the court was careful to say no evidence had been presented that Shahar had violated the law. Indeed, Shahar had provided expert witness testimony to the effect that most lesbians "prefer to engage in non-sodomy sexual practices, rather than anal or oral sex—the only two practices prohibited by Georgia's sodomy statute."[63] This evidence was deemed irrelevant by Bowers who argued that the people of Georgia were unaware of what lesbian sexual practices were and would, however wrongly, make the assumption that lesbians practiced sodomy.

When one reads between the lines of the *Shahar* opinion, the decision begins to sound like a military opinion in disguise. The court grants deference to the attorney general and says it will not look beyond his statements in determining whether his action was justified. He need produce no evidence in support of his conclusions. Even though he has never met Shahar, he can decide to dismiss her if he feels that he cannot trust her. Her openness about her sexual orientation might contribute to loss of cohesiveness and loss of morale in the AG's office. Those concerns are reasonable justifications for his actions. The court is also willing to agree with the attorney general's characterization of Shahar as someone likely to engage in sodomy. And echoing the military's claim, the court says the attorney general's discrimination is not on the basis of status, but rather on the basis of conduct. Presumably, Bowers, like the military, would hire a lesbian, so long as she did not tell and so long as she did not engage in any activity that might suggest to others that she was gay.

The *Shahar* decision was handed down by the Eleventh Circuit on May 30, 1997. Two days later, Michael Bowers resigned as attorney general of Georgia to seek the office of governor. On June 6, 1997, the *New York Times* reported:

> Former Georgia Attorney General Michael J. Bowers, who earned nationwide attention for aggressively defending his state's anti-sodomy law, announced today that he had carried on an adulterous affair for more than a decade with a woman who once worked in his office. In light of the raging discord in the military about adultery, Mr. Bowers, a West Point graduate, also said today that he had resigned his commission with the Air National Guard, in which he held the rank of major general.

Adultery is a misdemeanor under Georgia law. Shahar's lawyers filed for permission to supplement the record and have the case reconsidered in light of this new evidence. Their argument was that if Bowers had himself violated the laws of Georgia, then his purported motive for dismissing Shahar may have been a pretext. On August 1, 1997, the Court of Appeals for the Eleventh Circuit denied the attorneys' motion.

On January 12, 1998, the Supreme Court of the United States denied certiorari in *Shahar*. Ironically, in a totally unrelated case, the Supreme Court of Georgia struck down Georgia's sodomy statute under the Georgia constitution[64] just ten months later.

Although *Romer* has been interpreted too narrowly to help in subsequent cases involving antigay initiatives, the military, and a government employee such as Shahar, the case remains an important first step in gaining full recognition of lesbian and gay equal rights. Even at its narrowest, *Romer* can be cited for the principle that status-based classifications entitle lesbians and gay men to a claim of discrimination despite *Bowers v. Hardwick*. *Romer* was first cited for this principle successfully in a case brought by a gay youth against his school for allowing him to be harassed on the basis of his sexual orientation. In July 1996, the Court of Appeals for the Seventh Circuit, not known to be a particularly gay-friendly forum, ruled in favor of the youth and held that he had stated an equal protection claim. With respect to the relevance of *Bowers v. Hardwick,* the court said: "Of course

Bowers will soon be eclipsed in the area of equal protection by the Supreme Court's holding in *Romer v. Evans.*"[65]

In *Stemler v. City of Florence,*[66] the Sixth Circuit Court of Appeals relied on *Romer* to support its finding that a selective criminal prosecution in Boone County, Kentucky, on the basis of sexual orientation violated the Equal Protection Clause. In addition, two federal district courts have relied on *Romer*'s rule that antigay animus can never justify discrimination to rule in favor of two schoolteachers.[67]

Based on these positive decisions, *Romer* has clearly opened a door, or perhaps at least a window, for lesbian and gay civil rights lawyers. But as the *Shahar* case shows, even outside the military context, the *Hardwick* decision continues to cast a shadow over that opening.

USING STATE AND LOCAL LAWS TO GAIN PUBLIC SPHERE RIGHTS

Although Congress refuses to enact antidiscrimination legislation that would protect lesbians, bisexuals, and gay men in the public sphere, eleven states and hundreds of cities and counties throughout the states have enacted gay rights statutes and ordinances.[68] Gay people who live in jurisdictions covered by these laws can bring suit against employers for employment discrimination, against landlords or sellers for housing discrimination, and against public accommodations or business enterprises for denial of public benefits, or goods and services. To succeed, the plaintiff must show that the defendant is covered by the applicable law and that the defendant's action violates the specific provisions of the law. Employment and housing discrimination cases are fairly straightforward. All employers and housing providers are generally covered by the statutes or ordinances unless they are specifically exempted, as is sometimes the case with very small employers or homeowners who rent out part of their own homes. The application of public accommodations statutes has been less clear.

The Parade Cases

St. Patrick's Day celebrations around the country usually include a parade. Two of the most notable and visible celebrations occur in Boston and New York City. Boston residents have celebrated the saint's day since 1737. After 1776, the St. Patrick's Day celebration was combined with festivities that commemorated the evacuation of British troops from Boston, an event that occurred in March of 1776. The city of Boston organized the St. Patrick's Day–Evacuation Day Parade every year until 1947, when it began to cosponsor the event with a private group, the South Boston Allied War Veterans Council. In New York City, the first St. Patrick's Day parade occurred in 1762. A private Catholic fraternal group, the Ancient Order of Hibernians, has sponsored the New York parade since the early 1800s.

In 1990, a group of Irish gay men and lesbians asked to march in the 1991 New York parade. The parade organizers resisted. Under pressure from the city administration, a compromise was struck under which the group was allowed to march in the parade, but not as a separate, identifiable lesbian and gay contingent. In 1992, the Irish-American Gay, Lesbian & Bisexual Group of Boston (GLIB) submitted a request to march in the Boston parade. Although such requests were routinely granted to any group that asked to be included, the South Boston Allied War Veterans Council denied permission to GLIB. A state court ordered the parade organizers to allow the group to march carrying the group's banner. The group applied again in 1993, were denied permission again, and again a state court ordered the Veteran's Council to let the group march.

Both the New York and Boston gay groups sued to be admitted to the St. Patrick's Day parades in their respective cities, claiming that to deny them the benefit of marching was a violation of the applicable public accommodations law. The New York group claimed a violation of the New York City ordinance that prohibits discrimination in a public accommodation on the basis of sexual orientation. The City Human Rights Commission agreed that the parade was a public accommodation and ruled in favor of the gay group's right to march in the parade. In the meantime, the city of New York, for the first time in 150 years, refused to grant the St. Patrick's parade permit to the Ancient Order of Hibernians (AOH). AOH filed suit in federal court, claiming a violation of its First Amendment free speech rights. The district court agreed with AOH and ordered the city to grant the parade permit to AOH.[69] According to the court, parades are speech, not public accommodations. Thus, the organizers have the right to exclude any group that proposes to engage in speech that is counter to the message of the parade organizers.

The Boston litigation produced similar results. The Massachusetts trial and appellate courts both ruled in favor of the gay and lesbian group. The Massachusetts Supreme Court found that the parade was a public accommodation under the Massachusetts statute. Furthermore, the court held that the parade organizers could not exclude the gay and lesbian group. Finally, the court held that applying the Massachusetts public accommodations statute to the parade organizers did not infringe upon their first amendment speech rights. The Boston case, *Hurley v. Irish-American Gay, Lesbian and Bisexual Group of Boston*,[70] went to the U.S. Supreme Court and resulted in a unanimous decision in favor of the free speech rights of the parade sponsors.

Given the Supreme Court's First Amendment jurisprudence, the *Hurley* opinion came as no surprise to many gay rights litigators. Parades do constitute speech and when a private party conducts a parade, the parade's message ought to be protected. *Hurley* did not break new ground on this point. When the Ku Klux Klan wanted to conduct a march and exclude the NAACP from marching in the same parade, a federal court ruled in favor of the Klan's right to exclude.[71] Similarly, if the NAACP had wanted to march for black civil rights, that organization's free speech rights would be invaded if it were forced to include the Ku Klux Klan. A gay rights parade should not be forced to include a contingent with banners condemning homosexuality as a sin. First Amendment jurisprudence, in the parade context, allows the parade organizers to exclude groups from the parade if the contested group's message will interfere with the parade's message. No one can be excluded from the parade's audience, however, and people along the parade route can engage in their own speech disagreeing with the message of the parade.

Where the *Hurley* decision created disagreement was in its characterization of the Boston St. Patrick's Day/Evacuation Day Parade as a private parade. Given that parade's particular history, many view the parade as a public civic celebration, sponsored in part by the city. As such, the parade is either a public celebration that has no particular message other than "we are all Bostonians who celebrate with the Irish on March 17,"[72] or it is a public forum in which no particular message can be censored. The Supreme Court may have turned the case into an easy one by mischaracterizing the parade as a private one with a private message.

St. Patrick's Day parades continue and the New York and Boston parades continue to exclude identifiable lesbian, gay, and bisexual groups from marching. March 2000 marks the ten-year anniversary of the exclusion of the Irish Lesbian and Gay Organization (ILGO) from the New York parade. Every year, ILGO applies for permission to join the parade and every year the application is denied. Every year the group protests by holding its own parade on Fifth Avenue at approximately the same time as the official St. Patrick's Day parade is held. And every year the police arrest members of the group for disorderly conduct and obstructing traffic.[73] ILGO has tried for years to obtain its own parade permit for St. Patrick's Day, but it insists on marching the same route as the AOH parade. Since New York City parade regulations prohibit two parades at the same time and place, those requests have been denied. In February 2000, a federal district court, after a jury trial, upheld the city's denial of the requested permit. For the 2000 St. Patrick's Day protest parade in New York, ILGO was joined by gays and lesbians from Ireland, where apparently St. Patrick's Day parades have been including gay and lesbian marchers without incident.

The Boy Scout Cases

The Boy Scouts of America excludes gays from its membership. Nor can gay men serve as adult scout leaders. The organization also excludes women. These exclusions have been tested under various state and federal public accommodations statutes. Some courts have ruled that the Boy Scouts organization is not a "place of public accommodation" as that term is used in the applicable statute.[74] These holdings resemble earlier cases in which women had challenged the gender exclusionary rules of such clubs as the Jaycees and Kiwanis but lost in states that defined "place of public accommodation" narrowly.

The Connecticut Supreme Court has construed its public accommodations statute broadly enough to cover the Boy Scouts but found no violation of the statute when the organization denied a woman's application to be a scoutmaster. The court found that the statute only prohibited discriminatory denials of goods, services, or similar items, none of which covered her request to be a scoutmaster.[75]

In 1999 the New Jersey Supreme Court similarly found that its public accommodations statute covered the Boy Scouts of America (BSA). The court also found that the organization's denial of adult membership and an accompanying scout leadership position to James Dale, who is openly gay, deprived Dale of a benefit that was protected under the New Jersey Law Against Discrimination (LAD).[76] BSA countered that its exclusionary membership policy was an expression of its belief that homosexuality is inconsistent with boy scouting and, further, that any state law requiring the organization to include Dale would violate BSA's right to express its antigay views, a right protected by the First Amendment. The New Jersey court rejected the First Amendment claim. On June 28, 2000, by a vote of 5 to 4, the Supreme Court reversed the New Jersey court, holding that BSA's right to exclude Dale was protected under the First Amendment.[77]

James Dale had been a scout since the age of 8. He had earned over twenty-five merit badges and had been admitted into the Order of the Arrow, an honor awarded to scouts who "best exemplify the Scout Oath and Law in their daily lives." Ultimately he achieved the status of Eagle Scout, an honor achieved by only two percent of all scouts.

When Dale went to college, he began to admit that he was gay. He told friends and family and became active in the Rutgers Lesbian/Gay Alliance. He also remained active in the Boy Scouts as an adult member and continued to embrace scout ideals. Then, a news story focusing on a gay conference on the Rutgers campus included an interview with Dale in which he talked about being gay. He never mentioned his connection with the Boy Scouts. Nonetheless, a month after the story appeared, he received a letter revoking his membership in the Boy Scouts.

Evan Wolfson, of Lambda Legal Defense, was counsel for Dale. In his brief to the U.S. Supreme Court he made two key arguments. First, he argued that BSA in fact had no expressive interest in making statements regarding homosexuality. The organization had never issued any public statement mentioning homosexuality and morality until it had expelled Dale. Furthermore, official guidelines stated that sexuality was a matter that boys should discuss with their families and not with their scoutmasters. Thus, to the extent there was any official policy, that policy was one of silence. In addition, BSA's adoption of a gay exclusionary rule stood at odds with the message of inclusion contained in all its other policies. In the absence of any record that the organization actually had an expressive antigay message in need of protection, the First Amendment claim should fail.

Wolfson's next argument was that even if BSA were found to have a right of expressive association in an antigay message, that right was trumped by the state of New Jersey's compelling interest in ending discrimination. Wolfson argued that the state's interest was particularly compelling in the case of BSA because of the organization's close entanglement with government. Like the USOC, another "private" organization that had defended its antigay position before the Court just two decades earlier, the BSA was chartered by the federal government. It receives substantial support from public schools and governmental entities such as the police and the military. BSA's partnership with government makes it a particularly harmful discriminator. New Jersey's interest in distancing itself from the BSA message is thus particularly strong and justifies the application of the LAD to require nondiscrimination in BSA's public activities.

The Supreme Court, in a decision written by Justice Rehnquist, rejected both arguments, finding that Dale's inclusion would force BSA to adopt a message different from the one it wished to maintain. Two key points in the decision are troubling. First, the Court found that the BSA did have an anti-gay message that needed protecting despite the lack of any evidence that it had fostered this message over time. Rehnquist stated: "We accept the Boy Scouts' assertion. We need not inquire further...." Such an approach gives great deference to the organization's own view of the facts and engages in no independent judicial review, an approach that the four dissenting justices found disconcerting. Second, the Rehnquist opinion explained that Dale's inclusion would burden the organization's speech rights even more than the inclusion of a nongay scoutmaster who supported gay rights because "[t]he presence of an avowed homosexual and gay rights activist in an assistant scoutmaster's uniform sends a distinctly different message from the presence of a heterosexual assistant scoutmaster who is on record as disagreeing with Boy Scouts policy." This view of "gay difference" conflates status and conduct. It presumes that just being gay is sufficient "speech" in and of itself to justify treating gay people differently.

THE FIRST AMENDMENT DEFENSE

The parade cases and *Dale* pose similar problems. In both sorts of cases defendants are asked to conform to the legislative mandate of nondiscrimination. In both sorts of cases, the defendants defend by claiming a right to exclude on the basis of free speech, or in some cases, on the basis of religious freedom. It is too soon to predict the ramifications of the *Dale* decision. At the very least it has extended the First Amendment defense to organizations other than parades. It is thus likely that a number of organizations will argue on First Amendment grounds that they are not subject to any laws that require them to treat gay people fairly. Yet, the specific First Amendment holding in *Dale* is not likely to be extended to many other organizations. BSA is a sufficiently unique organization that other organizations can be easily distinguished. Follow-up litigation involving BSA, however, is likely to raise issues that may once again find their way to the Supreme Court. I have in mind litigation over the right of government entities to withdraw support from the Boy Scouts with BSA making a plausible

First Amendment claim that the organization is being punished for its anti-gay viewpoint.

The religious freedom defense has been raised by landlords who refuse to rent to unmarried couples even though local legislation prohibits such discrimination. Currently a case is pending before the Ninth Circuit to determine whether or not religious liberty can trump the antidiscrimination laws in such a case.[78] More recently, the defense has been raised by a doctor in Kentucky who claims that his religious liberty will be infringed if city and county ordinances prohibiting discrimination against gays and lesbians are applied to him. The ACLU Lesbian and Gay Rights Project has intervened in the Kentucky case.

This "religious right to discriminate," as Matt Coles dubs it, is not new in the lesbian and gay civil rights movement. Bob Jones University claimed it had a religious right to discriminate on the basis of race.[79] Religious employers do enjoy limited protection from the provisions of Title VII insofar as they make employment decisions regarding church positions. Thus, the courts will not interfere with church decisions about who is qualified to be a pastor. But the religious exemption does not leave such employers free generally to discriminate on the basis of sex, even when religious beliefs include the idea that the male is the rightful head of the household. Thus, for example, a religious school that provided health insurance to married male employees but not to married females violated Title VII.[80] Thus, broad claims to a religious right to discriminate have failed in prior civil rights movements regarding race and gender equality. It remains to be seen how seriously these claims will be taken by courts when the issue is gay and lesbian civil rights.

NOTES

1. *See,* for example, Note, "The Constitutional Status of Sexual Orientation: Homosexuality as a Suspect Classification," 98 *Harvard Law Review* 1285 (1985); Harris M. Miller II, Note, "An Argument for the Application of Equal Protection Heightened Scrutiny to Classifications Based on Homosexuality," 57 *Southern California Law Review* 797 (1984).

2. City of Cleburne v. Cleburne Living Center, 473 U.S. 432 (1985).

3. Padula v. Webster, 822 F.2d 97 (D.C. Cir. 1987).

4. Padula, 822 F.2d 97 at 103.

5. Ibid.

6. Missouri appears to be an exception. Missouri defines deviate sexual conduct as "any act involving the genitals of one person and the mouth, tongue, or anus of another person or a sexual act involving the penetration, however slight, of the male or female sex organ or the anus by a finger, instrument or object done for the

purpose of arousing or gratifying the sexual desire of any person." Mo. St. 566.010. Thus mutual masturbation would violate Missouri's sodomy law.

7. Rich v. Secretary of the Army, 735 F.2d 1220 (10th Cir. 1984).

8. See Jantz v. Muci, 976 F.2d 623 (10th Cir. 1992), rev'g. 759 F.Supp. 1543 (D. Kan. 1991), which had held that as of 1991 gay men and lesbians were a suspect class).

9. See David G. Savage, "Crusading Liberal Judge Keeps High Court Busy," *Los Angeles Times*, Part A, March 3, 1996.

10. High Tech Gays v. Defense Industrial Security Clearance Office, 895 F.2d 563 (9th Cir. 1990).

11. Ibid. at 571.

12. U.S. Government Accounting Office, Defense Force Management: DOD's Policy on Homosexuality at 11 (Report to Congressional Requesters June 1992).

13. See DOD Directive 1332.14 (H) (1) (b) (3).

14. Cammermeyer v. Aspin, 850 F.Supp 910 (W.D. Wash. 1994).

15. Cammermeyer, 850 F.Supp. 910 at 925.

16. Ibid.

17. 10 U.S.C. § 654.

18. Under the 1982 Army Regulations, for example, a member was subject to separation if "[t]he member has stated that he is a homosexual or bisexual unless there is a further finding that the member is not a homosexual or bisexual." Army Regulations 635–200, Chapter 15 (May 1, 1982).

19. *See* Halley, *Don't: A Reader's Guide to the Military's Anti-Gay Policy.*

20. Pruitt v. Cheney, 963 F.2d 1160 (9th Cir. 1991), *cert. denied*, 506 U.S. 1020 (1992).

21. Meinhold v. United States, 34 F.3d 1469 (9th Cir. 1994). The panel consisted of Judge Pamela Rymer (appointed by Bush), Judge David R. Thompson (appointed by Reagan) and Judge Otto R. Skopil (appointed by Carter).

22. Holmes v. California Army National Guard, 155 F.3d 1049 (9th Cir. 1998).

23. Able v. United States, 155 F.3d 628 (2d Cir. 1998).

24. Baker v. Wade, 769 F.2d at 292.

25. 119 S.Ct. 794 (1999).

26. The first appeal resulted in a remand to the district court. *See* 88 F.3d 1280 (2d Cir. 1996). On remand, the district court held that the "Don't Ask/Don't Tell" policy violated the servicemembers' constitutional rights. *See* 968 F.Supp. 850 (E.D. N.Y. 1997). On appeal, this decision was reversed. *See* 155 F.3d 628 (2d Cir. 1998).

27. Able v. United States, 968 F. Supp. 850 (E.D. N.Y. 1997).

28. Prior to the passage of Title VII of the Civil Rights Act of 1964, there was minimal protection for women in employment at the state level. A few states had passed "equal pay acts" (e.g., Massachusetts and Pennsylvania), but states did not add "sex" to their fair employment laws until the federal law was passed.

29. *See generally* Arthur Earl Bonfield, "The Origin and Development of American Fair Employment Legislation," 52 *Iowa Law Review* 1043 (1967).

30. Button et al., *Private Lives, Public Conflicts: Battles over Gay Rights in American Communities* at 65.

31. See William E. Adams Jr., "Is It Animus or a Difference of Opinion? The Problems Caused by the Invidious Intent of Anti-gay Ballot Measures," 34 *Willamette Law Review* 449 (1998).

32. Keen and Goldberg, *Strangers to the Law* at 15.

33. Reitman v. Mulkey, 387 U.S. 369 (1967).

34. Hunter v. Erickson, 393 U.S. 385 (1969).

35. Richard B. Collins and Dale Oesterle, "Structuring the Ballot Initiative: Procedures That Do and Don't Work," 66 *University of Colorado Law Review* 47, 49–50 (1995).

36. The Colorado constitution provides: "The first power hereby reserved by the people is the initiative, and signatures by registered electors in an amount equal to at least five percent of the total number of votes cast for all candidates for the office of secretary of state at the previous general election shall be required to propose any measure by petition, and every such petition shall include the full text of the measure so proposed. Initiative petitions for state legislation and amendments to the constitution, in such form as may be prescribed pursuant to law, shall be addressed to and filed with the secretary of state at least three months before the general election at which they are to be voted upon."

C.R.S.A. Const. Art. 5, Sec. 1.

37. Evans v. Romer, 882 P.2d 1335, 1339–1340 (Colo. 1994).

38. *Strangers to the Law* at 196.

39. Matthew Coles, "Equal Protection and the Anti-Civil-Rights Initiatives: Protecting the Rights of Lesbian and Gay Men to Bargain in the Pluralist Bazaar," 55 *Ohio State Law Review* 563 at 575 (1994).

40. 402 U.S. 137 (1971).

41. The organization mentioned is the Society of American Law Teachers.

42. Romer v. Evans, 517 U.S. at 635 (1996).

43. Ibid. at 633.

44. Romer, 517 U.S. at 635.

45. Romer v. Evans, Brief for Respondents.

46. Tribe, "Saenz Sans Prophecy" at 177–178.

47. *Strangers to the Law* at 237.

48. *See* Cass R. Sunstein, "Foreword: Leaving Things Undecided," 110 *Harvard Law Review* 4 (1996).

49. Equality Foundation of Greater Cincinnati, Inc. v. City of Cincinnati, 54 F.3d 261 (6th Cir. 1995), *cert. granted, vacated and remanded* 518 U.S. 1001 (1996).

50. 518 U.S. 1001.

51. 128 F.3d 289 (6th Cir. 1997).

52. 119 S.Ct. 365 (1998).

53. 155 F.3d 628 at 634.

54. *See* EEOC Guidelines on Sex Discrimination.

55. Palmore v. Sidoti, 466 U.S. 429 (1984).

56. City of Cleburne v. Cleburne Living Center, 473 U.S. 432 (1985).

57. Shahar v. Bowers, 836 F.Supp. 859 (N.D. Ga. 1993), *aff'd in part, rev'd in part*, 70 F.3d 1218 (11th Cir. 1995), *vacated and rehearing en banc granted*, 78 F.3d (1996), rev'd, 114 F.3d 1097 (11th Cir. 1997) *(en banc)*, cert denied, 522 U.S. 1049 (1998).

58. Her final class rank was No. 4.
59. See "A.G. Refuses to Hire Lesbian," *A.B.A. Journal* at 32 (December 1991).
60. Shahar v. Bowers, Defendant's Reply, at 11 n.5.
61. 70 F.3d 1218 at 1223.
62. 114 F.3d 1097.
63. 114 F.3d 1097 at 1127 (dissenting opinion).
64. Powell v. State, 510 S.E.2d 18 (Ga. 1998).
65. Nabozny, 92 F.3d 446 at 458 (7th Cir. 1996).
66. 126 F.3d 856, 873–874 (6th Cir. 1997).
67. See Glover v. Williamsburg Local School District Board of Education, 20 F.Supp. 2d 1160 (S.D. Ohio 1998); Weaver v. Nebo School District, 29 F.Supp. 2d 1279 (D. Utah 1998).
68. Button et al., *Private Lives, Public Conflicts.*
69. Ancient Order of Hibernians v. Dinkins, 814 F.Supp. 358 (S.D.N.Y. 1993).
70. 515 U.S. 557 (1995).
71. Ku Klux Klan v. Town of Thurmont, 700 F.Supp. 281 (D. Md. 1988).
72. See Gretchen Van Ness, "Parades and Prejudice: The Incredible True Story of Boston's St. Patrick's Day Parade and the United States Supreme Court," 30 *New Engand Law Review* 625 (1996).
73. See People v. Arbeiter, 650 N.Y.S.2d 915 (N.Y. Sup. App. 1996), *appeal denied,* 677 N.E.2d 292 (N.Y. 1996), *cert. denied* 520 U.S. 1213 (1997).
74. *See,* for example, Welsh v. Boy Scouts of America, 993 F.2d 1267, 1269 (7th Cir.) (holding that the Boy Scouts is not a "place of public accommodation" under Title II of Civil Rights Act of 1964). The plaintiff in this case challenged the Boy Scout rule that required scouts to affirm their belief in God. This rule implicated Title II's provision prohibiting discrimination on the basis of religion. *See also* Schwenk v. Boy Scouts of America, 551 P.2d 465 (Ore. 1976) (Boy Scouts not a place of public accommodation under Oregon statutes, at least insofar as gender discrimination is the claim); Curran v. Mount Diablo Council of the Boy Scouts, 952 P.2d 218 (Cal. 1998) (holding that Boy Scouts are not a business enterprise and thus could exclude gays).
75. Quinnipiac Council, Boy Scouts of America, Inc. v. Commission on Human Rights and Opportunities, 528 A.2d 352 (Conn. 1987).
76. Dale v. Boy Scouts of America, 734 A.2d 1196 (N.J. 1999).
77. Dale v. Boy Scouts of America, 120 S. Court. 2446 (2000).
78. Thomas v. Anchorage Equal Rights Commission, 165 F.3d 692 (9th Cir. 1998) *opinion withdrawn and en banc rehearing ordered.* 192 F.3d 1208 (9th Cir. 1999).
79. See Bob Jones University v. United States, 639 F.2d 147 (4th Cir. 1980), *aff'd.* 461 U.S. 574 (1983).
80. *See* EEOC v. Fremont Christian Schools, 781 F.2d 1362 (9th Cir. 1986).

8

Private Sphere Rights Post–
Bowers v. Hardwick

Bowers v. Hardwick ended the battle in federal court for recognition of privacy rights or due process claims on behalf of gay men and lesbians. Federal litigation post-*Hardwick* would have to focus on equal protection claims instead, and, as we saw in the last chapter, even those claims would be hampered by a broad reading of *Hardwick*. But the fight against sodomy statutes did not stop merely because federal courts were no longer a friendly forum. Before the decision in *Hardwick* was handed down, litigation at the state level had successfully challenged state sodomy statutes. Most of these state challenges had been on federal constitutional grounds. Often state constitutional claims were included as a pro forma part of the argument, but the state courts always focused on the federal constitution in rendering their opinions. Once the U.S. Supreme Court had determined that no protected privacy right existed under the federal constitution for same-sex sodomy, gay rights litigators wondered about the continued validity of the sodomy statutes in those states whose courts had determined that the federal constitution did protect same-sex sodomy.

In most states, the issue was more academic than real. Since arguments against sodomy statutes were typically made on the basis of both state and federal constitutional claims, most state courts had ruled the statutes unconstitutional under the state constitution as well as the federal. Statutes that were held to violate a state's constitution were unaffected by the *Hardwick* decision since that decision was based on the federal constitution. Even if a state court had ruled the statute unconstitutional solely on federal grounds, the *Hardwick* decision could have no immediate impact on decisions in earlier cases because those decisions were final. Besides, in states where the state legislatures had repealed their sodomy statutes once they had been found unconstitutional,[1] no statute was on the books for the police to enforce anymore. But for those states with statutes still on the books and with prosecutors willing to enforce them, the effect of *Hardwick* on a prior state court ruling against the statute was a real question.

The problem was particularly pressing in the state of New York, where in 1980 the Court of Appeals had struck down the state sodomy law on federal constitutional grounds, without ever addressing the state constitutional arguments made in the case. The sodomy statute had remained on the books despite annual attempts to convince the legislature to repeal it. Given the opinion in *Hardwick,* a prosecutor could take the position that the statute could now be enforced in new cases because it was, after all, constitutional.

New York's attorney general at the time, Robert Abrams, decided otherwise. After reviewing the case, he determined that although the New York court had relied solely on the federal constitution in striking down the statute, the court had found the statute unconstitutional under both privacy/due process *and* equal protection grounds. Since the *Hardwick* case only addressed the privacy/due process claim, the New York case remained good law on the basis of the equal protection claim.

The New York legislature's refusal to repeal the sodomy statute, even after it had been ruled unconstitutional, is evidence of the difficulty gay rights activists have had in gaining repeal of sodomy statutes around the country. Having lost their biggest case in the Supreme Court, gay rights lawyers needed a new strategy to challenge sodomy statutes. The Ad Hoc Task Force suggested several routes of attack, including litigation. The best forum for litigation against sodomy after *Hardwick* was in state court. Thus, a new campaign against sodomy statutes was begun in the state courts, arguing that the statute violated the state constitution even though it had been held not to violate the federal constitution.

FEDERAL COURTS, STATE COURTS, AND CIVIL RIGHTS

Although the Supreme Court is insulated from politics more than any other institution in the federal government, it is not completely immune. The president nominates candidates to serve on the Court, and the Senate must confirm those nominations before they can take effect. As we have witnessed in recent years, some judicial nominations become quite political, even at the Supreme Court level. Judge Robert Bork, for example, was nominated by a

Republican president and rejected by a Senate that responded to questions raised by progressive Democrats about Bork's impartiality. Douglas Ginsberg withdrew his nomination during the same highly publicized nomination period once members of Congress discovered that he had smoked marijuana. Judge Clarence Thomas was nominated, seriously challenged, but then ultimately confirmed. Political battles over the makeup of the Supreme Court have raged in earlier times as well. President Roosevelt, upset at the Court's rejection of much of his New Deal legislation, threatened to retaliate by increasing the number of justices on the Court. This tactic was one that he had learned from history. Congress had approved a tenth justice in 1863, and President Abraham Lincoln appointed Justice Field from California to that slot to counter the influence of the five justices from the South who had carried the day in the infamous *Dred Scott* decision. The makeup of the Court at any given time will vary depending on which president has the ability to make nominations and on who is in control of the Senate. And the makeup of the Court necessarily changes over time.

Although the Warren Court handed down important progressive decisions expanding the rights of African Americans and other racial minorities, it resisted claims to equal protection made by women. By the time the Court was willing to read women into the Constitution, Chief Justice Warren had retired and the Court had become the Burger Court. The Burger Court, and later the Rehnquist Court, proved to be less ready to expand civil rights. In the middle of the African American civil rights movement, for example, the Burger Court began cutting back on earlier Warren Court decisions that had interpreted the state action requirement of the Fourteenth Amendment expansively enough to reach private discrimination. And even though the Burger Court was willing to read women into the Constitution, it was never willing to grant them equal status with racial minorities. Sex classifications would be accorded heightened judicial scrutiny but they would never be subjected to the more rigorous compelling state interest test applied to racial classifications.

In the midst of this slow-down in the expansion of civil rights at the federal level, civil rights litigators began pressing more claims in state court, arguing for greater protection under the state constitution than the U.S. Supreme Court seemed willing to give under the federal constitution. Feminist litigators in the state of California, for example, managed to convince the California Supreme Court that sex was a suspect classification subject to the same exacting review as racial classifications, even before the U.S. Supreme Court had recognized sex as a "quasi-suspect" classification. The California decision was based on the California constitution's Equal Protection Clause.[2] Additionally, in the 1970s many states added an equal rights amendment to their state constitutions, thereby explicitly granting their women citizens greater protection than the federal constitution afforded.

By the early 1980s, the trend was apparent. Many state courts were willing to interpret their own constitutions to afford greater protection in civil rights claims. Indeed, as Justice Brennan reported in a published speech, "Between 1970 and 1984, state courts, increasingly reluctant to follow the federal lead, have handed down over 250 published opinions holding that the constitutional minimums set by the United States Supreme Court were insufficient to satisfy the more stringent requirements of state constitutional law."[3] Several state courts have been more willing than the Supreme Court to protect the exercise of free speech rights in quasi-public forums.[4] The Minnesota Supreme Court has recognized greater protection for religious freedom under the Minnesota constitution than the U.S. Supreme Court has recognized under the federal constitution.[5] And after the U.S. Supreme Court refused to provide relief in a case challenging Texas's discriminatory school finance system,[6] litigants, following the lead in other states, finally turned to the Texas courts and met with success.[7]

SODOMY CHALLENGES IN
STATE COURTS

Lesbian and gay rights litigators in the post-*Hardwick* years followed this trend of turning to state courts for greater civil rights protections and began bringing sodomy challenges in state court. In some of these cases, the litigators were aided by language in state constitutions that differs from the U.S. Constitution. For example, many state constitutions actually mention the right of privacy, rather than implying its existence through other constitutional guarantees.

At the same time that Michael Hardwick's case was before the U.S. Supreme Court, Huber Walsh's case was before the Missouri Supreme Court. Walsh had been arrested for violating Missouri's deviate sexual intercourse statute. The Missouri statute applies only to same-sex sexual conduct. The definition of intercourse in the statute is so broad that it applied to Walsh, whose only offense was that he had touched another man's genitals with his hand through the other man's clothing. Walsh's lawyer claimed the statute violated equal protection, and the trial judge readily agreed, reasoning that Walsh was the victim of gender discrimination because if he'd been a woman who had touched a man he would not have been arrested. The Supreme Court of Missouri disagreed. Handing down its opinion less than a month after the *Hardwick* decision was handed down, the Missouri Supreme Court rejected all federal constitutional claims and refused to read Missouri's constitutional right of privacy any broader than the *Hardwick* Court had read the federal right. As to the equal protection claim, the court rejected the claim of gender discrimination, pointing out that women were equally prevented from touching other women. The court correctly identified another equal protection claim, that the statute discriminated against homosexual persons because it prevented them from engaging in conduct that was permitted for heterosexuals. But because homosexual persons were not perceived to be a suspect or quasi-suspect class, mere rational basis review was sufficient to justify the statute. The legitimate interests of the state were protecting public morality and health.[8]

Four years later, a Michigan court held the Michigan sodomy statute unconstitutional under the Michigan constitution.[9] Unfortunately, that case never reached the Michigan Supreme Court so the reach of the ruling is uncertain, but at least in Wayne County, the sodomy statute is no longer enforceable. In 1992, gay rights activists and litigators won an important and clear victory in a challenge to the sodomy statute of Kentucky. The Supreme Court of Kentucky held that the state's sodomy statute, which applied only to same-sex sodomy, violated both the privacy and equality provisions of the Kentucky constitution. In its decision, the court stressed that the state constitution came into being before the federal constitution was adopted, and, thus, the state constitution was the true harbinger of individual freedom, rather than the federal constitution.

> Contrary to popular belief, the Bill of Rights in the United States Constitution represents neither the primary source nor the maximum guarantee of state constitutional liberty. Our own constitutional guarantees against the intrusive power of the state do not derive from the Federal Constitution. The adoption of the Federal Constitution in 1791 was preceded by state constitutions developed over the preceding 15 years, and, while there is, of course, overlap between state and federal constitutional guarantees of individual rights, they are by no means identical. State constitutional law documents and the writings on liberty were more the source of federal law than the child of federal law.[10]

Ask, Don't Tell was discussed in the last chapter. Because the Texas statute applied only to same-sex sodomy, litigators had hoped the Supreme Court would grant certiorari separately from *Hardwick* and consider the equal protection arguments posed by the Texas case. Instead, the Supreme Court denied review of the case shortly after *Hardwick* was decided.

Since that time, the Texas statute has twice been ruled unconstitutional under the Texas constitution by an intermediate state appellate court. In the first case, *Morales,*[15] a group of gay rights activists challenged the statute, claiming they were harmed not only by threat of prosecution, but also by other effects of the statute. Specifically, they claimed the statute encouraged discrimination against lesbians and gay men as well as acts of violence against them. Further, the "stigma of criminality" created by the statute affected their rights in family law matters, housing, and employment. The trial court agreed that the plaintiffs had sufficient standing to challenge the statute and ruled that the statute violated the privacy rights explicitly guaranteed in the Texas constitution. A three-judge appellate court in Austin agreed. The state appealed the decision to the Texas Supreme Court.

The other case, in litigation at approximately the same time, grew out of an employment discrimination claim. The Dallas police department refused to hire Mica England because she was a lesbian.[16] As in the later Georgia case involving Robin Shahar, the primary justification for the police department's action was that, as a lesbian, England was likely to violate the criminal law of Texas, presumably a relevant consideration for an employee who was supposed to enforce the law. But unlike Shahar, England challenged the validity of the state sodomy statute. The trial court agreed with England's arguments, held that the sodomy statute violated the right of privacy under the Texas constitution, and enjoined the city of Dallas and its police chief from enforcing both the statute and the police department's exclusionary hiring policy. The trial court dismissed the state as defendant in the case. Thus, the injunction was against only the city of Dallas. Another three-judge appellate court in Austin upheld the trial court's decision. The defendants neglected to take the steps necessary to perfect their appeal and, thus, the decision in *England* became final under Texas law on May 5, 1993, when the Texas Supreme Court dismissed the writ of appeal.

Then in 1994, after sitting on the appeal from the first case for almost two years, the Texas Supreme Court finally issued its opinion in *Morales.* The court did not rule on the merits of the claim, nor did the court rule that the plaintiffs lacked standing because they had not suffered the harm of criminal prosecution. Instead, the court ruled that in Texas a plaintiff cannot enter the civil court system to challenge the constitutionality of a criminal statute. Rather, the plaintiff must await arrest and prosecution and then challenge the statute in criminal court. That ruling created a problem for anyone wanting to challenge the Texas statute. By the state's own admission, the statute was never enforced. As the Court of Appeals had observed:

> [Plaintiffs] are confronted with this dilemma: They suffer actual harm from the existence of [the sodomy statute], harm that the State acknowledges, yet they are unable to attack the statute's constitutionality because of the State's apparent refusal to enforce the statute. [They], therefore, claim that they lack an adequate remedy at law. We agree.[17]

In the current Arkansas challenge, the Arkansas Supreme Court appears to agree with the Texas Supreme Court that constitutional challenges to criminal statutes ought to be brought in criminal courts rather than civil courts. But the Arkansas court disagrees with the further holding in the Texas case, that a plaintiff must await arrest and prosecution before the statute can be challenged. Thus, Arkansas has adopted a unique and creative solution to the problem created by the Texas court opinion. Arkansas has authorized the plaintiffs to bring a declaratory judgment action claiming the sodomy statute is unconstitutional in a criminal court of law.

As for Texas, the event that no one thought would happen finally happened. On September 17, 1998, Houston police burst into a private apartment, discovered two men engaged in a private, consensual act of sodomy, and arrested them on the spot. The police had not gone there seeking sodomites, but rather were responding to a false report that an armed burglar was inside the apartment. In December 1998, a county criminal court refused to dismiss the charges despite the plea that the same-sex sodomy statute violates the Texas constitution. The two defendants pled "no contest" to the criminal charge, but with the help of gay rights lawyers, appealed the case to the Court of Appeals for the Houston District, claiming that the Texas statute is unconstitutional.

Lambda lawyers are representing the two defendants together with local cooperating attorneys. The lawyers are challenging the constitutionality of the sodomy statute on both privacy and equality grounds, under both the Texas and the federal constitution.

There are two types of equality arguments: (1) that the statute discriminates on the basis of sex because it criminalizes conduct depending on the sex of one's partner, and (2) that the statute discriminates against gay and lesbian couples because it only criminalizes same-sex sodomy. In response to both arguments, the state is making an "equal application" argument similar to the argument put forward in early race discrimination cases such as *Buchanan v. Warley* and *Loving v. Virginia.* In response to the gay litigants' first equality argument, the state's position is that the statute does not classify on the basis of sex because two women who engage in the prohibited conduct are as guilty as two men who engage in the conduct. In response to the second equality argument, the state's position is that the statute does not classify on the basis of sexual orientation because two heterosexual men who engage in the prohibited conduct are as guilty as two gay men who engage in the conduct.

On June 8, 2000, the intermediate appellate court in Houston issued its opinion in the case, striking down the sodomy statute by a vote of 2 to 1.[18] The court addressed only equality argument number one. Finding that the statute classified on the basis of sex, and applying the Texas equal rights amendment, the court held that the state had not met the required compelling state interest justification for classifications based on sex. Although the case is a clear victory for the lawyers and clients most directly involved in the case, it is questionable whether the decision will stand. Appeal lies to the Texas Court of Criminal Appeals, a court that is notoriously conservative. Furthermore, the equal application defense works better in this case than it did in *Loving.* In *Loving,* the effect of the restriction on opposite race marriages was clearly to stigmatize those persons who were not white. The effect of the sex restriction in the Texas sodomy statute, by contrast, does not stigmatize women, but rather stigmatizes gays and lesbians. And, if sexual orientation is the classification, rather than gender, the Texas equal rights amendment will not be available to accord strict scrutiny. Fortunately, the lawyers have preserved additional equal protection and privacy arguments. It remains to be seen how the Texas Court of Criminal Appeals will respond to those arguments.

CURRENT STATUS OF SODOMY STATUTES

As of March 2000 at least thirty-three states, if one includes Michigan, have no effective statute on the books criminalizing consensual acts in private. Five states, including Texas and Arkansas, in which challenges are proceeding, have statutes criminalizing only same-sex sodomy. The statutes in Oklahoma, Kansas, and Missouri, the other three same-sex sodomy states, have so far survived constitutional challenges.

Of the twelve states with sodomy statutes that apply to both same-sex and opposite-sex sodomy, the current effectiveness of the Massachusetts statute is questionable. Massachusetts has two private sex statutes, one that prohibits anal intercourse (the crime against nature) and another that prohibits other acts defined as "unnatural and lascivious acts." The latter statute has been held not to apply to consensual, private sex[19] and some lawyers believe that this limitation should logically be extended to the "crime against nature" statute. In July 2000, GLAD of Boston filed suit asking the state court to declare the Massachusetts sodomy statute unconstitutional. The gay rights challenge to the recently upheld Louisiana statute continues. The other ten states with good solid effective, but rarely enforced, sodomy statutes are Arizona, Utah, Idaho, Mississippi, Alabama, Florida, Minnesota, South Carolina, North Carolina, and Virginia. Of these, Minnesota appears something of an anomaly since its state legislature has passed statewide gay civil rights legislation. Repeal efforts would seem to be worthwhile in that state.

Repeal efforts have been successful in other states despite the *Hardwick* decision's reinforcement of the notion that legislatures have full constitutional power to enact sodomy statutes. In 1993, the Nevada legislature repealed its sodomy statute, and, in 1998, Rhode Island repealed its statute. Maryland's sodomy statute was effectively repealed in 1998 through a combined effort of litigation and lobbying. An intermediate appellate court ruled that the statute should not be construed to apply to private consensual conduct and rather than appeal, the litigants and the state agreed that the statute should be so interpreted throughout the state. Thus, even if the statute remains on the books, the governor, on behalf of the state, has signed a binding agreement that the statute will not be enforced against private consensual acts.

Justice White's opinion in *Bowers v. Hardwick* cited twenty-four states that prohibited sodomy, even when committed in private between consenting adults. Since that time, the number has decreased to fifteen or sixteen. If current challenges in state court are successful, that number will be cut even further. By these repeals, state courts and legislatures have accorded their lesbian and gay citizens the constitutional right to privacy denied by the Supreme Court in *Hardwick*.

REVERSING *HARDWICK*

For the Supreme Court to reverse *Hardwick*, the right case will have to find its way onto the Court's certiorari docket. When state courts rule sodomy statutes unconstitutional or constitutional under the state constitution, no grounds for appeal to the Supreme Court exists. An appeal would be possible in a case in which the state upheld the statute on both state and federal constitutional grounds. An appeal would be more difficult in a case in which the state court struck the statute down on both state and federal constitutional grounds. In such a case, the Supreme Court could deny certiorari because the state constitutional claim would resolve the issue in the case and the Court would thus not be required to consider whether or not the federal constitutional claim had been decided correctly. In any event, if a sodomy case is presented to the Supreme Court, the plaintiff would have to meet the Court's strict standing rules. Challenges brought by gay rights activists who have not been threatened with arrest, but who have suffered stigmatic harm, may satisfy state standing requirements under state declaratory judgment acts, but such cases are not likely to meet the more stringent standing test that the Supreme Court applies.

The problem is that most sodomy statutes are not enforced against consenting adults in private. Of the current or recent challenges to sodomy statutes, the Texas case presents the best fact situation for testing the constitutionality of the statute. The Texas litigants clearly have standing because they were arrested. *State v. Smith*,[20] recently decided by the Louisiana Supreme Court, also involves an arrest. Mr. Smith, however, was not arrested for consensual sodomy, but rather for forcible rape. Unable to prove lack of consent, the prosecutors included a charge for consensual oral sex, which ultimately was the only crime proved. As a result Mr. Smith should have sufficient standing to challenge the constitutionality of the Louisiana statute, which the state court upheld against both state and federal constitutional challenges. However, one Louisiana Supreme Court Justice, concurring in the decision, stated that he did not believe Mr. Smith was in a position to bring a privacy challenge to the statute since his arrest and prosecution resulted from a charge of rape. If he could meet the standing requirements, Smith's case would be an interesting one to take to the U.S. Supreme Court since he is claiming a constitutionally protected right to engage in heterosexual sodomy, an issue not addressed by *Bowers v. Hardwick*. The best case to challenge the Hardwick decision directly, however, is the Texas case, because those defendants, like *Hardwick*, were arrested in the privacy of their own bedroom for engaging in same-sex sodomy.

Suppose, however, that lesbian and gay rights litigators are successful in the Texas challenge. Suppose further that lesbian and gay rights activists are successful in every state so that they manage either to convince every state legislature to repeal the sodomy statute or every state's supreme court to strike it down. Suppose they even manage to convince the military to amend the Code of Military Justice to repeal sodomy. Would *Hardwick* have any vitality at that point? Yes, it would because its rationale was that a state legislature was justified in taking action against a particular kind of private consensual sexual conduct solely because the majority believed it immoral. So long as that rationale can be cited to support other state actions taken against similar conduct, or, in the case of the military and other governmental employers, against persons who have a propensity to engage in such conduct, *Hardwick* will continue to be the nemesis of the lesbian and gay civil rights movement. Repealing sodomy statutes will not take care of the stigma caused by that decision any more than the integration of all railroad cars would have taken care of the stigma created by *Plessy*. *Hardwick* has to be officially overruled and litigators must not stop looking for the best case to do that.

FAMILY RIGHTS

Family law in general has been through a number of major changes in the past few decades. In 1969, the year of the Stonewall Rebellion, another revolution was taking place, this one in the traditional arena of families and family law. "No-fault" divorce was first introduced in 1969 in California. Supported at the time by feminists, who believed that easier exits from bad marriages would help emancipate women both personally and economically, these laws took hold throughout the country. But as later feminist scholars have shown, easy divorce was not always in the best interest of women. Despite the enactment of statutory revisions, such as equitable distribution rules, intended to ameliorate the effect of the new divorce laws on women, women nonetheless appear to suffer disproportionately from postdivorce poverty. The ideal of equality, embraced by many feminists, required that family law rules be gender neutral. Although the primary feminist argument was for equal participation in parenting generally, the application of equality rules at divorce created windfalls for men. In the 1970s, men began to win custody battles or to bargain for other things by threatening to challenge custody. Some states adopted rules under which joint custody was the presumption. Many divorced spouses, influenced by feminism, struggled to make custody and visitation rules work to ensure a significant presence of both mother and father in the lives of their children.

More recently, national attention has shifted from feminist concerns about the welfare of women postdivorce and equal parenting to concern about the breakdown of the traditional American family. Family law scholars have begun to suggest alternative forms of marriage, those that embrace more indestructible covenants than the current marriage contract provided by most states.[21] Louisiana has recently enacted a covenant marriage law as an alternative to the existing law, and other states, including Iowa, are considering such statutes. Under covenant marriage laws, spouses assume more obligations and restrict the grounds for divorce, thereby rejecting the notion of no-fault divorce.

National attention has also been focused on the deterioration of the black family. More and more black teenage girls are having children out of wedlock. More and more black teenage boys are going to prison rather than to school. With no quick fix in sight, commentators have argued whether the breakdown of the family is the cause of the increase in black crime or whether the increase is black crime is a major cause of the breakdown of the family. Others place the blame on a government that has never recognized that black families are different from white families.[22] And others theorize about the breakdown in the black community generally, focusing on the current generation's rejection of the established black community that was built up in the 1960s.[23]

In the midst of this revolution in family law and national debate over the nature of families, lesbian and gay families have claimed their part in the revolution and the debate. The Census Bureau has made lesbian and gay families more visible by finally asking questions that measure their existence. As of March 1997, the Census Bureau reported that there were almost 6.0 million households consisting of unmarried adult couples who were unrelated to each other. Of these, slightly over 4.0 million households consisted of opposite-sex couples and approximately 2.0 million consisted of same-sex couples.[24] Of these same-sex couples, 132,000 were raising a child under age fifteen.[25] Family law, especially its concern about the "best interests of the child," can no longer ignore the existence of lesbian and gay families.

CHILD CUSTODY

The custody battles that predated *Hardwick* continue. Indeed, *Hardwick* has made it more difficult for family lawyers to argue that societal discrimination against gay men and lesbians should not be a valid consideration in custody decision. The antigay argument based on *Hardwick,* so often used in other discrimination cases, has been presented just as often in family law courts. In the family law context, the argument is as follows: if the state can legitimately throw a lesbian or gay man in jail for sodomy, surely the state can do something less burdensome, like merely restrict their access to their children.

The success of state challenges to state sodomy statutes has been a tremendous boost to family lawyers who no longer have to go into court buttressed with character witnesses for their lesbian mother clients, only to hear the other side exclaim: "But your honor, this woman is a criminal." A lesbian (or gay) parent who is no longer a potential criminal is more likely to be viewed as a fit mom (or dad).

Nonetheless, primarily in states where sodomy is still a crime, bad decisions continue to abound. Virginia, for example, although claiming not to apply a rule that lesbians are per se unfit as parents, continues to consider sexual orientation an important factor in making custody decisions. In a 1995 case, the court explained that the fact that "conduct inherent in lesbianism is punishable as a felony . . . is an important consideration in determining custody."[26] After denying custody to the mother, Sharon Bottoms, and instead awarding custody to the child's grandmother, the trial court further punished the mother for her lesbian lifestyle by severely restricting the mother's visitation and prohibiting all contact between the child and the mother's lesbian partner. This decision was affirmed by the Virginia Court of Appeals on June 29, 1999.[27]

Missouri is another bad jurisdiction for lesbian and gay custody battles. In a 1998 case, *DeLong v. DeLong,* a trial court awarded custody of three minor children to the father rather than the lesbian mother because she had engaged in extramarital lesbian relationships and stated her intention to continue her search for romance. In explaining its decision, the trial court focused exclusively on the mother's lesbianism, the fact that she engaged in lesbian relationships, that she concealed the relationships, that she introduced her children to lesbians, and that she had demonstrated her "immaturity in seeking after repeated new love relationships." The court ignored the mother's testimony that she only engaged in lesbian relationships once the marriage had broken down, that the husband had also engaged in an extramarital relationship, that the mother was discreet and kept the sexual nature of her relationships with other women secret from her children, and that she introduced her lesbian friends to her children not as lesbians or lovers, but rather as friends. In addition to denying the mother's request for custody, the court restricted the mother's visitation with her children instructing her not to visit the children in the presence of any known lesbian nor in the presence of any woman unrelated to the mother with whom the mother might be living.

On appeal, the intermediate appellate court noted that Missouri had considered seven appellate cases in which the homosexuality of the parent was either a consideration in the custody award, a grounds for a subsequent change in custody, or a reason to restrict the visitation rights of the homosexual parent. In every case, the trial court's decision in favor of the nongay parent had been upheld. Even though Missouri courts claimed they were not applying a per se rule, this appellate court viewed the matter differently. Behind every negative opinion was a judge's view that the parent's homosexuality might lead to conduct that could have a negative impact on the child. As one Missouri court had said: a parent's homosexual conduct "can never be kept private enough to be a neutral factor in the development of a child's values and character."[28] The intermediate appellate court in *DeLong* rejected the application of a per se rule, whether express or implied, and adopted the nexus rule, which requires the court to find that the homosexual conduct in fact causes an adverse impact on the children.[29] Before remand to the trial court occurred, however, the case was referred to the Missouri Supreme Court, which held that the trial court's award of custody to the father was justified because it was not based on the mother's homosexuality alone, but also on other factors, including the mother's conduct.[30] The Supreme Court did remand to the trial court to reconsider the restrictions that the trial court had placed on visitation, instructing the court to reject only third parties whose conduct might be harmful to the children. Although eschewing the claim that Missouri courts were applying a per se rule, the Supreme Court's reaction to the visitation limitation is revealing. The trial court had barred two types of third parties from being present during the mother's time with her children: lesbians and nonlesbians. The Supreme Court, in asking the trial court to focus on potentially harmful conduct, expressed the opinion that lesbians were more likely to cause harm to children than nonlesbians were. Thus, although the Court rejects a per se rule, it makes decisions based on the presumption that a child's association with a lesbian is likely to be more harmful than association with a nonlesbian.

Both Missouri and Virginia have sodomy statutes. The statutes have been challenged in litigation in both states and upheld. The family law courts in states with sodomy statutes often cite the criminality of homosexual conduct in making decisions regarding custody. The criminality of the conduct is also evidence of the immorality of the conduct. Since many states stress the morality of the parents as a key factor in making custody determinations, sodomy statute states are bound to have more antigay custody decisions.

Lesbian and gay rights activists and litigators have discussed the possibility of appealing an adverse family law case to the Supreme Court in an attempt to obtain a ruling in favor of lesbian and gay parents, similar to the ruling in *Palmore v. Sidoti.* Although the Supreme Court does not hear many family law cases (only two in the past twenty-five years, according to the ACLU), the Court had readily granted certiorari in *Palmore* to clarify that state judges should not award custody on the basis of society's prejudices. Although *Palmore* was a case about racial prejudices, the same principle should apply in cases dealing with antigay bias. Once the Supreme Court ruled in *Romer* that antigay bias was an impermissible justification for state action, the *Palmore* argument seemed even stronger in lesbian and gay custody cases.

Lambda Legal Defense (LLDEF), the Lesbian and Gay Rights Project of the ACLU, and the National Center for Lesbian Rights (NCLR) have all increased their participation in family law custody disputes. Since many states apply fair custody laws in which sexual orientation is not a relevant factor, these public interest law firms have concentrated in states with antigay family law precedents. Virginia is one such state. The ACLU and NCLR have both pressed the *Palmore/Romer* argument in separate lesbian custody cases in Virginia.[31] Despite a short-lived success in an interim appeal of the *Bottoms* case, the Virginia appellate courts have uniformly rejected the argument by finding that the trial judge did not base his decision on societal prejudice, but rather on other factors. In one such case, the conclusion of the appellate court regarding the grounds of the trial court's decision was seriously questioned by a dissenting judge who pointed out that the trial judge focused on the mother's lesbianism when he awarded custody to the father, despite the fact that there was no evidence offered to establish that the mother's sexuality was in fact harmful to the child.[32]

The *Palmore/Romer* argument was successful in a recent Lambda custody case litigated in Ohio. In a case involving a gay man living in an "open homosexual relationship," the Ohio appellate court reversed a trial court's change of custody from the father to the mother and awarded custody back to the gay father. Not only did the court reiterate the rule that sexual orientation was only relevant if it could be proved to cause direct harm to the child, the court went through all the evidence relied on by the trial court and threw out everything that stemmed from society's prejudice against homosexuals. Finding no evidence that the father's gayness had harmed the child, the court ruled in favor of the father.[33]

All three public interest law firms, NCLR, ACLU, and LLDEF have been active in cases litigated in Florida, where a nexus test has been adopted and continues to be delineated by appellate courts. In a case decided May 26, 2000, the District Court of Appeal of Florida, Second District, fully endorsed the *Palmore/Romer* thesis in a lesbian custody case, holding that sexual orientation is irrelevant unless there is direct proof of harm to the children caused by the parent's sexual conduct.[34] As to the potential harm caused by society's stigmatization of gays and lesbians, the court said that "reliance on perceived biases was an improper basis for a residential custody determination." The court also made the insightful observation that even if society's biases were to be considered, the stigma that the child might experience would stem from the fact that her mother was a lesbian rather than from the fact that the child was living with her mother.

To take a lesbian or gay custody case to the Supreme Court, gay rights litigators need a case in which the decision is clearly based on society's prejudice against gay men and lesbians. The *Palmore* case was an easy one for the Supreme Court because the trial judge stated clearly that he was basing his decision on his belief that the child might be harmed by society's prejudice against interracial marriages. Because trial courts look at a number of factors when making custody determinations, identifying one factor as the determinative one is often difficult. Even when custody decisions are made on the basis of prejudice and stereotypical thinking about gay men and lesbians, courts say they are looking at other factors. However, three recent cases present factual situations where no one would have any difficulty concluding that the custody decision was based on bias or prejudice. These cases all occurred in states with sodomy statutes.

In a 1998 Alabama case, the state supreme court affirmed the trial court's change of custody from the lesbian mother, who had been raising her child with her lesbian partner for six years with the full knowledge of the father, to the father who had recently married and could thereby provide the child with a more normal two-parent home.[35] Because the case involved a change in custody rather than a determination of initial custody, the father had to show "that the positive good brought about by the modification would more than offset the inherently disruptive effect caused by uprooting the child." The state supreme court agreed with the trial court that the positive influence of a heterosexual family environment over a homosexual one was sufficient to demonstrate the required "positive good." In an attempt to insulate its decision against the charge, which had been pressed in amicus briefs, that the court was awarding custody solely on the basis of sexual orientation, the court stressed that the main reason for its decision was not the lesbian relationship of the mother, but that the mother did not conceal the relationship from her children. The court also cited the Alabama sodomy statute. The National Center for Lesbian Rights participated in the representation of the lesbian mother in this case.

A similar ruling was handed down just one month later in a Lambda case that was before the North Carolina Supreme Court. In *Pulliam v. Smith*,[36] the court took custody away from a gay male father who had raised his two sons from birth and also restricted his visitation to one month in the summer with a requirement that he not allow his sons in the home he shared with his gay partner. The court found no evidence that Smith had been anything other than a stellar parent. The sons had lived with him alone in California when their mother moved to Kansas to live with another man. The sons later moved with their father from California to North Carolina. Several years later, the father began a long-term committed relationship with another man, Tim Tipton, who moved into the family home with Smith and his sons. When the ex-wife learned that Smith was gay, she began seeking custody of the two boys. Based on the fact that the two men engaged in homosexual conduct, including private sex and public expressions of affection, the trial court found that such activity "will likely create emotional difficulties for the two minor children," and awarded a change of custody to the mother. The North Carolina Supreme Court upheld the lower court decision, claiming that the decision was not based on the fact that the father was a "practicing homosexual," but rather on the fact that he "was regularly engaging in sexual acts with Mr. Tipton in the home while the children were present and upon other improper conduct by these two men." The court failed to mention that the sex occurred in the privacy of the father's bedroom. Nor did it explain why demonstrations of affection between two men were improper apart from the fact that they constitute the practice of homosexuality. Nor did the court address the argument, raised in the father's brief, that the trial court's reliance on societal prejudice to determine the best interest of the child is contrary to the Supreme Court's decision in *Palmore v. Sidoti*.

The third case hails from the state of Mississippi. In an opinion that gay rights activists across the nation describe as "shocking," the Mississippi Supreme Court on February 4, 1999, upheld a trial court decision refusing to grant a gay father's request to have his son's custody transferred to him, despite the fact that the mother was now married to a man who had twice beaten her and threatened to kill the son.[37] Because of his concerns for his son's safety, David Weigand petitioned for custody of his son, Paul. Despite the fact that the stepfather's violent behavior had caused the family to be evicted, despite the fact that the son, in fear of his stepfather, had called 911 to report the violent behavior, despite the fact that the mother had to hold down two jobs to support the family, thereby reducing her time with her son, and despite the fact that the gay father had a stable job and home life in California, the trial court said:

> The conscience of this Court is shocked by the audacity and brashness of an individual to come into court, openly and freely admit to engaging in felonious conduct on a regular basis and expect the Court to find such conduct acceptable, particularly with regard to the custody of a minor child. The parties are not in Kansas anymore, nor are they in California.

Weigand's felonious conduct refers to the fact that he was sexually intimate with his life partner, a fact he openly admitted under oath when questioned. Of course, the sexual intimacy occurs in the state of California where it is not a felony and where Mississippi does not have sufficient extraterritorial jurisdiction to make it a felony. The reference to Kansas is not a reference to the Wizard of Oz, but rather to the fact that the parties were originally domiciled in Kansas. No, they are not there any more. Wiegand has instead moved to California, which, to this judge, is either an irrelevant fact or contributes to Weigand's audacity.

The Mississipi Supreme Court upheld the trial court's custody ruling. However, it did reverse the trial court's order requiring Weigand's life partner to move out of the California home while the son, Paul, visited each summer. The *Palmore/Romer* argument was fully briefed by the ACLU counsel in the case. Only the dissent addressed the constitutional issues raised by this argument.

In reporting the decision not to take this case to the Supreme Court, Matt Coles, director of the ACLU's Lesbian and Gay Right Project, reported:

> The consensus was that this Court is still apprehensive about lesbian and gay issues, especially ones involving children, and that it would not want to say that state courts cannot take sexual orientation into account in custody cases.

In short, we thought the risk of a bad decision that would hurt us for years to come was too great.[38]

One cannot disagree with Coles's observations about the Court. The Court has issued only one progay decision, *Romer*. It has never explicitly backpedaled from the antigay position in *Bowers v. Hardwick*. And it has declined the chance to reverse antigay holdings in every post-*Romer* case in which a petition for certiorari has been filed. So long as the *Palmore/Romer* argument is meeting with success in some state courts, litigators are quite sensible to avoid the risk that the Supreme Court might demolish that particular legal strategy. Unlike the problem of finding good plaintiffs to bring sodomy challenges, so long as there are family law judges operating on the basis of prejudice and stereotype, good plaintiffs will exist in cases for years to come. Failure to appeal family law cases now does not seriously endanger the opportunity to ask the Supreme Court to endorse the *Palmore/Romer* argument in some future case.

NOTES

1. For example, Iowa.

2. Sail'er Inn, Inc. v. Kirby, 485 P.2d 529 (Cal. 1971).

3. William J. Brennan Jr., "The Bill of Rights and the States: The Revival of State Constitutions as Guardians of Individual Rights," 61 *New York University Law Review* 535 (1986).

4. Batchelder v. Allied Stores International, Inc., 445 N.E.2d 590, 593–595 (1983); Alderwood Associates v. Washington Environmental Council, 96 Wash. 2d 230, 237–246, 635 P.2d 108, 112–117 (1981).

5. *See* State v. French, 460 N.W.2d 2 (Minn. 1990).

6. San Antonio Independent School District v. Rodriguez, 411 U.S. 1 (1973).

7. Edgewood Independent School District v. Kirby, 777 S.W.2d 391 (Tex. 1989).

8. Missouri v. Walsh, 713 S.W.2d 508 (Mo. 1986).

9. Michigan Organization for Human Rights v. Kelley, No. 88–815820 CZ (Wayne County Cir. Ct., July 9, 1990).

10. Commonwealth of Kentucky v. Wasson, 842 S.W.2d 487 at 492 (Ky. 1992).

11. Campbell v. Sundquist, 926 S.W.2d 250 (Tenn. App. 1996), permission to appeal denied; Gryczan v. State, 942 P.2d 112 (Mont. 1997).

12. Sawatzky v. City of Oklahoma City, 906 P.2d 785 (Okla. 1995).

13. Powell v. State, 510 S.E.2d 18 (Ga. 1998).

14. Buchanon v. Batchelor, 308 F.Supp. 729 (N.D. Tex. 1970), *vacated and remanded sub nom.*, Wade v. Buchanon and Buchanon v. Wade, 401 U.S. 989 (1971).

15. State v. Morales, 826 S.W.2d 201 (Tex. Ct. App. 1992), *vacated on jurisdictional grounds*, 869 S.W.2d 941 (Tex. 1994).

16. City of Dallas v. England, 846 S.W.2d 957 (Tex. App. 1993).

17. 826 S.W.2d at 203.

18. Lawrence v. Texas, 2000 WL 729417 (slip opinion).

19. Commonwealth v. Balthazar, 318 N.E.2d 478 (Mass. 1974).

20. Smith v. State 2000 La. Lexis 1911.

21. *See,* for example, Margaret F. Brinig, "Economics, Law and Covenant Marriage," 16 *Gender Issues* 1 (1998); Elizabeth S. Scott and Robert E. Scott, "Marriage as Relational Contract," 84 *Virginia Law Review* 1125 (1998).

22. June Jordan, *Technical Difficulties: African-American Notes on the State of the Union* 67 (1992).

23. Regina Austin, "The Black Community, Its Lawbreakers, and a Politics of Identification," 65 *Southern California Law Review* 1769 (1992).

24. *See* Census Bureau, Marital Status and Living Arrangements: March 1997 (Update), Table 8.

25. There were 1.47 million unmarried opposite-sex couples with children under the age of fifteen and 132,000 same-sex couples with children under the age of fifteen. Ibid.

26. Bottoms v. Bottoms, 457 S.E.2d 102 at 108 (Va. 1995).

27. Bottoms v. Bottoms, 1999 WL 1129720 (Va. App. 1999).

28. G.A. v. D.A., 745 S.W.2d 726, 728 (Mo. App. 1987).

29. DeLong v. DeLong, 1998 WL 15536 (Mo.App. 1998).

30. J.A.D. v. F.J.D, 978 S.W.2d 336.

31. See Bottoms, 1999 WL 1129720 (Va. App. 1999) and Piatt v. Piatt, 499 S.E.2d 567 (Va. App. 1998).

32. See Piatt, 499 S.E.2d at 572–574.

33. Inscoe v. Inscoe, 700 N.E. 2d 70 (Ohio App. 1997).

34. Jacoby v. Jacoby, 2000 WL 678997 (Fla. App. 2000)(slip opinion).

35. Ex parte J.M.F., 730 So.2d 1190 (Ala. 1998).

36. 501 S.E.2d 898 (N.C. 1998).

37. Weigand v. Houghton, 730 So.2d 581 (Miss. 1999).

38. Letter from Matt Coles dated May 20, 1999.

9

Public Recognition of Private Relationships Post–*Bowers v. Hardwick*

Lesbian and gay relationships exist. Courts and legislatures now know more about these relationships than they did in the early days of the movement. In the 1970s, family law judges were surprised by lesbian mothers who admitted their lesbianism but nonetheless demanded custody rights. Judges rarely understood lesbianism or lesbian relationships. Litigants and their lawyers often report instances in which judges cross-examined lesbian mothers about their sex lives, unable to understand what exactly two women could do in bed. In one early Ohio case, the judge asked the lesbian mother's expert witness, Dr. Richard Green, if he could explain how "the sex act between lesbians [was] accomplished?"[1] Judges in those early days assumed not only that relationships were immoral or criminal, but also that relationships did not last and that gay parents would unduly influence their children's choice of sexuality. The view that such relationships are immoral remains, but courts now have a clearer and more accurate view of what it means to be a lesbian and to share a family life with a partner and children.

In the equal protection litigation following the *Hardwick* decision, lesbian and gay litigators argued that when the state discriminated against homosexual persons as a class, lesbians and gay men were entitled to heightened judicial scrutiny. In courtrooms around the country lawyers debated the nature of the class. Did gay men and lesbians have more political power than racial minorities or women? Did they suffer prejudice? What exactly qualified as homosexuality? Was particular conduct necessary or was personal identification sufficient? In making these arguments, lesbian and gay rights litigators have educated numerous judges and the American public about the nature of sexual orientation. Many of these debates spread to forums beyond the courtroom. For example, the debate over whether one is born gay or chooses to be gay has been the subject of numerous articles, opinion pieces, and letters to the editor in mainstream newspapers and magazines around the country.

These debates about gay and lesbian families and the nature of sexual orientation have contributed to what has now become the biggest debate of all: the legitimacy of same-sex marriage. The marriage issue is more contested than any other lesbian and gay issue. It has captured the attention of the general public, politicians, and the religious community. Emotions run high on both sides of the debate. The primacy of this issue has, in the short run, occluded practically all other lesbian and gay issues.

The issue at stake for lesbians and gay men is whether their committed relationships will be accorded any deference by state law. Failure to recognize the reality of these relationships results in two intimately connected people being treated by the law as strangers to one another. At some core level of rationality, such treatment is simply absurd. Treating intimates as strangers denies the reality of a couple's life together and accords them no individual human dignity.

On the other side of the debate stand centuries of religious and social teaching about the sanctity of marriage. Proponents of the unique superiority of male-female marriage are so committed to their beliefs that they often fail to see the real human concerns on the other side. Nowhere is this more obvious than in the reported responses to surveys that continually show that even when a person thinks discrimination against lesbians and gay men is bad, that person is nonetheless opposed to the recognition of lesbian and gay marriage.[2]

Marriage is not the only route to legal recognition of same-sex relationships. Domestic partner registration laws have been enacted by a number of municipalities around the country. Under such laws, same-sex partners, who meet certain legislative requirements that range from sharing the basic necessities of life to obligating themselves to provide emotional and financial support for each other, enjoy the benefit of being publicly recognized as a couple within the jurisdiction of the city in which they live or work. Whether that recognition carries any additional benefits depends on the particular provisions of that city's ordinance. Although some municipalities provide fringe benefits to the domestic partners of city employees, municipalities generally lack the legal capacity to legislate on behalf of domestic partners generally. Although a city may have the power to require businesses within its borders to recognize domestic partners as family members, a city cannot define domestic partners as family for any purpose that is otherwise covered under state or federal law. In other words, a city can only legislate regarding matters within its jurisdiction. Even then, a city may not legislate contrary to state or federal legislation. Thus, in most cases, domestic partner ordinances are of little benefit to partners who are not employed by the city. Nonetheless, same-sex couples who desire some official status register as domestic partners for the sole intangible benefit of public recognition.

The opponents of same-sex marriage often oppose these domestic partnership laws as well, viewing them as uncomfortably similar to the union in marriage of one man and one woman. The arguments are necessarily different, for the Bible says nothing directly about domestic partnerships. Emotions run high on this issue, but they never reach the same intensity as with marriage. Thus, some activists in the movement believe a workable political strategy is to fight for marriage as the ultimate goal, but to settle for domestic partnership.

At a lower level of visibility than marriage and domestic partnership are the individual cases that, one by one, are establishing some protected core of family life for lesbians and gay men. Indeed, so long as issues regarding marriage and domestic partnership steal the limelight, these lesser, but important, litigation victories may be easier to maintain. They include such cases as *Braschi*[3] in which a New York court was willing to read a statutory definition of "family" broadly enough to include the same-sex partner of a deceased gay man, thereby protecting the partner from eviction from his home. They also include the increasing number of judicially approved second-parent adoptions that allow both same-sex partners to be recognized as the legal parents of their children.

This chapter will look at all three of these battles for public recognition of private relationships: (1) marriage, (2) domestic partnerships, and (3) judicial recognition of rights that help to stabilize families that are not otherwise recognized by statute. I will call this latter topic Nonstatutory Recognitions of Lesbian and Gay Families. All three battles are important, and the work done in each contributes to the possibility of success in the others by providing public education about the needs of lesbian and gay families.

MARRIAGE

The marriage battle is not a new one in the lesbian and gay civil rights movement. As discussed in an earlier chapter, that battle was fought in court in the early 1970s. Courts uniformly held that marriage was a union of one man and one woman. The litigation ended, and the movement took up other issues that seemed more likely to be won in court.

During this period, from the early 1970s to the mid-1980s, the lesbian and gay marriage issue languished in what William Eskridge calls a "generational purgatory."[4] Not only were there no gay activists visibly supporting the cause of same-sex marriage, lesbian and gay activists were surprisingly silent as the issue was used negatively in other campaigns, such as the campaign against the Equal Rights Amendment. As right-wing conservatives battled state by state passage of the equal rights amendment, they latched onto the homophobic and religious convictions of middle America by arguing that passage of the ERA would legalize homosexual marriage. Feminists, primarily for strategic reasons, responded not with a defense of same-sex marriage, but with an insistence that the ERA would do no such thing. Then, by the early 1980s, the ERA debates lost steam as time ran out on the ratification possibility for the federal constitution.

The Supreme Court decision in *Bowers v. Hardwick* galvanized the lesbian and gay legal community, causing national organizations to step up their calls for stronger laws to protect gay men and lesbian, including marriage laws. In October 1986, just months after the *Hardwick* decision, the ACLU became the first national civil rights organization to support the "elimination of legal barriers to homosexual and lesbian marriages." The ACLU directors adopted a new formal policy statement proclaiming that legal recognition of same-sex marriages and of economic benefits for gay and lesbian life partners is "imperative for the complete legal equality of lesbians and gay men."

Sometime in the mid-1980s, the lawyers and board members of Lambda Legal Defense and Education Fund began debating whether impact litigation regarding marriage rights should be added to Lambda's docket. The issue was a divisive one, even in the gay community. The Lambda internal debates reflected this division, which often broke down along gender lines. Lesbian feminists, who had been part of the feminist deconstruction of marriage as a patriarchal institution, were opposed to fighting for marriage rights for the lesbian and gay community. Gay men, especially those in stable relationships, supported the idea. But the lines were not always drawn on the basis of gender. Some radical lesbian feminists believed that opening marriage up to same-sex couples would transform the institution in positive ways for everyone. Once the gender dynamic present in opposite-sex marriages was removed, they believed marriage could become an egalitarian institution genuinely supportive of its members and a positive force in the larger community. And there were feminist men who agreed with lesbian feminists who opposed gay marriage, as well as men who believed that marriage was a conservative institution that ought to be abolished altogether.

This intracommunity debate was made public in the often re-created and reprinted dialogue between Tom Stoddard, at that time executive director of Lambda, and Paula Ettelbrick, Lambda's legal director.[5] Although Stoddard recognized the historical oppressiveness of the institution, he supported adding marriage litigation to the movement's agenda for three basic reasons: (1) marriage creates rights and benefits to marital partners that support the continuation of their relationships and their individual security, (2) win or lose, fighting for the right to marry presumes that same-sex relationships should be treated with equal dignity as opposite-sex relationships, and (3) once lesbians and gay men have the right to enter the institution of marriage, the institution will be transformed for the good. Ettelbrick offers two main arguments against litigating for marriage rights on behalf of lesbians and gay men: (1) marriage will not liberate gay men and lesbians as individuals, but will instead assimilate us into a mainstream institution, and (2) if gay men and lesbians do enter the institution of marriage, they will defeat a primary goal of gay liberation: family diversity. In short, Stoddard's position supports the claim that discrimination against lesbians and gay men will not end until our relationships are understood to be the *same* as nongay ones. And Ettelbrick's position supports the claim that gay men and lesbians will not attain equal respect with nongays until the *difference* of our relationships from nongay ones is honored and respected.

These two positions encapsulate two long-standing and competing legal arguments of the lesbian and gay civil rights movement: (1) that we are the same and thus should be equally respected, and (2) that we are different and our difference should be accorded equal respect. Equality arguments support the sameness thesis. Liberty and fundamental rights arguments support the difference thesis.

The key marriage case decided by the Supreme Court in 1967, *Loving v. Virginia,* recognized the relevance of both equality and liberty arguments. Although the case involved arguments in support of mixed-race marriages, which at the time were outlawed by a number of states, lesbian and gay rights activists and scholars have relied on this case as a central tool in making their own arguments in favor of same-sex marriage. In *Loving,* the Supreme Court held that entrance into the institution of marriage could not be regulated on the basis of race. Racial restrictions violated both the Equal Protection Clause and the Due Process (liberty) Clause. In the 1970s, courts were unwilling to entertain either equality or liberty arguments in favor of same-sex marriage. But in 1993, the lesbian and gay civil rights movement experienced a surge of support for gay marriage when the Supreme Court of Hawaii relied on the equality argument in *Loving* to find that same-sex couples had a similar right to enter the institution of marriage free from gender restrictions.

The Hawaii Litigation and Its Effect

On November 26, 1990, the following news item from Honolulu was reported in several newspapers across the country: "25 gay couples are expected to file for marriage licenses to protest state ban on same-sex marriages. Legal challenges to such bans failed in Washington, Kentucky, Minnesota."[6] A related item appeared a month later: "3 gay couples—2 pairs of women, 1 pair of men—applied for marriage licenses to challenge '81 ban on same-sex marriages. State health officials say they won't process applications without attorney general's OK."[7]

In April 1991, Hawaii became the third state in the United States to enact statewide civil rights protections for gay men and lesbians. One month later, Ninia Baehr and her partner, Genora Dancel, along with another female couple and a male couple, sued the Hawaii director of health, John Lewin, claiming that denying their applications for marriage licenses violated their fundamental right to marry as well as their equal protection rights under the Hawaii constitution. Five months later, the circuit court dismissed their case, and the plaintiffs appealed to the Hawaii Supreme Court.

In May 1993, the Hawaii Supreme Court shocked the rest of the country by ruling in favor of the plaintiffs.[8] The legal theory endorsed by the court was that the equal protection rights of the individuals had been violated because their marriage partners were limited by sex. Thus, the marriage law constituted an instance of sex discrimination, which, under the Hawaii constitution, triggered strict judicial scrutiny. The state could only prevail if it could show a compelling reason for restricting choice of marital partners on the basis of sex. The decision proved that the earlier ERA opponents had been correct in their arguments against adding equal rights on the basis of sex to state constitutions. The Equal Rights Amendment of the state of Hawaii was the basis for this court's holding that the state constitution protected same-sex marriages.

The decision in Hawaii became the focus of the entire nation. Almost immediately, the nation divided into camps supporting and camps opposing same-sex marriage. Citizens in every state began to wonder: "If it can happen in Hawaii, will my state be next?" By 1995, antigay forces had organized around the country and had begun to lobby state legislatures to adopt antimarriage bills. The Hawaii case was not yet final. The state of Hawaii, now required to produce a compelling justification for its exclusionary marriage laws, had not yet put on its evidence at trial in support of the ban on same-sex marriage. No other state recognized same-sex marriages. Yet a national campaign soon developed to prevent recognition of same-sex marriage in each and every state. Within a year, still before the trial in the Hawaii case, fifteen states had adopted statutes that proclaimed same-sex marriages void in that state, even if recognized in another state. By 1999, that number had doubled.

On December 3, 1996, the trial court in Hawaii issued its ruling in the *Baehr* case. After weeks of testimony, including much gay-positive expert witness testimony, the trial judge ruled that the state had failed to demonstrate a compelling reason for its discrimination. The state immediately appealed to the state supreme court and asked for a stay of the trial court's opinion. Therefore, despite two positive court rulings, no moment in Hawaii ever came into being during which the plaintiffs could exercise their marriage rights.

The Supreme Court of Hawaii delayed its ruling. In the meantime, antigay marriage groups campaigned to amend the Hawaii constitution to prevent the court's ruling from ever taking effect. In November 1998, voters in Hawaii approved an amendment to the state constitution that authorized the legislature to restrict marriage. Specifically, the amendment provided: "The legislature shall have the power to reserve marriage to opposite-sex couples." Unclear about what the amendment's effect might be on the ongoing litigation, the Hawaii Supreme Court asked the parties to submit additional briefs addressing the amendment's effect. The gay plaintiffs argued that the amendment delegated to the legislature the ability to define marriage as a constitutional matter, but could have no effect on their case unless and until the legislature so acted. Since the legislature had taken no action, the status of the case was unchanged. The state argued otherwise, saying that the amendment merely ratified the current legislative definition of marriage, a definition that restricts the institution to one man and one woman.

On December 9, 1999, the Supreme Court of Hawaii finally issued its ruling in the case. After taking judicial notice of the fact that the marriage amendment to the Hawaii constitution had been ratified in November 1998, the court proceeded to address the constitutionality of the Hawaii statute, HRS §572-1, the statute that limited marriage to opposite-sex couples. The court stated:

> The marriage amendment validated HRS §572-1 by taking the statute out of the ambit of the equal protection clause of the Hawaii Constitution. . . . Accordingly, whether or not in the past it was violative of the equal protection clause, HRS §572-1 no longer is. In light of the marriage amendment, HRS §572-1 must be given full force and effect.

With this short opinion, the Court informed the plaintiffs that their case was now moot. The plaintiffs' request that they be issued a marriage license was denied.

The Vermont Litigation

At the same time the Hawaii courts were considering the constitutionality of Hawaii's marriage laws, a similar challenge to Vermont's marriage laws began. In *Baker v. Vermont,* the plaintiffs argued that the state's denial of marriage rights, including all the benefits that attach to marriage, constitutes a denial of equality under the Vermont constitution. In particular, they argued that the restrictive marriage laws violated the common benefits provision of the Vermont constitution, which provides as follows:

> That government is, or ought to be, instituted for the common benefit, protection, and security of the people, nation, or community, and not for the particular emolument or advantage of any single person, family, or set of persons, who are a part only of that community. . . .

In an opinion handed down in January 2000, the Vermont Supreme Court agreed that the restrictive marriage laws violated the common benefits clause. The court then turned to the question of how to remedy the violation. The simplest way to extend the benefits enjoyed by married couples to same-sex couples who wished to marry would be to allow same-sex couples to marry. The court, however, recognizing that there were other ways to accomplish this result, held as follows:

> The State is constitutionally required to extend to same-sex couples the common benefits and protections that flow from marriage under Vermont law. Whether this ultimately takes the form of inclusion within the marriage laws themselves or a parallel "domestic partnership" system or some equivalent

statutory alternative, rests with the Legislature. Whatever system is chosen, however, must conform with the constitutional imperative to afford all Vermonters the common benefit, protection, and security of the law.

Baker is an amazing decision, even though the Court did not require the state to recognize same-sex marriage. All justices agreed that the Vermont law restricting marriage to opposite-sex couples, together with the Vermont laws that confer benefits on married couples, violates the Vermont constitution. The only dissent from the majority opinion was by Justice Johnson, who disagreed with the remedy. Johnson thought the court should grant an immediate remedy (i.e., issue marriage licenses to the plaintiffs) rather than delegating the choice of remedy to the legislature. On April 26, 2000, the Vermont legislature responded to the *Baker* decision by enacting a statute that creates a new legal status, a "civil union."[9] The legislature elected to reserve the institution of marriage to opposite-sex couples, but declared that the "state has a strong interest in promoting stable and lasting families, including families based upon a same-sex couple." To carry out that interest, the legislature has provided that same-sex couples may enter a "civil union" that parallels marriage in that parties to a civil union shall have all the same benefits and responsibilities under Vermont law that spouses have. Specifically, the new law provides:

> Parties to a civil union shall have all the same benefits, protections and responsibilities under law, whether they derive from statute, administrative or court rule, policy, common law or any other source of civil law, as are granted to spouses in a marriage.[10]

With the enactment of this law, Vermont has adopted two separate institutions, marriage and civil unions, that are treated equally by the law. Only opposite-sex couples can marry and only same-sex couples can be parties to a civil union. The result is a true case of separate but equal in that the equality of state-provided benefits is real. One might argue, however, that by maintaining a separate institution, domestic partnership, for gay men and lesbians creates a stigma by saying that gay men and lesbians are not worthy of the institution of marriage. Other than this stigmatic harm, Vermont's proposed law will accomplish equality of treatment.

One additional problem is that Vermont law applies only to Vermont. Vermont's recognition of two lesbians as domestic partners will determine their legal benefits and burdens only within Vermont. The Vermont legislature cannot make the federal government recognize the couple as a legal entity, nor can Vermont create a legal status of domestic partnership that will extend beyond its state borders into other states. Once the lesbian couple moves to another state or even travels through another state, the laws of other states become applicable. Another state could elect to recognize the relationship created under Vermont law, but that decision would have to be made by the other state, not by Vermont. Legal scholars have debated whether gay marriages in any state that recognizes such marriages would be recognized in other states. Full faith and credit, comity, and conflicts of law principles generally are available to support arguments in favor of extraterritorial recognition of gay marriages. The same arguments would be available to support extraterritorial recognition of Vermont domestic partnerships. The arguments regarding domestic partnership recognition suffer one major drawback, however. Since no other state recognizes domestic partner status, no state law other than Vermont's would contain any substantive provisions with respect to the rights and responsibilities of domestic partners. Thus, for the state of Iowa to agree to recognize two Vermont lesbians as domestic partners would mean nothing unless Iowa were to import the substantive law of Vermont dealing with domestic partnership. Although it is possible for courts to apply the substantive law of another state under its conflicts of law rules, a court would not apply Vermont law unless Vermont had an important present connection with the dispute. Thus, conflicts of law principles might fully protect Vermont domestic partners who are only temporarily outside Vermont borders, but no protection would be available for any Vermonters who abandoned Vermont as a domicile.

The battle over marriage is one that will have to be won state by state unless and until the U.S. Supreme Court rules that gay and lesbian couples have a fundamental right to marry that is protected by the U.S. Constitution. We are, to be sure, a long way away from seeing any such ruling by the Supreme Court. The lesbian and gay community is still fighting at the national level for equal access to jobs. As earlier civil rights movements have shown, courts will grant equal access to public arenas well before they will tinker with rights that are linked to marriage.

MARRIAGE RIGHTS BY LITIGATION OR LEGISLATION?

Litigation efforts on behalf of same-sex marriage necessarily rely on legal arguments that courts can recognize and enforce. If marriage is a fundamental right, then litigants can argue in court that the state's failure to make that right available to lesbians and gay men is unconstitutional. Since the Supreme

Court of the United States has recognized marriage as a fundamental right on more than one occasion, this argument is an obvious one to press in court. The Supreme Court has ruled that prisoners cannot be denied the right to marry,[11] so how can a state deny that right to lesbians and gay men? The easy judicial response is that marriage in general is not a fundamental right unless it is marriage between two opposite-sex persons, whether prisoners or not. *Bowers v. Hardwick* supports this position because the effect of its holding is that privacy, another recognized fundamental right, is not a fundamental right for same-sex intimacy. The "marriage as a fundamental right" argument will thus only work in state courts under state constitutions where *Hardwick* is not necessarily the law. But note that the fundamental right argument did not carry the day in Hawaii, where the court ruled that same-sex marriage was not a fundamental right under the Hawaii constitution, even though the court did rule favorably on equal protection grounds.

Another legal argument can be made against recognizing same-sex marriage as a fundamental right. This alternative argument is that marriage itself is not a fundamental right for anyone, although some of the rights within marriage are fundamental. Under this view of fundamental rights and marriage, gay rights litigators ought to claim a denial of fundamental rights not because their clients are denied access to marriage, but because they are denied access to specific fundamental rights within marriage. To elaborate, marriage is an institution with many different attributes. As recognized by the state, marriage carries benefits and imposes obligations. The benefits of marriage are of two primary types: (1) benefits that protect the intimacy and togetherness of the couple, and (2) financial benefits that protect the economic integrity of the marital unit. For married couples with children, the benefits include both intimacy and economic benefits that extend to the expanded family unit. The Constitution does not require the government to provide economic benefits to married couples, or even to couples with children. Indeed, in a number of situations, legislation actually imposes financial costs on married couples. The current marriage tax penalty that applies to two-income spouses is a prime example. Legislation creating such burdens has been challenged by married couples who claim that the burdens violate their fundamental right to marry, but none of these cases have been successful. Such cases support the conclusion that the constitution does not require government to provide married couples with financial benefits. Thus, financial benefits associated with marriage are not considered fundamental rights.

Marriage does create fundamental personal intimacy interests, however, which the state cannot unduly burden. The Supreme Court first recognized this right to marital privacy in *Griswold v. Connecticut.* Based on *Griswold,* one can conclude that the fundamental right to marry is really nothing more than the right to protected marital intimacy. In states where same-sex intimacy can be protected under state constitutional provisions free from the limitations of *Hardwick,* a state need not confer marital status in order to offer the protection contemplated by *Griswold.* Indeed, some states have protected the fundamental intimacy rights of same-sex couples by striking down state criminal laws that regulate the sexual aspects of that intimacy.

Does the state grant any other personal intimacy rights to married couples and not to same-sex couples? If so, then lesbian and gay litigators could challenge the deprivation of those rights directly rather than making the secondary claim that same-sex marriage should be recognized so that such benefits can flow to gay men and lesbians. Other personal intimacy rights include the right to be together, whether sexual activity is contemplated or not. Rights of this sort are implicated in cases in which same-sex partners are denied access to each other when one partner becomes incapacitated or institutionalized. These rights are also implicated when partners are denied the right to live together or when an alien partner is forced to leave the country because the federal government will not grant the legal status necessary for that partner to remain in this country. These rights are also implicated after one partner dies and the survivor is prohibited from having any contact with the deceased's body or any involvement in funeral or burial arrangements. When a state grants some, but not all, couples these personal intimacy rights, it can be sued for violating the fundamental rights of those who have been denied these rights. The specific legal theory is the fundamental rights branch of equal protection doctrine.

As an alternative legal theory, litigators have also claimed that state laws denying marital status to same-sex couples create classifications that violate the Equal Protection Clause. Under equal protection, there are two possible arguments. One, the opposite-sex restriction on the status of marriage constitutes discrimination on the basis of sex. Two, the restriction constitutes discrimination on the basis of sexual orientation. Clearly, the first argument is superior since sex discrimination will trigger heightened judicial scrutiny. This argument was accepted by the Hawaii Supreme Court and by one concurring justice in the Vermont case. But other courts could find that the restriction was intended to prevent lesbian and gay couples from marrying and thus, at its core, the restriction is discrimination on the basis of sexual orientation. Under low-level rational basis review, courts should have no difficulty justifying the sex restriction in state marriage law.

Litigation under the federal constitution, whether the claim is based on equal protection or the liberty clause of the Fourteenth Amendment, is unlikely to succeed. Although many state courts are likely to find that their state marriage laws do not violate the federal constitution, the Vermont case creates the hope that other successful state constitutional challenges are possible. Vermont is not the only state with an equal benefits clause in its constitution.

Litigation victories in the marriage arena may be short-lived, however, as the Hawaii victory proved to be. If courts rule in favor of gay marriage before the general population is ready to accept the premise, then a majority of citizens who oppose the notion can effectively repeal the decision by amending the state constitution to forbid gay marriage. For this reason, a number of gay and lesbian activists believe that obtaining statewide domestic partnership laws similar to the new Vermont "civil union" statute would be a positive interim step. And although activists in the past have presumed that legislative action would be required to create domestic partner legislation, we now know from the Vermont litigation that litigation may prove to be a successful catalyst in inspiring legislators to act on the matter. Additionally, before the people of Hawaii adopted the marriage amendment to the Hawaii constitution, the legislature passed legislation that provided some rights to unmarried couples. The details of this "reciprocal beneficiary" legislation will be discussed in the next section. What the experience in Hawaii shows, however, is that even litigation that fails in the end can spur legislative action that benefits same-sex couples.

The legislative alternative to same-sex marriage is domestic partnership law. If ultimately what most couples want are the personal and economic benefits attached to marriage, then state recognition of some status other than marriage will meet most couples' needs, provided the new status carries all or most of the same benefits as marriage. Others believe that equal dignity will never be accomplished by this separate but equal approach. For them, no matter how many benefits lesbian and gay rights activists are able to acquire for same-sex couples, marriage must be equally available for all couples. Thus, in their opinion, neither litigation nor legislative efforts should cease until full marriage equality is achieved.

DOMESTIC PARTNERSHIPS

Many of the benefits of marriage, including the benefit of public recognition, can be obtained through domestic partner legislation. Some domestic partner benefits can be obtained by litigating against employers who offer fringe benefits to spouses of employees. The basic legal claim in such cases is that failure to offer benefits on an equal basis is a form of discrimination. When advocates began to file suits making these claims they broke new ground in the world of civil rights arguments. The employee's claim was not a typical discrimination claim, that is, that an individual employee had been discriminated against because of some unrelated personal characteristic such as race or sex. Rather, the claim depended on something external to the individual employee, the fact that he or she had a partner. Since the partner was obviously not a spouse, lawyers had to argue either that the same-sex partner of the employee was so similar to a spouse that to deny the benefit violated the principle that likes should be treated alike or that the spousal classification on its face discriminated on the basis of sexual orientation.

The first litigated case on domestic partner benefits was a case brought by attorney Roberta Achtenberg of the Lesbian Rights Project, with assistance from local counsel Rosie Metrailer in Sacramento. They filed suit on behalf of Boyce Hinman, a California state employee who claimed that his employer's refusal to extend the benefit of dental insurance to his partner of twelve years was discriminatory.[12] Their main argument was that since the employer knew that gay and lesbian marriages were not possible, adoption of the classification "spouse" was intended to discriminate against gay and lesbian employees. The argument was a good one in California because earlier litigation had established that discrimination on the basis of sexual orientation was actionable, and the governor had issued an executive order banning such discrimination against employees in the executive branch of state government.

The court, however, dismissed the claim, holding that the benefits plan did not discriminate on the basis of sexual orientation, but rather on the basis of marital status. The court explained its holding as follows:

Rather than discriminating on the basis of sexual orientation, therefore, the dental plans distinguish eligibility on the basis of marriage. There is no difference in the effect of the eligibility requirement on unmarried homosexual and unmarried heterosexual employees. Thus, plaintiffs are not similarly situated to heterosexual state employees with spouses. They are similarly situated to other unmarried state employees. Unmarried employees are all given the same benefits; plaintiffs have not shown that unmarried homosexual employees are treated differently than unmarried heterosexual employees.

In a subsequent California case, *Brinkin v. Southern Pacific Transportation Company*,[13] the plaintiff included a claim of marital status discrimination. The plaintiff's life partner of eleven years had committed suicide, and the plaintiff requested the same three days of bereavement leave that the employer granted in the case of the death of an employee's "father, mother, wife, husband, brother, sister, son or daughter, including mother-in-law, father-in-law, step parents [or] step children." The judge denied the claim, despite the fact that the Fair Employment and Housing Act barred discrimination on the basis of marital status, holding that the line drawn on the basis of marriage was necessary to administer the leave plan. Instead, the judge focused on the sexual orientation discrimination claim and reasoned that the real complaint was against the marriage laws, which she opined should be changed to include same-sex couples, but which could only be done by the legislature.

Responding to her opinion, which was hailed by some activists as gay-positive in that it recognized the fundamental right of lesbians and gay men to marry, the plaintiff in the case wrote, in a letter to the editor:

As the plaintiff in Brinkin vs. Southern Pacific, I would like to point out the fact that Judge Ollie Marie-Victoire completely missed the point of my case in her decision (Wednesday, August 28, 1985).

Though she made some nice comments about the bias of present marriage laws against gay people, her comments were not relevant to my case, which asserted that state laws against marital status discrimination would prevent basing funeral leave benefits on marital status. A reading of her decision reveals that our testimony about the bitter unfairness of denying unmarried people funeral leave when our loved ones die meant nothing to her. She states in her decision that a funeral leave plan naming a loved one would be "difficult, if not impossible" to administer. This is patently false; city employees and department store workers, for instance, have such a plan and it is easily administered. Judge Marie-Victoire did not bother to mention the circumstances of my bereavement—the time it took for funeral arrangements and the devastation of the experience which required me to stay home from work.

The ploy of changing the subject to the need for gay marriages will hopefully not blind the gay and civil rights communities to Judge Marie-Victoire's very anti-gay decision.

Litigation efforts in other states have met with the same resistance as these two early cases in California demonstrate. Even plaintiffs who have brought cases under state civil rights statutes banning discrimination on the basis of sexual orientation have not prevailed. In Wisconsin[14] and New Jersey,[15] the courts have so far rejected such claims, explaining that the discrimination is not on the basis of sexual orientation, but rather on the basis of marital status. However, a claim lodged against the city of Seattle claiming both marital status discrimination and sexual orientation discrimination resulted in a positive ruling by the city's human rights commission that resulted in the extension of domestic partner benefits to city employees.

Thwarted by judicial rejection of equality claims to domestic partner benefits, gay rights activists have centered their attention on lobbying their employers to extend the benefits. A minirevolution has occurred in response to these lobbying efforts. Beginning with the city of Berkeley, California, in 1984, cities across the country have begun to adopt domestic partner benefit plans under which some or all of the benefits extended to employee's spouses would also be extended to an employee's domestic partner. "Domestic partner" is a term that was coined in San Francisco in the early 1980s. No single definition of "domestic partner" exists and wide variances can be found among different jurisdictions regarding the conditions a couple must meet before they qualify. As of 1999, approximately 100 cities and counties offered some form of domestic partner registry or extension of domestic partner benefits.

Having met with success in city and county legislative bodies in establishing domestic partner benefits, the legal battle soon became focused on keeping the benefits. As happened when antidiscrimination laws benefiting lesbians and gay men were passed, opponents of domestic partner benefits fought to repeal the legislative actions. But in addition to lobbying their city councilpeople and collecting signatures for initiatives, they took their claims to court. The basic legal argument they made was that cities did not have the power to pass legislation that had the effect of redefining marriage and family. The specifics of the argument varied from state to state since the power of municipalities is determined by the state law. Courts in three states have ruled that cities within the state are without power to extend domestic partner benefits to the partners of city employees. Based on an intermediate appellate court ruling, the city of Minneapolis is not able to extend domestic partner benefits to its lesbian and gay employees even though, in its role as employer, not as political subdivision, it had voted to do so.[16] Generally a "home rule city" can enact whatever legislation it likes so long as the legislation does not directly conflict with state legislation. To determine whether Minneapolis, a "home rule city," had the power to enact legislation in favor of domestic partners, the court first considered whether the Minneapolis ordinance conflicted with state statutes. State statutes did define the term "dependent" for purposes of insurance benefits provided to governmental employees, but the language in the state provision was permissive only. That is, the statute only said that cities *may* provide benefits to certain dependents. The statute did not say that cities must provide benefits to any limited group. Nor did it explicitly state that cities could not provide benefits to persons other than dependents. Recognizing the permissive nature of the state statute, the court had to admit there was no direct conflict between the city ordinance and the state definition of "dependent." Nonetheless, the court ruled that Minneapolis lacked the power to enact the domestic partner ordinance because home rule cities could only legislate on matters of local concern. The court viewed the domestic partner issue as part of the larger issue of discrimination and held that since discrimination was a matter of statewide concern, evidenced by the recent enactment of statewide laws banning discrimination on the basis of sexual orientation, Minneapolis was without power to address the issue as a matter of local concern. Thus, in the short run at least, domestic partner legislation is unlikely to be upheld in Minnesota until the Minnesota legislature acts on the matter. The reasoning in this case has not been adopted in other states and may, in the end, be limited to Minnesota.

The Supreme Court of Massachusetts, however, has also ruled that, under the home rule provisions of Massachusetts, the city of Boston may not provide domestic partner benefits to city employees.[17] The reasoning in the Massachusetts case is a bit different from the Minnesota case. The Massachusetts legislature has enacted a statute stating which dependents may be included in insurance benefits programs provided to governmental employees. The Massachusetts statute, however, goes beyond mere permissive inclusion and mandates that all cities adopt plans that conform to the state requirements. Thus, the Massachusetts court has read the state statutory scheme as requiring uniformity among municipalities and thereby taking away a city's power to define eligible dependents differently.

The Virginia Supreme Court has also ruled that local governments in that state lack the power to extend health benefits to domestic partners of their employees because the state statute authorizing the extension of benefits is limited to "dependents" of the employee.[18] Despite the fact that the state statute does not define dependent, the court held that Arlington County did not have the power to define dependent as someone who was financially interdependent with the employee. Only someone who received over half of his support from an employee could meet the definition of dependent. Spouses, although not necessarily dependent, could be covered because spouses have always been covered. Despite these recent negative state court rulings, a number of positive rulings also exist. Recent positive court opinions upholding the power of local governments to award domestic partnership benefits have been issued in Georgia,[19] Illinois,[20] and New York.[21]

Litigation over domestic partner benefits has become particularly complex in San Francisco. The City of San Francisco has enacted an ordinance requiring all employers that contract with the city to provide domestic partner benefits. Litigation over its ability to take such action has been challenged under ERISA, a federal statute that specifically preempts state law with respect to any benefit plans that are covered by ERISA. That litigation continues. In addition, the city of Atlanta, having established its right to extend domestic partner benefits in successful litigation before the Georgia Supreme Court, is now battling with the state insurance commissioner, who is resisting the request to provide such benefits.

Perhaps the most impressive litigation in a domestic partner benefits case is the recent victory in an Oregon case. In *Tanner v. Oregon Health Sciences University,*[22] a claim brought by three lesbians against their employer for the extension of spousal benefits to their domestic partners resulted in a final ruling from an appellate court that has important implications for future gay rights litigation in that state. Despite the defendant's argument that the class burdened by the benefit plan was unmarried individuals, the court determined that the burdened class should be defined as unmarried same-sex couples. Defining the class in this manner was important because the Oregon constitution explicitly provides: "No law shall be passed granting to any citizen or class of citizens privileges or immunities, which, upon the same terms, shall not equally belong to all citizens." This clause is similar to the equal benefits clause in the Vermont constitution. Furthermore, the court ruled that the class, unmarried same-sex couples, was a suspect one, thereby entitled to heightened judicial scrutiny. To deny this class of couples a state benefit, the state must prove that something exists about their difference, viewed by the court as their sexual orientation, that warrants the denial. The state could not provide a justification in *Tanner* and the court could not think of one. This ruling effectively creates a statewide domestic partner law. Under the court's reasoning, any benefit that the state grants to married couples, but denies to an unmarried same-sex couple, is subject to serious challenge in the courts.

Other than Vermont, Hawaii is the only state that has enacted statewide legislation that can benefit same-sex domestic partners. The Hawaii legislature, in response to the equality arguments raised in the marriage case, passed a law called the Reciprocal Beneficiaries Act. Any two individuals who are unable to marry each other, who meet the minimal statutory requirements, and register with the state can qualify as "reciprocal beneficiaries." Under Hawaii law, such couples are entitled to many, although not nearly all, of the benefits extended to married couples. Key benefits include (1) the right to own a life insurance policy insuring the life of one's partner, (2) the right to family health insurance on the same terms as married couples, (3) the right to visit one's partner in the hospital, (4) the right to inherit from one's partner under the intestacy laws, and (5) the right to a minimum share of the partner's estate at death. The Vermont legislation, discussed earlier in this chapter, goes much further and provides to domestic partners all of the same benefits the state provides to spouses. The Vermont legislation also includes a reciprocal beneficiary law that is similar to Hawaii's. Reciprocal beneficiary status is available for a broader class of persons than same-sex domestic partners because it includes all persons who can't marry. Thus, for example, siblings or a parent and child could elect to be reciprocal beneficiaries. An interesting aspect of the Vermont legislation is that same-sex couples could elect to be either domestic partners or reciprocal beneficiaries, depending on which status more accurately reflects their commitment and interdependence. Some family law scholars have argued that marriage should similarly be divided into different sorts of regimes so that married couples could select which type of marriage they wanted (e.g., full merger or partial merger). The current version of the Hawaii and Vermont reciprocal beneficiary statutes, however, would prevent opposite sex couples from choosing that status so long as they have the legal option of marriage. Thus opposite-sex couples are limited to choosing marriage or nothing.

Under *Tanner*, the Oregon domestic partner case, every unmarried lesbian or gay couple can presumably assert a claim to all of the state-provided rights and benefits enjoyed by spouses. Indeed, the mere fact that these rights have been granted to same-sex couples by two other states is evidence that nothing about the sexual orientation of the same-sex couple requires denying them these rights.

NONSTATUTORY RECOGNITION OF LESBIAN AND GAY FAMILIES

In addition to the rare successful case establishing the right of lesbian and gay couples to domestic partner benefits, other cases have arisen that recognize some rights of lesbian and gay families. A prime example of such a case is *Braschi,* handed down by the New York Court of Appeals in 1989. In *Braschi,* the surviving life partner of a deceased gay man was threatened with eviction from his New York apartment. The landlord wanted the partner to leave so that he could rent to a new tenant free of the city's rent control restrictions. Had Braschi been recognized as a "family member" of the deceased, the issue would not have arisen. The two men had lived together in the apartment for ten years. They had combined their finances, named each other as beneficiaries in their insurance policies and in their wills, and executed powers of attorney that gave each other power to make financial and personal decisions affecting the other in the case of incapacity. The New York Court of Appeals construed the term "family member" in the applicable statute to mean "family" in the functional sense rather than the purely traditional sense. Braschi clearly met this definition and, thus, was allowed to continue living in his home after the death of his partner.

A key point in the *Braschi* case is that the statute being construed used the word "family," but did not define it. Thus, the court was left free to interpret the word in keeping with the purpose of the statute. But a court has less flexibility when the statutory language is more specific, such as using the term "spouse" or providing a definition of family member as one who is related by blood or marriage. Although the holding in *Braschi* cannot be easily transported to provide other spousal or family benefits to lesbian and gay partners, the decision nonetheless stands as an important gay litigation victory because it put the highest court of New York on record as supporting the idea of family justice for lesbian and gay couples.

Two key family justice issues affect lesbian and gay families with children. The first issue is legal recognition of parental status for both parents. The best way to establish parental status for persons with no biological connection to the child is through adoption. Despite archaic statutory language that was written by legislatures who never contemplated lesbian and gay parenting, numerous judges have been willing to interpret that language liberally to allow two same-sex unmarried partners to be parents to the same child. This process can involve several different fact situations, but the most common are the following two: (1) a biological or adoptive parent wants her or his same-sex partner to adopt the child without erasing the existing parent's legal relationship to the child, or (2) a same-sex couple wishes to adopt a child together. In the former case, positive decisions are hampered by statutory language that cancels the legal relationship of a parent with a child when that child is adopted by anyone other than a spouse of the existing parent. Since same-sex partners cannot marry, they cannot meet this exception. In the latter case, positive judicial rulings are hampered by statutory language that authorizes adoption by a single person or a married couple, but makes no mention of adoption by unmarried couples.

Despite these drawbacks, lower courts in a number of states have allowed same-sex partners to enter into adoption arrangements that result in what is best for the child: two legal parents. Known as "second-parent adoption" this process has been successful in approximately half the states. In at least three states (New York, Vermont, Masachusetts),[23] the highest state court has approved the procedure. Connecticut has recently amended its adoption statute to allow same-sex couples to adopt children.[24] The amendment is necessary because that state's top court had interpreted the Connecticut statute as precluding adoptions by same-sex parents.[25]

More recently, several California superior courts have been willing to issue a declaration of parentage in certain types of lesbian parent cases. For example, when one woman agrees to carry the child and the genetic material comes from her partner, judges are willing to declare that both women are parents under California's version of the Uniform Parentage Age.[26] In addition, some judges have been willing to declare the lesbian mother's partner a parent even when the partner contributed no genetic material.[27] The theory in such cases is that the nonbiological mother is an "intentional parent," a doctrine that has been recognized by California courts in cases involving alternative reproductive technology used by heterosexual couples.[28] Once a declaration of parentage is issued, further legal action to establish the parent-child relationship, such as adoption, is unnecessary.

The second key family issue involving children is whether a court, in the absence of formal adoption, will recognize the right of the second parent to visit the child in the event the partner relationship ends. Courts have been less willing to be creative in these cases. In part, since no statute is before the court that can be liberally construed and since visitation rights, by statute, go to parents, and in some rare cases, to grandparents, the courts have concluded that their ability to intervene is limited. In addition, the adoption cases present the court with two adults both agreeing that recognizing them both as parents is in the child's best interest. By contrast, visitation cases often pit the biological parent against the nonbiological parent who disagree about what is in the child's best interest. When the two partners specifically have agreed that visitation would occur in such cases, however, the court is faced with the evidence that at one point in time the two thought such visitation would be in the best interest of the child. Fact situations in which there is evidence of such agreements present stronger cases. In such situations, a handful of state courts have been willing to recognize the nonlegal parent's right to visit the child.[29]

Cases such as *Braschi* that recognize a liberal definition of family and cases that allow gay and lesbian families with children to cement their legal status through adoption or contract are important gains in the battle toward legal recognition of lesbian and gay families. Gaining family rights bit by bit not only creates immediate benefit to the individual litigants, but contributes to a litigation strategy that should help eventually to produce broader gains such as domestic partner rights and perhaps, eventually, marriage.

NOTES

1. *See* Transcript at 46, Hall v. Hall, No. 55900 (Ohio C.P. Div. Dom. Rel., April 26, 1974), described in Rhonda R. Rivera, "Our Straight-Laced Judges: The Legal Position of Homosexual Persons in the United States," 30 *Hastings Law Journal* 799 at 1117 (1979).

2. *See* Alan Yang, "From Wrongs to Rights: Public Opinion on Gay & Lesbian Americans Moves Toward Equality" (NGLTF Publications: December 1999).

3. Braschi v. Stahl Associates Co., 543 N.E.2d 49 (N.Y. 1989).

4. William N. Eskridge Jr. *The Case for Same-Sex Marriage* at 57 (1996).

5. The debate is reproduced in Suzanne Sherman, *Lesbian and Gay Marriage: Private Commitments, Public Ceremonies* at 13–26 (Temple University Press 1992).

6. *See*, for example, *USA Today*, November 26, 1990.

7. *USA Today*, December 19, 1990.

8. Baehr v. Lewin, 852 P.2d 44 (Haw. 1993) (holding that the state's refusal to recognize same-sex marriages is a form of sex discrimination that can only be justified by a compelling state interest under the Equal Protection Clause of the Hawaii constitution).

9. *See* 15 Vermont Statutes Annotated §§ 1201 et. seq.

10. 15 Vermont Statutes Annotated §1204.

11. Turner v. Safley, 482 U.S. 78 (1987).

12. Hinman v. Department of Personnel Administration, 213 Cal Rptr. 410 (Cal. App. 1985).

13. Brinkin v. Southern Pacific Transportation Co., 572 F.Supp. 236 (N.D. Cal. 1985).

14. Phillips v. Wisconsin Personnel Commission., 482 N.W.2d 121 (Wisc. App. 1992).

15. Rutgers Council of AAUP Chapters v. Rutgers, 689 A.2d 828 (N.J. Super. 1997), *cert. denied*, 707 A.2d 151 (N.J. 1998).

16. Lilly v. City of Minneapolis, 527 N.W.2d 107 (Minn. App. 1985) (holding that city council exceeded authority when it extended health care benefits to same-sex domestic partners).

17. Connors v. City of Boston, 714 N.E.2d 335 (Mass. 1999).

18. Arlington County v. White, 528 S.E.2d 706 (Va. 2000).

19. City of Atlanta v. Morgan, 492 S.E.2d 193 (Ga. 1997) (upholding Atlanta's domestic partner ordinance).

20. Crawford v. City of Chicago, 710 N.E.2d 91 (Ill. App. 1999) (upholding Chicago's domestic partner ordinance).

21. Slattery v. City of New York, 697 N.Y.S.2d 603 (App. Div. 1999).

22. Tanner v. Oregon Health Science University, 971 P.2d 435 (Ore. App. 1998).

23. Matter of Jacob, 660 N.E.2d 397 (N.Y. 1995) (allowing lesbian partner to adopt her partner's child without forcing biological mother to terminate her parental rights); Adoption of B.L.V.B. and E.L.V.B., 628 A.2d 1271 (Vt. 1993) (lesbian partner can adopt partner's child and biological mother need not terminate parental rights); Adoption of Tammy, 619 N.E.2d 315 (Mass. 1993) (statute did not prevent same-sex couple from jointly adopting child when adoption was in child's best interest).

24. *See* Connecticut General Statutes Annotated §45a–724(a)(3).

25. In re Adoption of Baby Z, 724 A.2d 1035 (Conn. 1999) (holding that biological mother must terminate her rights before her lesbian life partner of ten years could adopt their child).

26. *See* In the Matter of Doe (genetic mother) and Roe (gestational mother), Case No. PA008168, Super. Ct. Santa Cruz CA, (April 27, 1999, J. Stevens).

27. Petition of Carhart and Hollingsworth, Case No. F054887, Super. Ct. San Mateo, (June 11, 1999, J. Pfeiffer).

28. *See* Buzzanca. 72 Cal.Rptr.2d 280 (1998) (recognizing the doctrine of intentional parenthood in the case of a surrogate arrangement involving heterosexual couples).

29. *See,* for example, V.C. v. M.J.B., 748 A.2d 539 (N.J. 2000) (granting visitation to lesbian ex-partner). *See also* A.C. v. C.B., 829 P. 2d 660 (N.M. App. 1992) (holding that nonbiological mother had standing to seek enforcement of joint custody agreement with her lesbian ex-partner).

10

Conclusion

Relying on successful courtroom arguments made in the African American civil rights movement and the women's movement, the lesbian and gay civil rights movement has litigated for equal access in the public sphere and for the right to be left alone in the private sphere. As was true in both earlier movements, the first lesbian and gay rights case to reach the U.S. Supreme Court was not successful.

Gay and lesbian activists have learned from earlier civil rights movements that the most workable legal arguments, especially in litigation, are sameness arguments. Translated into a constitutional argument, the argument based on sameness is that similarly situated individuals should be accorded equal treatment under the law. But we have also learned from earlier civil rights movements that the sameness thesis has its limits. Sameness arguments simply won't work when the court perceives difference rather than sameness.

Another problem with the sameness thesis is its blandness, its tendency to maintain the status quo—not a particularly strong rallying cry for a vibrant civil rights movement. In the gay rights movement, as in earlier civil rights movements, activists often disavow sameness arguments because of their tendency to devalue the very thing that makes us who we are. For example, Kate Kendell, executive director of NCLR, writes that she is biased against making the sameness argument because:

> It denies that as a lesbian I am in any essential important way different from say, my sister, who is straight—but I am essentially and proudly different—my erotic, passionate, emotional desire is captivated and fulfilled by another woman. That folks is an essential, core difference between me and my sister and to deny the difference is to deny that sexuality and that I will not do.

This sameness/difference dichotomy plagued earlier civil rights movements in many of the same ways it plagues the lesbian and gay civil rights
movement. Sameness arguments won African Americans important equal
access rights in the public sphere in the 1950s. Before that time, sameness
arguments were hampered by application of the "separate but equal" doctrine, a doctrine that was founded on the assumption that there were core
differences between the races that justified the separation. Sameness arguments were necessary to attack those assumptions of difference, assumptions based on faulty racial stereotypes. Once the core sameness of being a
human being, regardless of race, was recognized, it became possible to embrace real and valid differences, differences that are not based on stereotype. That embrace is nowhere near complete. In some people's lives, it may
not even have begun. But for many of us, especially those of us who lived
through "separate but equal" and Jim Crow, the discussions of racial difference today are light-years away from the discussions in the old days. The
new discussions would not be possible if the old stereotypes had not been
shattered by connecting individuals through their sameness.

Building on the sameness arguments that had been made for racial equality and on the equal protection tests that the Supreme Court developed to
handle those arguments, feminist litigators in the 1970s also won important equal access rights in the public sphere for women. In doing so, they
fought the stereotype of the past that had defined "woman" as properly belonging only in her sphere of home and family. But women faced a new and
different problem from that faced by racial minorities in making their
sameness arguments. In cases in which the biological differences between
men and women seemed relevant, courts had difficulty seeing the sameness
between men and women and thus found it difficult to rule in favor of
equal treatment. Thus, for women, sameness arguments under equal protection could not always accomplish the desired goals. For example, sameness arguments in the courtroom did not gain medical benefits or medical
leave for pregnant women in the workplace. But, as with arguments about
race, once the sameness arguments established that, at the core, women and
men are equally able, a new starting point was established for discussing
difference. The proper treatment of pregnant workers, for example, was
not a serious topic of discussion until sameness arguments had transformed
the workplace into a place where women and men were viewed as equal
workers. As with race, the embrace of difference is nowhere near complete.
But the dialogue about difference has been meaningfully changed, and the
discussion is filled with more promise, because the sameness argument has

created a sufficiently new landscape in which women are no longer confined to private spheres.

Lesbian and gay rights litigators have also made the sameness argument to gain equal public access for lesbians and gay men. They have asked the courts to apply equal protection doctrine to protect lesbian and gay rights in the same way the courts have used equal protection doctrine to protect the rights of racial minorities and women. Although these arguments have worked in some cases, the rights attained for gays and lesbians lag far behind the rights attained for blacks and women. This current lag can be explained in part by the fact that the lesbian and gay civil rights movement is more recent. To measure the relative success of lesbian and gay rights arguments in the courts, one must consider where each movement began.

The black civil rights movement and the modern women's movement began their battles for equal rights using equality arguments based on sameness. For African Americans, the primary target of these arguments was *Plessy v. Ferguson,* the case that established the separate but equal doctrine, and the various Jim Crow laws that mandated racial segregation. For women, the primary target was a trilogy of old Supreme Court cases, *Bradwell, Goesaert,* and *Hoyt,* cases that reflected the stereotypical view that women belonged in the private sphere of home and family rather than in the public sphere of employment and jury service.

Plessy was decided in 1896 and finally overruled in 1954. The NAACP spent almost thirty years litigating primarily against segregated schools before it gained its ultimate victory in *Brown v. Board of Education.* But, in the meantime, the NAACP and the black civil rights movement scored litigation victories against segregation in housing in 1917 *(Buchanan v. Warley)* and 1948 *(Shelley v. Kraemer).* The NAACP also scored a major litigation victory against segregation in higher education in 1950 *(Sweatt v. Painter).* Thus, even though the road from *Plessy* to *Brown* took over fifty years to travel, the NAACP's litigation efforts took a mere twenty-five years from the time of its initial funding by the Garland Fund[1] to its victory in *Sweatt v. Painter.*

Bradwell was decided in 1873. Although the case was argued under the privileges and immunities clause of the fourteenth amendment, the Court's action and especially Justice Bradley's concurring opinion, endorsed the view that women belonged in the private and unequal sphere of home and family. *Goesaert v. Cleary,*[2] decided in 1948, embraced the same stereotypical view of women, as did *Hoyt v. Florida,*[3] decided in 1961. These cases were effectively reversed in the first ACLU Women's Rights Project case to reach the Supreme Court, *Reed v. Reed,* decided in 1971. Thus, although the road from *Bradwell* to *Reed* took ninety-eight years, the road from *Hoyt* to *Reed* took a mere ten.

Modern gay rights litigators focused on state sodomy statutes as their primary target because these statutes worked to endorse discrimination against gay men and lesbians. *Doe v. Commonwealth's Attorney* was the first gay rights case challenging the criminalization of sodomy to reach the Supreme Court. In 1976, twenty-two years after *Brown* and five years after *Reed*, the Supreme Court refused even to hear oral arguments in the gay rights case and summarily affirmed the constitutionality of the Virginia sodomy statute without opinion. Ten years later, in *Hardwick*, despite the benefit of oral argument and amici briefs in support of Hardwick from organizations as diverse as the American Jewish Congress, the American Psychological Association, the American Public Health Association, the National Organization for Women, the Presbyterian Church (USA), and the attorneys general of New York and California, a majority of the Supreme Court again failed to recognize lesbian and gay equality.

As in the civil rights movements for race and gender equality, gay rights lawyers argued sameness and equality in *Hardwick*. Although *Hardwick* was structured as a fundamental rights/privacy case, at its core the case is about equality and sameness. Only the four dissenters, however, saw the case in that light. For Justice White and the majority, the case was a simple one about homosexual sodomy, a practice that, in their view, was not similar to any recognized constitutional right and thus a practice that raised no issues of equality. But gay rights lawyers had seen the Court grant sexual privacy rights to married couples in *Griswold* and to unmarried couples in *Eisenstadt* and believed the sexual rights of interest to lesbians and gay men were within the same sphere of protection. The litigators did argue for privacy, but on the grounds that the claim was for the *same* privacy that heterosexuals enjoyed. Instead, the Court heard "homosexual sodomy," not privacy. The Court said gay people are different.

Post-*Hardwick*, gay rights litigators have continued to make sameness/equality arguments, primarily in cases of public sphere rights. *Romer v. Evans* gives hope that gay people will not always be "strangers to the law." The argument in *Romer* focused primarily on the right of individuals to be free from discrimination in the public sphere. At its narrowest, the opinion proclaims that gays, lesbians, and bisexuals cannot be cordoned off from other citizens in a state and made to go through extra hoops solely to ask for equal protection of the law. At its narrowest, it is a decision about equal access to the persons who make the law, and it establishes no substantive personal rights for lesbians and gay men. Indeed, as Professor Tribe has explained, laws such as Amendment 2 should be struck down even if the people targeted by the law are criminals. So long as sodomy statutes remain on the books, *Romer* does nothing to dispel their effectiveness in discriminating generally against gay men and lesbians. *Romer,* the Supreme Court's first positive decision in a gay rights case, is not a victory for the gay rights movement of the same caliber as *Buchanan v. Warley* was for the NAACP in its battle against segregation. In *Buchanan,* at least, one form of segregation, racial zoning by ordinance, was struck down, thereby reducing the state's ability to enforce apartheid. *Romer* in no way reduces any state's ability to regulate same-sex sexual intimacy. Indeed, by not even mentioning *Hardwick,* the majority opinion in *Romer* indicates that the *Romer* decision does not reduce *Hardwick*'s potency.

For the gay rights movement, the primary target has not changed. Litigators must continue to make sameness arguments in the private sphere in order to cabin *Hardwick,* if not outright reverse it. Under the sameness argument, if litigators can prove that lesbians and gay men are sufficiently similar in their abilities and needs to similarly situated nongay persons, then lesbians and gay men should enjoy the same rights as nongay persons, including the same rights of sexual intimacy. If the sameness/equality argument worked for blacks and for women, gaining them equal access to both public and private sphere rights, then why should the argument not work similarly for gays and lesbians? One answer, of course, is that the argument will work in the end, as it did ultimately for blacks and women. Just as they struggled over time, gay rights litigators must patiently struggle over the requisite time period. Although modern civil rights movements should gain successes more quickly than in the past because they have the benefit of the work of past movements, law, especially judge-made law, is often slow to change. Law is rooted in the past and its consistency over time is one of its values. Legislatures can change the law to deal with changing times, but judges are more constrained. Nonetheless, judges can extend existing legal principles derived from old cases to new cases, provided the new case is sufficiently similar to the old case.

But even if gay rights litigators can establish the required similarity, obstacles exist that will make it difficult for the lesbian and gay civil rights movement to build on the litigation successes of past movements. These difficulties arise for a number of different reasons. Some arise because of the nature of the claims being pursued and the views of judges and the public about the morality of homosexuality. Other difficulties arise because legal doctrine, especially constitutional jurisprudence, has changed since blacks and women won their early litigation victories. Lesbian and gay rights litigators need to grapple with these obstacles as they plan strategies for the future.

OBSTACLE NUMBER ONE: NO RESPECT

By comparison to the black civil rights movement, the lesbian and gay civil rights movement has not yet even attained the "separate but equal" stage, the stage at which black Americans began their litigation efforts. *Bowers v. Hardwick* has been described as the lesbian and gay movement's *Plessy v. Ferguson*. But as a starting point, the case presents a difficulty that *Plessy* did not. For African Americans, courts, at a minimum, embraced the rhetoric of separate but equal. That is, although courts approved of apartheid, they nonetheless espoused a belief that black Americans were entitled to equality. *Plessy* and its progeny never said that black men and women were not entitled to travel on trains or entitled to enjoy other public accommodations. In fact, the command of separate but *equal* was that accommodations be made available to all people, regardless of race, albeit on a segregated basis.

As hollow as the promise of equal separate accommodations was in the realities of black lives, the rhetoric of equality enabled litigators to build on judicial precedents that accorded some respect to black Americans. The black civil rights movement was able to chip away at the doctrine of separate but equal, in part, by showing that things that were purported to be equal were, in fact, not equal. Finally, the black civil rights movement was able to argue that separate is never equal. These arguments would have been much more difficult had litigators begun with precedents holding that African Americans were not entitled to the respect that a right to equality implicitly carries with it.

The women's liberation movement and its litigation efforts began from a similar position of respect in combating antifeminist Court precedent. The ACLU Women's Right's Project sought to reverse earlier negative Supreme Court precedent embodied in *Bradwell, Goesaert,* and *Hoyt.* The core message of *Bradwell, Goesaert,* and *Hoyt* was that keeping women at home, that is, approving the gendered separation of home and work, was consistent with the norm of equality. The Court never said that women were not to be respected because they were incapable of performing the tasks of lawyering, bartending, or serving on juries. Rather, the Court embraced the notion that women had nobler callings and needed protection from the ugliness of public life. Fighting these earlier precedents required feminist litigators to debunk these stereotypes, but they began with precedent that, on its face, purported to respect women in their separate space.

Gay rights litigators, by contrast, begin their arguments from a different position. Gay rights litigators must attack a Supreme Court precedent that is totally devoid of any rhetoric of respect. The majority opinion in *Bowers v. Hardwick* says that gay people are criminals, that their relationships have nothing to do with family, and that even to suggest such a connection is facetious at best. While *Romer* can be cited for the principle that gay men and lesbians are worthy of equal respect in the public sphere, it does not speak to private sphere concerns. Nor is the *Dale* case comforting, despite its presumably limited effect. Because the Boy Scouts believe that gay people are immoral, they can exclude gay men and boys from their otherwise open organization. Morality was the justification for criminalizing gay people in *Bowers v. Hardwick*. *Dale* reinforces that notion. The only positive aspect of the *Dale* majority opinion is that it did not cite *Bowers v. Hardwick* as relevant precedent.

So long as *Bowers v. Hardwick* remains on the books, gays and lesbians will have difficulty mounting a legal argument that they are the same as heterosexual persons. We, as gay and lesbian people, argue that our private choices about love and sex are the same as heterosexual choices, but *Bowers v. Hardwick* says that they are not. We, as gay and lesbian couples, argue that our relationships are the same as heterosexual relationships, but *Bowers v. Hardwick* is cited to show that they are not. And in our separate sphere of gay space, our relationships are accorded no recognition, no protection, and no respect. To overcome this deficit of respect, gay rights litigators face tougher negative precedent than any group has faced since the *Dred Scott* case. At least no court has yet claimed that gay people are not citizens.

OBSTACLE NUMBER TWO:
EQUAL PROTECTION DOCTRINE

There are two types of sameness arguments relevant to equal protection claims. The first argument is that gays, like blacks and women, have suffered from a history of discrimination, lack sufficient political power to protect themselves in the legislature, and thus are a sufficiently discrete and insular minority to warrant heightened judicial scrutiny under footnote 4 of *Carolene Products*. Gay rights litigators have been making this argument for at least twenty years. Unfortunately, gay equal protection claims reached the courts at the very time that the Supreme Court began to cut back on its heightened scrutiny jurisprudence. By the end of the 1970s, the list of suspect or quasi-suspect classifications was closed. The Rehnquist Court has not added a single new classification to the list and additions are unlikely to occur unless and until there is a major shift in Court personnel.[4] Thus, gay people are confined to a classification category under which only low-level scrutiny is available. Although low-level scrutiny produced a victory in *Romer,* further victories are doubtful unless litigators can prove the requisite prejudice or bias behind the state action.

The other way to gain heightened scrutiny under equal protection doctrine is to claim an infringement of a fundamental right. Personal rights to privacy, sexual intimacy, marriage, and family intimacy have been recognized as fundamental. The task for lesbian and gay rights litigators is to convince the courts that gay privacy, sexual intimacy, and family relationships are sufficiently similar to nongay ones. To make these arguments requires a direct challenge to *Bowers v. Hardwick* since that case held that gay sexual intimacy was not protected. Given the Court's reluctance to recognize new suspect classifications, this latter approach to equal protection litigation seems the most promising.

OBSTACLE NUMBER THREE: THE NEW FEDERALISM

A recent string of Supreme Court decisions indicates that the Court is concerned about protecting the states' rights to make decisions free of federal control. In some cases, the Court has ruled that the federal Congress cannot compel states to act in a certain way with respect to its employees solely because Congress thinks the state might be engaging in discrimination. Thus, for example, the Court recently held the Age Discrimination Act unconstitutional as applied to state decisions regarding its own employees.[5] The Court did not believe Congress should regulate state employment decisions unless there was clear proof that a state had engaged in systematic discrimination against a particular group. In short, the Court indicated that congressional power to reach state employment discrimination was limited to types of discrimination for which there was such a long history of state discrimination that the group had been classified as a suspect classification.

This move by the Court toward increased protection of state autonomy has been called the new federalism. Coupled with the Court's refusal to name additional suspect classifications, the new federalism means that nonsuspect groups, such as gays and lesbians, may have to focus their civil rights litigation and lobbying efforts in state courts and legislatures to gain protection state by state. Perhaps after a sufficient number of state battles are won, the lesbian and gay rights movement could renew a federal claim to certain basic substantive rights that should be equally available to all citizens. But in the meantime, state by state battles may be required.

OBSTACLE NUMBER FOUR:
TALKING ABOUT SEX

In an ideal world, lesbian and gay coupling would be equally respected with heterosexual coupling. If it were, we wouldn't need to talk so loudly in public about our lesbian and gay intimate relationships, a phenomenon that often results in charges of "flaunting." But we are not in an ideal world yet. We are in transition, trying to reach the ideal. While in transition and attempting to reach the ideal, we need to publicize the ways in which we are treated inhumanely. For us in the lesbian and gay civil rights movement that includes making revelations about our private spheres so that our plight is better understood.

On a recent NPR broadcast featuring one of the authors of the book *Out For Good,* an African American woman called in during the discussion portion of the program. She wanted to give the gay and lesbian civil rights movement a warning. The warning was that we couldn't have it both ways. We couldn't ask for inclusion in humanity arguing that we were the same, and then, when it suits us, emphasize our difference. We couldn't complain about public discrimination against gays and lesbians and at the same time ask to keep our sexual identities private. We couldn't be gay only some of the time. In part, she was complaining about the ability of lesbians and gay men to pass, an ability that she did not think was available to other civil rights groups. But she also made a larger point. That point was that civil rights movements are aimed at erasing differences that have been imposed on a group of people by others, differences that construct the individuals in the group as less than fully human. In accomplishing that goal of erasure of negative differences, civil rights movements argue that every individual is a full member of the human race. The argument is not that blacks are fully human *despite* their race. Instead, the argument is that blacks are fully human *because* of their race. The race is always there. It can never be ignored.

I think she is right. The claim to be part of humanity should be the driving argument in the lesbian and gay civil rights movement as it has been in other civil rights movements. And our argument, as with race, should be that gays are fully human, not despite our gayness, but because of it. To make this argument, lesbian and gay rights advocates need to focus on what it is that makes us gay. And that, I believe, requires us to focus on sex and intimacy. We need to make the private more public.

There is a difficulty with this tactic. Many Americans appear to be uncomfortable talking about private matters such as sex and intimacy. Lesbian and gay advocates need to find a way to talk about such private matters without destroying the sanctity of the private sphere, the gay private sphere as well as the nongay private sphere. We need to applaud the value of intimacy and sex in heterosexual as well as same-sex relationships. We need to identify that core of being that we all share, that core of human nature that makes us part of the same race. It isn't what we *do* in bed that makes us human. Rather it is what we *feel*. And we all need a zone of privacy in which we express our feelings, most especially our sexual feelings. At the core of our sexual experience is something that is at the core of the human condition: the angst of being separate and the desire to be connected.

When we talk about our private spheres, we need to convince the courts and the public that our relationships consist of something that is essential for all human beings: the connectedness of family. *Bowers v. Hardwick* is an insult because it said our relationships have nothing to do with family. It is precisely because our relationships are family ones that we make our claim to be part of the human race. It is within our families of choice that we experience the human condition of trying to overcome our separation with connection. We, too, need intimacy, love, and yes, sex. And these needs are met in our relationships, relationships that make it possible for us as individuals to realize our full potential as human beings.

The Court of Public Opinion

When Atticus Finch, in *To Kill a Mockingbird,* said that our courts were the great levelers, he described the potential that courts have to be countermajoritarian. Courts are where justice is tendered and mob rule is denied. Of course the jury convicted Tom Robinson in Harper Lee's book. Thus, for Atticus and his client, the appellate court was the only potential forum for denying mob rule.

Modern civil rights movements have similarly viewed the countermajoritarian potential of appellate courts as a prime ally in their battles for justice. But appellate courts face constraints. When appellate courts move too quickly and take positions that find insufficient support in society at large, their decisions will fail to be enforced. The gay rights movement saw this phenomenon in Hawaii when that state court recognized a right that the people of Hawaii were not ready to accord gay people. Before the Court could enter a final decree in the marriage rights case, the people of Hawaii had amended the constitution to deny such rights to same-sex couples.

A study summarizing public opinion on gay and lesbian issues shows that most Americans favor laws that would protect lesbians and gay men in their public sphere rights, such as employment and housing.[6] Support for equal rights in employment has grown from slightly over 50 percent in the 1970s to over 80 percent in the 1990s. This indication of broad support helps to explain why eleven states have enacted legislation banning discrimination by employers on the basis of sexual orientation. Gallup polls show that a majority of Americans even support gays in the military. Although only 51 percent indicated such support in 1977, 70 percent supported hiring gays in the military by 1999. These high percentages of support make it difficult to understand why Congress cannot pass employment protections for gays and why neither Congress nor courts have supported gays in the military. One partial explanation is that feelings run deep on these issues so that although a majority may support nondiscrimination, the minority opposed to legal protections for gays may be particularly vocal. This phenomenon might help explain legislative reluctance, but it fails to explain adequately why courts are also dragging their feet on offering legal protection.

Although public opinion polls indicate broad support for equal public sphere rights for gay men and lesbians, only about a third of Americans support equal marriage rights.[7] Public support for adoptions by gay couples is around 35 percent to 40 percent.[8] In addition, the most recent polls on the question of whether Americans viewed "homosexuality" as an acceptable "alternative lifestyle" show that about half the populace still disapproves of homosexuality.[9]

Thus, both society at large and the courts in general have been willing to support public sphere rights for gays. Earlier civil rights movements have contributed to the breadth of this support. Earlier civil rights movements have helped Americans to understand that discrimination in employment and housing is wrong, that all Americans need basic benefits like jobs and housing to survive. But earlier civil rights movements have not been as much help in gaining broad support for private sphere rights such as gay marriage. The gay civil rights movement needs to win that support in the courts of public opinion. Lesbian and gay rights litigators elect to pursue cases that they believe will help the movement win that support. *Baehr v. Lewin* was such a case even though the plaintiffs ultimately lost. The Hawaii case sparked a nationwide debate that may not have increased support for gay marriage, but has certainly made the issue better understood. In every year after the first opinion in *Baehr*, polls indicate that a majority of Americans believe same-sex couples should be entitled to spousal benefits. This change in public attitudes was crucial to the recent legislative activity in Vermont.

Judicial opinions cannot change the hearts and minds of Americans, but the arguments that litigators make in courtrooms can—provided they are heard beyond the courtrooms. Our sameness arguments must continue to be made to our neighbors and to the people in the streets, as well as to the courts, until we have convinced enough nongay persons that we, as gays and lesbians, share life experiences with them that are extremely special. It is this shared experience—this similarity—that makes us all human. If the courts understand our arguments before the people in the streets do, then the courts may take our side and support us in this movement. And there is something about the courts in this country that makes us believe it is possible for them to lead the way. After all, they are said to be the great levelers, and, as such, they did lead the way for at least two earlier civil rights movements, abolishing invidious distinctions and recognizing our common humanity. Judge Irving Goldberg, a courageous judge of the Fifth Circuit who often ruled against public opinion in order to protect the rights of blacks and women, explained the role of courts as follows:

> Preachers and writers have been preaching and writing for generations that we should do certain things for our brothers and they have been heard, but not heeded. And that's where the courts come in. The courts not only are heeded, but what's important in their being heeded is . . . that the courts do speak for the moral heights of our society. And when they don't, they forfeit their responsibility.[10]

NOTES

1. Tushnet at 4.
2. 335 U.S. 464 (1948) (upholding Michigan law that prohibited women from serving as barmaids unless the bar was owned by her husband or father on theory that husbands and fathers would protect them).
3. 368 U.S. 57 (1961)(jury exclusion case).
4. *See* Evan Gerstmann, *The Constitutional Underclass* (1999).
5. Kimel v. Florida Board of Regents, 120 S.Ct. 631 (2000).
6. See Alan Yang, "From Wrongs to Rights: Public Opinion on Gay & Lesbian Americans Moves Toward Equality" (NGLTF Publications: December 1999).
7. Yang at 14.
8. Yang at 15.
9. Yang at 21.
10. Jack Bass, *Unlikely Heroes* 328 (1981) (quoting Judge Goldberg).

Table of Cases

Able v. United States, 968 F.Supp. 850 (E.D.N.Y. 1997) (holding "Don't Ask/Don't Tell" policy unconstitutional), *rev'd* 155 F.3d 628 (2d Cir. 1998)(holding policy constitutional under principle of deference to military)

Adams v. Howerton, 486 F. Supp. 1119 (C.D. Cal. 1980), *aff'd,* 673 F.2d 1036 (9th Cir. 1982), *cert. denied* 458 U.S. 1111 (1982) (marriage between two men is not valid for purposes of immigration law)

Adickes v. S. H. Kress & Co., 398 U.S. 144 (1970) (state action requirement of Fourteenth Amendment is met when city policeman assists private business in furthering racially discriminatory practices)

Adoption of B.L.V.B. and E.L.V.B., 628 A.2d 1271 (Vt. 1993) (Lesbian partner can adopt partner's child without requiring biological mother to terminate her parental rights)

Adoption of Tammy, 619 N.E.2d 315 (Mass. 1993) (adoption statute did not preclude same-sex couple from jointly adopting child when adoption was in child's best interest)

Alderwood Associates v. Washington Environmental Council, 635 P.2d 108 (Wash. 1981) (environmental group has right to solicit on premises of privately owned shopping mall under speech and initiative provisions of state constitution)

Ancient Order of Hibernians v. Dinkins, 814 F.Supp 358 (S.D.N.Y. 1993) (city violates parade organizer's free speech rights by requiring that gay organization be allowed to march in St. Patrick's Day parade)

Arlington County v. White, 528 S.E.2d 706, 2000 WL 429453 (Va. 2000) (county's grant of domestic partner benefits not a reasonable method of implementing its implied authority under relevant statutes and constitutes an ultra vires act)

Associated Students of Sacramento State College v. Butz, Civil No. 200795 (Super. Ct. Sacramento, February 15, 1971) (university recognition of student gay group required by the First Amendment)

Aumiller v. University of Delaware, 434 F.Supp. 1273 (D. Del. 1977) (university's firing of employee who made progay statements to press violated employee's First Amendment rights)

Baehr v. Lewin, 852 P.2d 44 (Haw. 1993) (state's refusal to recognize same-sex marriages is a form of sex discrimination that can only be justified by a compelling state interest under the Equal Protection Clause of the Hawaii constitution)

Baker v. Nelson, 191 N.W.2d 185 (Minn. 1971) (same-sex marriage case holding marriage can be constitutionally limited to persons of the opposite sex)

Baker v. Vermont, 744 A.2d 864 (Vt. 1999) (same-sex couples entitled to the same benefits and protections as opposite-sex couples under the common benefits clause of Vermont constitution)

ering on remand and holding that Romer did not affect earlier decision); *cert. denied,* 119 S. Ct. 365 (1998).

Evans v. Abney, 396 U.S. 435 (1970) (Georgia court's determination that cy pres doctrine could not be used to remove racial restriction from charitable gift in trust of park for whites only, a determination that returned the park land to heirs of grantor, was not discriminatory state action under the Fourteenth Amendment, but rather neutral application of state trust law)

Evans v. Newton, 382 U.S. 296 (1966) (operation of municipal park in a racially discriminatory manner violates the Fourteenth Amendment, even when management of the park has been turned over to private trustees)

Evans v. Romer, 882 P.2d 1335 (Colo. 1994) (holding that antihomosexual referendum could not pass constitutional scrutiny since it burdened the fundamental right of participation in the political process), *aff'd on different grounds;* Romer v. Evans, 517 U.S. 620 (1996)

Ex parte J.M.F., 730 S.2d 1190 (Ala. 1998) (Change in custody from mother to father warranted when father can provide traditional heterosexual family environment and mother's once discreet lesbian affair has become an open relationship)

Florida Board of Bar Examiners v. N.R.S., 403 So.2d 1315 (Fla. 1981) (struck down Board of Bar Examiners' policy of making overly personal inquiry into sexual conduct of gay applicant)

Fricke v. Lynch, 491 F.Supp. 381 (D.R.I. 1980) (gay high school senior had First Amendment right to make a political statement by bringing male escort to senior prom)

Frontiero v. Richardson, 411 U.S. 677 (1973) (plurality of Supreme Court justices found sex a suspect classification)

G.A. v. D.A., 745 S.W.2d 726 (Mo. App. W.D. 1987) (family court holding that welfare of preschool-age son better served if custody awarded to the husband rather than his former wife, a lesbian living with her lover and two teenage daughters)

Gay Activists Alliance v. Board of Regents of University of Oklahoma, 638 P.2d 1116 (Okla. 1981) (gay student organization has First Amendment right to organize and gain recognition from a university)

Gay Alliance of Students v. Matthews, 544 F.2d 162 (4th Cir. 1976) (First and Fourteenth Amendments require university to grant gay student organization equal access to campus facilities for social functions)

Gay Law Students Association v. Pacific Telephone & Telegraph, 595 P.2d 592 (Cal. 1979) (gay and lesbian employees of public utility protected from arbitrary employment actions by equal protection provision of state constitution)

Gay Lesbian Bisexual Alliance v. Pryor, 110 F.3d 1543 (11th Cir. 1997) (Alabama statute prohibiting recognition or funding of any group promoting gay or lesbian lifestyles held unconstitutional because it infringed on the First Amendment speech rights of a gay student organization)

Gay Lib v. University of Missouri, 558 F.2d 848 (8th Cir. 1977), *cert. denied,* 434 U.S. 1080 (1978) (University of Missouri must recognize gay student group)

Gay Student Services v. Texas A&M University, 737 F.2d 1317 (5th Cir. 1984) (Texas A&M must recognize gay student group), *cert denied,* 471 U.S. 1001 (1985).

J.E.B. v. Alabama, 511 U.S. 127 (1994) (use of peremptory challenges by private defense attorney to exclude women from jury a violation of the Fourteenth Amendment's Equal Protection Clause)

James v. Valtierra, 402 U.S. 137 (1971) (upheld state constitutional provision requiring that low-rent housing project be approved by majority of qualified eligible voters)

Jantz v. Muci, 976 F.2d 623 (10th Cir. 1992) (plaintiff claimed that defendant high school principal had violated the Fourteenth Amendment by refusing to hire plaintiff as a teacher on grounds that plaintiff exhibited "homosexual tendencies"; Court of Appeals ruled that even if homosexual status was a protected class under equal protection analysis, the state of the law was too uncertain to hold government official liable and thus granted the defendant immunity from suit)

Jones v. Alfred Mayer Co., 392 U.S. 409 (1968) (right of blacks to buy and own property protected under the Thirteenth Amendment and appropriately codified in the 1866 Civil Rights Act)

Kahn v. Shevin, 416 U.S. 351 (1974) (state property tax law favoring women does not violate equal protection since it constitutes benign discrimination)

Katzenbach v. McClung, 379 U.S. 294 (1964) (restaurant's use and purchase of goods through interstate commerce sufficient in the aggregate to warrant application of Civil Rights Act of 1964 under the Commerce Clause)

Kelly v. State, 412 A.2d 1274 (Md. App. 1980) (sodomy statute not a violation of a right to privacy, and imposition of criminal sanctions not cruel and unusual punishment)

Kimel v. Florida Board of Regents, 120 S.Ct. 631 (2000) (held that the Eleventh Amendment gives states immunity from suit under the Age Discrimination in Employment Act by private individuals and that Congress can only legislate against states under section five of the Fourteenth Amendment if the discrimination involves suspect classifications)

Kirchberg v. Feenstra, 450 U.S. 455 (1981) (state marital property statute giving husband unilateral control over marital property a violation of equal protection)

Korematsu v. United States 323 U.S. 214 (1944) (mandatory imprisonment of Japanese citizens and noncitizens during World War II survives Fourteenth Amendment scrutiny because of compelling need to prevent espionage and sabotage)

Kotteman v. Grevemberg, 96 So.2d 601 (La. 1957) (suspension of liquor license upheld by evidence of inordinate number of arrests and police officer testimony that premises were place of congregation for "sex deviates")

Ku Klux Klan v. Town of Thurmont, 700 F.Supp. 281 (D. Md. 1988) (town's imposition of nondiscrimination condition on grant of parade permit to Ku Klux Klan that requested right to march with only Klan members, all of whom were white, created unconstitutional burden on Klan's free speech rights)

Lassiter v. Department of Social Services of Durham County, N.C., 452 U.S. 18 (1981) (failure to provide counsel for an indigent parent in termination of parental rights case is not a violation of due process unless criminal charges are evident)

Lawrence v. Texas, 2000 WL 729417 (Tex. App. 2000) (holding Texas same-sex sodomy statute unconstitutional under Texas Equal Rights Amendment)

Stemler v. City of Florence, 126 F.3d 856 (6th Cir. 1996) (citing *Romer v. Evans,* held selective prosecution on the basis of sexual orientation violates Equal Protection Clause)

Stoumen v. Reilly, 234 P.2d 969 (Cal. 1951) (evidence that premises catered to homosexuals without further evidence of illegal conduct on the premises insufficient to warrant revocation of liquor license), *rev'g* 222 P.2d 678 (Cal. App. 1950) (holding suspension of liquor license warranted when premises at issue were a "regular meeting place for known homosexuals")

Student Services for Lesbians/Gays and Friends v. Tex. Tech University, 635 F.Supp. 776 (N.D. Tex. 1986) (university officials not liable for damages for initial failure to recognize gay student group under Eleventh Amendment immunity principles)

Sullivan v. INS, 772 F.2d 609 (9th Cir. 1985) (No abuse of discretion by trial court in upholding INS deportation order where gay partner of American male contends deportation will separate him from partner and subject him to discrimination in his home country)

Sullivan v. Little Hunting Park, Inc., 396 U.S. 229 (1969) (affirmed black's rights under the 1866 Civil Rights Act to "inherit, purchase, lease, sell, hold and convey real and personal property" by striking down a community park's refusal to transfer ownership rights to a black purchaser)

Sweatt v. Painter, 339 U.S. 629 (1950) (refusal by University of Texas to admit black law school applicant a violation of the Equal Protection Clause of the Fourteenth Amendment)

Sweezy v. State of New Hampshire 354 U.S. 234 (1957) (professor's refusal to answer questions regarding political party and its adherents is protected academic freedom and political expression under the First Amendment)

Tanner v. Oregon Health Science University, 971 P.2d 435 (Ore. App. 1998) (holding that university's refusal to extend insurance benefits to employee's same-sex domestic partner violates the Privileges and Immunities Clause of the Oregon constitution, which guarantees equal privileges to classes of citizens and finding that same-sex couples are a suspect class who must be granted equal privileges with married couples in absence of a compelling state reason for denying the privilege)

Taylor v. Louisiana, 419 U.S. 522 (1975) (male criminal defendant has standing to challenge constitutionality of state law excluding women from jury service, since the right to a jury trial made up of a representative sample of the community is a constitutional Sixth Amendment right)

Thom, Application of, 301 N.E.2d 542 (N.Y. 1973) (New York Court of Appeals orders lower court to grant Lambda Legal Defense and Education Fund's application for charter as a public interest law firm serving the lesbian and gay community)

Thom, Application of, 350 N.Y.S.2d 1 (1973) (lower court granted Lambda's charter request, but required removal of charter language stating one of the corporation's purposes was "to promote legal education among homosexuals by recruiting and encouraging potential law students who are homosexuals . . . ")

Thomas v. Anchorage Equal Rights Commission, 165 F.3d 692 (9th Cir. 1998) (creating a religious exemption for landlords under state fair housing acts who refuse

Bibliography

Achtenberg, Roberta, ed. *Sexual Orientation and the Law*.: St. Paul, Minn.: West Group, 1998.

Adam, Barry D. *The Rise of a Gay and Lesbian Movement*. Boston: Twayne Publishers, 1987.

Adams, William E., Jr. "Is it Animus or a Difference of Opinion? The Problems Caused by the Invidious Intent of Anti-gay Ballot Measures." 34 *Willamette Law Review* 449 (1998).

Austin, Regina. "The Black Community, Its Lawbreakers, and a Politics of Identification." 65 *Southern California Law Review* 1769 (1992).

Bass, Jack. *Unlikely Heroes: The Dramatic Story of the Southern Judges of the Fifth Circuit Who Translated the Supreme Court's* Brown *Decision into a Revolution for Equality*. Tuscaloosa, Ala.: University of Alabama Press, 1990.

Bérubé, Allan. *Coming Out Under Fire: The History of Gay Men and Women in World War II*. New York: Free Press, 1990.

Bonfield, Arthur Earl. "The Origin and Development of American Fair Employment Legislation." 52 *Iowa Law Review* 1043–1092 (1967).

Bourdonnay, Katherine, R. Charles Johnson, Joseph Schuman, and Bridget Wilson. *Fighting Back: Lesbian and Gay Draft, Military and Veterans Issues*. Chicago: Midwest Committee for Military Counseling, 1985.

Branch, Taylor. *Parting the Waters: America in the King Years 1954–63*. New York: Simon and Schuster, 1988.

Brennan, William J., Jr. "The Bill of Rights and the States: The Revival of State Constitutions as Guardians of Individual Rights." 61 *New York University Law Review* 535 (1986).

Brinig, Margaret F. "Economics, Law and Covenant Marriage." 16 *Gender Issues* 1 (1998).

Bullough, Vern L. "Lesbianism, Homosexuality, and the American Civil Liberties Union." *Journal of Homosexuality* 13 (1986):23.

Button, James W., Barbara A. Rienzo, and Kenneth D. Wald. *Private Lives, Public Conflicts: Battles over Gay Rights in American Communities*. Washington, D.C.: CQ Press, 1997.

Cammermeyer, Margarethe, and Chris Fisher. *Serving in Silence*. New York: Viking, 1994.

Carter, Robert L. "A Reassessment of Brown v. Board." In *Shades of Brown: New Perspectives on School Desegregation*, ed. Derrick Bell. New York: Teachers College Press, 1980.

Chauncey, George. *Gay New York*. New York: Basic Books, 1994.

Chemerinsky, Erwin. "Rethinking State Action." 80 *Northwestern University Law Review* 503 (1985).

Clendinen, Dudley, and Adam Nagourney. *Out for Good: The Struggle to Build a Gay Rights Movement in America*. New York: Simon and Schuster, 1999.

Cruikshank, Margaret. *The Gay and Lesbian Liberation Movement*. New York: Routledge, 1992.

D'Emilio, John. *Sexual Politics, Sexual Communities: The Making of a Homosexual Minority in the United States, 1940–1970*. Chicago: University of Chicago Press, 1983.

D'Emilio, John, and Estelle B. Freedman. *Intimate Matters: A History of Sexuality in America*. New York: Harper and Row, 1988.

Duberman, Martin. *Stonewall*. New York: Dutton, 1993.

Elshtain, Jean Bethke. *Democracy on Trial*. New York: Basic Books, 1995.

Eskridge, William N., Jr. *The Case for Same-Sex Marriage*. New York: The Free Press, 1996.

Eskridge, William N., Jr. *Gaylaw: Challenging the Apartheid of the Closet*. Cambridge, Mass.: Harvard University Press, 1999.

Evans, Sara M. *Born for Liberty*. New York: The Free Press, 1989.

Faderman, Lillian. *Odd Girls and Twilight Lovers*. New York: Columbia University Press, 1991.

Frantz, Laurent B, "Congressional Power to Enforce the Fourteenth Amendment Against Private Acts." 73 *Yale Law Journal* 1353 (1964).

Fricke, Aaron. *Reflections of a Rock Lobster: A Story About Growing Up Gay*. Boston: AlyCat Books, 1981.

Friedan, Betty. *It Changed My Life: Writings on the Women's Movement*. New York: Random House, 1976.

Gerstmann, Evan. *The Constitutional Underclass*. Chicago: University of Chicago Press, 1999.

Grahn, Judy. *Another Mother Tongue: Gay Words, Gay Worlds*. Boston: Beacon Press, 1984.

Greenberg, Jack. *Crusaders in the Courts: How a Dedicated Band of Lawyers Fought for the Civil Rights Revolution*. New York: Basic Books, 1994.

Halley, Janet E. *Don't: A Reader's Guide to the Military's Anti-Gay Policy*. Durham, N.C.: Duke University Press, 1999.

Harrison, Cynthia. *On Account of Sex: The Politics of Women's Issues 1945–1968*. Berkeley: University of California Press, 1988.

Heilbrun, Carolyn G. *The Education of a Woman: The Life of Gloria Steinem*. New York: Dial Press, 1995.

Higginbotham, A. Leon, Jr. *Shades of Freedom, Racial Politics and Presumptions of the American Legal Process*. Oxford: Oxford University Press, 1996.

Hirshman, Linda R., and Jane E. Larson. *Hard Bargains: The Politics of Sex*. Oxford: Oxford University Press, 1998.

Hitchens, Donna Hitchens, and Barbara Price, "Trial Strategy in Lesbian Mother Custody Cases: The Use of Expert Testimony." 9 *Golden Gate University Law Review* 451–479 (1978–1979).

Hunter, Nan D., and Nancy D. Polikoff. "Custody Rights of Lesbian Mothers: Legal Theory and Litigation Strategy." 25 *Buffalo Law Review* 691–733 (1976).

Hunter, Nan D., Sherryl E. Michaelson, and Thomas B. Stoddard. *The Rights of Lesbians and Gay Men: The Basic ACLU Guide to a Gay Person's Rights,* 3d ed. Carbondale: Southern Illinois University Press, 1992.

James, Marlise. *The People's Lawyers.* New York: Holt, Rinehart and Winston, 1973.

Jennings, Kevin, ed. *Becoming Visible.* Boston: Alyson Publications, Inc., 1994.

Jordan, Barbara, and Shelby Hearon. *Barbara Jordan: A Self-Portrait.* New York: Doubleday and Co., 1979.

Kaiser, Charles. *The Gay Metropolis: The Landmark History of Gay Life in America Since World War II.* New York: Harcourt Brace and Co., 1997.

Kaplan, Morris B. *Sexual Justice: Democratic Citizenship and the Politics of Desire.* New York: Routledge, 1997.

Katz, Jonathan Ned. *Gay American History: Lesbians and Gay Men in the U.S.A.,* rev. ed. New York: Meridian, 1992.

Keen, Lisa, and Suzanne B. Goldberg. *Strangers to the Law: Gay People on Trial.* Ann Arbor: University of Michigan Press, 1998.

Kennedy, Elizabeth Lapovsky, and Madeline D. Davis. *Boots of Leather, Slippers of Gold: The History of a Lesbian Community.* New York, Routledge, 1993.

Kerber, Linda K. *No Constitutional Right to Be Ladies.* New York: Hill and Wang, 1998.

Kinsman, Gary. *The Regulation of Desire,* 2d ed. Montreal: Black Rose Books, 1996.

Klarman, Michael J. "An Interpretive History of Modern Equal Protection." 90 *Michigan Law Review* 213 (1991).

Kluger, Richard. *Simple Justice.* New York: Alfred A. Knopf, 1976.

Knutson, Donald C., ed. *Homosexuality and the Law.* New York: Haworth Press, 1980.

Leonard, Arthur S. *Sexuality and the Law: An Encyclopedia of Major Legal Cases.* New York: Garland Publishing, 1993.

Lopez, Gerald P. *Rebellious Lawyering: One Chicano's Vision of Progressive Law Practice.* Boulder, Colo: Westview Press, 1992.

Loughery, John. *The Other Side of Silence: Men's Lives and Gay Identities: A Twentieth Century History.* New York: Henry Holt & Co., 1998.

Lusky, Louis. "Footnote Redux: A Carolene Products Reminiscence." 82 *Columbia Law Review* 1093 (1982).

Marcus, Eric. *Making History: The Struggle for Gay and Lesbian Rights, 1945–1990.* New York: HarperCollins, 1992.

Morello, Karen Berger. *The Invisible Bar: The Woman Lawyer in America, 1638 to the Present.* Boston: Beacon Press, 1988.

Motley, Constance Baker. *Equal Justice Under Law.* New York: Farrar, Straus and Giroux, 1998.

Murray, Pauli, and Mary O. Eastwood. "Jane Crow and the Law: Sex Discrimination and Title VII." 34 *George Washington Law Review* 232 (1965).

Newton, David E. *Gay and Lesbian Rights.* Denver: ABC-CLIO, 1994.

Polikoff, Nancy D. "Am I My Client? The Role Confusion of a Lawyer Activist." *Harvard Civil Rights–Civil Liberties Law Review* 31 (1996):443.

Price, Deb. "Rainbow Flag is a Symbol of a United Gay People." *Star Tribune,* April 19, 1995:4-E.

Rhode, Deborah L. "Moral Character as a Professional Credential." 94 *Yale Law Journal* 491 (1985).

Richards, David A. J. *Women, Gays, and the Constitution: The Grounds for Feminism and Gay Rights in Culture and Law.* Chicago: University of Chicago Press, 1998.

Rivera, Rhonda R. "Our Straight-Laced Judges: The Legal Position of Homosexual Persons in the United States." 30 *Hastings Law Journal* 799 (1979).

Rivera, Rhonda R. "Recent Developments in Sexual Preference Law." 30 *Drake Law Review* 311 (1980–1981).

Rosenberg, Gerald N. *The Hollow Hope: Can Courts Bring About Social Change.* Chicago: University of Chicago Press, 1991.

Rubinstein, Ronald A., and Patricia B. Fry. *Of a Homosexual Teacher.* Frederick, Md.: Associated Faculty Press, Inc., 1981.

Rubenstein, William. *Sexual Orientation and the Law.* 2d ed. St. Paul, Minn.: West Publishing Co., 1997.

Schrecker, Ellen W. *No Ivory Tower: McCarthyism & The Universities.* New York: Oxford University Press, 1986.

Shilts, Randy. *Conduct Unbecoming.* New York: St. Martin's Press, 1993.

Siegel, Reva. "Home as Work: The First Woman's Rights Claims Concerning Wives' Household Labor, 1850–1880." 103 *Yale Law Journal* 1073 (1994).

Spann, Girardeau A. *Race Against the Court: The Supreme Court and Minorities in Contemporary America.* New York: New York University Press, 1993.

Strossen, Nadine. "The American Civil Liberties Union and Women's Rights." 66 *New York University Law Review* 1940 (1991).

Symposium. "Gay Rights and the Courts: The Amendment 2 Controversy." *Colorado Law Review* 68 (1997).

Symposium. "Sexual Orientation and the Law." *Virginia Law Review* 79 (1993).

Symposium. "The Legal System and Homosexuality—Approbation, Accommodation, or Reprobation?" *University of Dayton Law Review* 10 (1985).

tenBroek, Jacobus, Edward N. Barnhart, and Floyd W. Matson, *Prejudice, War and the Constitution.* Berkeley: University of California Press, 1968.

Tribe, Laurence H. "Saenz Sans Prophecy: Does the Privileges or Immunities Revival Portend the Future—or Reveal the Structure of the Present?" 113 *Harvard Law Review* 110 (1999).

Tushnet, Mark V. *The NAACP Legal Strategy Against Segregated Education, 1925–1950.* Chapel Hill: University of North Carolina Press, 1987.

Vaid, Urvashi. *Virtual Equality: The Mainstreaming of Gay and Lesbian Liberation.* New York: Doubleday, 1995.

Vetri, Dominick. "Almost Everything You Always Wanted to Know About Lesbians and Gay Men, Their Families, and the Law." 26 *Southern University Law Review* 1 (1998).

Walker, Samuel. *In Defense of American Liberties*. New York: Oxford University Press, 1990.

Warren, Carol. *Identity and Community in the Gay World*. Ann Arbor: University Microfilms, 1972.

Weiss, Andrea, and Greta Schiller. *Before Stonewall: The Making of a Gay and Lesbian Community*. Tallahassee, Fla.: Naiad Press, 1988.

Witt, Stephanie, and Suzanne McCorkle, eds. *Anti-Gay Rights: Assessing Voter Initatives*. Westport, Conn.: Praeger, 1997.

Wolfenden Report (authorized American ed.). New York: Stein and Day, 1963.

Yang, Alan. *From Wrongs to Rights: Public Opinion on Gay & Lesbian Americans Moves Toward Equality*. Washington, D.C.: NGLTF Publications, 1999.

Index